James Foxall

Wendy Haro-Chun, Contributor

SAMS
Teach Yourself
C#
in 24 Hours

SAMS

201 West 103rd St., Indianapolis, Indiana, 46290 USA

Sams Teach Yourself C# in 24 Hours
Copyright © 2002 by Sams Publishing

International Standard Book Number: 0-672-32287-0

Library of Congress Catalog Card Number: 2001093572

Printed in the United States of America

First Printing: February 2002

05 04 03 02   4 3 2 1

Trademarks

Warning and Disclaimer

ASSOCIATE PUBLISHER
Linda Engelman

ACQUISITIONS EDITOR
Sondra Scott

DEVELOPMENT EDITOR
Ginny Bess

MANAGING EDITOR
Charlotte Clapp

PROJECT EDITOR
Carol Bowers

COPY EDITOR
Barbara Hacha

INDEXER
Erika Millen

PROOFREADER
Jody Larsen

TECHNICAL EDITORS
Joel Mueller
Deon Schaffer

TEAM COORDINATOR
Lynne Williams

MEDIA DEVELOPER
Dan Scherf

INTERIOR DESIGNER
Gary Adair

COVER DESIGNER
Aren Howell

PAGE LAYOUT
D&G Limited, LLC

Contents at a Glance

Contents

Part III Making Things Happen—Programming!   233

Hour 11 Creating and Calling Methods   235

Hour 12 Using Constants, Data Types, Variables, and Arrays   257

About the Authors

James Foxall is Vice President of Development and Support for Tigerpaw Software, Inc. (www.tigerpawsoftware.com)—an Omaha, Nebraska, Microsoft Certified Partner specializing in commercial database applications. James manages a commercial suite of programs designed to automate contact management, marketing, service and repair, proposal generation, and inventory control and purchasing. James's experience in creating certified Office-compatible software has made him an authority on application interface and behavior standards of applications for the Microsoft Windows and Microsoft Office environments.

James has personally written more than 150,000 lines of commercial production code, both in single programmer and multiple programmer environments. He is the author of numerous books, including *Practical Standards for Microsoft Visual Basic* and *MCSD in a Nutshell: The Visual Basic Exams*, and he has written articles for *Access-Office-VBA Advisor* and *Visual Basic Programmer's Journal*. James is a Microsoft Certified Solution Developer and an international speaker on Microsoft programming technologies. When not programming or writing about programming, he enjoys spending time with his family, playing guitar, doing battle over the chess board, listening to Pink Floyd, playing computer games, and (believe it or not) programming! You can reach James at jamesf@tigerpawsoftware.com.

Wendy Haro-Chun, MCSD, holds a B.S. in Computer Science and an M.B.A. with an emphasis in International Business. She is Assistant Vice President of Research and Development for SunGard Insurance Systems. Her areas of technological expertise include .NET, C#, ASP, DHTML, JavaScript, XML, COM, VB, ADO, and Microsoft SQL Server. Wendy has also served as technical editor and reviewer on numerous computer technology books. She lives in Miami with her husband, Dave, and her two beagles, Buster and Belle. She can be reached at wharo@bellsouth.net.

Dedication

To my children, Ethan and Tess.

—James Foxall

To my parents, Olga and Alfonso, and my love, Dave.

—Wendy Haro-Chun

Acknowledgments

James's acknowledgements:

To Sondra Scott, both for the opportunity to do this book as well as just being a great person to work for!

To Wendy for her wonderful contributions, Carol Bowers, Ginny Bess, Joel Mueller, Deon Schaffer, and everyone else that had a hand in this book—thanks guys!

To Matt Wagner at Waterside Productions for all his help behind the scenes.

To my wife and children for always supporting and encouraging me through these projects. You are the best!

Finally, a special thanks to Mike Pizzo at Microsoft for his contributions to the ADO.NET chapter.

Wendy's acknowledgements:

I would like to thank Sondra Scott for giving me the opportunity to work on this great project. I would also like to thank Ginny Bess and Carol Bowers for making sure everything came together and technical editors Joel and Deon for making sure this new technology worked the way I said it did. Also, special thanks to Peter Farquharson, David Marcato, Deon Schaffer, and Larry Wall for helping to get this project started on a good foundation.

To James Foxall, I have enjoyed reading your VB .NET book, and it has been a great pleasure working with you on this C# book.

A big thanks goes out to my husband, Dave, for his constant support in all my projects and for always believing in me.

To Olga and Alfonso, thank you for all the support, encouragement, and love you have always given me.

Finally, thanks to all my relatives and friends for buying this book!

Tell Us What You Think!

As the reader of this book, *you* are our most important critic and commentator. We value your opinion and want to know what we're doing right, what we could do better, what areas you'd like to see us publish in, and any other words of wisdom you're willing to pass our way.

As an Associate Publisher for Sams Publishing, I welcome your comments. You can fax, e-mail, or write me directly to let me know what you did or didn't like about this book—as well as what we can do to make our books stronger.

Please note that I cannot help you with technical problems related to the topic of this book, and that because of the high volume of mail I receive, I might not be able to reply to every message.

When you write, please be sure to include this book's title and author as well as your name and phone or fax number. I will carefully review your comments and share them with the author and editors who worked on the book.

Fax: 317-581-4770
E-mail: feedback@samspublishing.com
Mail: Linda Engelman
         Sams Publishing
         201 West 103rd Street
         Indianapolis, IN 46290 USA

Introduction

With Microsoft's introduction of the .NET platform, a new, exciting programming language was born. C# is the language of choice for developing on the .NET platform, and Microsoft has even written a majority of the .NET Framework using C#. C# is a modern object-oriented language designed and developed from the ground up with a best-of-breed mentality, implementing and expanding on the best features and functions found in other languages. C# combines the power and flexibility of C++ with the simplicity of Visual Basic.

Audience and Organization

This book is targeted toward those who have little or no programming experience. The book has been structured and written with a purpose, and that is to get you productive as quickly and as smoothly as possible. I've used my experiences from writing large commercial applications to create a book that, hopefully, cuts through the fluff and teaches you *what* you need to know. All too often, authors fall into the trap of focusing on the technology rather than on the practical application of the technology. I've worked hard to keep this book focused on teaching you practical skills that you can apply immediately toward a development project. Please feel free to send me your suggestions or success stories at jamesf@tigerpawsoftware.com.

This book is divided into five parts, each of which focuses on a different aspect of developing applications with C#. These parts generally follow the flow of tasks you'll perform as you begin creating your own programs using C#. I recommend that you read them in the order in which they appear.

- **Part I** *The Visual Studio Environment* teaches you about the Visual Studio's C# development environment, including how to navigate and access 'numerous tools. In addition, you'll learn some key development concepts such as objects, collections, and events.

- **Part II** *Building a User Interface* shows you how to build attractive and functional user interfaces. In this part, you'll learn about forms and controls—the user-interface elements such as text boxes and list boxes.

- **Part III** *Making Things Happen—Programming!* teaches you the nuts and bolts of C# programming—and there's a lot to learn. You'll discover how to create methods, as well has how to store data, perform loops, and make decisions in code. After you've learned the core programming skills, you'll move into object-oriented programming and debugging applications.

- **Part IV** *Working with Data* introduces you to working with a database and shows you how to automate external applications such as Word and Excel. In addition, this part teaches you how to manipulate a user's file system.

- **Part V** *Deploying Solutions and Beyond* shows you how to distribute an application that you've created to an end user's computer. Then, the focus is brought back a bit to take a look at Web programming and Microsoft's .NET initiative from a higher, less-technical level.

Conventions Used in This Book

This book uses several conventions to help you prioritize and reference the information it contains:

- **Tips** highlight information that can make your C# programming more effective.
- **Cautions** focus your attention on problems or side effects that can occur in specific situations.
- **Notes** provide useful sidebar information that you can read immediately or circle back to without losing the flow of the topic at hand.
- **New Term** icons signal places where new terminology is first used and defined. Such terminology appears in an italic typeface for emphasis.

In addition, this book uses various typefaces to help you distinguish code from regular English. Code is presented in a monospace font. Placeholders—words or characters used temporarily to represent the real words or characters you would type in code—are typeset in *italic monospace*.

Some code statements presented in this book are too long to appear on a single line. In these cases, a line-continuation character (an underscore) is used to indicate that the following line is a continuation of the current statement.

Onward and Upward!

This is an exciting time to be learning how to program, and it's my sincerest wish that when you finish this book, you will feel capable of creating, debugging, and deploying modest C# programs using many C# and Visual Studio tools. Although you won't be an expert, you'll be surprised at how much you've learned. And hopefully, this book will help you determine your future direction as you proceed down the road to C# mastery.

PART I

The Visual Studio Environment

Before you can begin to create C# applications for Windows and the Web, you need to have a thorough grasp of the C# environment as well as some key development concepts. In this part, you'll get an overview of developing a project in C#, you'll learn all about the C# interface, and you'll learn about objects, collections, and events—concepts that are critical to your success as a C# developer.

- Hour 1: A C# Programming Tour
- Hour 2: Navigating C#
- Hour 3: Understanding Objects and Collections
- Hour 4: Understanding Events

HOUR 1

A C# Programming Tour

Learning a new programming language can be intimidating. If you've never programmed before, the act of typing seemingly cryptic text to produce sleek and powerful applications probably seems like a black art, and you may wonder how you'll ever learn everything you need to know. The answer is, of course, one step at a time. The first step to learning a language is the same as that of any other activity—building confidence. Programming is part art and part science. Although it may seem like magic, it's more akin to illusion; after you know how things work, a lot of the mysticism goes away, freeing you to focus on the mechanics necessary to produce the desired result.

In this hour, you'll complete a quick tour that takes you step-by-step through creating a complete, albeit small, C# program. I've yet to see a "Hello World" program that's the least bit helpful (they usually do nothing more than print "hello world" to the screen—oh, fun). So instead, you'll create a picture-viewer application that lets you view Windows bitmaps and icons on your computer. You'll learn how to let a user browse for a file and how to display a selected picture file on the screen, both of which are skills that will come in handy in later applications that you create. Creating large, commercial solutions is accomplished by way of a series of small steps. After you've finished creating this small project, you'll have an overall feel for the development process.

The highlights of this hour include the following:

- Building a simple, yet functional, C# application
- Letting a user browse a hard drive
- Displaying a picture from a file on disk
- Getting familiar with some programming lingo
- Learning about the Visual Studio—C# IDE

I hope that by the end of this hour, you'll realize just how much fun it is to program using C#.

Starting C#

You must become familiar with a few terms before you begin to create programs in C#:

- Distributable Component   The final, compiled version of a project. Components can be distributed to other people and other computers and do not require C# to run (although the .NET Framework is required, which you'll learn about in coming hours). Distributable components are also called programs. In Hour 22, "Deploying a Solution," you'll learn how to distribute the Picture Viewer program that you're about to build to other computers.

- Project   A collection of files that can be compiled to create a distributable component (program). There are many types of projects, and complex applications may consist of many projects, such as a Windows Application project and support DLL projects.

- Solution   A collection of projects and files that compose an application or component.

NEW TERM   C# is a complete development environment; every tool you'll need to create your C# projects is accessed from within Visual Studio. The Visual Studio-C# environment is called the IDE, short for Integrated Development Environment, and it is the design framework in which you build applications. To work with C# projects, you must first start the Visual Studio IDE.

Start the C# IDE now by choosing Microsoft Visual Studio .NET from within the Microsoft Visual Studio .NET folder on your Start menu.

Creating a New Project

When you first start Visual Studio .NET, you're shown the Visual Studio Start Page tab within the IDE. Using this page, you can open projects created previously or create new ones (see Figure 1.1). For this quick tour, you're going to create a new Windows application, so click New Project to display the New Project dialog box shown in Figure 1.2.

If you don't see the Visual Studio Start page, chances are that you've changed the default settings. Hour 2, "Navigating C#," shows you how to change them back. For now, be aware that you can create a new project from the File menu in addition to using the techniques described in this hour.

FIGURE 1.1

You can open existing projects or create new projects from the Visual Studio Start page.

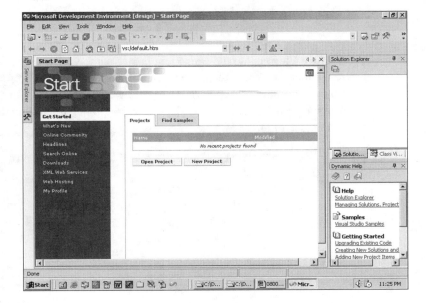

You can create many types of projects with C#, as well as with the other supported languages of the .NET platform. The New Project dialog box is used to specify the type of C# project you want to create. If the Visual C# Projects folder isn't selected, click it to display the C# project types and then make sure the Windows Application icon is selected (if it's not, click it once to select it). At the bottom of the New Project dialog box is a Name text box, in which you specify the name of the project you're creating; in the Location text box, you can enter the location in which to save the project files.

You should always set these values to something meaningful before creating a project, or you'll have more work to do later if you want to move or rename the project.

FIGURE 1.2

The New Project dialog box allows you to create many types of .NET projects.

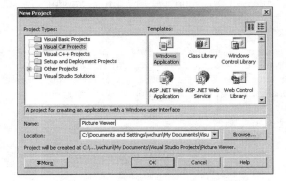

Type **Picture Viewer** into the Name text box to name your project. There's no need to change the location where the project files are to be saved at this time, so go ahead and create the new Windows Application project by clicking OK. C# creates the new project, complete with one form (design window) for you to begin building the interface for your application (see Figure 1.3).

FIGURE 1.3

New Windows applications start with a blank form; the fun is just beginning!

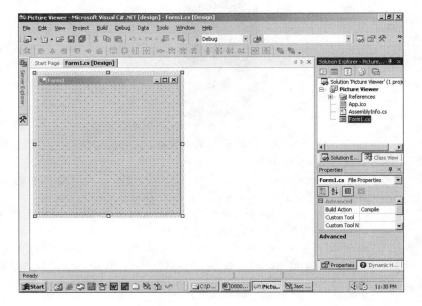

Your C# environment may look different from that shown in the figures of this hour, depending on the edition of C# you're using, whether you've already played with C#, and other factors such as the resolution of your monitor. All the elements discussed in this hour, however, exist in all editions of C#. (If your IDE doesn't have a window displayed that is shown in a figure, use the View menu to display the window.)

To create a program that can be run on another computer, you start by creating a project, and then you compile the project into a component, such as an executable (a program a user can run) or a DLL (a component that can be used by other programs and components). The compilation process is discussed in detail in Hour 22, "Deploying a Solution." The important thing to note at this time is that when you hear someone refer to creating or writing a program, just as you are creating the Picture Viewer program now, they're referring to the completion of all steps up to and including compiling the project to a distributable file.

Understanding the C# Environment

The first time you run C#, you'll notice that the IDE contains a lot of windows, such as the Properties window on the right, which is used to view and set properties of objects. In addition to these windows, the IDE contains a lot of tabs, such as the Toolbox tab on the left edge of the IDE (refer to Figure 1.3). Clicking a tab displays an associated window. Try this now: click the Toolbox tab to display the Toolbox window. You can also hover the mouse over a tab for a few seconds to display the window. To hide the window, simply move the mouse off the window. To close the window completely, click the Close (X) button in the window's title bar.

You can adjust the size and position of any of these windows, and you can even hide and show them at will. You'll learn how to customize your design environment in Hour 2, "Navigating C#."

Unless specifically instructed to do so, do not double-click anything in the C# design environment. Double-clicking most objects produces an entirely different outcome than single-clicking does. If you mistakenly double-click an object on a form, a code window is displayed. At the top of the code window is a set of tabs: one for the form design and one for the code. Click the tab for the form design to hide the code window and return to the form.

The Properties window at the right side of the design environment is perhaps the most important window, and it's the one you'll use most often. If your computer's display is set for 640×480, you can probably see only a few properties at this time. This makes it difficult to view and set properties as you create projects. I highly recommend that you don't attempt development with Visual Studio at a resolution below 800×600. Personally, I prefer 1024×768 because it offers plenty of work space. To change your display settings, right-click your desktop and select Properties.

Changing the Characteristics of Objects

Almost everything you work with in C# is an object. Forms, for instance, are objects, as are all the items you can put on a form to build an interface, such as list boxes and buttons. There are many types of objects (Hour 3, "Understanding Objects and Collections," discusses objects in detail). Objects, in turn, are classified by type. For instance, a form is a Form object, whereas items you can place on a form are called Control objects, or controls. Some objects don't have a physical appearance, but exist only in code. You'll learn about these kinds of objects in later hours.

NEW TERM   Every object, regardless of whether it has a physical appearance, has a distinct set of attributes known as *properties*. You have certain properties about you, such as your height and hair color, and C# objects have properties as well, such as Height and BackColor. Properties define the characteristics of an object. When you create a new object, the first thing you need to do is set its properties so that the object appears and behaves in the way you desire. To display the properties of an object, click the object in its designer. Click the form now to ensure that its properties are displayed in the Properties window.

Naming Objects

The property you should set first for any new object is the Name property. Press F4 to display the Properties window (if it's not already visible), and notice the Name given to your default form (the first property listed in the Properties window)—Form1. When you first create an object, C# gives the object a unique, generic name based on the object's type. Although these names are functional, they aren't very descriptive. For instance, C# named your form Form1, but it's common to have dozens of forms in a project, and it would be extremely difficult to manage a complicated project if all forms were distinguishable only by a number (Form2, Form3, and so forth).

In actuality, what you're creating is a form *class*, or template, that will be used to create and show forms at runtime. For the purpose of this quick tour, I simply refer to it as a form. See Hour 5, "Building Forms—Part I," for more information.

To better manage your forms, you should give each one a descriptive name. C# gives you the chance to name new forms as they're created. Because C# created this default form for you, you didn't get a chance to name it, so you must change both the filename and name of the form. Change the name of the form now by clicking the Name property and changing the text from Form1 to **fclsViewer**. Notice that this did not change the filename of the form as it is displayed in the Solution Explorer window. Change the filename now by right-clicking Form1.cs in the Solution Explorer window, choosing Rename from the context menu, and changing the text from Form1.cs to **fclsViewer.cs**. In future examples, I won't have you change the filename each time because you'll have enough steps to accomplish as it is. I do recommend, however, that you always change your filenames to something meaningful in your 'real' projects.

I use the fcls prefix here to denote that the file is a form class. There are different types of classes, so using a prefix helps differentiate the classes in code. You're not required by C# to use object prefixes, but I highly recommend that you do so. In Hour 12, "Using Constants, Data Types, Variables, and Arrays," you'll learn the benefits of using a naming convention as well as the standard prefixes for many .NET objects.

Setting the Text Property of the Form

Notice that the text that appears in the form's title bar says Form1. This is because C# sets the form's title bar text to the name of the form when it is first created, but doesn't change it when you change the name of the form. The text in the title bar is determined by the value of the Text property of the form. Click the form once more so that its properties appear in the Properties window. Use the scrollbar in the Properties window to locate the Text property in the Properties window and then change the text to **Picture Viewer**.

Giving the Form an Icon

Everyone who has used Windows is familiar with icons, which are the little pictures used to represent programs. Icons most commonly appear in the Start menu next to the name of their respective programs. In C#, you not only have control over the icon of your program file, you can also give every form in your program a unique icon if you want to.

> The instructions that follow assume you have access to the source files for the examples in this book. They are available at www.samspublishing.com/ detail_sams.cfm?item=0672320800. You don't have to use the icon I've provided for this example; you can use any icon of your choice. If you don't have an icon available, you can skip this section without affecting the outcome of the example.

To give the form an icon, follow these steps:

1. In the Properties window, click the Icon property to select it.
2. When you click the Icon property, a small button with three dots appears to the right of the property. Click this button.
3. To locate the HourOne.ico file or another ico file of your choice, use the Open dialog box that appears. When you've found the icon, double-click it, or click it once to select it and then click Open.

After you've selected the icon, it appears in the Icon property along with the word (Icon). A small version of the icon appears in the upper-left corner of the form, as well. Whenever this form is minimized, this is the icon that's displayed on the Windows taskbar. (Note: This doesn't change the icon for the project as a whole. In Hour 22, you'll learn how to assign an icon to your distributable file.)

Changing the Size of the Form

Next, you're going to change the Width and Height properties of the form. The Width and Height values are shown collectively under the Size property; Width appears to the left of the comma, Height to the right. You can change the Width or Height by changing the corresponding number in the Size property. Both values represent the number of pixels of the dimension. To display and adjust the Width and Height properties separately, click the small plus sign (+) next to the Size property (see Figure 1.4).

FIGURE 1.4

Some properties can be expanded to show more specific properties.

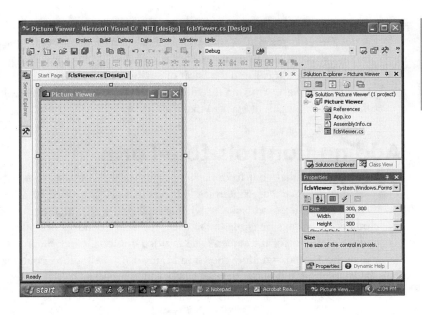

Change the Width property to **400** and the Height to **325**. To commit a property change, press Tab or click a different property or window. Your screen should now look like the one in Figure 1.5.

FIGURE 1.5

A change in the Properties window is reflected as soon as the change is committed.

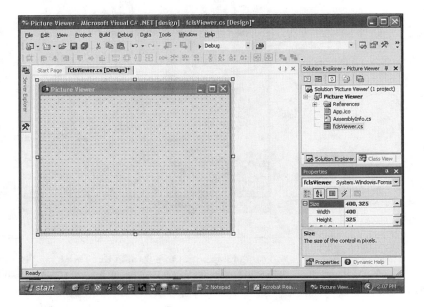

When you first created this project, C# saved a copy of the source files in their initial state. The changes you've made so far exist only in memory; if you were to turn your computer off at this time (don't do this), you would lose any and all work up to this point. You should get into the habit of saving your work frequently. Save the project now by choosing Save All from the File menu or by clicking the Save All button on the toolbar (it has a picture of stacked disks on it).

Adding Controls to a Form

NEW TERM Now that your form has its properties set, you need to add objects to the form to produce a user interface. Objects that can be placed on a form are called *controls*. Some controls have a visible interface with which a user can interact, whereas others are always invisible to the user. You'll use controls of both types in this example. On the left side of the screen is a tab titled Toolbox. Click the Toolbox tab now to display the Toolbox window shown in Figure 1.6. The toolbox contains all the controls available in the project, such as labels and text boxes.

FIGURE 1.6

The toolbox is used to select controls to build a user interface.

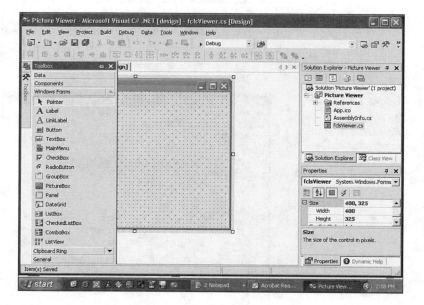

You can add a control to a form in three ways, and Hour 5 explains them in detail. In this hour, you'll use the technique of double-clicking a tool in the toolbox.

The toolbox closes itself soon after you've added a control to a form and the pointer is no longer over the toolbox. To make the toolbox stay visible, click the little picture of a pushpin located in the toolbox's title bar.

> Refer to Hour 2, "Navigating C#," for more information on customizing the design environment.

Your Picture Viewer interface will consist of the following controls:

- Two Button controls
- A PictureBox control
- An OpenFileDialog control

Designing an Interface

It's generally best to design the user interface of a form and then add the code behind the interface that makes the form functional. The user interface for your Picture Viewer program will consist of a View Picture button, a Close button, and a PictureBox in which to display a picture.

Adding a Visible Control to a Form

Start by adding a Button control to the form. Do this by double-clicking the Button item in the toolbox. C# then creates a new button and places it in the upper-left corner of the form (see Figure 1.7).

Using the Properties window, set the button's properties as follows (note that you may want to change the Properties list to alphabetical, if it is not already, to make it easier to find these properties by name):

Property	Value
Name	btnSelectPicture
Text	Select Picture
Location	301,10 (Note: 301 is the x coordinate, 10 is the y coordinate.)
Size	85,23

FIGURE 1.7

When you double-click a control in the toolbox, the control is added to the upper-left corner of the form.

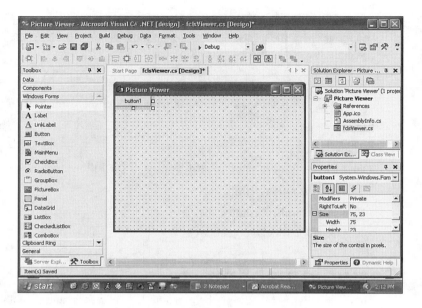

You're now going to create a button that the user can click to close the Picture Viewer program. Rather than adding a new button to the form, you're going to create a copy of the button you've already defined. To do this, right-click the button on the form and choose Copy from its shortcut menu. Next, right-click anywhere on the form and choose Paste from the form's shortcut menu. The new button appears over the button you copied, and it is selected by default. Change the properties of the new button as follows:

Property	Value
Name	btnQuit
Text	Quit
Location	301,40

The last control you need to add to the form is a PictureBox control. A PictureBox has many capabilities, but its primary purpose is to show pictures—which is precisely what you'll use it for in this example. Add a new PictureBox control to the form and set its properties as follows:

Property	Value
Name	picShowPicture
BorderStle	FixedSingle
Location	8,8
Size	282, 275

After you've made these property changes, your form will look like the one in Figure 1.8. Click the Save All button on the toolbar to save your work.

FIGURE 1.8

An application's interface doesn't have to be complex to be useful.

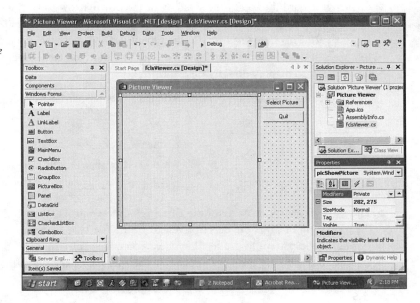

Adding an Invisible Control to a Form

NEW TERM So far, all the controls that you've used sit on a form and have a physical appearance. However, not all controls have a physical appearance. Such controls, referred to as *invisible-at-runtime controls*, aren't designed for user interactivity, but they're designed to give you, the programmer, functionality beyond the standard features of C#.

To allow the user to select a picture to display, you need to give her the capability to locate a file on her hard drive. You've probably noticed in the past that whenever you choose to open a file from within any Windows application, the dialog box displayed is almost always the same. It doesn't make any sense to force each and every developer to write the code necessary to perform standard file operations. Instead, Microsoft has exposed the functionality via a control that you can use in your project. This control is called the OpenFileDialog control, and it will save you dozens of hours that you would otherwise spend trying to duplicate common functionality.

Other controls besides the OpenFileDialog control give you file functionality. For example, the SaveFileDialog control provides features for enabling the user to save a file.

Scroll the toolbox until you can see the OpenFileDialog control, and then double-click it to add it to your form. (You may have to scroll the toolbox, which is done by clicking the up arrow toward the top of the window or the down arrow toward the bottom.) Note that the control isn't placed on the form, but it appears in a special area below the form (see Figure 1.9). This happens because the OpenFileDialog control has no interface to display to a user. It does have an interface, a dialog box that you can display as necessary, but it has nothing to display directly on a form.

Select the OpenFileDialog control and change its properties as follows:

Property	Value
Name	ofdSelectPicture
Filter	Windows Bitmaps|*.BMP|JPEG Files|*.JPG
Title	Select Picture

The Filter property determines the filtering of the control. The text that appears before the pipe symbol (|) is the descriptive text of the file type, whereas the text after the pipe symbol is the pattern to use to filter files; you can specify more than one filter type. Text entered into the Title property appears in the title bar of the Open File dialog box.

FIGURE 1.9

Controls that have no interface appear below the form designer.

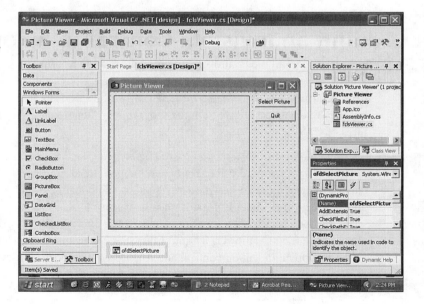

Coding an Interface

The graphical interface for your Picture Viewer program is now complete, so click the pushpin in the title bar of the toolbox to close it. Now, you have to write code for the program to be capable of performing actions. C# is an event-driven language, which means that code is executed in response to events. These events may come from users, such as a user clicking a button, or from Windows itself (see Hour 4, "Understanding Events," for a complete explanation of events). Currently, your application looks nice but it won't do a darn thing. The user can click the Select Picture button, for example, until the cows come home, but nothing will happen because you haven't told the program what to do when the user clicks the button.

You're going to write code to accomplish two tasks. First, you're going to write code that lets the user browse his or her hard drives to locate and select a picture file and then display the file in the picture box (this sounds a lot harder than it is). Second, you're going to add code to the Quit button that shuts down the program when the user clicks the button.

Letting a User Browse for a File

The first bit of code you're going to write will allow the user to browse his or her hard drives, select a file, and then show the selected picture in the PictureBox control. This code will execute when the user clicks the Select Picture button; therefore, it's added to the Click event of that button (you'll learn all about events in later hours). When you double-click a control on a form in Design view, the default event for that control is created and displayed in a code window. The default event for a Button control is its Click event, which makes sense because clicking a button is its most common purpose. Double-click the Select Picture button now to access its Click event in the code window (see Figure 1.10).

NEW TERM When you access an event, C# builds an *event handler*, which is essentially a template procedure in which you add the code that executes when the event is fired. The cursor is already placed within the code procedure, so all you have to do is add code. You will also notice that the open and closing braces are preset for your new event procedure. The braces, in this case, define the beginning and end of your procedure. You will soon see that C# requires many open and closing braces({ }). By the time you're done with this book, you'll be madly clicking away as you write your own code to make your applications do exactly what you want them to do—well, most of the time. For now, just enter the code as I present it here.

FIGURE 1.10
You will write all code in a window such as this.

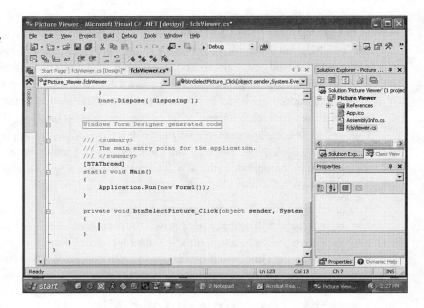

It's very important that you get in the habit of commenting your code, so the first line you're going to enter is a comment. Beginning a statement with the characters // designates the statement as a comment; the compiler won't do anything with the statement, so you can enter whatever text you want after the double slashes. Type the following statement exactly as it appears and press the Enter key at the end of the line.

> For more information on creating good comments, see Hour 16, "Debugging Your Code."

```
// Show the open file dialog box.
```

The next statement you'll enter triggers a method of the OpenFileDialog control that you added to the form. You'll learn all about methods in Hour 3, "Understanding Objects and Collections." For now, think of a method as a mechanism to make a control take action. The ShowDialog method tells the control to show its Open dialog box and let the user select a file. The ShowDialog method returns a value that indicates its success or failure, which we are then comparing to a predefined result (DialogResult.OK). Don't worry too much about what is happening here, because you'll be learning the details of this in later hours. In a nutshell, the ShowDialog method is called to let a user browse for a file, and if the user selects a file, more code gets executed. Of course, there is a lot more to using the OpenFileDialog control than I present in this basic example, but this simple statement gets the job done. Enter the following if statement followed by an open brace:

```
if (ofdSelectPicture.ShowDialog() == DialogResult.OK)
 {
```

Open and closing braces are necessary for this if statement because they denote that multiple lines will be part of this construct.

Time for another comment. Enter this statement and remember to press Enter at the end of each code line.

```
// Load the picture into the picture box.
```

Don't worry about indenting the code by pressing the Tab key or using spaces. C# .NET automatically indents code for you.

You're now going to enter the next line of code. This statement, which appears within the if construct, is the line of code that actually displays the picture in the picture box. (If you're itching to know more about graphics, take a look at Hour 10, "Drawing and Printing.")

Enter the following statement:

```
picShowPicture.Image = Image.FromFile(ofdSelectPicture.FileName);
```

In addition to displaying the selected picture, your program is going to display the path and filename of the picture in the title bar. When you first created the form, you changed the Text property of the form using the Properties window. To create dynamic applications, properties need to be constantly adjusted at runtime, and this is done using code. Enter the following three lines of code:

```
// Show the name of the file in the form's caption.
this.Text = String.Concat("Picture Viewer (" + ofdSelectPicture.FileName + ")");
 }
```

C# is case sensitive! You must enter all code using the same case as shown in the text.

Checking Your Program Entry Point

All C# programs must contain an entry point. The Main() method is the entry point. In this sample you need to change the reference from Form1 to **fclsViewer** (this is necessary because we renamed the form earlier) . This statement will invoke the constructor on the form. C++ programmers will be familiar with the Main() entry point method, but they should take notice of the capitalization of Main. We will talk a bit more about the program entry point later in the book.

To update the entry point in this sample, press Ctrl+F to open the Find window, enter **Form1**, and click Find Next. Close the Find window and replace the text Form1 with **fclsViewer**. The updated statement should now read:

```
Application.Run(new fclsViewer());
```

After you've entered all the code, your editor should look like that shown in Figure 1.11.

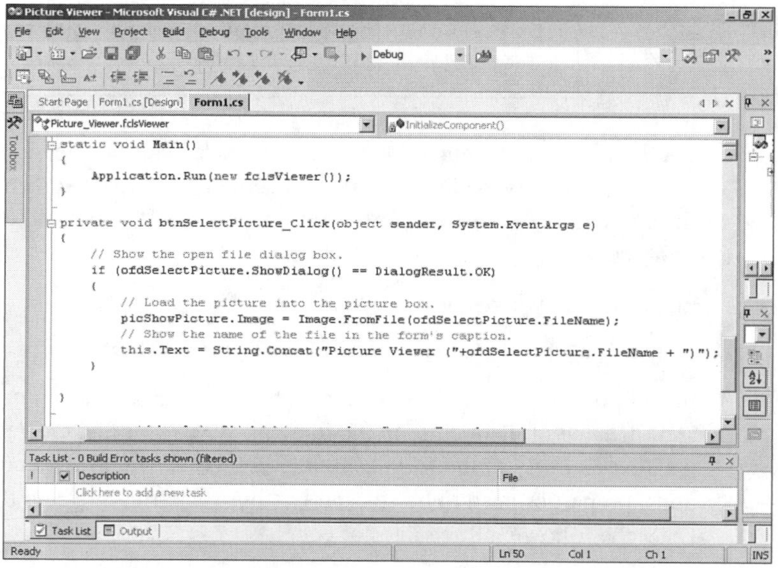

FIGURE 1.11

Make sure your code exactly matches the code shown here.

Terminating a Program Using Code

The last bit of code you'll write will terminate the application when the user clicks the Quit button. To do this, you'll need to access the Click event handler of the btnQuit button. At the top of the code window are two tabs. The current tab has the text fclsViewer.cs. Next to this is a tab that contains the text fclsViewer.cs [Design]. Click this tab now to switch from Code view to the form designer. If you receive an error when

1

you click the tab, the code you entered is incorrect, and you need to edit it to make it the same as I've presented it. After the form designer is displayed, double-click the Quit button to access its Click event.

Enter the following code in the Quit button's Click event handler:

```
this.Close();
```

The Close statement closes the current form. When the last loaded form in a program is closed, the application shuts itself down—completely. As you build more robust applications, you'll probably want to execute all kinds of clean-up routines before terminating your application, but for this example, closing the form is all you need to do.

Running a Project

Your application is now complete. Click the Save All button (it looks like a stack of disks) on the toolbar, and then run your program by pressing F5. You can also run the program by clicking the button on the toolbar that looks like a right-facing triangle and resembles the Play button on a VCR (this button is also found on the Debug menu, and it is called Start). However, learning the keyboard shortcuts will make your development process move along faster. When you run the program, the C# interface changes, and the form you've designed appears floating over the design environment (see Figure 1.12).

FIGURE 1.12

When in Run mode, your program executes the same as it would for an end user.

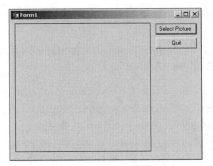

You're now running your program as though it were a standalone application running on another user's machine; what you see is exactly what someone else would see if they ran the program (without the C# design environment in the background, of course). Click the Select Picture button to display the Select Picture dialog box (see Figure 1.13). Use the dialog box to locate a picture file. When you've found a file, double-click it, or click once to select it and then click Open. The selected picture is then displayed in the PictureBox control, as shown in Figure 1.14.

FIGURE 1.13

The OpenFileDialog control handles all the details of browsing for files. Cool, huh?

FIGURE 1.14

C# makes it easy to display pictures with very little work.

Summary

When you're done playing with the program, click the Quit button and then save your project by clicking Save All on the C# toolbar.

That's it! You've just created a bona fide C# program. You've used the toolbox to build an interface with which users can interact with your program, and you've written code in strategic event handlers to empower your program to do things. These are the basics of application development in C#. Even the most complicated programs are built using this basic approach; you build the interface and add code to make the application do things. Of course, writing code to do things exactly the way you want things done is where the process can get complicated, but you're on your way.

If you take a close look at the organization of the hours in this book, you'll see that I start out by teaching you the C# environment. I then move on to building an

1

interface, and later I teach you all about writing code. This organization is deliberate. You might be a little anxious to jump in and start writing serious code, but writing code is only part of the equation. As you progress through the hours, you'll be building a solid foundation of development skills.

Soon, you'll pay no attention to the man behind the curtain—you'll be that man (or woman)!

Q&A

Q. Can I show bitmaps of file types other than BMP and JPG?

A. Yes. The PictureBox supports the display of images with the extensions BMP, JPG, ICO, EMF, WMF, and GIF. The PictureBox can even save images to a file.

Q. Is it possible to show pictures in other controls?

A. The PictureBox is the control to use when you are just displaying images. However, many other controls allow you to display pictures as part of the control. For instance, you can display an image on a Button control by setting the button's Image property to a valid picture.

Workshop

The Workshop is designed to help you anticipate possible questions, review what you've learned, and get you thinking about how to put your knowledge into practice. The answers to the quiz are in Appendix A, "Answers to Quizzes/Exercises."

Quiz

1. What type of C# project creates a standard Windows program?
2. What window is used to change the attributes (location, size, and so on) of a form or control?
3. How do you access the default event (code) of a control?
4. What property of a PictureBox do you set to display an image?
5. What is the default event for a Button control?

Exercise

1. Change your Picture Viewer program so that the user can also locate and select GIF files. (Hint: Change the Filter property of the OpenFileDialog control.)
2. Alter the form in your Picture Viewer project so that the buttons are side by side in the lower-right corner of the form, rather than vertically aligned in the upper-right corner.

HOUR 2

Navigating C#

The key to expanding your knowledge of C# is to become as comfortable as possible—as quickly as possible—with the C# design environment. Just as a carpenter doesn't think much about hammering a nail into a piece of wood, performing actions such as saving projects, creating new forms, and setting object properties should become second nature to you. The more comfortable you are with the tools of C#, the more you can focus your energies on what you're creating with the tools.

In this hour, you'll learn how to customize your design environment. You'll learn how to move, dock, float, hide, and show design windows, as well as how to customize menus and toolbars; you'll even create a new toolbar from scratch. After you've gotten acquainted with the environment, I'll teach you about projects and the files that they're made of (taking you beyond what was briefly discussed in Hour 1, "A C# Programming Tour"), and I'll introduce you to the design windows with which you'll work most frequently. Finally, I'll show you how to get help when you're stuck.

The highlights of this hour include the following:

- Navigating C#
- Using the Visual Studio .NET Start Page to open and create projects
- Showing, hiding, docking, and floating design windows
- Customizing menus and toolbars
- Adding controls to a form using the toolbox
- Viewing and changing object attributes using the Properties window
- Working with the files that make up a project
- How to get help

Using the Visual Studio .NET Start Page

By default, the Visual Studio Start Page shown in Figure 2.1 is the first thing you see when you start C# (if C# isn't running, start it now). The Visual Studio Start Page is a gateway for performing tasks with C#. From this page, you can open previously edited projects, create new projects, edit your user profile, and browse information provided by Microsoft.

FIGURE 2.1

The Visual Studio Start Page is the default starting point for all Visual Studio programming languages, including C#.

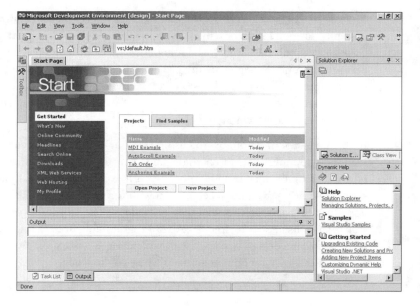

From this page, you can have C# load the last solution you edited, show the Open Project dialog box, show the New Project dialog box, or show an empty design environment. To view or edit the startup options, choose Options from the Tools menu to display the Options dialog box shown in Figure 2.2. By default, the General section of the Environment folder is selected, which happens to contain the At Startup option.

If the Visual Studio Start Page doesn't appear when you start C#, check the settings on the Options form; you may need to change At Startup to Show Start Page.

2

FIGURE 2.2

Use the At Startup setting to control the first thing you see when C# starts.

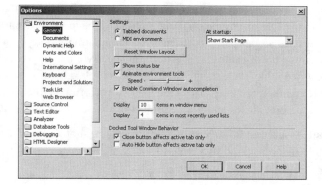

Creating New Projects

To create new projects, click New Project on the Visual Studio Start Page. This shows the New Project dialog box shown in Figure 2.3. The Project Types list varies from machine to machine, depending on which products of the Visual Studio .NET family are installed. Of course, we're interested only in the C# Project types in this book.

You can create many types of projects with C#, but this book focuses mostly on creating Windows Applications, perhaps the most common of the project types. You will learn about some of the other project types as well, but when you're told to create a new project, make sure the Windows Application template is selected unless you're told otherwise.

FIGURE 2.3

Use the New Project dialog box to create C# projects from scratch.

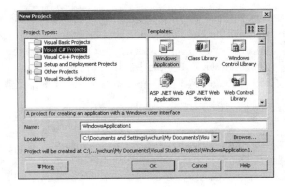

When you create a new project, be sure to enter a name for it in the Name text box before clicking OK or double-clicking a project type icon. This ensures that the project is created with the proper path and filenames, eliminating work you would otherwise have to do to change these values later. After you specify a name, you can create the new project either by double-clicking the project type template icon or by clicking an icon once to select it and then clicking OK. After you've performed either of these actions, the New Project dialog box closes and a new project of the selected type is created.

By default, Visual Studio saves all your projects in subfolders of your My Documents folder. The hierarchy used by C# is

```
\My Documents\Visual Studio Projects\<Project Name>
```

Notice how the name you give your project is used as its folder name. This makes it easy to find the folders and files for any given project and is one reason that you should always give your projects descriptive names. You can use a path other than the default by specifying a specific path on the New Project dialog box, although you probably won't often need to do so.

You can create a new project at any time (not just when starting C#) by opening the New submenu on the File menu and choosing Project.

Opening an Existing Project

Over time, you'll open more projects than you create. There are essentially two ways to open projects from the Visual Studio Start Page. If it's one you've recently opened, the project name will appear in a list within a rectangle in the middle of the Start Page (refer to Figure 2.1). Because the name displayed for the project is the one given when it was created, this is yet another reason to give your projects descriptive names. Clicking a project name opens the project. I'd venture to guess that you'll use this technique 95% of the time. To open a project for the first time (such as when opening sample projects), click Open Project on the Visual Studio Start Page. Clicking this link displays a standard dialog box that you can use to locate and select a project file.

As with creating new projects, you can open an existing project at any time, not just when starting C#, by selecting File, Open.

Navigating and Customizing the C# Environment

C# lets you customize many of its interface elements, such as windows and toolbars, enabling you to be more efficient in the work that you do. Create a new Windows Application now (use the New Project dialog box or select File, New) so that you can see and manipulate the design environment. Name this project **Environment Tutorial**. (This exercise won't create anything reusable, but it will help you learn how to navigate the design environment.) Your screen should look like the one shown in Figure 2.4.

Your screen may not look exactly like that shown in Figure 2.4, but it'll be close. For example, the Output window won't be visible unless you've built a project. If you completed Hour 1, the window will be visible. By the time you've finished this hour, you'll be able to change the appearance of the design environment to match this figure—or to any configuration you prefer.

Working with Design Windows

Design windows, such as the Properties and Solution Explorer windows shown in Figure 2.4, provide functionality for building complex applications. Just as your desk isn't organized exactly like that of your co-workers, your design environment doesn't have to be the same as anyone else's, either.

A design window may be placed into one of four primary states:

- Closed
- Floating
- Docked
- Auto hidden

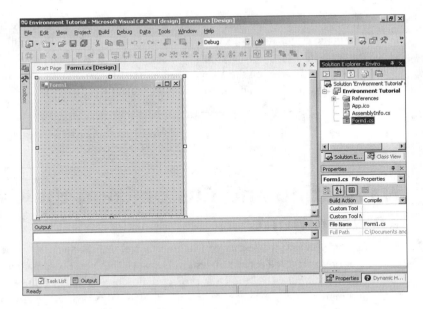

FIGURE 2.4

This is pretty much how the IDE appears when you first install C#.

Showing and Hiding Design Windows

When a design window is closed, it doesn't appear anywhere. There is a difference between being closed and being hidden, as you'll learn shortly. To display a closed or hidden window, choose the corresponding menu item from the View menu. For example, if the Properties window isn't displayed in your design environment, you can display it by choosing Properties Window on the View menu (or press its keyboard shortcut—F4). Whenever you need a design window and can't find it, use the View menu to display it. To close a design window, click its Close button (the button on the right side of the title bar with the X on it), just as you would close an ordinary window.

Floating Design Windows

Floating design windows are visible windows that float over the workspace, as shown in Figure 2.5. Floating windows are like typical application windows in that you can drag them around and place them anywhere you please, even on other monitors when you're using a multiple-display setup. In addition to moving a floating window, you can also change its size by dragging a border.

Docking Design Windows

Visible windows appear docked by default. A docked window is a window that appears attached to the side, top, or bottom of the work area or to some other window. The Properties window in Figure 2.4, for example, is docked to the right side of the design environment. To make a floating window a docked window, drag the title bar of the window toward the edge of the design environment to which you want to dock the window. As you drag the window, you'll drag a rectangle that represents the outline of the window. When you approach an edge of the design environment, the rectangle will change shape and "stick" in a docked position. If you release the mouse while the rectangle appears this way, the window will be docked. Although this is hard to explain, it's very easy to do.

FIGURE 2.5

Floating windows appear over the top of the design environment.

You can size a docked window by dragging its edge opposite the side that's docked. If two windows are docked to the same edge, dragging the border between them enlarges one while shrinking the other.

To try this, you'll need to float a window that's already docked. To float a window, you "tear" the window away from the docked edge by dragging the title bar of the docked window away from the edge to which it is docked. Note that this technique won't work if a window is set to Auto Hide (which is explained next). Try docking and floating windows now by following these steps:

1. Ensure that the Properties window is currently displayed (if it's not, show it using the View menu). Make sure the Properties window isn't set to Auto Hide by right-clicking its title bar and deselecting Auto Hide (if it's selected) from the shortcut menu, as shown in Figure 2.6.

2. Drag the title bar of the Properties window away from the docked edge. When the rectangle representing the border of the window changes shape, release the mouse button. The Properties window should now appear floating.

3. Dock the window once more by dragging the title bar toward the right edge of the design environment. Again, release the mouse button when the rectangle changes shape.

FIGURE 2.6

You can't float a window that's set to Auto Hide.

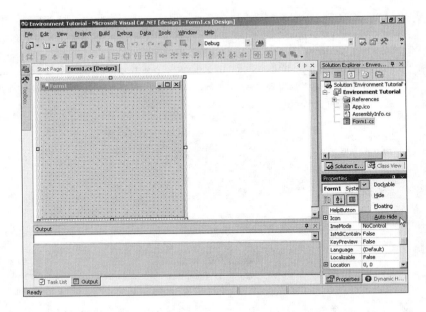

 If you don't want a floating window to dock, regardless of where you drag it to, right-click the title bar of the window and choose Floating from the context menu. To allow the window to be docked again, right-click the title bar and choose Dockable.

Auto Hiding Design Windows

A feature of C# design environment is the capability to auto hide windows. Although you might find this a bit disconcerting at first, after you get the hang of things, this is a very productive way in which to work because your workspace is freed up, yet design windows are available by simply moving the mouse. Windows that are set to Auto Hide are always docked; you can't set a floating window to Auto Hide. When a window auto hides, it appears as a tab on the edge to which it's docked—much like minimized applications are placed in the Windows taskbar.

Look at the left edge of the design environment in Figure 2.6. Notice the two tabs on the left side of the IDE. One tab has a picture of two computers, and the other is labeled Toolbox. These tabs represent auto-hidden windows. To display an auto-hidden window, move the pointer over the tab representing the window. When you move the pointer over a tab, C# displays the design window so that you can use its features. When you move the pointer away from the window, the window automatically hides itself—hence the name. To make any window hide itself automatically, right-click its title bar and select

Auto Hide from its shortcut menu. Alternatively, you can click the little picture of a pushpin appearing in the title bar next to the Close button to toggle the window's Auto Hide state.

Performing Advanced Window Placement

The techniques discussed in this section so far are basic methods for customizing your design environment. Things can actually get a bit more complicated if you want them to. Such complication presents itself primarily as the capability to create tabbed floating windows like the one shown in Figure 2.5. Notice that at the bottom of the floating window is a set of tabs. Clicking a tab shows its corresponding design window, replacing the window currently displayed. These tabs are created much the same way in which you dock and undock windows—by dragging and dropping. For instance, to make the Solution Explorer window a floating window of its own, you would drag the Solution Explorer window tab away from the floating window. As you do so, a rectangle appears, showing you the outline of the new window. Where you release the rectangle determines whether you dock the design window you're dragging or whether you make the window floating. To make a design window a new tab of an already floating window, drag its title bar and drop it in the title bar of a window that is already floating.

In addition to creating tabbed floating windows, you can dock two floating windows together. To do this, drag the title bar of one window over another window (other than over the title bar) until the shape changes, and then release the mouse. Figure 2.7 shows two floating windows that are docked to one another and a third window that is floating by itself.

FIGURE 2.7

Floating, docked, floating and docked— the possibilities are numerous!

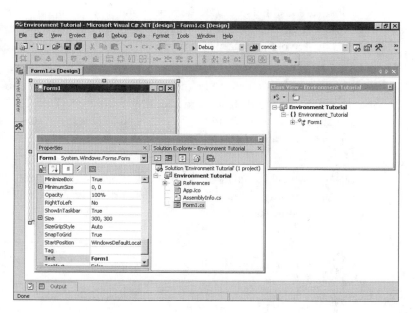

Using all the techniques discussed here, you can tailor the appearance of your design environment in all sorts of ways. There is no one best configuration. You'll find that different configurations work better for different projects and in different stages of development. For instance, when I'm designing the interface of a form, I want the toolbox to stay visible but out of my way, so I tend to make it float, or I turn off its Auto Hide property and leave it docked to the left edge of the design environment. However, after the majority of the interface elements have been added to a form, I want to focus on code. Then I dock the toolbox and make it auto hide itself; it's there when I need it, but it's out of the way when I don't. Don't be afraid to experiment with your design windows, and don't hesitate to modify them to suit your changing needs.

Working with Toolbars

Toolbars are the mainstay for performing functions quickly in almost all Windows programs (you'll probably want to add them to your own programs at some point, and Hour 9, "Adding Menus and Toolbars to Forms," shows you how). Every toolbar has a corresponding menu item, and buttons on toolbars are essentially shortcuts to their corresponding menu items. To maximize your efficiency when developing with C#, you should become familiar with the available toolbars. As your C# skills progress, you can customize existing toolbars and even create your own toolbars to more closely fit the way you work.

Showing and Hiding Toolbars

C# includes a number of built-in toolbars for you to use when creating projects. Two toolbars are visible in most of the figures shown so far in this hour. The one on the top is the Standard toolbar, which you'll probably want displayed all the time. The second toolbar is the Layout toolbar, which provides useful tools for building forms.

The previous edition of Visual Studio had about 5 toolbars; Visual Studio .NET, on the other hand, has more than 20 toolbars! The toolbars you'll use most often as a C# developer are the Standard, Text Editor, and Debug toolbars. Therefore, this hour discusses each of these. In addition to these predefined toolbars, you can create your own custom toolbars to contain any functions you think necessary, which you'll learn how to do later in this hour.

To show or hide a toolbar, choose View, Toolbars to display a list of available toolbars. Toolbars currently displayed appear selected (see Figure 2.8). Click a toolbar name to toggle its visible state.

A quick way to access the list of toolbars is to right-click any visible toolbar.

FIGURE 2.8
*Hide or show toolbars
to make your work
more efficient.*

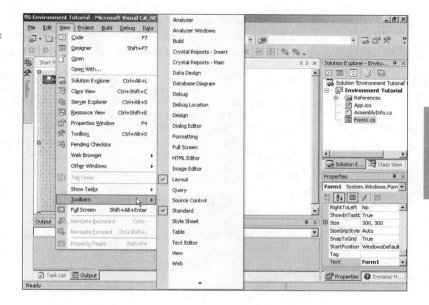

Docking and Resizing Toolbars

Just as you can dock and undock C#'s design windows, you can dock and undock the
toolbars. Unlike the design windows, however, C#'s toolbars don't have a title bar that
you can click and drag when they're in a docked state. Instead, each docked toolbar has a
drag handle (a set of horizontal lines along its left edge). To float (undock) a toolbar,
click and drag the grab handle away from the docked edge. After a toolbar is floating, it
has a title bar. To dock a floating toolbar, click and drag its title bar to the edge of the
design environment to which you want it docked. This is the same technique you use to
dock design windows.

A shortcut for docking a toolbar is to double-click its title bar.

Although you can't change the size of a docked toolbar, you can resize a floating toolbar
(a floating toolbar behaves like any other normal window). To resize a floating toolbar,
move the pointer over the edge you want to stretch and then click and drag to the border
to change the size of the toolbar.

Customizing Toolbars

As your experience with C# grows, you'll find that you use certain functions repeatedly.
To increase your productivity, you can customize any of C#'s toolbars, and you can

create your own from scratch. You can even customize the C# menu and create your own menus. To customize toolbars and menus, you use the Customize dialog box shown in Figure 2.9, which is accessed by choosing View, Toolbars, Customize.

 I strongly suggest that you don't modify the existing C# toolbars. Instead, create new toolbars. If you modify the predefined toolbars, you may find that you've removed tools that I refer to in later examples. If you do happen to change a built-in toolbar, you can reset it to its original state by selecting it in the Customize dialog box and clicking Reset.

FIGURE 2.9

Create new toolbars or customize existing ones to fit the way you work.

The Toolbars tab on the Customize dialog box shows you a list of all the existing toolbars and menus. The toolbars and menus currently visible have a check mark next to them. To toggle a toolbar or menu between visible and hidden, click its check box.

Creating a New Toolbar

You're now going to create a new toolbar to get a feel for how toolbar customization works. Your toolbar will contain only a single button, which will be used to call C#'s Help program.

To create your new toolbar, follow these steps:

1. From the Toolbars tab of the Customize dialog box, click New.
2. Enter **My Help** as the name for your new toolbar when prompted.
3. Click OK to create the new toolbar.

After you've entered a name for your toolbar and clicked OK, your new toolbar appears, floating on the screen—most likely somewhere outside the Customize dialog box (see Figure 2.10). Dock your toolbar now by double-clicking the blank area on the toolbar (the area where a button would ordinarily appear). Your screen should look like the one in Figure 2.11.

FIGURE 2.10

New toolbars are pretty tiny; they have no buttons on them.

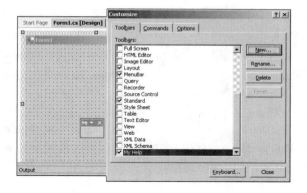

FIGURE 2.11

It's easier to customize toolbars when they're docked.

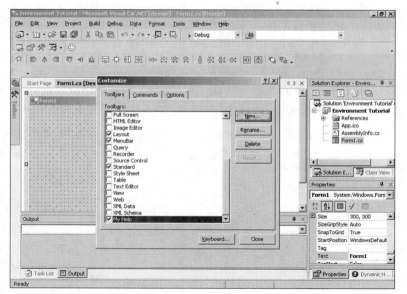

Adding Buttons to a Toolbar

Now that you have an empty toolbar, the next step is to add the desired command buttons to it. Click the Commands tab of the Customize dialog box to display all the available commands.

The Commands tab contains the following:

- A list of command categories
- A list of the commands for the selected command category

The Categories list shows all available command categories, such as File and Edit functions. When you select a category, all the available commands for that category are shown in the list on the right.

You're going to add a toolbar button that appears as a Help icon and that actually displays Help when clicked.

To add the command button to your toolbar, follow these steps:

1. Locate and select the category Help. All the available commands for the Help category will appear in the list on the right.

2. From the Commands list, click and drag the Contents command to your custom toolbar. As you drag, the pointer changes to an arrow pointing to a small gray box. At the lower-right corner of the pointer is a little hollow box with an x in it. This indicates that the location over which the pointer is positioned is not a valid location to drop the command.

3. As you drag the command over your toolbar (or any other toolbar for that matter), the x in the little box will change to a plus sign (+), indicating that the command can be placed in the current location. In addition, an insertion point (often called an I-beam because that's what it looks like) appears on the toolbar to indicate where the button would be placed if the command were dropped at that spot. When an I-beam appears on your toolbar and the pointer box contains a plus sign, release the mouse button. Your toolbar will now look like the one in Figure 2.12.

FIGURE 2.12

Building toolbars is a simple matter of dragging and dropping commands.

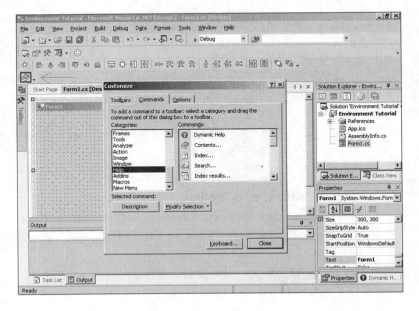

You can alter any button on a toolbar by right-clicking the button to access its shortcut menu and then choosing Change Button Image. Feel free to experiment with changing the image of the button on your custom toolbar, but be sure to leave the buttons on the built-in toolbars as they are.

2

To remove a button from a toolbar, drag the button to remove it from the toolbar and drop it somewhere other than on the same toolbar. If you drop the button onto another toolbar, the button is removed from the original toolbar and placed on the toolbar on which you dropped it. If you drop the button in a location where no toolbar exists, the button is simply removed from the toolbar.

You can drag command buttons only in Customize mode. If you attempt to drag an item during normal operation, you'll simply click the button.

Although these techniques are illustrated using toolbars, they apply to menus, as well.

Moving Buttons on a Menu or Toolbar

You should always attempt to group command buttons logically. For example, the Edit functions are all grouped together on the Standard toolbar, as are the File operations. A separator (space) is used to separate groups. To create a separator space, right-click the button that starts a new group and choose Begin a Group from the button's shortcut menu.

You probably won't get the exact groupings you want when you first add commands to a toolbar, but that's not a problem because you can change the position of a button at any time. To move a button on a toolbar, drag the button and drop it in the desired location (remember, you have to be in Customize mode to do this). To move a button from one toolbar to another, drag the button from its toolbar and drop it at the preferred location on the desired toolbar.

Now that your toolbar is complete (Hey, I never said it'd be fancy), click Close on the Customize dialog box to exit Customize mode. All toolbars, including the one you just created, are no longer in Customize mode and they can't be modified. Click the button you placed on your new toolbar and C#'s Help will appear.

Because your custom toolbar really doesn't do much, hide it now to save screen real estate by right-clicking any toolbar to display the Toolbar shortcut menu and then deselecting My Help.

As you work your way through this book, you should always have the Standard toolbar and menu bar displayed on your screen.

Typically, you should customize toolbars only after you're very familiar with the available functions and only after you know which functions you use most often. I recommend that you refrain from modifying any of the predefined toolbars until you're quite familiar with C#. As you become more comfortable with C#, you can customize the toolbars to make your project work area as efficient as possible.

Adding Controls to a Form Using the Toolbox

The toolbox is used to place controls, such as the common text box and list box, onto a form. The default toolbox you see when you first run C# is shown in Figure 2.13. The buttons labeled Data, Components, Windows Forms, and so on are actually tabs, although they don't look like standard tabs. Clicking any of these tabs causes a related set of controls to appear. The default tab is the Windows Forms tab, and it contains many great controls you can place on Windows forms (the forms used to build Windows applications, in contrast to Web applications). All the controls that appear by default on the tabs are included with C#, and these controls are discussed in detail in Hour 7, "Working with Traditional Controls," and Hour 8, "Advanced Controls." You'll learn how to add other controls to your toolbox as well.

FIGURE 2.13

The standard toolbox contains many useful controls you can use to build robust user interfaces.

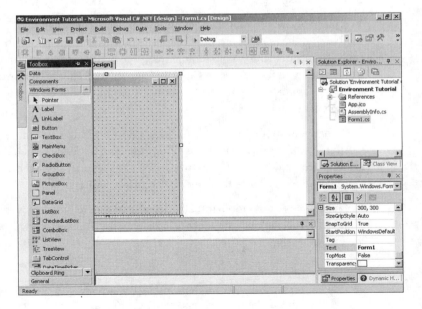

You can add a control to a form in one of three ways:

- In the toolbox, click the tool that you want to place on a form, and then click and drag on the form where you want the control placed (essentially, you're drawing the border of the control). The location at which you start dragging is used for the upper-left corner of the control, and the lower-right corner is the point at which you release the mouse button and stop dragging.

- Double-click the desired control in the toolbox. When you double-click a control in the toolbox, a new control of the selected type is placed in the upper-left corner of the form. The control's height and width are set to the default height and width of the selected control type.

- Drag a control from the toolbox and drop it somewhere on a form.

> If you prefer to draw controls on your forms by clicking and dragging, I strongly suggest that you dock the toolbox to the right or bottom edge of the design environment or float it; the toolbar tends to interfere with drawing controls when it's docked to the left edge, because it obscures part of the form.

The very first item on the Windows Forms tab, titled Pointer, isn't actually a control. When the pointer item is selected, the design environment is placed in a select mode rather than in a mode to create a new control. With the pointer item selected, you can select a control (by clicking it) to display all its properties in the Properties window; this is the default behavior.

Setting Object Properties Using the Properties Window

When developing the interface of a project, you'll spend a lot of time viewing and setting object properties using the Properties window (see Figure 2.14). The Properties window contains four items:

- An object drop-down list
- A list of properties
- A set of tool buttons used to change the appearance of the properties grid
- A section showing a description of the selected property

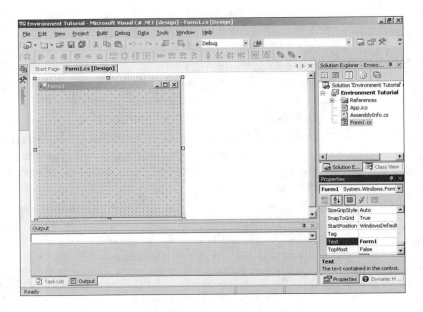

FIGURE 2.14
*Use the Properties
window to view and
change properties of
forms and controls.*

Selecting an Object and Viewing Its Properties

The drop-down list at the top of the Properties window contains the name of the form with which you're currently working and all the controls (objects) on the form. To view the properties of a control, select it from the drop-down list or click the control on the form. You must have the pointer item selected in the toolbox to select an object by clicking it.

Viewing and Changing Properties

The first two buttons in the Properties window (Categorized and Alphabetic), enable you to select the format in which you view properties. When you select the Alphabetic button, the selected object's properties are listed in the Properties window in alphabetical order. When you click the Categorized button, all the selected object's properties are displayed by category. For example, the Appearance category contains properties such as BackColor and BorderStyle. When working with properties, select the view you're most comfortable with and feel free to switch back and forth between the views.

The Properties pane of the Properties window is used to view and set the properties of a selected object. You can set a property in one of the following ways:

- Type in a value
- Select a value from a drop-down list
- Click a Build button for property-specific options

Many properties can be changed by more than one of these methods.

To better understand how changing properties works, follow these steps:

1. Start by creating a new Windows Application project. Name this project **Changing Properties**.

2. Add a new text box to a form by double-clicking the TextBox tool in the toolbox. You're now going to change a few properties of the new text box.

3. Select the Name property in the Properties window by clicking it, and then type in a name for the text box—call it **txtComments**.

4. Click the BorderStyle property and try to type in the word **Big**—you can't; the BorderStyle property supports only selecting values from a list. You can type a value that exists in the list, however. When you selected the BorderStyle property, a drop-down arrow appeared in the value column. Click this arrow now to display a list of the values that the BorderStyle property accepts. Select FixedSingle and notice how the appearance of the text box changes. To make the text box appear three dimensional again, open the drop-down list and select Fixed3D.

5. Select the BackColor property, type in some text, and press the Tab key to commit your entry. C# displays an Invalid Property Value error. This happened because, although you can type in text, you're restricted to entering specific values (in the case of BackColor, the value must be a number within a specific range or a named color). Click the drop-down arrow of the BackColor property and select a color from the drop-down list. (Selecting colors using the Color Palette is discussed later in this hour, and detailed information on using colors is provided in Hour 10, "Drawing and Printing.")

6. Select the Font property. Notice that a Build button appears (a small button with three dots on it). When you click the Build button, a dialog box specific to the property you've selected appears. In this instance, a dialog box that allows you to manipulate the font of the text box appears (see Figure 2.15). Different properties display different dialog boxes when you click their Build buttons.

By clicking a property in the Properties window, you can easily tell the type of input the property requires.

FIGURE 2.15

The Font dialog box gives you complete authority over the font of a control.

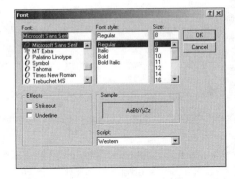

Working with Color Properties

Properties that deal with colors, such as BackColor and ForeColor, are unique in the way in which they accept values, yet all color-related properties behave the same way. In C#, all colors are expressed as a set of three numbers, each number having a value from 0 to 255. The set of numbers represents the Red, Green, and Blue (RGB) components of the color, respectively.

> The value 0,255,0, for instance, represents pure green, whereas the values 0,0,0 represent black and 255,255,255 represents white. (See Hour 10 for more information on the specifics of working with color.)

A color rectangle is displayed for each color property in the Properties window; this color is the selected color for the property. Text is displayed next to the colored rectangle. This text is either the name of a color or a set of RGB values that defines the color. Clicking in a color property causes a drop-down arrow to appear, but the drop-down you get by clicking the arrow isn't a typical drop-down list. Figure 2.16 shows what the drop-down list for a color property looks like.

FIGURE 2.16

The color drop-down list enables you to select from three sets of colors.

The color drop-down list is composed of three tabs: Custom, Web, and System. Most color properties use a system color by default. Hour 10 goes into great detail on system colors, so I only want to mention here that system colors vary from computer to computer; they are the colors determined by the user when he or she right-clicks the desktop and chooses Properties from the desktop's shortcut menu. Use a system color when you want a color to be one of the user's selected system colors. When a color property is set to a system color, the name of the color appears in the property sheet.

The Custom tab shown in Figure 2.17 is used to specify a specific color, regardless of the user's system color settings; changes to system colors have no effect on the property. The most common colors appear on the palette of the Custom tab, but you can specify any color you desire.

FIGURE 2.17

The Custom tab of the color drop-down list lets you specify any color imaginable.

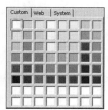

The colors visible in the various palettes are limited by the number of colors that can be produced by your video card. If your video card doesn't support enough colors, some will appear dithered, which means they will appear as dots of colors rather than as a true, solid color.

The bottom two rows in the Custom color palette are used to mix your own colors. To assign a color to an empty color slot, right-click a slot in one of the two rows to access the Define Color dialog box (see Figure 2.18). Use the controls on the Define Color dialog box to create the color you desire, and then click Add Color. The new color appears on the color palette in the slot you selected, and it is automatically assigned to the current property.

The Web tab is used to pick colors from a list of named colors for building Web pages.

Viewing Property Descriptions

It's not always immediately apparent just exactly what a property is or does—especially for new users of Visual Studio. The Description section at the bottom of the Properties window shows a simple description of the selected property (refer to Figure 2.14). To view a description, simply click a property or value area of a property.

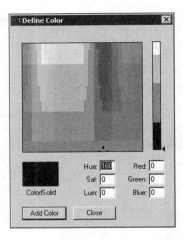

FIGURE 2.18
The Define Color dialog box lets you create your own colors.

You can hide or show the Description section of the Properties window at any time by right-clicking anywhere within the Properties window (other than in the value column or on the title bar) to display the Properties window shortcut menu and choosing Description. Each time you do this, you toggle the Description section between visible and hidden. To change the size of the Description box, click and drag the border between it and the Properties pane.

Managing Projects

Before you can effectively create an interface and write code, you need to understand what makes up a C# project and how to add and remove various components from within your own projects. In this section, you'll learn about the Solution Explorer window and how it's used to manage project files. You'll also learn specifics about projects and project files, as well as how to change a project's properties.

Managing Project Files with the Solution Explorer

As you develop projects, they'll become more and more complex, often containing many objects such as forms and modules. Each object is defined by one or more files. In addition, you can build complex solutions composed of more than one project. The Solution Explorer window shown in Figure 2.19 is the tool for managing all the files in a simple or complex solution. Using the Solution Explorer, you can add, rename, and remove project files, as well as select objects to view their properties. If the Solution Explorer window isn't visible on your screen, show it now by choosing Solution Explorer from the View menu.

FIGURE 2.19

Use the Solution Explorer window to manage all the files that make up a project.

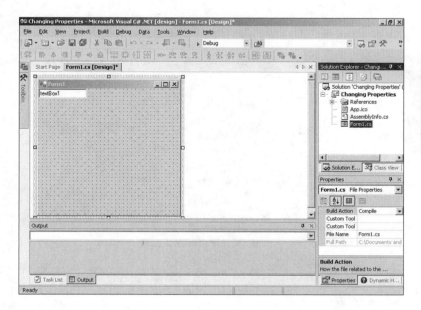

To better understand the Solution Explorer window, follow these steps:

1. Locate the Picture Viewer program you created in the Quick Tour by choosing File, Open, and then clicking Project.

2. Open the Picture Viewer project. The file you need to select is located in the Picture Viewer folder that C# created when the project was constructed. The file has the extension .sln (for solution). If you're asked whether you want to save the current project, choose No.

3. Select the Picture Viewer project item in the Solution Explorer. When you do, a button becomes visible toward the top of the window. This button has a picture of pieces of paper and has the ToolTip Show All Files (see Figure 2.20). Click this button and the Solution Explorer displays all files in the project.

Your design environment should now look like the one in Figure 2.20. If your screen looks much different from the one in this figure, use the techniques you've learned in this hour to change your design environment so that it's similar to the one shown here. Be sure to widen the Solution Explorer window so that you can read all the text it contains.

FIGURE 2.20

Notice that the form you defined appears as two files in the Solution Explorer.

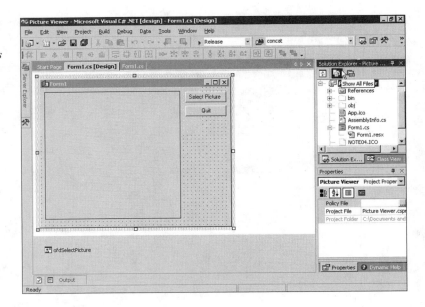

Some forms and other objects may be composed of more than one file. By default, C# hides project files that you don't directly manipulate. Click the plus sign (+) next to the form item and you'll see a sub item titled Form1.resx. You'll learn about these additional files in Hour 5, "Building Forms—Part I." For now, click the Show All Files button again to hide these related files.

You can view any object listed within the Solution Explorer using the object's default viewer by double-clicking the object. Each object has a default viewer but may actually have more than one viewer. For instance, a form has a Form Design view as well as a Code view. By default, double-clicking a form in the Solution Explorer displays the form in Form Design view, where you can manipulate the form's interface.

You've already learned one way to access the code behind a form—double-click an object to access its default event handler. You'll frequently need to get to the code of a form without adding a new event handler. One way to do this is to use the Solution Explorer. When a form is selected in the Solution Explorer, buttons are visible at the top of the Solution Explorer window that allow you to display the code editor or the form designer, respectively.

You'll use the Solution Explorer window so often that you'll probably want to dock it to an edge and set it to Auto Hide, or perhaps keep it visible all the time. The Solution Explorer window is one of the easiest to get the hang of in C#; navigating the Solution Explorer window will be second nature to you before you know it.

Working with Solutions

In truth, the Solution Explorer window is the evolution of the Project Explorer window from versions of Visual Studio prior to .NET, and the two are similar in many ways. Understanding solutions is easier to do when you understand projects.

A project is what you create with C#. Often, the words *project* and *program* are used interchangeably; this isn't much of a problem if you understand the important distinctions. A project is the set of source files that make up a program or component, whereas a program is the binary file that you build by compiling source files into something such as a Windows executable file (.exe). Projects always consist of a main project file and may be made up of any number of other files, such as form files, module files, or class module files. The main project file stores information about the project—all the files that make up the project, for example—as well as properties that define aspects of a project, such as the parameters to use when the project is compiled into a program.

What then, is a solution? As your abilities grow and your applications increase in complexity, you'll find that to accomplish your development goals, you'll have to build multiple projects that work harmoniously. For instance, you might build a custom user control such as a custom data grid that you use within other projects you design, or you may isolate the business rules of a complex application into separate components to run on isolated servers. All the projects used to accomplish those goals are collectively called a *solution*. Therefore, a solution (at its most basic level) is really nothing more than a grouping of projects.

> You should group projects into a single solution only when the projects relate to one another. If you have a number of projects that you're working on, but each of them is autonomous, work with each project in a separate solution.

Understanding Project Components

As I stated earlier, a project always consists of a main project file, and it may consist of one or more secondary files, such as files that make up forms or code modules. As you create and save objects within your project, one or more corresponding files are created and saved on your hard drive. All files that are created for C# source objects have the extension .cs, designating that they define C# objects. Make sure that you save your objects with understandable names, or things might get confusing as the size of your project grows.

All the files that make up a project are text files. Some objects, however, need to store binary information, such as a picture, for a form's BackgroundImage property. Binary data is stored in an XML file (which is still a text file). Suppose you had a form with an icon on it. You'd have a text file defining the form (its size, the controls on it, and the code behind it), and an associated *resource file* with the same name as the form file but with the extension .resx. This second file would be in XML format and would contain all the binary data needed to create the form.

If you want to see what the source file of a form file looks like, use Notepad to open a form file on your computer. Don't save any changes to the file, however, or it may never work again.

The following is a list of some of the components you may use in your projects:

- Forms   Forms are the visual windows that make up the interface of your application. Forms are defined using a special type of module.
- Class Modules   Class modules are a special type of module that enable you to create object-oriented applications. Throughout the course of this book, you're learning how to program using an object-oriented language, but you're mostly learning how to use objects supplied by C#. In Hour 17, "Designing Objects with Classes," you'll learn how to use class modules to create your own objects. Forms are derived from a special type of class module.
- User Controls   User controls (formerly ActiveX controls, which are formerly OLE controls) are controls that can be used on the forms of other projects. For example, you could create a User control with a calendar interface for a contact manager. Creating user controls requires the skill of an experienced programmer; therefore, I won't be covering them in this book.

Setting Project Properties

C# projects have properties, just as other objects do, such as forms and controls. Projects have lots of properties, many of them relating to advanced functionality that I won't be covering in this book. However, you need to be aware of how to access project properties and how to change some of the more commonly used properties.

To access the properties for a project, right-click the project in the Solution Explorer window and choose Properties from the shortcut menu. Do this now.

> In earlier versions of Visual Studio, you accessed the project properties via the Project menu. You can still do this, but you *must* have the project selected in the Solution Explorer, or the Properties menu won't appear on the Project menu. If you don't remember this, you could spend a lot of time trying to find the properties—I sure did.

The Tree View control on the left side of the dialog box is used to display a property page (see Figure 2.21). When you first open the dialog box, the General page is visible. On this page, the setting you'll need to worry about most is the Startup Object property. The Startup Object setting determines the name of the class that contains the Main() method that you want called on program startup. The (Not Set) option, as shown in Figure 2.21, is valid if only one Main() method exists in your application.

FIGURE 2.21

Project properties let you tailor aspects of the project as a whole.

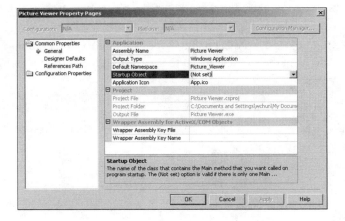

The Output Type option determines the type of compiled component defined by this source project. When you create a new project, you select the type of project to create (such as Windows Application), so this field is always filled in. At times, you might have to change this setting after the project has been created, and this is the place to do so.

Notice that the project folder, project filename, and output name are displayed on this page as well. If you work with a lot of projects, you may find this information valuable, and this is certainly the easiest spot to obtain it.

> The output name determines the filename created when you build a distributable component. Distributing applications is discussed in Hour 22.

As you work through the hours in this book, I'll refer to the Project Properties dialog box as necessary, explaining pages and items in context with other material.

Adding and Removing Project Files

When you first start C# and create a new Windows Application project, C# creates the project with a single form. You're not limited to having one form in a project, however; you can create new forms or add existing forms to your project at will. You can also create and add code files and classes, as well as other types of objects.

You can add a new or existing object to your project in one of three ways:

- Choose the appropriate menu item from the Project menu.
- Click the small drop-down arrow that is part of the Add New Item button on the Standard toolbar, and then choose the object type from the drop-down list that is displayed (see Figure 2.22).
- Right-click the project name in the Solution Explorer window, and then choose Add from the shortcut menu to access a submenu from which you can select object types.

FIGURE 2.22

This tool button is one of three ways to add objects to a project.

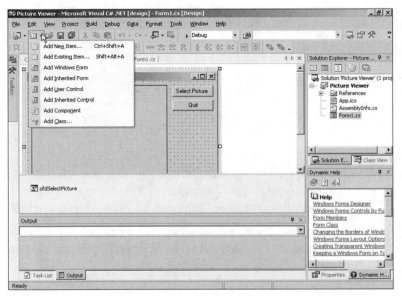

When you select Add *ObjectType* from any of these menus, a dialog box appears, showing you the objects that can be added to the project. Your chosen item is selected by default (see Figure 2.23). Simply name the object and click Open to create a new object of the selected type. To create an object of a different type, click the type to select it, name it, and then click Open.

FIGURE 2.23

Regardless of the menu option you select, you can add any type of object you want using this dialog box.

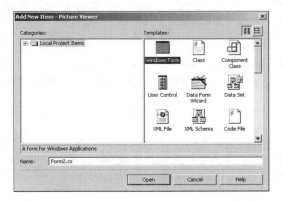

Adding new forms and modules to your project is easy, and you can add as many as you like. You'll come to rely more heavily on the Solution Explorer to manage all the objects in the project as the project becomes more complex.

Although it won't happen as often as adding project files, you may sometimes need to remove an object from a project. Removing objects from your project is even easier than adding them. To remove an object, simply right-click the object in the Solution Explorer window and select Exclude from Project. This removes the object from the file but does not delete the source file from the disk. Selecting Delete, on the other hand, removes the file from the project and deletes it from the disk. Don't select Delete unless you want to totally destroy the file and you're sure that you'll never need it again in the future.

Getting Help

Although C# was designed to be as intuitive as possible, you'll find that you occasionally need assistance in performing a task. It doesn't matter how much you know, C# is so complex and contains so many features that you'll have to use Help sometimes. This is particularly true when writing C# code; you won't always remember the command you need or the syntax of the command. Fortunately, C# includes a comprehensive Help feature.

To access Help from within the design environment, press F1. Generally speaking, when you press F1, C# shows you a help topic directly related to what you're doing. This is known as context-sensitive help, and when it works, it works well. For example, you can display help for any C# syntax or keyword (functions, objects, methods, properties, and so on) when writing C# code by typing the word into the code editor, positioning the cursor anywhere within the word (including before the first letter or after the last), and pressing F1. You can also get to help from the Help menu on the menu bar.

C#'s Help won't be displayed if your program is in Run mode when you press F1. Instead, the help for your application will appear—if you've created Help.

Help displays topics directly within the design environment instead of in a separate window. This is a new feature of .NET. Personally, I think this method is considerably inferior to the old style of Visual Studio having Help float above the design environment. When Help is displayed within the design environment, you can't necessarily see the code, form, or other object with which you're working. To make Help float above the design environment, choose Options from the Tools menu to display the Options dialog box, click Help in the Tree view on the left, and select External Help.

C# includes a Help feature called Dynamic Help. To display the Dynamic Help window, choose Dynamic Help from the Help menu. The Dynamic Help window shows Help links related to what it is you're working on (see Figure 2.24). For instance, if you select a form, the contents of the Dynamic Help window show you Help links related to forms. If you click a text box, the contents of the Dynamic Help window adjust to show you Help links related to text boxes. This is an interesting feature, and you may find it valuable.

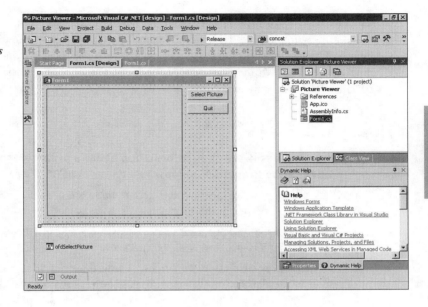

FIGURE 2.24
*Dynamic Help gives
you a list of Help links
related to the task
you're performing.*

2

Summary

In this hour, you learned how to use the Visual Studio Start page—your gateway to C#.
You learned how to create new projects and how to open existing projects. The C# environment is your workspace, toolbox, and so much more. You learned how to navigate the
environment, including how to work with design windows (hide, show, dock, and float).

You'll use toolbars constantly, and now you know how to modify them to suit your specific needs. You learned how to create new toolbars and how to modify existing toolbars.
This is an important skill that shouldn't be overlooked.

C# has many different design windows, and in this hour, you began learning about some
of them in detail. You learned how to get and set properties using the Properties window,
how to manage projects using the Solution Explorer, and how to add controls to a form
using the toolbox. You'll use these skills often, so it's important to get familiar with them
right away. Finally, you learned how to access C#'s Help feature, which I guarantee you
will find very important as you learn to use C#.

C# is a vast and powerful development tool. Don't expect to become an expert overnight; this is simply impossible. However, by learning the tools and techniques presented in this hour, you've begun your journey. Remember, you'll use most of what you learned in this hour each and every time you use C#. Get proficient with these basics and you'll be building cool programs in no time!

Q&A

Q. How can I easily get more information about a property when the Description section of the Properties window just doesn't cut it?

A. Click the property in question to select it, and then press F1; context-sensitive help applies to properties in the Properties window, as well.

Q. I find that I need to see a lot of design windows at one time, but I can't find that "magic" layout. Any suggestions?

A. Run at a higher resolution. Personally, I won't develop in less than 1024×768. As a matter of fact, all my development machines have two displays, both running at this resolution. You'll find that any investment you make in having more screen real estate will pay you big dividends.

Workshop

The Workshop is designed to help you anticipate possible questions, review what you've learned, and get you thinking about how to put your knowledge into practice. The answers to the quiz are in Appendix A, "Answers to Quizzes/Exercises."

Quiz

1. How can you make the Visual Studio Start Page appear at startup if this feature has been disabled?

2. Unless instructed otherwise, you are to create what type of project when building examples in this book?

3. To make a docked design window appear when you hover over its tab and disappear when you move the mouse away from it, you change what setting of the window?

4. How do you access the Toolbars menu?

5. What design window do you use to add controls to a form?

6. What design window is used to change the attributes of an object?

7. To modify the properties of a project, you must select the project in what design window?

8. Which Help feature adjusts the links it displays to match what it is you are doing?

Exercises

1. Create a custom toolbar that contains Save All, Start, and Stop Debugging—three buttons you'll use a lot throughout this book.

2. Use the Custom Color dialog box to create a color of your choice, and then assign the color to the BackColor property of a form.

HOUR 3

Understanding Objects and Collections

So far, you've gotten an introduction to programming in C# by building a Picture Viewer project. You spent the previous hour digging into the IDE and learning skills critical to your success with C#. In this hour, you're going to start learning about some important programming concepts, namely *objects*.

NEW TERM The term *object*, as it relates to programming, may have been new to you prior to this book. The more you work with C#, the more you'll hear about objects. C# is a true object-oriented language. This hour isn't going to discuss object-oriented programming in any detail, because object-oriented programming is a very complex subject and is well beyond the scope of this book. Instead, you'll learn about objects in a more general sense. Everything you use in C# is an object, so understanding this material is critical to your success with C#. Forms are objects, for example, as are the controls you place on a form. Pretty much every element of a C# project is an object and belongs to a collection of objects. All objects have attributes (called properties), most have methods, and many have events. Whether creating simple applications or building large-scale enterprise solutions, you must understand what an object is and how it works. In this hour, you'll learn what makes an object an object, and you'll learn about collections.

The highlights of this hour include the following:

- Understanding objects
- Getting and setting properties
- Triggering methods
- Understanding method dynamism
- Writing object-based code
- Understanding collections
- Using the Object Browser

 If you've listened to the programming press at all, you've probably heard the term *object oriented*, and perhaps words such as polymorphism, encapsulation, and inheritance. In truth, these object-oriented features of C# are very exciting, but they're far beyond Hour 3. You'll learn a little about object-oriented programming in this book, but if you're really interested in taking your programming skills to the next level, you should buy a book dedicated to the subject after you've completed this one.

Understanding Objects

Object-oriented programming has been a technical buzzword for quite some time. Almost everywhere you look—the Web, publications, books—you read about objects. What exactly is an object? Strictly speaking, it is a programming structure that encapsulates data and functionality as a single unit and for which the only public access is through the programming structure's interfaces (properties, methods, and events). In reality, the answer to this question can be somewhat ambiguous because there are so many types of objects—and the number grows almost daily. However, all objects share specific characteristics, such as properties and methods.

The most commonly used objects in Windows applications are the form object and the control object. Earlier hours introduced you to working with forms and controls and even showed you how to set form and control properties. In your Picture Viewer project from Hour 1, for instance, you added a picture box and two buttons to a form. Both the PictureBox and the Button control are *control objects*, but each is a specific type of control object. Another, less-technical example uses pets. Dogs and cats are definitely different entities (objects), but they both fit into the category of Pet objects. Similarly, text boxes and buttons are each a unique type of object, but they're both considered a control object. This small distinction is important.

Understanding Properties

All objects have attributes used to specify and return the state of the object. These attributes are properties, and you've already used some of them in previous hours using the Properties window. Indeed, every object exposes a specific set of properties, but not every object exposes the same set of properties. To illustrate this point, I will continue with the Pet object concept. Suppose you have an object, and the object is a dog. This Dog object has a certain set of properties that are common to all dogs. These properties include attributes such as the dog's name, the color of its hair, and even the number of legs it has. All dogs have these same properties; however, different dogs have different values for these properties. Figure 3.1 illustrates such a Dog object and its properties.

FIGURE 3.1
Properties are the attributes that describe an object.

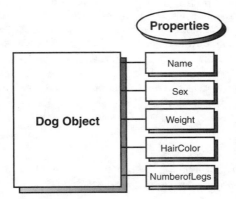

Getting and Setting Properties

You've already seen how to read and change properties using the Properties window. The Properties window is available only at design time, however, and is used only for manipulating the properties of forms and controls. Most reading and changing of properties you'll perform will be done with C# code, not by using the Properties window. When referencing properties in code, you specify the name of the object first, followed by a period (.), and then the property name, as in the following syntax:

```
{ObjectName}.{Property}
```

If you had a Dog object named Bruno, for example, you would reference Bruno's hair color this way:

```
Bruno.HairColor
```

This line of code would return whatever value was contained in the HairColor property of the Dog object Bruno. To set a property to some value, you use an equal (=) sign. For example, to change the Dog object Bruno's Weight property, you would use a line of code such as the following:

```
Bruno.Weight = 90;
```

> A little later in this hour, I discuss *instantiation*, which is the process of creating an object based on a template. It's important to note here that Bruno is a named instance of an object derived from a template or blueprint (called a class). Each object instance has its own set of data, such as property values. For example, you could also have a Dog object named Bonnie, which has a unique set of properties. In a more real-world example, consider how you can have two buttons on a form. Although they have different property values (such as Name), and they have different code within their Click events, they are both Button objects.

When you reference a property on the left side of an equal sign, you're setting the value. When you reference a property on the right side of the equal sign, you're getting (reading) the value.

```
Bruno.Weight = 90;
```

It's easier to see here that referencing the property on the left side of the equal sign indicates that you are setting the property to some value.

The following line of code places the value of the Weight property of the Dog object called Bruno into a temporary variable. This statement retrieves the value of the Weight property because the Weight property is referenced on the right side of the equal sign.

```
fltWeight = Bruno.Weight;
```

Variables are discussed in detail in Hour 12, "Using Constants, Data Types, Variables, and Arrays." For now, think of a variable as a storage location. When the processor executes this code statement, it retrieves the value in the Weight property of the Dog object Bruno and places it in the variable (storage location) titled Weight. Assuming that Bruno's Weight is 90, as set in the previous example, the computer would process the following code statement:

```
fltWeight = 90;
```

Just as in real life, some properties can be read but not changed. Suppose you had a Sex property to designate the gender of a Dog object. It's impossible for you to change a dog from a male to a female or vice versa (at least I think it is). Because the Sex property can be retrieved but not changed, it is a *read-only* property. You'll often encounter properties that can be set in Design view but become read-only when the program is running.

One example of a read-only property is the Height property of the Combo Box control. Although you can view the value of the Height property in the Properties window, you cannot change the value—no matter how hard you try. If you attempt to change the Height property using C# code, C# simply changes the value back to the default.

> The best way to determine which properties of an object are read-only is to consult the online help for the object in question.

Working with an Object and Its Properties

Now that you know what properties are and how they can be viewed and changed, you're going to experiment with properties in a simple project. In Hour 1, you learned how to set the Height and Width properties of a form using the Properties window. Now, you're going to change the same properties using C# code.

The project you're going to create consists of a form with some buttons on it. One button will enlarge the form when clicked, whereas the other will shrink the form. This is a very simple project, but it illustrates rather well how to change object properties in C# code.

1. Start by creating a new Windows Application project (from the File menu, choose New, Project).

2. Name the project **Properties Example**.

3. Use the Properties window to change the name of the form to **fclsShrinkMe**. (Click the form once to select it and press F4 to display the Properties window.)

4. Next, change the Text property of the form to **Grow and Shrink**.

5. Click the View Code button in Solution Explorer to view the code behind the form. Scroll down and locate the reference to Form1 and change it to **fclsShrinkMe**.

6. Click the Form1.cs [Design] tab to return to the form designer.

When the project first runs, the default form will have a Height and Width as specified in the Properties window. You're going to add buttons to the form that a user can click to enlarge or shrink the form at runtime.

Add a new button to the form by double-clicking the Button tool in the toolbox. Set the
new button's properties as follows:

Property	Set To
Name	btnEnlarge
Location	111,70
Text	Enlarge

Now for the Shrink button. Again, double-click the Button tool in the toolbox to create a
new button on the form. Set this new button's properties as follows:

Property	Set To
Name	btnShrink
Location	111,120
Text	Shrink

Your form should now look like the one shown in Figure 3.2.

FIGURE 3.2

*Each button is an
object, as is the form
the buttons sit on.*

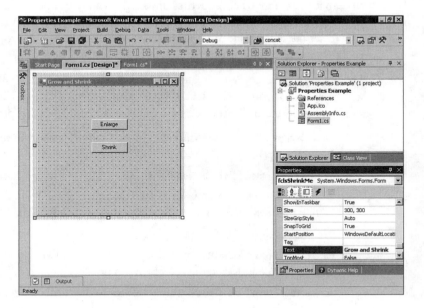

To complete the project, you need to add the small amount of C# code necessary to
modify the form's Height and Width properties when the user clicks a button. Access
the code for the Enlarge button now by double-clicking the Enlarge button. Type the

following statement exactly as you see it here. Do not hit the Enter key or add a space after you've entered this text.

```
this.Width
```

When you typed the period, or "dot," as it's called, a small drop-down list appeared, like the one shown in Figure 3.3. C# is smart enough to realize that this represents the current object (more on this in a moment), and to aid you in writing code for the object, it gives you a drop-down list containing all the properties and methods of the form. This feature is called *IntelliSense*, and it is relatively new to Visual Studio. Because C# is fully object-oriented, you'll come to rely on IntelliSense drop-down lists in a big way; I think I'd rather dig ditches than program without them.

FIGURE 3.3

IntelliSense drop-down lists, or auto-completion drop-down lists, make coding dramatically easier.

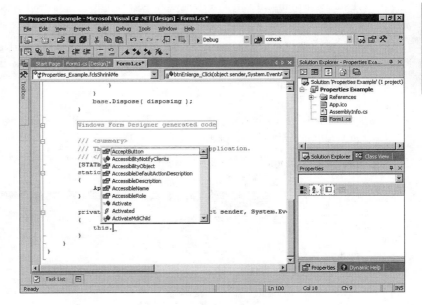

Use the Backspace key to completely erase the code you just entered and enter the following code in its place (press Enter at the end of each line):

```
this.Width = this.Width + 20;
this.Height = this.Height + 20;
```

Again, the word this refers to the object to which the code belongs (in this case, the form). The word this is a *reserved* word; it's a word that you cannot use to name objects or variables because C# has a specific meaning for it. When writing code within a form module, as you are doing here, you should always use the this reserved word rather than using the name of the form. this is much shorter than using the full name of the current form, and it makes the code more portable (you can copy and paste the code into another form module and not have to change the form name to make the code work). Also, should you change the name of the form at any time in the future, you won't have to change references to the old name.

> The word this is the equivalent to the Me reserved word in Visual Basic.

The code you've entered simply sets the Width and Height properties of the form to whatever the current value of the Width and Height properties happens to be, plus 20 pixels.

Redisplay the form designer by selecting the tab titled Form1.cs [Design]; then double-click the Shrink button to access its Click event and add the following code:

```
this.Width = this.Width - 20;
this.Height = this.Height - 20;
```

This code is very similar to the code in the Enlarge_Click event, except that it reduces the Width and Height properties of the form by 20 pixels.

Your screen should now look like Figure 3.4.

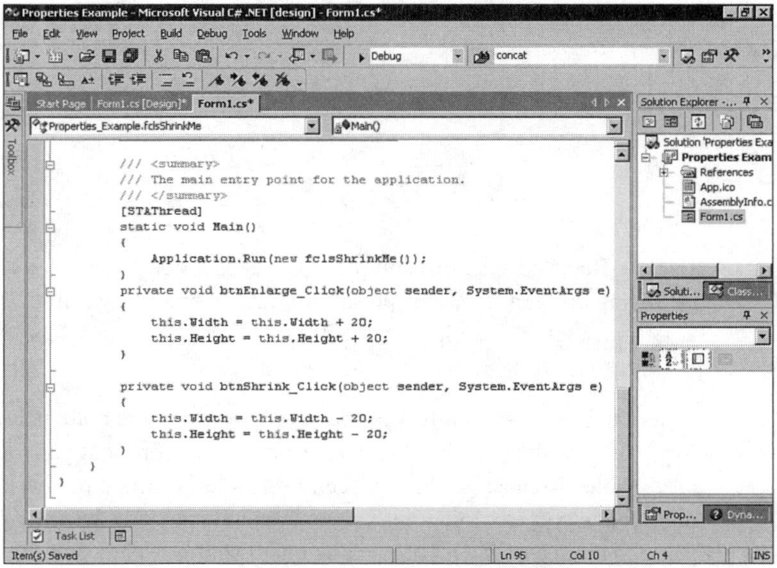

FIGURE 3.4

The code you've entered should look exactly like this.

As you create projects, it's a very good idea to save frequently. Save your project now by clicking the Save All button on the toolbar.

Again, display the form designer by clicking the tab Form1.cs [Design]. Your Properties Example is now ready to be run! Press F5 to put the project in Run mode (see Figure 3.5).

Figure 3.5

What you see is what you get—the form you created should look just as you designed it.

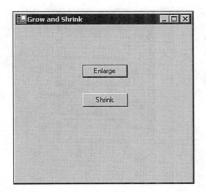

3

Click the Enlarge button a few times and notice how the form gets bigger. Next, click the Shrink button to make the form smaller. When you've clicked enough to satisfy your curiosity (or until you get bored), end the running program and return to Design mode by clicking the Stop Debugging button on the toolbar.

Understanding Methods

In addition to properties, most objects have methods. Methods are actions the object can perform, in contrast to attributes that describe the object. To understand this distinction, think about the Pet object example. A Dog object has a certain set of actions that it can perform. These actions, called methods in C#, include barking and tail wagging. Figure 3.6 illustrates the Dog object and its methods.

Triggering Methods

Think of methods as functions—which is exactly what they are. When you invoke a method, code is executed. You can pass data to the method, and methods may return values. However, a method is neither required to accept parameters (data passed by the calling code) nor required to return a value; many methods simply perform an action in code. Invoking (triggering) a method is similar to referencing the value of a property;

you first reference the object's name, then a "dot," then the method name, followed by a set of parentheses, which can optionally contain any parameters that must be passed to the method.

```
{ObjectName}.{Method}();
```

FIGURE 3.6

Invoking a method causes the object to perform an action.

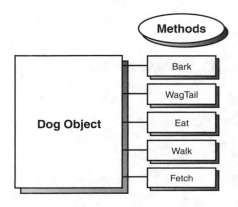

For example, to make the hypothetical Dog object Bruno bark using C# code, you would use this line of code:

```
Bruno.Bark();
```

Method calls in C# must always have parentheses. Sometimes they'll be empty, but at other times they'll contain data.

Invoking methods is simple; the real skill lies in knowing what methods an object supports and when to use a particular method.

Understanding Method Dynamism

Properties and methods go hand in hand, and at times a particular method may become unavailable because of one or more property values. For example, if you were to set the NumberofLegs on the Dog object Bruno equal to zero, the Walk and Fetch methods would obviously be inapplicable. If you were to set the NumberofLegs property back to four, you could then trigger the Walk or Fetch methods again. In C#, a method or property won't physically become unavailable—you can still call it, but doing so might cause an exception (error) or the call may be ignored.

Building an Object Example Project

The only way to really grasp what objects are and how they work is to use them. I've said this before but I can't say it enough: everything in C# is an object.

You're about to create a sample project that uses objects. If you're new to programming with objects, you'll probably find this a bit confusing. However, I'll walk you through step by step, explaining each section in detail.

The project you're going to create consists of a single form with one button on it. When the button is clicked, a line will be drawn on the form beginning at the upper-left corner of the form and extending to the lower-right corner.

 In Hour 10, "Drawing and Printing," you'll learn all about the drawing functionality within C#.

3

Creating the Interface for the Drawing Project

Follow these steps to create the interface for your project:

1. Create a new Windows Application project titled **Object Example**.
2. Change the form's Text property to **Object Example** using the Properties window.
3. Add a new button to the form and set its properties as shown in the following table:

Property	Value
Name	btnDraw
Location	112,120
Text	Draw

Writing the Object-Based Code

You're now going to add code to the Click event of the button. I'm going to explain each statement, and at the end of the steps, I'll show the complete code listing.

Object Example Project

1. Double-click the button to access its Click event.
2. Enter the first line of code as follows (remember to press Enter at the end of each statement):

```
System.Drawing.Graphics objGraphics = null;
```

Objects don't materialize out of thin air; they have to be created. When a form is loaded into memory, it loads all its controls (that is, creates the control objects), but not all objects are created automatically like this. The process of creating an instance of an object is called *instantiation*. When you load a form, you instantiate the form object, which in turn instantiates its control objects. You could load a second instance of the form, which in turn would instantiate a new instance of the form and new instances of all controls. You would then have two forms in memory and two of each used control.

To instantiate an object in code, you create a variable that holds a reference to an instantiated object. You then manipulate the variable as an object. The statement you wrote in step 2 creates a new variable called objGraphics, which holds a reference to an object of type Graphics from the .NET Framework System.Drawing class. You also initialized the value for objGraphics to null. You learn more about variables in Hour 12, "Using Constants, Data Types, Variables, and Arrays."

3. Enter the second line of code exactly as shown here:

```
objGraphics = CreateGraphics();
```

CreateGraphics is a method of the form. The CreateGraphics method is pretty complicated under the hood, and I discuss it in detail in Hour 10. For now, understand that the method CreateGraphics instantiates a new object that represents the client area of the current form. The client area is the gray area within the borders and title bar of a form. Anything drawn onto the objGraphics object appears on the form. What you've done is set the variable objGraphics to point to an object that was returned by the CreateGraphics method. Notice how values returned by a property or method don't have to be traditional values such as numbers or text; they can also be objects.

4. Enter the third line of code as shown next:

```
objGraphics.Clear(System.Drawing.SystemColors.Control);
```

This statement clears the background of the form using whatever color the user has selected as the Windows forms color.

How does this happen? In step 3, you used the CreateGraphics method of the form to instantiate a new graphics object in the variable objGraphics. With the code statement you just entered, you're calling the clear method of the objGraphics object. The Clear method is a method of all Graphics objects used to clear the graphics surface. The Clear method accepts a single parameter—the color to which you want the surface cleared.

The value you're passing to the parameter looks fairly convoluted. Remember that "dots" are a method of separating objects from their properties and methods.

Knowing this, you can discern that System is an object (technically it's a Namespace, as discussed in Hour 24, "The 10,000-Foot View," but for our purposes it behaves just like an object) because it appears before any of the dots. However, there are multiple dots. What this means is that Drawing is an *object property* of the System object; it's a property that returns an object. So the dot following Drawing is used to access a member of the Drawing object, which in turn is a property of the System object. We're not done yet, however, because there is yet another dot. Again, this indicates that SystemColors, which follows a dot, is an object of the Drawing object, which in turn is...well, you get the idea. As you can see, object references can and do go pretty deep, and you'll use many dots throughout your code. The key points to remember are the following:

- Text that appears to the left of a dot is always an object (or Namespace).

- Text that appears to the right of a dot is a property reference or a method call.

- Methods are never objects. In addition, methods are *always* followed by parentheses. If the text in question isn't followed by parentheses, it's definitely a property. Therefore, text that appears between two dots is a property that returns an object. Such a property is called an *object property*.

The final text in this statement is the word *Control*. Because Control is not followed by a dot, you know that it's not an object; therefore, it must be a property or a method. Because you expect this string of object references to return a color value to be used to clear the Graphics object, you know that Control must be a property or a method that returns a value. A quick check of the documentation (or simply realizing that the text isn't followed by a set of parentheses) would tell you that Control is indeed a property. The value of Control always equates to the color designated on the user's computer for the face of forms. By default, this is a light gray (often fondly referred to as battleship gray), but users can change this value on their computers. By using this property to specify a color rather than supplying the actual value for gray, you are assured that no matter the color scheme used on a computer, the code will clear the form to the proper system color. System colors are explained in Hour 10.

5. Enter the following statement:

```
objGraphics.DrawLine(System.Drawing.Pens.Chartreuse, 0, 0,
    this.DisplayRectangle.Width, this.DisplayRectangle.Height);
```

This statement draws a chartreuse line on the form. Within this statement is a single method call and three property references. Can you tell what's what? Immediately following objGraphics (and a dot) is DrawLine. Because no equal sign is present (and the text is followed by parentheses), you can deduce that this is a method call. As with the Clear() method, the parentheses after DrawLine() are used to enclose a value passed to the method. The DrawLine() method accepts the following parameters in the order in which they appear here:

- A Pen
- X value of first coordinate
- Y value of first coordinate
- X value of second coordinate
- Y value of second coordinate

The DrawLine() method draws a straight line between coordinate one and coordinate two, using the pen specified in the Pen parameter. I'm not going to go into detail on pens here (refer to Hour 10), but suffice it to say that a pen has characteristics such as width and color. Looking at the dots once more, notice that you're passing the Chartreuse property of the Pens object. Chartreuse is an object property that returns a predefined Pen object that has a width of 1 pixel and the color chartreuse.

You're passing 0 as the next two parameters. The coordinates used for drawing are defined such that 0,0 is always the upper-left corner of a surface. As you move to the right of the surface, X increases, and as you move down the surface, Y increases; you can use negative values to indicate coordinates that appear to the left or above the surface. The coordinate 0,0 causes the line to be drawn from the upper-left corner of the form's client area.

The object property DisplayRectangle is referenced twice in this statement. DisplayRectangle is a property of the form that holds information about the client area of the form. Here, you're simply getting the Width and Height properties of the client area and passing them to the DrawLine method. The result is that the end of the line will be at the lower-right corner of the form's client area.

6. Last, you have to clean up after yourself by entering the following code statement:

```
objGraphics.Dispose();
```

Objects often make use of other objects and resources. The underlying mechanics of an object can be truly boggling and almost impossible to discuss in an entry-level programming book. The net effect, however, is that you must explicitly destroy most objects when you're done with them. If you don't destroy an object, it may persist in memory and it may hold references to other objects or resources that exist in memory. This means you can create a *memory leak* within your application that slowly (or rather quickly) munches system memory and resources. This is one of the cardinal no-no's of Windows programming, yet the nature of using resources and the fact you're responsible for telling your objects to clean up after themselves makes this easy to do.

Objects that must explicitly be told to clean up after themselves usually provide a Dispose method. When you're done with such an object, call Dispose on the object to make sure it frees any resources it might be holding.

For your convenience, following are all the lines of code:

```
System.Drawing.Graphics objGraphics = null;

objGraphics = CreateGraphics();
objGraphics.Clear(System.Drawing.SystemColors.Control);
objGraphics.DrawLine(System.Drawing.Pens.Chartreuse, 0, 0,
    this.DisplayRectangle.Width, this.DisplayRectangle.Height);
objGraphics.Dispose();
```

Testing Your Object Example Project

Now the easy part. Run the project by pressing F5 or by clicking the Start button on the toolbar. Your form looks pretty much like it did at design time. Clicking the button causes a line to be drawn from the upper-left corner of the form's client area to the lower-right corner (see Figure 3.7).

If you receive any errors when you attempt to run the project, go back and make sure the code you entered exactly matches the code I've provided.

FIGURE 3.7
Simple lines and complex drawings are accomplished using objects.

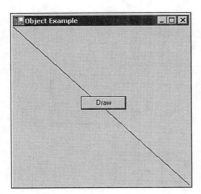

Resize the form, larger or smaller, and click the button again. Notice that the form is cleared and a new line is drawn. If you were to omit the statement that invokes the Clear method (and you're welcome to stop your project and do so), the new line would be drawn, but any and all lines already drawn would remain.

> If you use Alt+Tab to switch to another application after drawing one or more lines, the lines will be gone when you come back to your form. In Hour 10, you'll learn why this is so and how to work around this behavior.

Stop the project now by clicking Stop Debugging on the C# toolbar and then click Save All to save your project. What I hope you've gained from building this example is not necessarily that you can now draw a line (which is cool), but rather an understanding of how objects are used in programming. As with learning almost anything, repetition aids in understanding. Therefore, you'll be working with objects a lot throughout this book.

Understanding Collections

A collection is just what its name implies: a collection of objects. Collections make it easy to work with large numbers of similar objects by enabling you to create code that performs iterative processing on items within the collection. *Iterative processing* is an operation that uses a loop to perform actions on multiple objects, rather than writing the operative code for each object. In addition to containing an indexed set of objects, collections also have properties and may have methods. Figure 3.8 illustrates the structure of a collection.

FIGURE 3.8
Collections contain sets of like objects, and they have their own properties and methods.

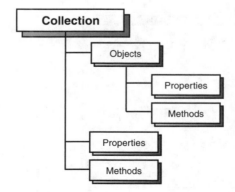

Continuing with the Dog/Pet object metaphor, think about what an Animals collection might look like. The Animals collection could contain one or more Pet objects, or it could be empty (containing no objects). All collections have a Count property that returns the total count of objects contained within the collection. Collections may also have methods, such as a Delete method used to remove objects from the collection or an Add method used to add a new object to the collection.

To better understand collections, you're going to create a small C# project that cycles through the Controls collection of a form, telling you the value of the Name property of every control on the form.

To create your sample project, follow these steps:

1. Start C# now (if it's not already loaded) and create a new Windows Application project titled **Collections Example**.

2. Change the text of the form to **Collections Example** by using the Properties window.

3. Add a new button to the form by double-clicking the Button tool in the toolbox. Set the button's properties as follows:

Property	Value
Name	btnShowNames
Location	88,112
Size	120,23
Text	Show Control Names

4. Next, add some text box and label controls to the form. As you add the controls to the form, be sure to give each control a unique name. Feel free to use any name you like, but you can't use spaces in a control name. You may want to drag the controls to different locations on the form so that they don't overlap.

5. When you are finished adding controls to your form, double-click the Show Control Names button to add code to its Click event. Enter the following code:

```
for (int intIndex=0; intIndex < this.Controls.Count; intIndex++)
{
    MessageBox.Show ("Control # " + intIndex.ToString() +
        " has the name " + this.Controls[intIndex].Name);
}
```

Every form has a Controls collection, which may or may not contain any controls. Even if no controls are on the form, the form still has a Controls collection.

The first statement (the one that begins with for) accomplishes a few tasks. First, it initializes the variable intIndex to 0, and then tests the variable. It also starts a loop executing the statement block (loops are discussed in Hour 15, "Looping for Efficiency"), incrementing intIndex by one until intIndex equals the number of controls on the form, less one. The reason that intIndex must always be less than the Count property is that when referencing items in a collection, the first item is always item zero—collections are zero based. Thus, the first item is in location zero, the second item is in location one, and so forth. If you tried to reference an item of a collection in the location of the value of the Count property, an error would occur because you would be referencing an index that is one higher than the actual locations within the collection.

The MessageBox.Show() method (discussed in detail in Hour 18, "Interacting with Users ") is a class available in the .NET Framework that is used to display a simple dialog box with text. The text that you are providing, which the MessageBox.Show() method will display, is a concatenation of multiple strings of text. (*Concatenation* is the process of adding strings together; it is discussed in Hour 13, "Performing Arithmetic, String Manipulation, and Date/Time Adjustments.")

Run the project by pressing F5 or by clicking Start on the toolbar. Ignore the additional controls that you placed on the form and click the Show Control Names button. Your program will then display a message box similar to the one shown in Figure 3.9 for each control on your form (because of the loop). When the program is finished displaying the names of the controls, choose Stop Debugging from the Debug toolbar to stop the program, and then save the project.

FIGURE 3.9

The Controls collection enables you to get to each and every control on a form.

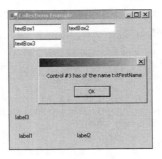

Because everything in C# is an object, you can expect to use numerous collections as you create your programs. Collections are powerful, and the quicker you become comfortable using them, the more productive you'll become.

Using the Object Browser

C# includes a useful tool that lets you easily view members, such as properties and methods, of all the objects in a project: the Object Browser (see Figure 3.10). This is extremely useful when dealing with objects that aren't well documented, because it enables you to see all the members an object supports. To view the Object Browser, display the Other Windows submenu of the View menu and choose Object Browser.

FIGURE 3.10

The Object Browser lets you view all properties and methods of an object.

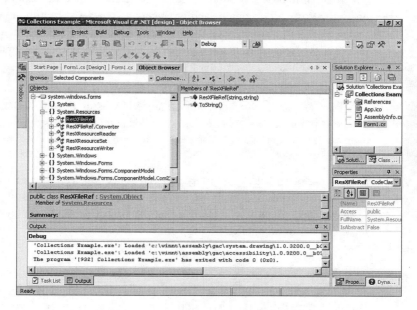

The Browse drop-down list in the upper-left corner of the Object Browser is used to determine the *browsing scope*. You can choose Active Project to view only the objects referenced in the active project, or you can choose Selected Components (the default) to view a set of selected objects. The Object Browser shows a preselected set of objects for Selected Components, but you can customize the object set by clicking the Customize button next to the Browse drop-down list. I wouldn't recommend changing the custom object set until you have some experience using C# objects and some experience using the Object Browser, as well.

The top-level nodes in the Objects tree are *libraries*. Libraries are usually DLL or EXE files on your computer that contain one or more objects. To view the objects within a library, simply expand the library node. As you select objects within a library, the list to the right of the Objects tree will show information regarding the members of the selected object (refer to Figure 3.10). For even more detailed information, click a member in the list on the right, and the Object Browser will show information about the member in the gray area below the two lists.

Summary

In this hour, you learned all about objects. You learned how objects have properties, which are attributes that describe the object. Some properties can be set at design time using the Properties window, and most can also be set at runtime in C# code. You learned that referencing a property on the left side of the equal sign has the effect of changing a property, whereas referencing a property on the right side of the equal sign retrieves the property's value.

In addition to properties, you learned that objects have executable functions, called methods. Like properties, methods are referenced by using a "dot" at the end of an object reference. An object may contain many methods and properties, and some properties can even be objects themselves. You learned how to "follow the dots" to interpret a lengthy object reference.

Objects are often used as a group, called a collection. You learned that a collection often contains properties and methods, and that collections let you easily iterate through a set of like objects. Finally, you learned that the Object Browser can be used to explore all the members of an object in a project.

The knowledge you've gained in this hour is fundamental to understanding programming with C#, because objects and collections are the basis on which applications are built. After you have a strong grasp of objects and collections—and you will have by the time you've completed all the hours in this book—you'll be well on your way to fully understanding the complexities of creating robust applications using C#.

Q&A

Q. Is there an easy way to get help about an object's member?

A. Absolutely. C#'s context-sensitive Help extends to code as well as to visual objects. To get help on a member, write a code statement that includes the member (it doesn't have to be a complete statement), position the cursor within the member text, and press F1. For instance, to get help on the Count property of the controls collection, you could type **this.Controls.Count**, position the cursor within the word Count, and press F1.

Q. Are there any other types of object members besides properties and methods?

A. Yes. An event is actually a member of an object, although it's not always thought of that way. Not all objects support events, however, but most objects do support properties and methods.

Workshop

The Workshop is designed to help you anticipate possible questions, review what you've learned, and get you thinking about how to put your knowledge into practice. The answers to the quiz are in Appendix A, "Answers to Quizzes/Exercises."

Quiz

1. True or False: C# is a true object-oriented language.

2. An attribute that defines the state of an object is called a what?

3. To change the value of a property, the property must be referenced on which side of an equal sign?

4. What is the term for when a new object is created from a template?

5. An external function of an object (one that is available to code using an object) is called a what?

6. True or False: A property of an object can be another object.

7. A group of like objects is called what?

8. What tool is used to explore the members of an object?

Exercises

1. Create a new project and add text boxes and a button to the form. Write code that, when clicked, places the text in the first text box into the second text box. Hint: Use the Text property of the text box controls.

2. Modify the collections example in this hour to print the Height of all controls, rather than the name.

HOUR 4

Understanding Events

It's fairly easy to create an attractive interface for an application using C#'s integrated design tools. You can create beautiful forms that have buttons to click, text boxes in which to type information, picture boxes in which to view pictures, and many other creative and attractive elements with which users can interact. However, this is just the start of producing a C# program. In addition to designing an interface, you have to empower your program to perform actions in response to how a user interacts with the program and how Windows interacts with the program. This is accomplished by using *events*. In the previous hour, you learned about objects and their members—notably, properties and methods. In this hour, you'll learn about object events and event-driven programming, and you'll learn how to use events to make your applications responsive.

The highlights of this hour include the following:

- Understanding event-driven programming
- Triggering events
- Avoiding recursive events
- Accessing an object's events

- Working with event parameters
- Creating event handlers
- Dealing with orphaned events

Understanding Event-Driven Programming

With "traditional" programming languages (often referred to as *procedural* languages), the program itself fully dictates what code is executed and when it's executed. When you start such a program, the first line of code in the program executes, and the code continues to execute in a completely predetermined path. The execution of code may, on occasion, branch and loop, but the execution path is completely controlled by the program. This often meant that a program was rather restricted in how it could respond to the user. For instance, the program might expect text to be entered into controls on the screen in a predetermined order, unlike in Windows, where a user can interact with different parts of the interface, often in any order the user chooses.

NEW TERM C# incorporates an event-driven programming model. Event-driven applications aren't bound by the constraints of procedural programs. Instead of the top-down approach of procedural languages, event-driven programs have logical sections of code placed within *events*. There is no predetermined order in which events occur, and often the user has complete control over what code is executed in an event-driven program by interactively triggering specific events, such as by clicking a button. An event, along with the code it contains, is called an *event procedure*.

Triggering Events

In the previous hour, you learned how a method is simply a function of an object. Events are a special kind of method; they are a way for objects to signal state changes that may be useful to clients of that object. Events are methods that can be called in special ways—usually by the user interacting with something on a form or by Windows itself, rather than being called from a statement in your code.

There are many types of events and many ways to trigger those events. You've already seen how a user can trigger the Click event of a button by clicking it. User interaction isn't the only thing that can trigger an event, however. An event can be triggered in one of the following four ways:

- Users can trigger events by interacting with your program.
- Objects can trigger their own events, as needed.
- The operating system (whichever version of Windows the user is running) can trigger events.
- You can trigger events by calling them using C# code.

Events Triggered Through User Interaction

The most common way an event is triggered is by a user interacting with a program. Every form, and almost every control you can place on a form, has a set of events specific to its object type. For example, the Button control has a number of events, including the Click event, which you've already used in previous hours. The Click event is triggered, and then the code within the Click event executes when the user clicks the button.

The Textbox control allows users to enter information using the keyboard, and it also has a set of events. The Textbox control has some of the same types of events as the Button control, such as a Click event, but the Textbox control also has events not supported by the Button control, such as a TextChanged event. The TextChanged event occurs each time the contents of the text box change, such as when the user types information into the text box. Because you can't enter text within a Button control, it makes sense that the Button control wouldn't have a TextChanged event. Each and every object that supports events supports a unique set of events.

Each type of event has its own behavior, and it's important to understand the events with which you work. The TextChanged event, for instance, exhibits a behavior that may not be intuitive to a new developer because the event fires each time the contents of the text box change. If you were to type the following sentence into an empty text box:

```
C# is very cool!
```

the Change event would be triggered 16 times—once for each character typed—because each time you enter a new character, the contents of the text box are changed. Although it's easy to think that the Change event fires only when you commit your entry, such as by leaving the text box or pressing Enter, this is simply not how it works. Again, it's important to learn the nuances and the exact behavior of the events you're using. If you use events without fully understanding how they work, your program may exhibit unusual, and often very undesirable, results.

 Triggering events (which are just a type of procedure) using C# code is discussed in detail in Hour 11, "Creating and Calling Methods."

Events Triggered by an Object

Sometimes an object triggers its own events. The most common example of this is the Timer control's Timer event. The Timer control doesn't appear on a form when the program is running; it appears only when you're designing a form. The Timer control's sole purpose is to trigger its Timer event at an interval that is specified in its Interval property.

By setting the Timer control's Interval property, you control the interval, in milliseconds, when the Timer event executes. After firing its Timer event, a Timer control resets itself and again fires its Timer event when the interval has passed. This occurs until the interval is changed, the Timer control is disabled, or the Timer control's form is unloaded. A common use of timers is to create a clock on a form. You can display the time in a label and update the time at regular intervals by placing the code to display the current time in the Timer event. You'll create a project with a Timer control in Hour 8, "Advanced Controls."

Events Triggered by the Operating System

Finally, Windows can trigger certain events within your program —events that you may not even know exist. For example, when a form is fully or partially obstructed by another window, the program needs to know when the offending window is resized or moved so that it can repaint the area of its window that's been hidden. Windows and C# work together in this respect. When the obstructing window is moved or resized, Windows tells C# to repaint the form, which C# does. This also causes C# to raise the form's Paint event. You can place code into the Paint event to create a custom display for the form, such as drawing shapes on the form using a Graphics object. That way, every time the form repaints itself, your custom drawing code executes.

Avoiding Recursive Events

NEW TERM You must make sure never to cause an event to endlessly trigger itself. An event that continuously triggers itself is called a *recursive* event. To illustrate a situation that causes a recursive event, think of the text box's TextChanged event discussed earlier. The TextChanged event fires every time the text within the text box changes. Placing code into the TextChanged event that alters the text within the text box would cause the Change event to be fired again, which could result in an endless loop. Recursive events terminate when Windows returns a StackOverFlow exception (see Figure 4.1), indicating that Windows no longer has the resources to follow the recursion.

> When you receive a StackOverFlow exception, you should look for a recursive event as the culprit.

Recursive events can involve more than one event in the loop. For example, if Event A triggers Event B, which in turn triggers Event A, you can have recursion of the two events. Recursion can take place among a sequence of many events, not just one or two.

FIGURE 4.1

Recursive events eventually exhaust Windows's resources until an exception (error) occurs.

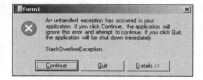

Uses for recursive procedures actually exist, such as when you are writing complex math functions. For instance, recursive events are often used to compute factorials. However, when you purposely create a recursive event, you must ensure that the recursion isn't infinite.

Accessing an Object's Events

Accessing an object's events is simple, and if you've been following the examples in this book, you've already accessed a number of objects' default events. To access all of an object's events, you can use the Events icon (the lightning bolt) in the Properties window.

You're now going to create a project to get the feel for working with events. Start C# and create a new Windows Application project titled **View Events,** and then follow these steps:

1. Use the toolbox to add a picture box to the form.
2. Change the name of the picture box to **picText.**
3. Click the Events button on the Properties window toolbar (the lightning bolt icon).

Your screen should look like the one in Figure 4.2. Notice that the Properties window now lists all the events for the selected object; in your case, it is the picText PictureBox object.

When you access a control's events, the default event for that type of control is selected. As you can see, the Click event is the default for a PictureBox. Scroll through the picText events and select the MouseDown event. Double-click the word MouseDown and C# will create the MouseDown event procedure and position you within it, ready to enter code (see Figure 4.3).

NEW TERM   The code statement above the cursor is the *event declaration*. An event declaration is a statement that defines the structure of an event handler. Notice that this event declaration contains the name of the object, an underscore character (_), and then the event name. Following the event name is a set of parentheses. The items within the parentheses are called *parameters,* which is the topic of the next section. This is the standard declaration structure for an event procedure.

FIGURE 4.2

Double–click an event in the Properties window to create the desired event.

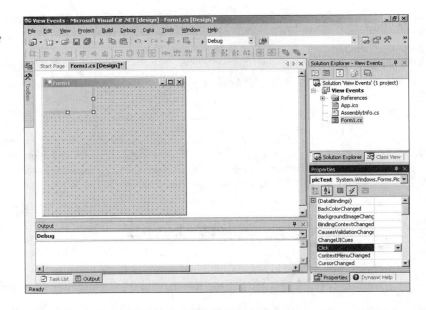

FIGURE 4.3

C# creates an empty event procedure when you select an object's event for the first time.

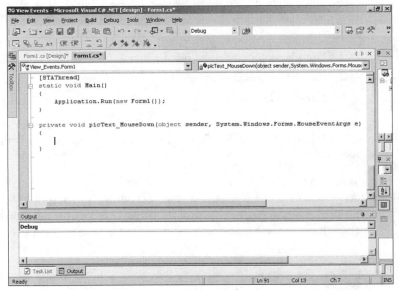

The full event declaration for the Click event is the following:

```
private void picText_MouseDown(object sender, _
    System.Windows.Forms.MouseEventArgs e)
```

> The words *Private* and *Void* are reserved words that indicate the scope and type of the method. Scope and type are discussed in Hour 11.

Working with Event Parameters

NEW TERM   As mentioned previously, the items within the parentheses of an event declaration are called *parameters*. An event parameter is a variable that is created and assigned a value by C#. These parameter variables are used to get, and sometimes set, relevant information within the event. Multiple parameters within an event procedure are always separated by commas. A parameter contains data that relates to the event. This data may be a number, text, an object—almost anything. As you can see, the MouseDown event has two parameters. When the Click event procedure is triggered, C# automatically creates the parameter variables and assigns them values for use in this one execution of the event procedure; the next time the event procedure occurs, the values in the parameters are reset. You use the values in the parameters to make decisions or perform operations in your code.

The MouseDown event of a form has the following parameters:

```
object sender
```

and

```
System.Windows.Forms.MouseEventArgs e
```

The first word identifies the type of data the parameter contains, followed by the name of the parameter. The first parameter, sender, holds a generic object. Object parameters can be any type of object supported by C#. It's not critical that you understand data types right now, just that you're aware that different parameter variables contain different types of information. Some contain text, others contain numbers, and still others (many others) contain objects. In the case of the sender parameter, it will always hold a reference to the control causing the event.

NEW TERM   The *sender* parameter returns a reference to the control that causes the event. It's often best to use the *sender* parameter rather than referencing the control by name, so that if you change the name of the control, you won't have to update the code. Also, by referencing the *sender* object, the code becomes portable; you can copy and paste it into the event of a different control of the same type, and the code should work without modification.

The *e* parameter, on the other hand, is where the real action is with the MouseDown event. The *e* parameter also holds an object; in this case the object is of the type

`System.WinForms.MouseEventArgs`. This object has properties that relate to the MouseDown_event. To see them, type in the following code, but don't press anything after entering the dot (period):

```
e.
```

When you press the period, you'll get a drop-down list showing you the members (properties and methods) of the *e* object (see Figure 4.4). Using the *e* object, you can determine a number of things about the occurrence of the MouseDown event. I've listed some of the more interesting items in Table 4.1.

FIGURE 4.4

IntelliSense drop-down lists alleviate the need for memorizing the makeup of hundreds of objects.

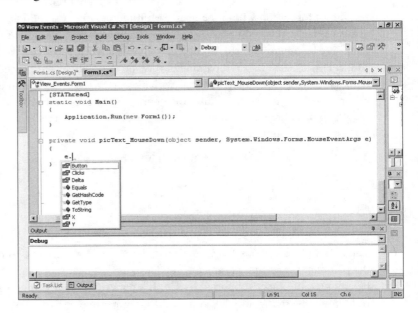

TABLE 4.1 Commonly used members of `System.WinForms.MouseEventArgs`

Property	Description
Clicks	Returns the number of times the user clicked the mouse button.
Button	Returns the button that was clicked (left, middle, right).
X	Returns the horizontal coordinate at which the pointer was located when the user clicked.
Y	Returns the vertical coordinate at which the pointer was located when the user clicked.

Each time the event occurs, the parameters are initialized by C# so that they always reflect the current occurrence of the event.

Each event has parameters specific to it. For instance, the TextChanged event returns parameters different from the MouseDown event. As you work with events—and you'll work with a lot of events—you'll quickly become familiar with the parameters of each event type. You'll learn how to create parameters for your own methods in Hour 11.

Deleting an Event Handler

Deleting an event handler involves more than just deleting the event procedure. When you add a new event handler to a class, C# automatically creates the event procedure for you and positions you to enter code within the event. However, C# does a little bit more for you "under the covers" to hook the event procedure to the control. It does this by creating a code statement in the hidden code of the class. Ordinarily, you don't have to worry about this statement. However, when you delete an event procedure, C# doesn't automatically delete the hidden code statement, and your code won't compile. The easiest way to correct this is to run the project; when C# encounters the error, it will show you the offending statement, which you can delete. Try this now:

1. Delete the MouseDown procedure (don't forget to delete the open and close brackets of the procedure, as well as any code within them). This deletes the procedure.

2. Press F5 to run the project. You'll receive a message that a build error has occurred. Click No to return to the code editor.

3. A task for the error has been created in the Task List. Double-click the task and C# will take you to the offending statement. It will read:
   ```
   this.pictureBox1.MouseDown += new
       System.Windows.Forms.MouseEventHandler(this.pictureBox1_MouseDown);
   ```

4. Delete this statement, and now your code will compile and run.

Whenever you delete an event procedure, you will have to delete the corresponding statement that links the procedure to its object before the code will run.

Building an Event Example Project

You're now going to create a very simple project in which you'll use the event procedures of a text box. Specifically, you're going to write code to display a message when a user presses a mouse button on the text box, and you'll write code to clear the text box

4

when the user releases the button. You'll be using the *e* parameter to determine which button the user has pressed.

Creating the User Interface

Create a new Windows application titled **Events Example**. Change the form's Text property to **Events Demo**.

Next, add a text box to the form by double-clicking the TextBox tool in the toolbox. Set the properties of the text box as follows:

Property	Value
Name	txtEvents
Location	48,120
Size	193,20
Text	Click Me!

The only other control you need on your form is a label. Label controls are used to display static text; users cannot type text into a label. Add a new label to your form now by double-clicking the Label tool in the toolbox and then setting the Label control's properties as follows:

Property	Value
Name	lblMessage
Location	48,152
Size	192,16
Text	(*make blank*)
TextAlign	MiddleCenter

Your form should now look like the one in Figure 4.5. It's a good idea to save frequently, so save your project now by clicking the Save All button on the toolbar.

Creating Event Handlers

The interface for the Events Example project is complete—on to the fun part. You're now going to create the event procedures that empower your program to do something. The event that we're interested in first is the MouseDown event. Select the TextBox on your design form, and then click the Events icon on the Properties window toolbar.

The default event for text boxes is the TextChanged event, so it's the one now selected. You're not interested in the TextChanged event at this time, however. Scroll through the event list for the MouseDown event. Double-click MouseDown; C# then creates a new MouseDown event procedure for the text box (see Figure 4.6).

FIGURE 4.5

A Label control that has no value in its Text property can be hard to see unless selected.

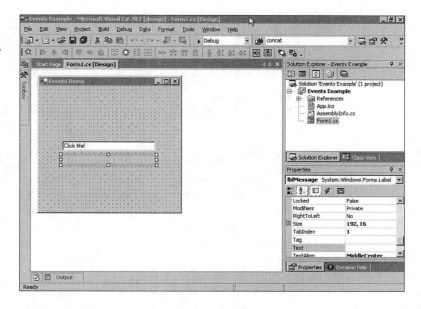

FIGURE 4.6

Each time you double-click a new event, C# creates an empty event procedure if one hasn't been created previously for the event.

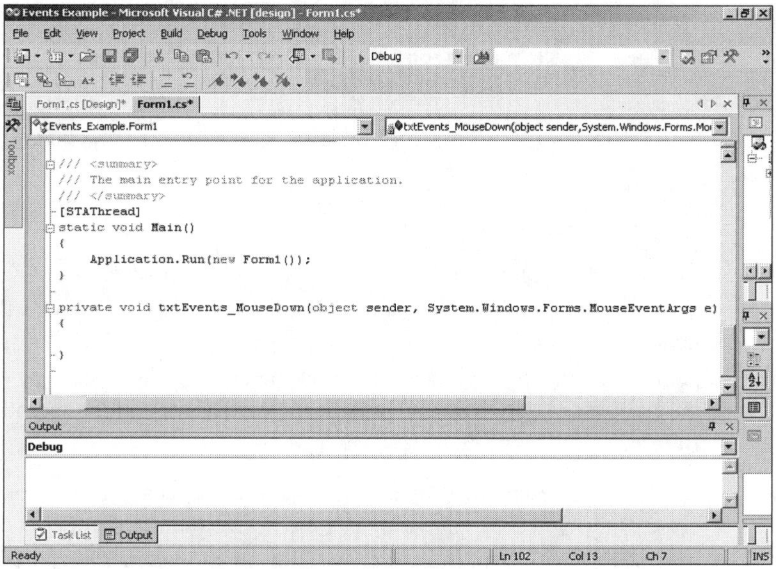

Enter the following code into the MouseDown event procedure:

```
switch(e.Button)
{
```

```
case MouseButtons.Left:
    lblMessage.Text = "You are pressing the left button!";
    break;
case MouseButtons.Right:
    lblMessage.Text = "You are pressing the right button!";
    break;
case MouseButtons.Middle:
    lblMessage.Text = "You are pressing the middle button!";
    break;
}
```

The Switch construct, which is discussed in detail in Hour 14, "Making Decisions in C# Code," compares the value of an expression to a list of possible values. In this instance, the expression is the value of e.Button (the Button property of the object *e*). When this code executes, the expression is compared to each Case statement in the order in which the statements appear. If and when a match is found, the code immediately following the Case statement that was matched gets executed. Therefore, the code you wrote looks at the value of e.Button and compares it to three values, one at a time. When the Switch construct determines which button has been pressed, it displays a message about it in the Label control.

 In a more robust application, you would probably perform more useful and more complicated code. For instance, you may want to display a custom pop-up menu when the user clicks with the right button and execute a specific function when the user clicks with the middle button. All this is possible, and more.

The nice thing about objects is that you don't have to commit every detail about them to memory. For example, you don't need to memorize the return values for each type of button (who wants to remember MouseButtons.Left anyway?). Just remember that the *e* parameter contains information about the event. When you type **e** and press the period, the IntelliSense drop-down list appears and shows you the members of *e*, one of which is Button.

Don't feel overwhelmed by all the object references you'll encounter throughout this book. Simply accept that you can't memorize them all, nor do you need to; you'll learn the ones that are important, and you'll use Help when you're stuck. Also, after you know the parent object in a situation, such as the *e* object in this example, it's easy for you to determine the objects and members that belong to it by using the IntelliSense drop-down lists.

You're now going to add code to the MouseUp event to clear the label's Text property when the user releases the button. First, you'll need to create the MouseUp event procedure. To do this, return to the Form Design view (click the Form1.cs[Design] tab). The Properties should still have the txtEvents object's events listed. If the events aren't shown in the Properties window, select txtEvents from the drop-down list box in the Properties window and click the events icon. Locate and double-click the MouseUp event from the events list.

All you're going to do in the MouseUp event is clear the label. Enter the following code:

```
lblMessage.Text = "";
```

Testing Your Events Project

Run your project now by pressing F5. If you entered all the code correctly and you don't receive any errors, your form will be displayed as shown in Figure 4.7.

FIGURE 4.7
A simple but functional example.

> Remember that C# is case sensitive. Entering only one character in the wrong case will cause your project to fail to compile.

Click the text box with the left mouse button and watch the label. It will display a sentence telling you which button has been clicked. When you release the button, the text is cleared. Try this with the middle and right buttons, as well. When you click the text box with the right button, Windows displays the standard shortcut menu for text boxes. When this menu appears, you have to select something from it or click somewhere off the menu to trigger the MouseUp event. In Hour 9, "Adding Menus and Toolbars to Forms," you'll learn how to add your own shortcut menus to forms and controls. When you're satisfied that your project is behaving as it should, from the Debug menu choose Stop Debugging to stop the project (or click the Close button on your form), and then save your work by clicking Save All on the toolbar.

Summary

In this hour, you learned about event-driven programming, including what events are, how to trigger events, and how to avoid recursive events. In addition, you've learned how to access an object's events and how to work with parameters. Much of the code you'll write will execute in response to an event of some kind. By understanding how events work, including being aware of the available events and their parameters, you'll be able to create complex C# programs that react to a multitude of user and system input.

Q&A

Q. Is it possible to create custom events for an object?

A. You can create custom events for objects created from your custom classes (see Hour 17, "Designing Objects with Classes"), but you cannot create custom events for existing C# objects such as forms and controls (without using some seriously advanced object-oriented techniques that are beyond the scope of this book).

Q. Is it possible for objects that don't have an interface to support events?

A. Yes. However, to use the events of such an object, the object variable must be dimensioned a special way or the events aren't available. This gets a little tricky and is beyond the scope of this book. If you have an object in code that supports events, look in Help for the keyword WithEvents for information on how to use such events.

Workshop

The Workshop is designed to help you anticipate possible questions, review what you've learned, and get you thinking about how to put your knowledge into practice. The answers to the quiz are in Appendix A, "Answers to Quizzes/Exercises."

Quiz

1. Name three things that can cause events to occur.
2. True or False: All objects support the same set of events.
3. What is the default event type for a button?
4. The act of an event calling itself in a loop is called what?
5. What is the easiest way to access a control's default event handler?
6. All control events pass a reference to the control causing the event. What is the name of the parameter that holds this reference?

Exercises

1. Create a project with a single text box. In the Resize event of the form, show the Width of the form in the text box.

2. Create a project with a form and a text box. Add code to the TextChange event to cause a recursion when the user types in text. Hint: Concatenate a character to the end of the user's text using a statement such as `txtMyTextBox.Text = String.Concat(this. txtMyTextBox.Text,"a");`

4

PART II

Building a User Interface

The Visual Studio .NET Integrated Development Environment (IDE) excells at allowing you to make attractive and functional user interfaces very quickly and efficiently. In this part, you'll learn how to build a solid user interface. You'll learn how to start with a form, which behaves much like a blank canvas, and you'll learn how to use the many controls, such as text boxes and list boxes with which users can interact. You'll also learn how to add menus and toolbars to your forms, and you'll get some experience with C#'s exciting drawing capabilities.

- Hour 5: Building Forms—Part I
- Hour 6: Building Forms—Part II
- Hour 7: Working with Traditional Controls
- Hour 8: Advanced Controls
- Hour 9: Adding Menus and Toolbars to Forms
- Hour 10: Drawing and Printing

HOUR 5

Building Forms—Part I

With few exceptions, forms are the cornerstone of every Windows application's interface. Forms are essentially windows and the two terms are often used interchangeably. More accurately, "window" refers to what's seen by the user and what the user interacts with, whereas "form" refers to what you see when you design. Forms let users view and enter information in a program (such as the form you built in your Picture Viewer program in Hour 1, "A C# Programming Tour"). Such information may be text, pictures, graphs—almost anything that can be viewed onscreen. Understanding how to design forms correctly will enable you to begin creating solid interface foundations for your programs.

 C# uses a new forms engine called Windows Forms.

Think of a form as a canvas on which you build your program's interface. On this canvas, you can print text, draw shapes, and place controls with which users can interact. The wonderful thing about C# forms is that they behave like a dynamic canvas; not only can you adjust the appearance of a form by manipulating what's on it, you can also manipulate specific properties of the form itself.

In previous hours, you manipulated the following form appearance properties:

- Text
- Height
- Left
- Top
- Width

The capability to tailor your forms, however, goes far beyond these simple manipulations.

There is so much to cover about Windows Forms that I've broken the material into two hours. In this hour, you'll learn the very basics of forms—adding them to a project, manipulating their properties, and showing and hiding them using C# code. Although you've done some of these things in previous hours, here you'll learn the nuts and bolts of the tasks you've performed. In the following hour, you'll learn more advanced form techniques.

The highlights of this hour include the following:

- Changing the name of a form
- Changing the appearance of a form
- Displaying text on a form's title bar
- Adding an image to a form's background
- Giving a form an icon
- Preventing a form from appearing in the taskbar
- Specifying the initial display position of a form
- Displaying a form in a normal, maximized, or minimized state
- Changing the mouse pointer
- Showing and hiding forms

Changing the Name of a Form

The first thing you should do when you create a new object is give it a descriptive name, so that's the first thing I'll talk about in this hour. Start C# now (if it's not already running) and create a new Windows Application titled **Forms Example**. Using the

Properties window, change the name of the form to **fclsExample**. When you need to create a new instance of this form, you'll use this name rather than the default generic name of Form1.

> Remember, when you change the name of the startup form for your application, you need to update the class name in the entry point of your application (static void Main()). Refer to Hour 1 for instructions on how to do this.

Changing the Appearance of a Form

Take a moment to browse the rest of the form's properties in the Properties window. In this hour, I'll show you how to use the more common properties of the form to tailor its appearance.

> Remember, to get help on any property at any time, select the property in the Properties window and press F1.

Displaying Text on a Form's Title Bar

You should always set the text in a form's title bar to something meaningful. (Note: Not all forms have title bars, as you'll see later in this hour.) The text displayed in the title bar is the value placed in the form's Text property. Generally, the text should be one of the following:

- The name of the program. This is most appropriate when the form is the program's main or only form.
- The purpose of the form. This is perhaps the most common type of text displayed in a title bar. For example, if a form is used to select a printer, consider setting the Text property to Select Printer. When you take this approach, use active voice (for instance, don't use Printer Select).
- The name of the form. If you choose to place the name of the form into the form's title bar, use the "English" name, not the actual form name. For instance, if you've used a naming convention and named a form fclsLogin, use the text **Login** or **Login Form**.

Change the Text property of your form to **Building Forms Example**. Your form should now look like the one in Figure 5.1.

FIGURE 5.1

Use common sense when setting title bar text.

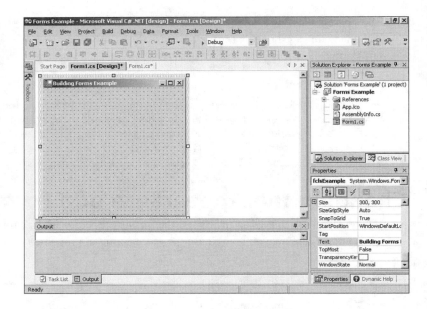

As with most other form properties, you can change the Text property at any time using C# code.

Changing a Form's Background Color

Although most forms appear with a gray background (this is part of the standard 3D color scheme in Windows), you can change a form's background to any color you like. To change a form's background color, you change its BackColor property. The BackColor property is a unique property in that you can specify a named color or an RGB value in the format Red, Green, Blue.

By default, the BackColor is set to the color named Control. This color is a system color and may not be gray. When Windows is first installed, it's configured to a default color scheme. In the default scheme, the color for forms and other objects is the familiar "battleship" gray. However, as a Windows user, you're free to change any system color you desire. For instance, some people with color blindness prefer to change their system colors to colors that have more contrast than the defaults so that objects are more clearly distinguishable. When you assign a system color to a form or control, the appearance of the object adjusts itself to the current user's system color scheme. This doesn't just occur when a form is first displayed; changes to the system color scheme are immediately propagated to all objects that use the affected colors.

Change the background color of your form to blue now by deleting the word Control in the BackColor property in the Properties window; in its place enter **0,0,255** and press Enter or Tab to commit your entry. Your form should now be blue because you entered an RGB value in which you specified no red, no green, and maximum blue (color values range from 0 to 255). In reality, you'll probably rarely enter RGB values. Instead, you'll select colors from color palettes. To view color palettes from which you can select a color for the BackColor property, click the drop-down arrow in the BackColor property in the Properties window (see Figure 5.2).

FIGURE 5.2

All color properties have palettes from which you can choose a color.

System colors are discussed in detail in Hour 10, "Drawing and Printing."

When the drop-down list appears, the color Blue on the Web tab is selected. This occurs because when you entered the RGB value 0,0,255, C# looked for a named color composed of the same values and it found blue. The color palettes were explained in Hour 2, "Navigating C#," so I'm not going to go into detail about them here. For now, select the System tab to see a list of the available system colors and choose Control from the list to change the BackColor of your form back to the default Windows color.

Adding an Image to a Form's Background

In addition to changing the color of a form's background, you can also place a picture on it. To add a picture to a form, set the form's BackgroundImage property. When you add an image to a form, the image is "painted" on the form's background. All the controls that you place on the form appear on top of the picture.

Add an image to your form now by following these steps:

1. Select the form.
2. Click the BackgroundImage property in the Properties window.

3. Click the Build button that appears next to the property (the small button with three dots).

4. Use the Open dialog box that appears to locate and select an image file from your hard drive. (I used Blue Lace 16.BMP, which I found in my \WinNT folder.)

C# always tiles an image specified in a BackgroundImage property (see Figure 5.3). This means that if the selected picture isn't big enough to fill the form, C# will display additional copies of the picture, creating a tiled effect. If you want to display a single copy of an image on a form, anywhere on the form, you should use a picture box, as discussed in Hour 10.

Notice that to the left of the BackgroundImage property is a small box containing a plus sign. This indicates that there are related properties, or *subproperties*, of the BackgroundImage property. Click the plus sign now to expand the list of subproperties (see Figure 5.3). In the case of the BackgroundImage property, C# shows you a number of properties related to the image assigned to the property, such as its dimensions and image format.

FIGURE 5.3

Images are tiled to fill the form.

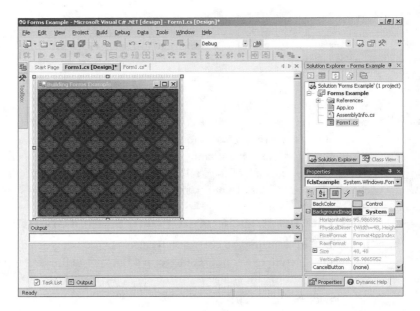

 Adding background images to forms can add pizzazz to a program, but it can also confuse users by making forms unnecessarily busy. Try to avoid adding images just because you can. Use discretion, and add an image to a form only when the image adds value to the interface.

Removing an image from a form is just as easy as adding the image in the first place. To remove the picture that you just added to your form, right-click the BackgroundImage property name and choose Reset from the shortcut menu that appears.

> You must right-click the Name column of the property, not the Value column. If you right-click the value of the property, you get a different shortcut menu that doesn't have a Reset option.

Giving a Form an Icon

The icon assigned to a form appears in the left side of the form's title bar, in the taskbar when the form is minimized, and in the iconic list of tasks when you press Alt+Tab to switch to another application. The icon often represents the application; therefore, you should assign an icon to any form a user can minimize. If you don't assign an icon to a form, C# supplies a default icon to represent it when the form is minimized. This default icon is generic and unattractive, and you should avoid it.

In the past, it was recommended that every form have a unique icon related to the form's purpose. This has proved very difficult to accomplish in large applications. As an alternative, I recommend that you set the icon of the main form in your program to the icon that you want to represent your application, and then assign that icon to other forms as they are loaded rather than assigning them at design time. If this proves to be a hassle, just assign the same icon to all your forms.

You assign an icon to a form in much the same way you assign an image to the BackgroundImage property. Add an icon to your form now by clicking the form's Icon property in the Properties window, clicking the Build button that appears, and selecting an icon file from your hard drive. After you've selected the icon, it appears in the form's title bar to the left.

Run your project by pressing F5, and then click the form's Minimize button to minimize it to the taskbar. Look at the form in the taskbar; you'll see both the form's caption and the form's icon displayed (see Figure 5.4).

FIGURE 5.4

Assigning meaningful icons to your forms makes your application easier to use.

Stop the project now by choosing Stop Debugging from the Debug menu.

Preventing a Form from Appearing in the Taskbar

Being able to display an icon for a minimized form is nice, but sometimes it's necessary to prevent a form from even appearing in the taskbar. For instance, if your application has a number of palette windows that float over a main form, it's unlikely that you'd want all but your main form to appear in the taskbar. To prevent a form from appearing in the taskbar, set the form's ShowInTaskbar property to false. If the user minimizes a form with its ShowInTaskbar property set to false, the user can still get to the application by pressing Alt+Tab, even though the program can't be accessed via the taskbar; C# won't allow the application to become completely inaccessible to the user.

Changing the Appearance and Behavior of a Form's Border

You may have noticed while working with other Windows programs that the borders of forms can vary. Some forms have borders that you can click and drag to change the size of the form, some have fixed borders that can't be changed, and still others have no borders at all. The appearance and behavior of a form's border is controlled by its FormBorderStyle property.

The FormBorderStyle property can be set to one of the following values:

- None
- FixedSingle
- Fixed3D
- FixedDialog
- Sizable
- FixedToolWindow
- SizableToolWindow

Run your project now by pressing F5, and move the mouse pointer over one of the borders of your form. This form has a sizable border, which means that the border can be resized by the user. Notice how the pointer changes from a large arrow to a line with arrows pointing on either side, indicating the direction you can stretch the border. When you move the pointer over a corner, you get a diagonal cursor that indicates you can stretch both of the sides that meet at the corner.

Stop the project now by choosing Stop Debugging from the Debug menu (or click the Close button on the form) and change the form's FormBorderStyle property to None. Your form should look like the one in Figure 5.5. When you choose to not give a form a border, the title bar of the form is removed. Of course, when the title bar is gone, there is no visible title bar text, no control box, and no Minimize or Maximize buttons. Run your project by pressing F5, and notice how the form appears as it did in Form Design view— with no border or title bar. Without a border, the form cannot be resized by the user, and without a title bar, the form cannot be repositioned. Rarely is it appropriate to specify None for a form's BorderStyle, but in the event you need to do this, it's entirely possible.

FIGURE 5.5

You can create forms without borders.

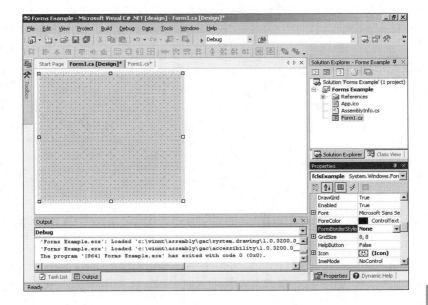

Stop the project (you should know how by now) and change the FormBorderStyle to FixedDialog. Press F5 to run the project again, and move the mouse pointer over a border of the form; the mouse pointer won't change, and you won't be able to stretch the borders of the form. Stop the project again and set the form's FormBorderStyle property to FixedToolWindow. This setting causes the title bar of the form to appear smaller than normal and the text to display in a smaller font (see Figure 5.6). In addition, the only thing displayed on the title bar besides the text is a Close button. C#'s various design windows, such as the Properties window and the toolbox, are good examples of tool windows.

The FormBorderStyle is a good example of how changing a single property can greatly affect the look and behavior of an object. Set the FormBorderStyle of the form back to Sizable, the default setting for new forms.

5

FIGURE 5.6

A tool window is a special window whose title bar takes up the minimum space possible.

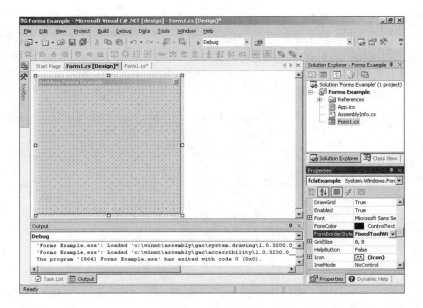

Adding Minimize, Maximize, and Control Box Buttons to a Form

Minimize and Maximize buttons make it easy for a user to quickly hide a form or make it fill the entire display. Adding a Minimize or Maximize button to your forms is as easy as setting a property (or two). To add a Minimize button to a form's title bar, set the form's MinimizeBox property to true. To add a Maximize button to a form, set its MaximizeBox property to true. Conversely, set the appropriate property to false to hide a button.

The form's ControlBox property must be set to true to display a Maximize and/or Minimize button on a form. When the ControlBox property of a form is set to true, a button with an X appears in the title bar at the right side, which the user can click to close the form. In addition, the form's icon is displayed in the left side of the title bar, and clicking it opens the form's System menu.

Notice that the title bar of your form shows all three buttons to the far right. From left to right, these are Minimize, Maximize, and Close. Run the project now and right-click the title bar to open the control box's menu, as shown in Figure 5.7. Notice that the icon isn't visible in the form's title bar. Some FormBorderStyle settings cause the icon to be hidden. When this occurs, right-clicking the title bar causes the menu to appear as though you clicked the icon. Close the form now by either selecting Close from the menu or clicking the Close button on the far right of the title bar.

FIGURE 5.7

Clicking the icon of a form with a control box (or right-clicking a title bar) displays a system menu.

Changing the MaximizeBox or MinimizeBox properties of a form enables or disables the corresponding item on the system menu in addition to the button on the toolbar. Save your project now by clicking the Save All button on the toolbar.

Specifying the Initial Display Position of a Form

The location on the display (monitor) where a form first appears isn't random but is controlled by the form's StartPosition property. The StartPosition property can be set to one of the values in Table 5.1.

TABLE 5.1 Values for the StartPosition Property

Value	Description
Manual	The Location property of the form determines where the form first appears.
CenterScreen	The form appears centered in the display.
WindowsDefaultLocation	The form appears in the Windows default location, which is toward the upper left of the display.
WindowsDefaultBounds	The form appears in the Windows default location with its bounds (size) set to the Windows default bounds.
CenterParent	The form is centered within the bounds of its parent form.

5

Generally, it's best to set the StartPosition property of all your forms to CenterParent, unless you have a specific reason to do otherwise. For the very first form that appears in you project, you might consider using the WindowsDefaultLocation (but I generally prefer CenterScreen).

Displaying a Form in a Normal, Maximized, or Minimized State

Using the Size and Location properties of a form in conjunction with the StartPosition property enables you to display forms at any location and at any size. You can also force a form to appear minimized or maximized. Whether a form is maximized, minimized, or shown normally is known as the form's *state*, and it's determined by the WindowState property.

Look at your form's WindowState property now. New forms have their WindowState property set to Normal by default. When you run the project, as you have several times, the form displays in the same size as it appears in the form designer, at the location specified by the form's Location property. Change the WindowState property now to Minimized. Nothing happens in the Form Design view, but run your project by pressing F5 and you'll see that the form is immediately minimized to the taskbar.

Stop the project and change the WindowState property to Maximized. Again, nothing happens in the Form Design window. Press F5 to run the project and notice how the form immediately maximizes to fill the entire screen.

When a form is maximized, it fills the entire screen regardless of the current screen resolution being used in Windows.

Stop the project and change the WindowState property back to Normal. Rarely will you set a form's WindowState property at design time to Minimize, but you'll probably encounter situations in which you need to change (or determine) the WindowState at runtime. As with most properties, you can accomplish this using code. For example, the following statement would minimize a form: `this.WindowState = FormWindowState.Minimized`. You don't have to remember the names of the values when entering code; you'll get an IntelliSense drop-down list when you type the period.

Changing the Mouse Pointer

You've no doubt used a program that altered the cursor when the pointer was moved over an object. This behavior is prevalent in Web browsers, in which the cursor is changed to the shape of a pointing hand when moved over a hyperlink. Using the Cursor property, you can specify the image of the pointer displayed when the pointer is over a form (or control).

Click the Cursor property of the form in the Properties window now and a drop-down arrow appears. Click the arrow to view a list of cursors (see Figure 5.8). Selecting a cursor from the list causes the pointer to change to that cursor when positioned over the form. Change the Cursor property of the form to AppStarting and press F5 to run the project. Move the pointer over the form and notice that the cursor changes to the AppStarting cursor while over the form and reverts to the default cursor when moved off the form. Stop the project now and click Save All on the toolbar to save your work.

FIGURE 5.8

Use the Cursor property to designate the image of the pointer when it's moved over the object.

5

Rarely will you want to change the cursor for a form, but you may find occasion to change the Cursor property for specific controls. Whenever you find yourself changing the default cursor for a form or control, choose a cursor that is consistent in purpose with well-known commercial applications.

Showing and Hiding Forms

Part III of this book is devoted to programming in C#, and I've avoided going into much programming detail in this hour so that you can focus on the concepts at hand. However, knowing how to create forms does nothing for you if you don't have a way to show and hide them. Because C# can display a single form automatically only when a program starts, you have to write code to show and hide other forms.

Showing Forms

In C#, everything is an object, and objects are based on classes (see Hour 17, "Designing Objects with Classes," for information on creating classes). Because the definition of a form is a class, you have to create a new Form object using the class as a template. In Hour 3, "Understanding Objects and Collections," I discussed objects and object variables, and these principles apply to creating forms.

As discussed in Hour 3, the process of creating an object from a class (template) is called instantiation. The syntax you'll use most often to instantiate a form is the following:

```
{ formclassname } {objectvariable} = new {formclassname()};
```

The parts of this declaration are as follows:

- *formclassname*   the name of the class that defines the form.
- *objectvariable*   This is the name for the form that you will use in code.
- The keyword *new*   Indicates that you want to instantiate a new object for the variable.

Last, you specify the name of the class used to derive the object—your form class. If you have a form class named fclsLoginDialog, for example, you could create a new Form object using the following code:

```
fclsLoginDialog frmLoginDialog = new fclsLoginDialog();
```

Thereafter, for as long as the object variable remains in scope (scope is discussed in Hour 12, "Using Constants, Data Types, Variables, and Arrays"), you can manipulate the Form object using the variable. For instance, to display the form, you call the Show method of the form or set the Visible property of the form to true using code such as this:

```
frmLoginDialog.Show();
```

or

```
frmLoginDialog.Visible = true;
```

The easiest way to get the hang of this is to actually do it. To begin, choose Add Windows Form from the Project menu to display the Add New Item dialog box. Change the name of the form to **fclsMyNewForm.cs** (as shown in Figure 5.9), and click Open to create the new form.

FIGURE 5.9

When you change the default name of a form, remember to leave the .cs extension.

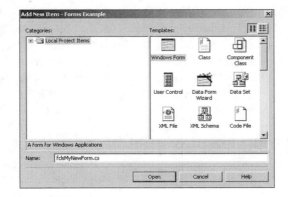

Your project now has two forms, as you can see by viewing the Solution Explorer window. The new form is displayed in the form designer, but right now you need to work with the main form. At the top of the main design area is a set of tabs. Currently, the tab fclsMyNewForm.cs [Design] is selected. Click the tab titled Form1.cs [Design] to show the designer for the first form.

Notice how the designer uses the filename rather than the object name on the tabs. You could right-click Form1.cs in the Solutions Explorer window and choose Rename to change the name of the file and therefore the name that appears on the tabs. You should actually do this in all your projects for the default forms. However, I haven't done this throughout the book because it adds yet another step to each example, and I don't want to complicate things too much.

Add a new button to your original form by double-clicking the Button item on the toolbox (be careful not to add the button to the new form by mistake). Set the button's properties as follows:

Property	Value
Name	btnShowForm
Location	112,112
Text	Show Form

5

Double-click the button to access its Click event (double-clicking a control is a shortcut for accessing its default event) and enter the following code:

```
fclsMyNewForm frmTest = new fclsMyNewForm();
frmTest.Show();
```

The first statement creates a new object variable and instantiates an instance of the fclsMyNewForm form. The second statement uses the object variable, now holding a reference to a Form object, to display the form. Press F5 to run the project and click the button. (If the button doesn't appear on the form, you may have accidentally added it to the wrong form). When you click the button, a new instance of the second form is created and displayed. Move this form and click the button again. Each time you click the button, a new form is created. Stop the project now and click Save All on the toolbar.

Understanding Form Modality

You can present two types of forms to the user: modal and nonmodal forms. The modality of a form is determined by how you show the form rather than by how you create the form (both modal and nonmodal forms are created the same way).

A nonmodal window is a window that doesn't cause other windows to be disabled. The forms you created in this example are nonmodal, which is why you were able to continue clicking the button on the first form even though the second form was displayed. Another example of a nonmodal window is the Find and Replace window in Word (and in C#, as well). When the Find and Replace window is visible, the user can still access other windows.

When a form is displayed as a modal form, on the other hand, all other forms in the same application become disabled until the modal form is closed; the other forms won't accept any keyboard or mouse input. The user is forced to deal only with the modal form. When the modal form is closed, the user is free to work with other visible forms within the program. Modal forms are most often used to create dialog boxes in which the user works with a specific set of data and controls before moving on. For instance, the Print dialog box of Microsoft Word is a modal dialog box. When the Print dialog box is displayed, the user cannot work with the document on the main Word window until the Print dialog box is closed. Most secondary windows in any given program are modal windows.

You can display one modal form from another modal form, but you cannot display a nonmodal form from a modal form.

To show a form as a modal form, you call the form's ShowDialog method rather than its Show method. Change the code in your button's Click event to read:

```
fclsMyNewForm frmTest = new fclsMyNewForm();
frmTest.ShowDialog();
```

When your code looks like this, press F5 to run the project. Click the button to create an instance of the second form. Then, move the second form away from the first window and try to click the button again. You can't—because you've created a modal form. Close the modal form now by clicking the Close button in the title bar. Now, the first form is enabled again and you can click the button once more. When you are done testing this, stop the running project.

 You can test to see whether a form has been shown modally by testing the form's Modal property.

Unloading Forms

After a form has served its purpose, you'll want it to go away. However, "go away" can mean one of two things. First, you can make a form disappear without closing it or freeing its resources (this is called *hiding*). To do so, set its Visible property to false. This hides the visual part of the form, but the form still resides in memory and can still be manipulated by code. In addition, all the variables and controls of the form retain their values when a form is hidden, so that if the form is displayed again, the form looks the same as it did when its Visible property was set to false.

Second, you can completely close a form and release the resources it consumes. You should close a form when it's no longer needed, so Windows can reclaim all resources used by the form. To do so, you invoke the Close method of the form like this:

```
this.Close();
```

In Hour 3, you learned how this is used to reference the current Form object. Because this represents the current Form object, you can manipulate properties and call methods of the current form using this. (this.Visible = false, and so forth).

The Close method tells C# to not simply hide the form, but to destroy it completely. If variables in other forms are holding a reference to the form you close, their references will be set to null and will no longer point to a valid Form object (refer to Hour 12 for information on null).

5

Select the fclsMyNewForm.cs [Design] tab to display the form designer for the second form, add a new button to the form, and set the button's properties as follows:

Property	Value
Name	btnCloseMe
Location	112,112
Text	Close Me

Double-click the button to access its Click event and then enter the following statement:

```
this.Close();
```

Next, run the project by pressing F5. Click the Show Form button to display the second form, and then click the second form's button. The form will disappear. Again, the form isn't just hidden; the form instance is unloaded from memory and no longer exists. You can create a new one by single-clicking the Show Form button on the first form. When you're finished, stop the running project and save your work.

Summary

In this hour, you've learned the basics of creating forms. You've learned how to add them to your project, how to set basic appearance properties, and how to show and hide them using C# code. In the next hour, you'll learn more advanced functionality for working with forms. After you've mastered the material in this hour as well as in the next hour, you'll be ready to dig into C#'s controls; that's where the fun of building an interface really begins!

Q&A

Q. How many form properties should I define at design time vs. runtime?

A. You should set all properties that you can at design time. First, it'll be easier to work with the form because you can see exactly what the user will see. Also, debugging is easier because there's less code.

Q. Should I let the user minimize and maximize all forms?

A. Probably not. First, there's no point in letting a form be maximized if you haven't anchored and aligned controls so that they adjust their appearance when the form is resized. In fact, if a form's contents don't change when a form is resized (including maximized), the form should not have a sizable border or a Maximize button.

Workshop

The Workshop is designed to help you anticipate possible questions, review what you've learned, and get you thinking about how to put your knowledge into practice. The answers to the quiz are in Appendix A, "Answers to Quizzes/Exercises."

Quiz

1. True or False: The text displayed in the form's title bar is determined by the value in the TitleBarText property.

2. The named color Control is what kind of color?

3. In what three places are a form's icon displayed?

4. A window with a smaller than normal title bar is called what?

5. For a Minimize or Maximize button to be visible on a form, what other element must be visible?

6. What, in general, is the best value to use for the StartPosition property of a form?

7. To maximize, minimize, or restore a form in code, you set what property?

8. True or False: To display a form, you must create a variable in code.

9. What property do you set to make a hidden form appear?

Exercises

1. Create a semitransparent form with a picture in its background. (Hint: Change the form's Opaque property.) Does the image become transparent? Add some controls to the form. Does the image appear behind or in front of the controls? (Hint: To create a transparent form, set the form's Opacity to something other than 100%—try 50%.)

2. Create a Windows Application with three forms. Give the startup form two buttons. Make the other two forms tool windows, and make one button display one tool window and the other button display the second tool window.

5

HOUR 6

Building Forms—Part II

A form is just a canvas, and although you can tailor a form by setting its properties, you'll need to add controls to it to make it functional. In the previous hour, you learned how to add forms to a project, how to set basic form properties, and how to show and hide forms. In this hour, you'll learn all about adding controls to a form, including arranging and aligning controls to create a pleasing and functional interface. You also learn how to create advanced multiple document interfaces (MDIs), as employed in applications such as Word. After you complete the material in this hour, you'll be ready to learn the details about the various controls available in C#.

The highlights of this hour include the following:

- Adding controls to a form
- Positioning, aligning, sizing, spacing, and anchoring controls
- Creating intelligent tab orders
- Adjusting the z-order of controls
- Creating transparent forms
- Creating forms that always float over other forms
- Creating multiple-document interfaces

Working with Controls

As discussed earlier, controls are the objects that you place on a form for users to interact with. If you've followed the examples in the previous hours, you've already added controls to a form. However, you'll be adding a lot of controls to forms, and it's important for you to understand all aspects of the process. Following the drill-down in this hour, the next two hours will teach you the ins and outs of the very cool controls provided by C#.

Adding Controls to a Form

All the controls that you can add to a form can be found in the toolbox. By default, the toolbox appears as a docked window on the left side of the design environment. This location is useful when you're only occasionally adding controls to forms. However, when doing serious form-design work, I find it best to dock the toolbox to the right side of the design environment, where it doesn't overlap so much (if at all) onto the form with which you're working.

 Remember that before you can undock a toolbar to move it to a new location, you must make sure it isn't set to Auto Hide.

The buttons on the toolbox are actually considered tabs because clicking one of them displays a specific page of controls. For most of your design, you'll use the controls on the Win Forms tab. However, as your skills progress, you may find yourself using more complex and highly specialized controls found on the other tabs.

You can add a control to a form in three ways, and you're now going to perform all three methods. Create a new Windows Application called **Adding Controls**. Change the name of the default form to **fclsAddingControls** and set its Text property to **Adding Controls**. Update the main entry point in the Main() function to reflect the new class name by clicking the View Code button on the Solution Explorer toolbar and then locating the reference to Form1 and replacing it with `fclsAddingControls`. Click Form1.cs [Design] to return to the form designer.

The easiest way to add a control to a form is to double-click the control in the toolbox. Try this now: display the toolbox and double-click the TextBox tool. C# creates a new text box in the upper-left corner of the form. Of course, you're free to move and size the text box as you please. Nevertheless, when you double-click a control in the toolbox, C# always creates the control in the upper-left corner, with the default size for the type of control you're adding.

If you want a little more authority over where the new control is placed, you can drag a control to the form. Try this now: display the toolbox and then click the Button control and drag it to the form. When the cursor is roughly where you want the button created, release the mouse button.

The last and most precise method of placing a control on a form is to "draw" the control on a form. Display the toolbox now and click the ListBox tool once to select it. Next, move the pointer to where you want the upper-left corner of the list box to appear and then click and hold the mouse button. Drag the pointer to where you want the bottom-right corner of the list box to be and release the button. The list box is created with its dimensions set to the rectangle you drew on the form. This is by far the most precise method of adding controls to a form.

> If you prefer to draw controls on your forms by clicking and dragging, I strongly suggest that you dock the toolbox to the right or bottom edge of the design environment or float it. The toolbox tends to interfere with drawing controls when it's docked to the left edge, because it obscures part of the form.

It's important to note that the very first item on the Windows Forms tab, titled Pointer, isn't actually a control. When the pointer item is selected, the design environment is placed in Select mode rather than in a mode to create a new control. With the pointer selected, you can select a control simply by clicking it, displaying all its properties in the Properties window. This is the default behavior of the development environment.

Manipulating Controls

Getting controls on a form is the easy part. Arranging them so that they create an intuitive and attractive interface is the challenge. Interface possibilities are nearly endless, so I can't tell you how to design any given interface. However, I can show you the techniques to move, size, and arrange controls so that they appear the way you want them to. By mastering these techniques, you'll be much faster at building interfaces, freeing your time for writing the code that makes things happen.

Using the Grid (Size and Snap)

When you first install C#, all forms appear with a grid of dots on them. When you draw or move controls on a form with a grid, the coordinates of the control automatically snap to the nearest grid coordinate. This offers some precision when adjusting the size and location of controls. In practical use, I often find the grid to be only slightly helpful because the size or location you want to specify often doesn't fit neatly with the grid locations. You can, however, control the granularity and even the visibility of the grid, and I suggest you do both.

You're now going to assign a higher level of granularity to the grid (the space between the grid points will be smaller). I find that this helps with design, without causing edges to snap to unwanted places.

To adjust the granularity of the grid on a form, you change the GridSize property (or the Width and Height subproperties of the GridSize property). Setting the Width or Height of the grid to a smaller number creates a smaller grid, which allows for finer control over sizing and placement, whereas using larger values creates a much larger grid and offers less control. With a larger grid, you'll find that edges snap to grid points much easier and at larger increments, making it impossible to fine-tune the size or position of a control. Change the GridSize property of your form now to **4,4**. Notice that a lot more grid dots appear (see Figure 6.1).

FIGURE 6.1

Grids can be distracting.

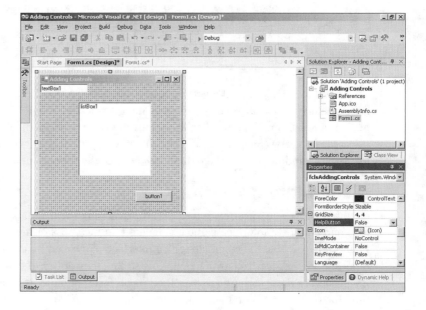

Try dragging the controls on your form or dragging their edges to size them. Notice that you have more control over the placement with the finer grid. Try changing the GridSize to a set of higher numbers, such as **25,25** and see what happens. When you're finished experimenting, change the GridSize values back to **4,4**.

An unfortunate side effect of a smaller grid is that the grid can become quite distracting. Again, you'll decide what you like best, but I generally turn grids off on my form. You do this by setting the DrawGrid property of the form to false. Try hiding the grid of your form now.

> This property determines only whether the grid is drawn, not whether it's active; grids are always active, regardless of whether they're visible.

Selecting a Group of Controls

As your skills grow, you'll find your forms becoming increasingly complex. Some forms may contain dozens, or even hundreds, of controls. C# has a set of features that makes it easy to align groups of controls.

Create a new Windows Application titled **Align Controls**. Change the name of the default form to **fclsAlignControls** and set its Text property to **Control Alignment Example**. Next, update the main entry point in the Main() function to reflect the new class name by clicking the View Code button on the Solution Explorer toolbar and then locating the reference to Form1 and replacing it with `fclsAlignControls`. Click Form1.cs [Design] to return to the form designer.

Double-click the TextBox tool in the toolbox to add a text box to the form. Set its properties as follows:

Property	Value
Name	txt1
Location	20, 20
Multiline	True
Size	100, 30
Text	txt1

> If you don't set the Multiline property of a text box to true, C# ignores the Height setting (the second value of the Size property) and instead, keeps the height at the standard height for a single-line text box.

Use the same technique (double-click the TextBox item in the toolbox) to add two more text boxes to the form. Set their properties as follows:

6

Text Box 2:

Property	Value
Name	txt2
Location	90, 80
Multiline	True
Size	50, 50
Text	txt2

Text Box 3:

Property	Value
Name	txt3
Location	140, 200
Multiline	True
Size	100, 60
Text	txt3

Your form should now look like the one in Figure 6.2. Save the project now by clicking the Save All button on the toolbar.

FIGURE 6.2

It's easy to align and size controls as a group.

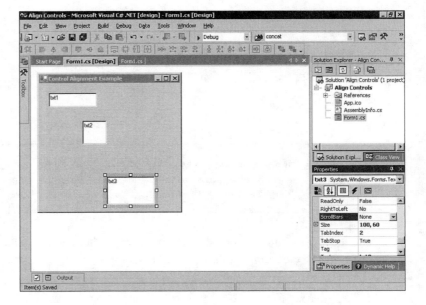

By default, clicking a control on a form selects it while deselecting any controls that were previously selected. To perform actions on more than one control, you need to select a group of controls. You can do so in one of two ways, the first of which is to *lasso* the controls. To lasso a group of controls, you first click and drag the mouse pointer anywhere on the form. As you drag the mouse, a rectangle is drawn on the form. When you release the mouse button, all controls intersected by the rectangle become selected. Note that you don't have to completely surround a control with the lasso (also called a marquee), you only have to intersect part of the control to select it. Try this now: click somewhere in the upper-right corner of the form and drag the pointer toward the bottom of the form without releasing the button (see Figure 6.3). When the rectangle has surrounded or intersected all the controls, release the button and the controls will be selected (see Figure 6.4).

FIGURE 6.3

Click and drag to create a selection rectangle.

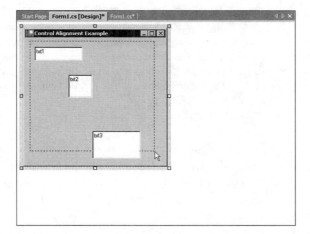

FIGURE 6.4

All selected controls appear with a hatched border and sizing handles.

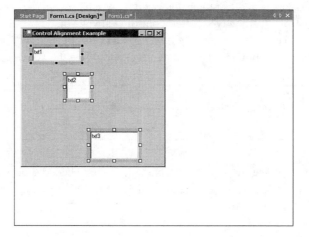

6

When a control is selected, it has a hatched border and a number of sizing handles (the rectangles in the hatched border at the corners and midpoints of the control). Pay careful attention to the sizing handles. The control with the black-centered sizing handles is the *active control* in the selected group. When you use C#'s tools, such as the alignment and formatting features, to work on a group of selected controls, the values of the active control are used. For example, if you were to align the left side of the selected controls shown in Figure 6.4, each of the controls would have its Left property value set to that of the active control. When you use the lasso technique to select a group of controls, you really don't have much authority over which control C# makes the active control. In this example, you want to align all controls to the control at the top, so you'll have to use a different technique to select the controls. Deselect all the controls now by clicking anywhere on the form (other than on a control).

When the sizing handle of an active control is colored white, you can click and drag the handle to alter the size of the control. Not all sizing handles are movable at all times. For example, before you set the Multiline property of a text box to true, C# won't allow you to change the height of the text box, so only the sizing handles at the left and right edges are movable and therefore are colored white.

The second technique for selecting multiple controls is to use the Shift or Ctrl key; this method is much like selecting multiple files in Windows Explorer. Click the bottom control (txt3) now to select it. Notice that its sizing handles are outlined in black; because it's the only control selected, it's automatically made the active control. Now hold down the Shift key and click the center control (txt2); txt2 and txt3 are now selected. However, txt2 is the active control (when multiple controls are selected, the active control has black-filled sizing handles rather than white). When you add a control to a group of selected controls, the newly selected control is always made the active control. Finally, with the Shift key still pressed, click txt1 to add it to the group of selected controls. All the controls should now be selected and txt1 should be the active control.

Clicking a selected control while Shift is held down deselects the control.

You can combine the two selection techniques when needed. For instance, you could first lasso all controls to select them. If the active control isn't the one you want it to be, you could hold the Shift key down and click the control you want made active, thereby deselecting it. Clicking the control a second time while still holding down the Shift key would again select the control. Because the control would then be the last control added to the selected group, it would be made active.

> If you must click the same control twice, such as to deselect and then reselect, do so slowly. If you click too fast, C# interprets your actions as a double-click, and it creates a new event handler for the control.

Aligning Controls

Now that you've selected all three controls, open C#'s Format menu (see Figure 6.5). The Format menu has a number of submenus containing functions to align, size, and format groups of controls. Open the Align submenu now to see the available options (see Figure 6.6).

FIGURE 6.5
Use the Format menu to quickly whip an interface into shape.

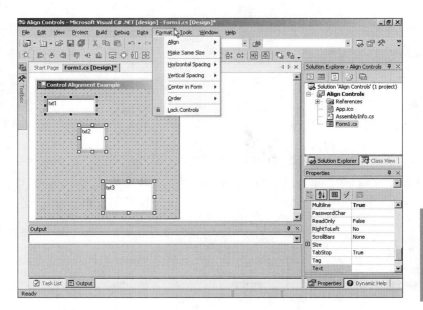

The top three items on the Align menu are used to align the selected controls horizontally, and the middle three items align the selected controls vertically. The last item, To Grid, will snap the corners of all the selected controls to the nearest grid points. Choose Align Lefts now, and C# aligns the left edges of the selected controls. Notice how the Left edge of the active control is used as the baseline for the alignment (see Figure 6.7).

FIGURE 6.6

The Align menu makes it easy to align an edge of a group of controls.

FIGURE 6.7

The property values of the active control are always used as the baseline values.

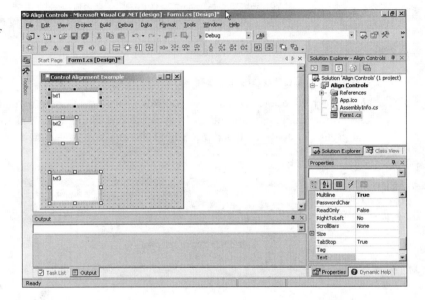

Making Controls the Same Size

In addition to aligning controls, you can als o make all selected controls the same size—Height, Width, or Both. To do this, use the Make Same Size submenu on the Format menu (see Figure 6.8). Make all your controls the same size now by choosing Both from the Make Same Size menu. As with the Align function, the values of the active control are used as the baseline values.

FIGURE 6.8

Use this menu to quickly make a group of controls the same size.

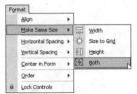

Evenly Spacing a Group of Controls

As many a salesman has said, "…and that's not all!" You can also make the spacing between controls uniform using the Format menu. Try this now: open the Vertical Spacing submenu of the Format menu and then choose Make Equal. All the controls are now evenly spaced. Next, choose Decrease from the Vertical Spacing menu and notice how the spacing between the controls decreases slightly. You can also increase the vertical spacing or completely remove vertical space from between controls using this menu. To perform the same functions on the horizontal spacing between controls, use the Horizontal Spacing submenu of the Format menu. Save your project now by clicking the Save All button on the toolbar.

Setting Property Values for a Group of Controls

You can change a property value in the Properties window when multiple controls are selected, and the change will be made to all controls. To do this, make sure all three controls are still selected and then display the Properties window.

When a group of controls is selected, the Properties window appears with some modifications (see Figure 6.9):

- No Name property is shown. This occurs because it's not allowable to have two controls with the same name, so C# won't even let you try.
- Only properties shared by all controls are displayed. If you had selected a label control and a text box, for example, only the properties shared by both control types would appear.
- For properties in which the values of the selected controls differ (such as the Location property in this example), the value is left empty in the Properties window.

Entering a value in any property changes the corresponding property for all selected controls. To see how this works, change the BackColor property to a shade of yellow, and you'll see that all controls have their BackColor set to yellow.

Anchoring and Autosizing Controls

One of my favorite additions to the forms engine in C# is the capability to anchor controls to one or more edges of a form so that controls can now size themselves appropriately when the user sizes the form. In the past, you had to use a (usually cumbersome) third-party component or resort to writing code in the form Resize event to get this behavior, but it's an intrinsic capability of C#'s form engine.

The default behavior is that controls are docked to the top and left edges. What if you want a control to always appear in the lower-left corner of a form? This is precisely what the Anchor property is designed to handle.

6

FIGURE 6.9

You can view the property values of many controls at once, with some caveats.

The easiest way to understand how anchoring works is to do it.

1. Create a new Windows Application called **Anchoring Example**.
2. Change the name of the default form to **fclsAnchoringExample** and set the form's Text property to **Anchoring Example**.
3. Change the main entry point to reflect the new form name.
4. Add a new button to the form and name it **btnAnchor**.
5. Run the project by pressing F5.
6. Click and drag the border of the form to change its size.

Notice that no matter what size you change the form to, the button stays in the upper-left corner of the form (see Figure 6.10).

FIGURE 6.10

By default, controls are anchored to the upper-left corner of the form.

Stop the running project now by choosing Stop Debugging from the Debug menu. Click the button on the form to select it, click the Anchor property, and then click the drop-down arrow that is displayed. You'll see a drop-down box that is unique to the Anchor property (see Figure 6.11).

FIGURE 6.11

You use this unique drop-down box to set the Anchor property of a control.

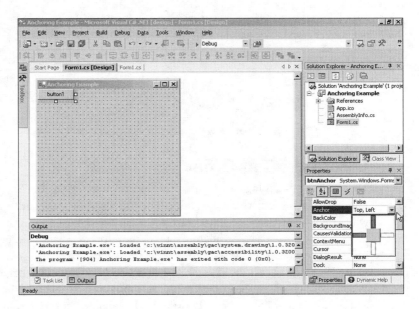

The gray square in the center of the drop-down box represents the control whose property you are setting. The thin rectangles on the top, bottom, left, and right represent the possible edges to which you can dock the control; if a rectangle is filled in, the edge of the control facing that rectangle is docked to that edge of the form.

1. Click the rectangle above the control so that it's no longer filled in, and then click the rectangle to the right of the control so that it is filled in.

2. Click any other property to close the drop-down box. The Anchor property should now read LeftRight.

3. Press F5 to run the project, and then drag an edge of the form to make it larger.

Pretty odd, huh? What C# has done is anchored the left edge of the button to the left edge of the form and anchored the right edge of the button to the right edge of the form (see Figure 6.12). Really, anchoring means keeping an edge of the control a constant relative distance from an edge of the form, and it's an unbelievably powerful tool for

6

building interfaces. Now you can make forms that users can resize, but you write little or no code to make the interface adjust accordingly. One caveat: depending on their anchor settings, controls may disappear if the form is shrunk quite small.

FIGURE 6.12

*Anchoring is a power-
ful feature for creating
adaptable forms.*

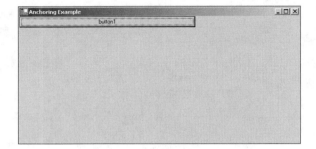

Creating a Tab Order

Tab order is something that is often (emphasis on *often*) overlooked. You're probably familiar with tab order as a user, although you may not realize it. When you press Tab while on a form, the focus moves from the current control to the next control in the tab order. This allows easy keyboard navigation on forms. The tab order for controls on a form is determined by the TabIndex properties of the controls. The control with the TabIndex value of 0 is the first control that receives the focus when the form is shown. When you press Tab, the control with the TabIndex of 1 receives the focus. When you add a control to a form, C# assigns the next available TabIndex value. Each control has a unique TabIndex value, and TabIndex values are always used in ascending order.

If the tab order isn't set correctly for a form, pressing Tab will cause the focus to jump from control to control in no apparent order. This really isn't a way to impress users.

The forms engine in C# has a far superior way to set the tab order for controls on a form. Create a new Windows Application named **Tab Order**, change the name of the default form to **fclsTabOrder**, set the Text property of the form to **Tab Order Example** and update the entry point with the **fclsTabOrder** reference.

Add three text box controls to the form and set their properties as follows:

Property	Value	Property	Value	Property	Value
Name	TextBox1	Name	TextBox2	Name	TextBox37
Location	90,120	Location	90,50	Location	90,190

Save the project by clicking the Save All button on the toolbar and then press F5 to run the project. Notice how the middle text box is the one with the focus. This is because it's the first one you added to the form and therefore has a TabIndex value of 0. Press Tab to move to the next control in the tab order (the top control); then press Tab once more and the focus jumps to the bottom control. Obviously, this isn't productive. Stop the project now by choosing Stop Debugging from the Debug menu (or simply close the form).

You're now going to set the tab order via the new visual method. Choose Tab Order from the View menu; notice how C# superimposes a set of numbers over the controls (see Figure 6.13). The number on a control indicates its TabIndex property value. Now it's very easy to see that the tab order is incorrect. Click the top control. Notice how the number over the control changes to 0. Click the middle control and you'll see its number change to 1. As you click controls, C# assigns the next highest number to the clicked control. Choose Tab Order from the View menu again to take the form out of Tab Order mode. Run the project again and you'll see that the top control is the first to get the focus, and pressing Tab now moves the focus logically.

FIGURE 6.13

The numbers over each control indicate the control's TabIndex.

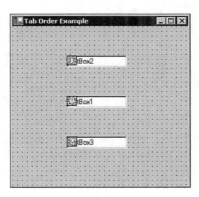

To programmatically move the focus via the tab order, use the SelectNextControl() method of a control or a form.

6

To remove a control from the tab sequence, set its TabStop property to false. When a control's TabStop property is set to false, users can still select the control with the mouse, but they can't enter the control using the Tab key. You should still set the TabIndex property to a logical value so that if the control receives the focus (such as by being clicked), pressing Tab will move the focus to the next logical control.

Layering Controls (Z-Order)

Tab order and visual alignment are key elements for effectively placing controls on forms. However, these two elements address control placement in only two dimensions—the x,y axis. At times, you may need to have controls overlap, although it's rare that you'll need to do so. Whenever two controls overlap, whichever control is added to the form most recently appears on top of the other (see Figure 6.14). You can control the ordering of controls using the Order submenu of the Format menu (see Figure 6.15).

FIGURE 6.14

Controls can overlap.

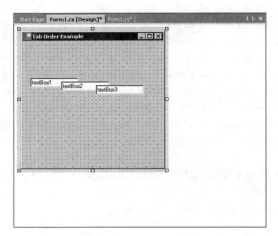

FIGURE 6.15

The Order menu is used to adjust the layering order of overlapping controls.

To send a control backward in the layering order, click it once to select it and then choose Send to Back from the Order menu. To bring the control forward in the layering order, select the control and choose Bring to Front from the Order menu.

 You can accomplish the same thing in C# code by invoking the BringToFront or SendToBack methods of a control.

Creating TopMost Windows

As you're probably aware, when you click a window it usually comes to the foreground and all other windows appear behind it. At times, you may want a window to stay on top of other windows, regardless of whether it's the current window (that is, it has the focus). An example of this is the Find window in C# and other applications such as Word. Regardless of which window has the focus, the Find form always appears floating over all other windows. Such a window is created by setting the form's TopMost property to true. Not exactly rocket science. However, that's the point; often a simple property change or method call is all it takes to accomplish what may otherwise seem to be a difficult task.

Creating Transparent Forms

A new property of forms that I think is very cool, yet I still can't come up with a reason to use it in a production application, is the Opacity property. This property controls the opaqueness of the form as well as all controls on the form. The default Opacity value of 100% means that the form and its controls are completely opaque (solid), whereas a value of 0% creates a completely transparent form (no real point in that). A value of 50% then, creates a form that is between solid and invisible (see Figure 6.16). I suppose you could write a loop that takes the Opaque property from 100% to 0% to fade out the form. Other than that, I don't know where to take advantage of this technique. *But ain't it cool?*

FIGURE 6.16
Ghost forms!

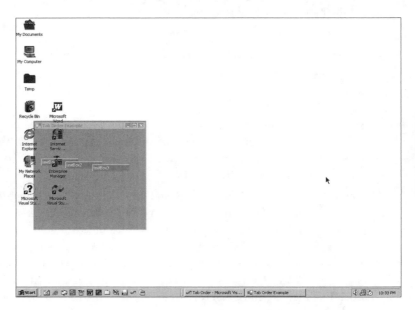

Creating Scrollable Forms

A scrollable form is a form that can display scrollbars when its contents are larger than the physical size of the form. Not only is this a cool and necessary feature, it's also trivial to implement in your own applications.

The scrolling behavior of a form is determined by the following three properties:

Property	Description
AutoScroll	This property determines whether scrollbars will ever appear on a form.
AutoScrollMinSize	The minimum size of the scroll region (area). If the size of the form is adjusted so that the client area of the form (the area of the form not counting borders and title bar) is smaller than the AutoScrollMinSize, scrollbars will appear.
AutoScrollMargin	This property determines the margin given around controls during scrolling. This essentially determines how far past the edge of the outermost controls you can scroll.

Again, it's easiest to understand this concept by doing it. Create a new Windows Application named **AutoScroll Example**, rename the default form to **fclsAutoScroll**, set the text of the form to **AutoScroll Example**, and update the entry point in Main().

Add a new Button control to the form by double-clicking the Button tool on the toolbox. Set the button's properties as follows:

Property	Value
Name	btnTest
Location	110,120
Text	Test

Save the project and press F5 to run it. Drag the borders of the control to make it larger and smaller. Notice that no matter how small you make the form, no scrollbars appear. This makes it possible to have controls on the form that are only partially visible or that can't be seen at all (see Figure 6.17).

Stop the project now by choosing Stop Debugging from the Debug menu or by closing the form. Change the **AutoScroll** property of the form to true. At this point you still won't get scrollbars, because you need to adjust at least one of the other scroll properties. Change the **AutoScrollMargin** property to **50,50** and run the project once more. Make the form smaller by dragging a border or a corner, and you'll see scrollbars appear (see Figure 6.18). The AutoScrollMargin property creates a virtual margin (in pixels) around all the outermost controls on the form. If the form is sized to within the margin area of a control, scrollbars automatically appear.

FIGURE 6.17

Without scrollbars, it's possible to have controls that can't be seen.

FIGURE 6.18

Scrollbars allow the user to view all parts of the form without needing to change the form's size.

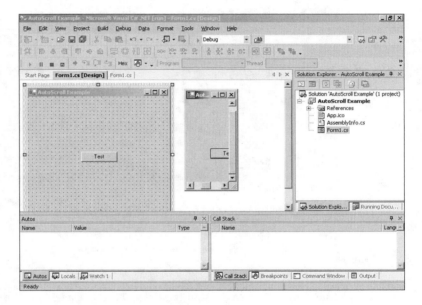

The final property that affects scrolling is the **AutoScrollMinSize**. Use the **AutoScrollMinSize** property to create a fixed-size scrolling region. If the form is ever sized such that the visible area of the form is smaller than the scrolling region defined by AutoScrollMinSize, scrollbars appear.

Creating MDI Forms

All the projects you've created so far have been single-document interface (SDI) projects. In SDI programs, every form in the application is a peer of all other forms; no intrinsic hierarchy exists between forms. C# also lets you create multiple-document interface (MDI) programs. A MDI program contains one parent window (also called a container) and one or more child windows. A classic example of a MDI program is Microsoft Word 95 (200 behaves slightly different, depending on how it's set up). When you run Word 97, a single parent window appears. Within this parent window, you can open any number of documents, which appear in child windows. In a MDI program, all child windows share the same toolbar and menu bar, which appears on the parent window. One restriction of child windows is that they can exist only within the confines of the parent window. Figure 6.19 shows an example of Word running with a number of child document windows open.

FIGURE 6.19

MDI applications consist of a single parent window and one or more child windows.

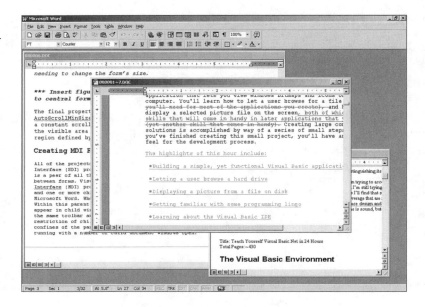

MDI applications can have any number of normal windows (dialog boxes, for example) in addition to child windows.

You're now going to create a simple MDI project. Create a new Windows Application named **MDI Example**. Change the name of the default form to **fclsMDIParent**, change its Text property to **MDI Parent,** update the entry point, and change its IsMdiContainer property to true (If you don't set the IsMdiContainer property to true, this example won't work). The first thing you'll notice is that C# changed the client area to a dark gray and gave it a sunken appearance. This is the standard appearance for MDI parent windows, and all visible child windows appear in this area.

Create a new form by choosing Add Windows Form from the Project menu. Name the form **fclsChild1.cs** and change its Text property to **Child 1**. Add a third form to the project in the same way. Name it **fclsChild2.cs** and set its Text property to **Child 2**. Any form can be a child form (except, of course, a MDI parent form). To make a form a child form, you set its MDIParent property to a form that is defined as a MDI container.

Make sure the fclsMDIParent parent form is visible in the form designer. If it's not, you can display it by double-clicking it in the Solution Explorer. Next, double-click the form to access its default event—the Load event. Enter the following code:

```
fclsChild1 objChild = new fclsChild1();
objChild.MdiParent = this;
objChild.Show();
```

By now, you should know what this code does. The first statement creates a new object
variable of type fclsChild1 and initializes it to hold a new instance of a form. The last
statement simply shows the form. What we're interested in here is the middle statement.
It sets the MdiParent property of the form to the current form (this always references the
current object), which is a MDI parent form because its IsMdiContainer property is set to
true. When the new form is shown, it's shown as a MDI child. Save your work and then
press F5 to run the project. Notice how the child form appears on the client area of the
parent form. If you size the parent form so that one or more child windows can't fully be
displayed, scrollbars appear (see Figure 6.20). If you were to remove the statement that
set the MdiParent property, the form would simply appear floating over the parent form
and would not be bound by the confines of the parent (it wouldn't be a child window).

FIGURE 6.20

*Child forms appear
only within the con-
fines of the parent
form.*

Stop the project by choosing Stop Debugging from the Debug menu. Display the
Solution Explorer and double-click the fclsChild1 form in its designer to display it in the
designer. Add a button to the form and set its properties as follows:

Property	Value
Name	btnShowChild2
Location	105,100
Size	85,23
Text	Show Child 2

Double-click the button to access its Click event, and then add the following code:

```
fclsChild2 objChild = new fclsChild2();
objChild.MdiParent = this.MdiParent;
objChild.Show();
```

6

This code shows the second child form. Note that two differences exist between this code and the code you entered earlier. First, the objChild variable creates a new instance of the fclsChild2 form rather than the fclsChild1 form. The second difference is how the parent is set. Because the child form is not a parent form, you can't simply set the second child's MdiParent property to this, because this doesn't refer to a parent form. However, you know that this.MdiParent references the parent form because this is precisely the property you set to make the form a child in the first place. Therefore, you can simply pass the parent of the first child to the second child, and they'll both be children of the same form.

Press F5 to run the project now. You'll see the button on the child form, so go ahead and click it (if you don't see the button, you may have mistakenly added it to the second child form). When you click the button, the second child form appears. Notice how this is also bound by the constraints of the parent form (see Figure 6.21).

The MDI parent form has an ActiveMdiChild property, which you can use to get a reference to the currently active child window.

FIGURE 6.21
Child forms are peers with one another.

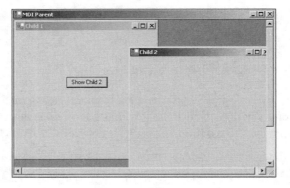

To make the parent form larger when the project is first run, you set the Height and Width properties of the form either at design time or at runtime in the Load event of the form.

One thing about forms that is important to note is that you can create as many instances of a form as you desire. For instance, you could change the code in the button to create a new instance of fclsChild1. The form that would be created would be the same as the form that created it, complete with a button to create yet another instance. Although you probably won't apply this technique because you're just getting started with C#, you may find it quite useful in the future. For instance, if you wanted to create a text editor, you might define the text entry portion as one form but create multiple instances of the form as new text files are opened, much like Word does with documents.

Setting the Startup Object

The Startup object in Windows Applications is, by default, the first form added to the project. This also happens to be the form that C# creates automatically when you create the new Windows Application project. Although the Startup object of a project was discussed briefly in a previous hour, it's worth mentioning here as well. Every project must have a Startup object as the entry point to the program.

The class that contains the *Main()* method that you want called as the entry point of the application is determined by the Startup Object property. You can change the Startup object by right-clicking the project name in the Solution Explorer and choosing Properties. The Startup Object property appears on the first property page that displays (see Figure 6.22).

FIGURE 6.22

The Startup Object property determines the first class that gets initialized and executed.

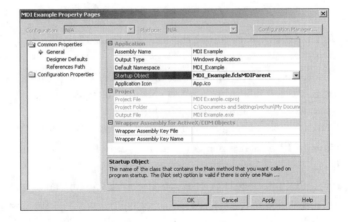

The setting of the Startup Object property isn't required if only one `Main()` method exists in the project.

If MDI forms still confuse you, don't worry. Most of the applications you'll write as a new C# programmer will be SDI programs. As you become more familiar with creating

C# projects in general, start experimenting with MDI projects. Remember, you don't have to make a program a MDI program simply because you can; make a MDI program if the requirements of the project dictate that you do so.

Summary

Understanding forms is critical because forms are the dynamic canvases on which you build your user interface. If you don't know how to work with forms, your entire application will suffer. Many things about working with forms go beyond simply setting properties, especially as you begin to think about the end user. As your experience grows, you'll get into the groove of form design and things will become second nature to you.

In this hour, you learned how to do some interesting things, such as creating transparent forms, as well as some high-end techniques, such as building an MDI application. You also learned how to create scrolling forms (an interface element that shouldn't be overlooked), and you spent a lot of time on working with controls on forms, which is important because the primary function of a form is as a place to host controls. In the next two hours, you'll learn the details of many of C#'s powerful controls that will eventually become important weapons in your vast development arsenal.

Q&A

Q. Do I need to worry about the anchoring and scrolling capabilities of every form I create?

A. Absolutely not. The majority of forms in most applications are dialog boxes. A dialog box is a modal form used to gather data from the user. A dialog box is usually a fixed size, which means that its border style is set to a style that cannot be sized. With a fixed-size form, you don't need to worry about anchoring or scrolling.

Q. How do I know if a project is a candidate for a MDI interface?

A. If the program will open many instances of the same type of form, it's a candidate for a MDI interface. For instance, if you're creating an image-editing program and the intent is to allow the user to open many images at once, MDI makes sense. Also, if you'll have many forms that will share a common toolbar and menu, you might want to consider MDI.

Workshop

The Workshop is designed to help you anticipate possible questions, review what you've learned, and get you thinking about how to put your knowledge into practice. The answers to the quiz are in Appendix A, "Answers to Quizzes/Exercises."

Quiz

1. True or False: The first control selected in a series is always made the active control.

2. How many methods are there to add a control to a form from the toolbox?

3. If you double-click a tool in the toolbox, where on the form is it placed?

4. Which property fixes an edge of a control to an edge of a form?

5. Which property do you change to hide the grid on a form?

6. Which menu contains the functions for spacing and aligning controls?

7. Which property do you set to make a form a MDI parent?

Exercises

1. Use your knowledge of the Anchor property and modify the Picture Viewer project you built in Hour 1 so that the main form can be sized. The buttons should always stay the size that they are and in the relative location in which they're placed, but the picture box should change size to show as much of the picture as possible, given the size of the form.

2. Modify the MDI Example project in this hour so that the first child form shows another instance of itself, rather than showing an instance of the second child form.

6

HOUR 7

Working with the Traditional Controls

The previous two hours described in considerable detail how to work with forms. Forms are the foundation of a user interface but are rather useless by themselves. To create a usable interface, you'll need to use *controls*. Controls are the various widgets and doodads on a form with which a user interacts. Dozens of different types of controls exist, from the simple Label control used to display static text to the rather complicated Tree View control used to present trees of data like that found in Explorer. In this hour, I'll introduce you to the most common (and most simple) controls, which I call traditional controls. In the next hour, you'll learn about the more advanced controls that you can use to create professional-looking applications.

The highlights of this hour include the following:

- Displaying static text with the Label control
- Allowing users to enter text using a text box
- Creating password fields
- Working with buttons

- Using panels, group boxes, check boxes, and option buttons
- Displaying lists with list boxes and combo boxes

Displaying Static Text with the Label Control

Label controls are used to display static text to the user. By static, I mean that the user can't change the text directly (but you can change the text with code). Label controls are one of the most common controls used; fortunately, they're also one of the easiest. Labels are most often used to provide descriptive text for other controls, such as text boxes. Labels are also great for providing status-type information to a user, as well as for providing general instructions on a form.

Begin by creating a new Windows Application named **Traditional Controls**. Change the name of the default form to **fclsControls**, and change its Text property to **Traditional Controls Example**. Next, change the Main entry point to use flcsControls.

Add a new Label control to the form by double-clicking the Label item in the toolbox. The primary property of the Label control is the Text property, which determines the text displayed to the user. When a Label control is first added to a form, the Text property is set to the name of control—this isn't very useful. Set the properties of the new Label control as follows:

Property	Value
Name	lblMyLabel
Location	5,6
Size	100,25
Text	Labels are for static text!

Notice how the label's text appears on two lines (see Figure 7.1). This occurs because the text is forced to fit within the size of a new Label control. In most cases, it's best to place label text on a single line. To do this, you could increase the width either by using the Properties window or by dragging the edge of the control, but there is an easier way. Double-click the Label control's AutoSize property now and notice how the label resizes itself automatically to fit the text on a single line. Double-clicking a property that accepts a set number of values cycles the property to the next value. The AutoSize property of new Label controls is false by default, so double-clicking this property changed it to true.

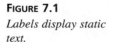

FIGURE 7.1

Labels display static text.

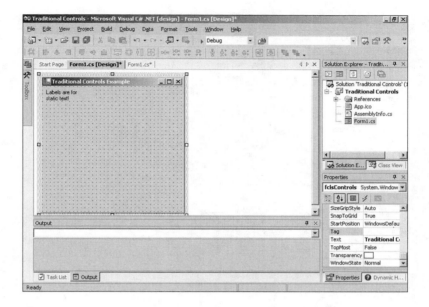

Allowing Users to Enter Text Using a Text Box

A Label control is usually the best control for displaying text a user can't change. However, when you need to let users enter or edit text, the text box is the tool for the job. If you've ever typed information on a form, you've almost certainly used a text box. Add a new text box to your form now by double-clicking the TextBox item in the toolbox. Set the text box's properties as follows:

Property	Value
Name	txtMyTextBox
Location	128,4
Size	136,20

When you first create a new text box, its Text property is set to its default name (see Figure 7.2). Unfortunately, the Text property isn't automatically changed when you change the name of the text box (which you should always do), so I recommend that you clear out the Text property of new text boxes. Delete the text in the Text property now and notice that the text box appears empty on the form.

7

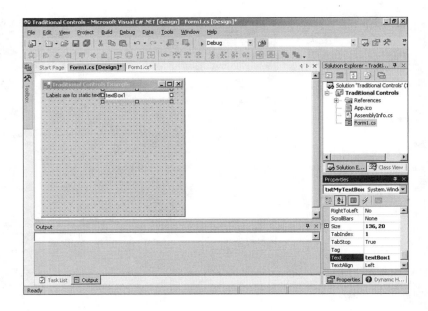

FIGURE 7.2

A new text box has its Text property set to its default name.

Although you'll probably want to clear the Text property of most of your text boxes at design time, understanding certain aspects of the text box is easier when a text box contains text. Set the text box's Text property to **This is sample text**. Remember to press Enter or Tab to commit your property change.

Specifying Text Alignment

Both the TextBox and the Label controls have a TextAlign property (as do many other controls). The TextAlign property determines the alignment of the text within the control—very much like the justification setting in a word processor. You can select from Left, Center, or Right.

Label controls allow you to set the vertical alignment and the horizontal alignment using the TextAlign property. This works best when AutoSize is set to false.

Change the TextAlign property of the text box to Right, and see how the text becomes right-aligned within the text box. Next, change TextAlign to Center to see what center alignment looks like. As you can see, this property is pretty straightforward. Change the TextAlign property back to Left before continuing.

Creating a Multiline Text Box

In the previous hour, I talked about the sizing handles of a selected control. I mentioned how handles that can be sized appear filled with white, and handles that are locked appear with a gray center. Notice how only the left and right edges of the text box have white sizing handles. This means that you can adjust only the left and right edges of the control (you can alter only the width, not the height). This is because the text box is defined as a single-line text box, meaning it will display only one line of text. What would be the point of a really tall text box that showed only a single line?

To allow a text box to display multiple lines of text, set its Multiline property to true. Set the Multiline property of your text box to true now, and notice that all the sizing handles become white.

Change the Text property of the text box to **This is sample text. A multiline text box will wrap its contents as necessary.** Press Enter or Tab to commit the property change. Notice how the text box displays only part of what you entered because the control simply isn't big enough to show all the text (see Figure 7.3). Change the Size property to **136,60**, and you'll then see the entire content of the text box (see Figure 7.4).

FIGURE 7.3

A text box may contain more text than it can display.

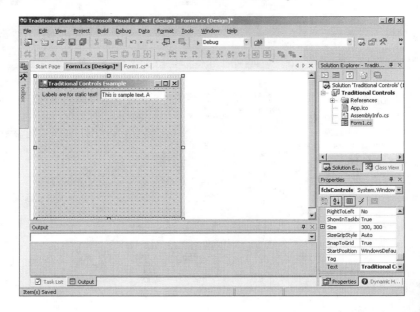

At times, you won't want a user to be able to interact with a control. For instance, you may implement a security model in your application, and if the user doesn't have the necessary privileges, you may not want the user to be able to alter data. The Enabled property, which almost every control has, determines whether the user can interact with the control. Change the Enabled property of the text box to false, and press F5 to run the

7

project. Although no noticeable change occurs in the control in Design view, there is a big change to the control at runtime: the text appears in gray rather than black, and the text box won't accept the focus or allow you to change the text (see Figure 7.5).

FIGURE 7.4

A multiline text box can be sized as large as necessary.

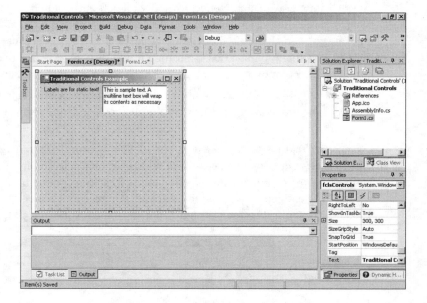

FIGURE 7.5

You can't interact with a text box whose Enabled property is set to false.

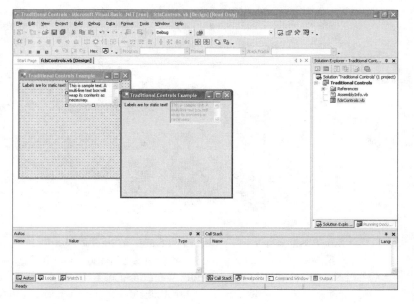

Stop the project now by choosing Stop Debugging from the Debug menu, and then change the control's Enabled property back to true.

Adding Scrollbars

Even though you can size a multiline text box, there may be times when the contents of the control are more than what can be displayed. If you believe that this is a possibility for a text box you're adding to a form, give the text box scrollbars by changing the ScrollBars property from None to Vertical, Horizontal, or Both.

> For a text box to display scrollbars, its Multiline property must be set to true.

Change the ScrollBars property of your text box to Vertical and notice how scrollbars appear in the text box (see Figure 7.6).

FIGURE 7.6

If a text box may contain lots of text, give it a scrollbar.

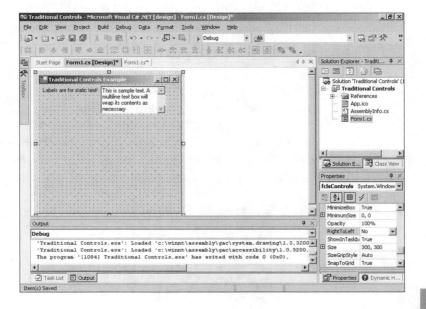

Limiting the Number of Characters a User Can Enter

You can limit the number of characters a user can type into a text box using the MaxLength property. All new text boxes are given the default value of 32767 for MaxLength, but you can change this as needed (up or down). Add a new text box to the form and set its properties as follows:

7

Property	Value
Name	txtRestrict
Location	128,80
MaxLength	10
Size	136,20
Text	*(make blank)*

Run the project by pressing F5 and then enter the following text into the text box: **So you run and you run.** Be sure to try to enter more than 10 characters of text—you can't (if you can, you're probably entering the text into the text box with scrollbars, rather than into the new text box). All that you're allowed to enter is **So you run** (10 characters). The text box allows only 10 characters, whether that's via entry using the keyboard or a Paste operation. The MaxLength property is most often used when the text box's content is to be written to a database, in which field sizes are usually restricted (using a database is discussed in Hour 21, "Working with a Database").

Stop the project by choosing Stop Debugging from the Debug menu and then click Save All on the toolbar.

Creating Password Fields

You've probably used a password field: a text box that displays an asterisk for each character entered. Any text box can be made a password field by assigning a character to its PasswordChar field. Select the PasswordChar property of the second text box now (txtRestrict) and enter an asterisk (*) for the property value. Run the project once more and enter text into the text box. Now an asterisk is displayed for each character you enter (see Figure 7.7). Although the user doesn't see the actual text contained in the text box, referencing the Text property in code always returns the true text.

FIGURE 7.7
A password field displays its password character for all entered text.

A text box will display password characters only if its Multiline property is set to false.

Stop the project by choosing Stop Debugging from the Debug menu. Delete the asterisk from the PasswordChar field, and then save the project by clicking Save All on the toolbar.

Creating Buttons

Every dialog box that Windows displays has at least one button on it. Buttons enable a user to invoke a function with a click of the mouse. Create a new project named **Button Example**, change the name of the default form to **fclsButtonExample**, set the form's Text property to **Button Example,** and update the entry point Main() to reference fclsButtonExample instead of Form1. Next, add a new button to the form by double-clicking the Button item in the toolbox. Set the button's properties as follows:

Property	Value
Name	btnClose
Location	104,90
Text	Close

Add a new text box to the form and set its properties as follows:

Property	Value
Name	txtTest
Location	92,40
TabIndex	0
Text	(make blank)

You're probably starting to see a pattern here. Whenever you add a new control to a form, the first thing you should do is give the control a descriptive name. If the control has a Text property, you should also change that to something meaningful. Your form should now look like Figure 7.8.

7

FIGURE 7.8

Users click buttons, such as the Close button, to make things happen.

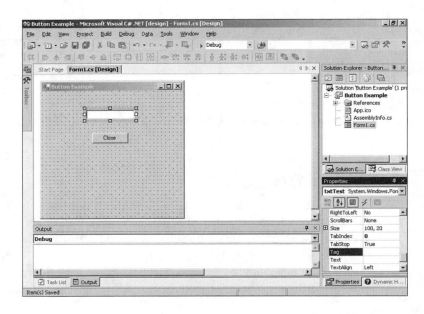

There's no point in having a button that doesn't do anything, so double-click the button now to access its Click event, and then add the following statement:

```
this.Close();
```

Recall from Hour 5, "Building Forms—Part I," that this statement closes the current form. Because you'll have only one form in the project, this has the effect of terminating the application. Press F5 to run the project. The cursor appears in the text box, which means that the text box has the focus (it has the lowest TabIndex property). Press Enter and note that nothing happens (this will make sense shortly). Next, click the button and the form will close.

Accept and Cancel Buttons

When creating dialog boxes, it's common to assign one button as the default button (called the Accept button). If a form has an Accept button, that button's Click event is fired when the user presses Enter, regardless of which control has the focus. This is great for dialog boxes in which the user enters some text and presses Enter to commit the data and close the form. To designate a button as an Accept button, use the following steps:

1. Select the AcceptButton property of the form.

2. Look at the AcceptButton property of your form now—it reads (none). Click the property to select it and a drop-down arrow appears.

3. Click the down arrow and you'll get a list of the buttons on the form (see Figure 7.9). Choose btnClose to make it the Accept button. Notice how the button now appears with a dark border, indicating that it is the Accept button.

FIGURE 7.9

You can designate only one button as a form's Accept button.

4. Press F5 to run the project. Again, the text box has the focus. Press Enter, and you'll find that the form closes. Again, pressing Enter on a form that has a designated Accept button causes that button's Click event to fire the same as if the user clicked it with the mouse, regardless of which control has the focus.

The Accept button is a useful concept, and you should take advantage of this functionality when possible. Keep in mind that when you do create an Accept button for a form, you should also create a Cancel button. A Cancel button is a button that fires its Click event when the user presses the Esc key, regardless of which control has the focus. Generally, you place code in a Cancel button to shut down the form without committing any changes made by the user. To designate a button as a Cancel button, choose it as the CancelButton property of the form.

Adding a Picture to a Button

Although it's not standard practice, and you shouldn't overuse the technique because doing so causes clutter and can reduce the usefulness of your interface, it's possible to add a picture to a button. The two primary methods of doing this are to add the picture to the button at design time by loading a picture into the Image property of the control using the Properties window, or to bind the button to an image list. I'll discuss loading a picture using the Properties window here and the Image List control in the next hour. (Note: You can load an image at runtime using the technique discussed for the Picture Viewer program in Hour 1, "A C# Programming Tour.")

To perform this operation, you'll need a small bitmap. I've provided one at www.samspublishing.com called Close.bmp.

7

Select the button and display its properties in the Properties window. Click the Image property to select it, and then click the button with the three dots. The Open File dialog box is displayed, allowing you to find and select a bitmap. Use this dialog box to locate and select the Close.bmp bitmap or another small bitmap of your choosing. Click Open to load the image into the button's Image property, and the picture will appear on your button (see Figure 7.10).

FIGURE 7.10

The picture loaded into the Image property of a button appears on the button.

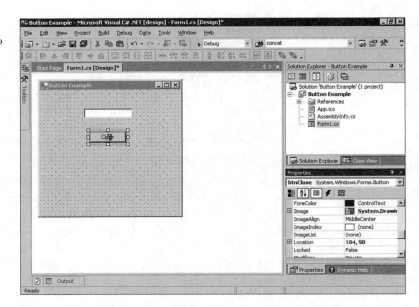

 Many controls have an Image property, and for the most part, they all work the same way as the Image property of the Button control.

Notice that there is a problem with how the picture appears on the button—the image overlays the text. This problem is easily corrected.

Although a picture is displayed in the center of a button by default, you can specify the placement using the ImageAlign property. Click the ImageAlign property to display a drop-down arrow, and then click the arrow. The drop-down list contains a special interface for specifying the alignment of the picture (see Figure 7.11). Each rectangle in the drop-down list corresponds to an alignment (center-left, center-center, center-right, and so on) Click the center-left rectangle now and the image will be moved to the left of the text. So much for problem one...

Figure 7.11

Click a rectangle to move the picture to the corresponding alignment.

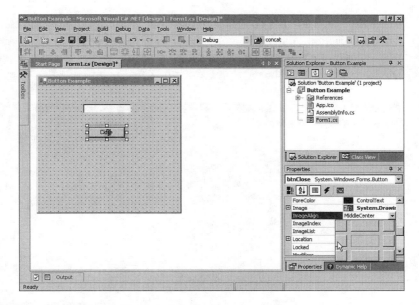

Creating Containers and Groups of Option Buttons

In this section, you'll learn how to create containers for groups of controls using panels and group boxes. You'll also learn how to use the Check Box and Option Button controls in conjunction with these container controls to present multiple choices to a user.

Begin by creating a new Windows Application titled **Options**. Change the name of the default form to **fclsOptions** and set the form's Text property to **Options**. Next, change the entry point Main() to reference fclsOptions instead of Form1.

Using Panels and Group Boxes

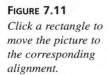

Controls can be placed on a form because the form is a *container* object—an object that can contain controls. A form is not the only type of container, however. Some controls act as containers as well, and a container may host one or more other containers. The Panel and Group Box controls are both container controls that serve a similar purpose, yet each is more suited to a particular application.

The Panel control is a slimmed-down version of the Group Box control, so I won't be discussing it in depth. If you need a very basic container control without the additional features offered by the group box, such as a border and a caption, use the Panel control.

7

The group box is a container control with properties that let you create a border (frame) and caption. Add a new group box to your form now by double-clicking the GroupBox item in the toolbox. When you create a new group box, it has a border by default, and its caption is set to the name of the control (see Figure 7.12).

FIGURE 7.12

A group box acts like a form within a form.

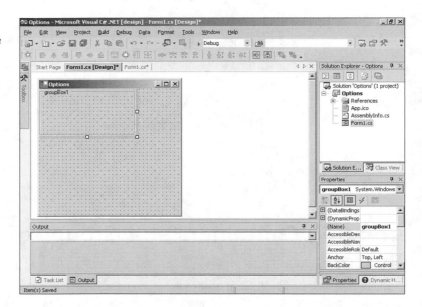

Set the properties of the group box as follows:

Property	Value
Name	grpMyGroupBox
Location	48,16
Size	200,168
Text	This is a group box

The group box is a fairly straightforward control. Other than defining a border and displaying a caption, the purpose of a group box is to provide a container for other controls. The next two sections, "Presenting Yes/No Options Using Check Boxes" and "Working with Radio Buttons," help demonstrate the benefits of using a group box as a container.

Presenting Yes/No Options Using Check Boxes

The check box is used to display true/false values on a form. You're now going to add a check box to your form—but not in the way you have been adding other controls. As you know by now, double-clicking the CheckBox item in the toolbox will place a new Check Box control on the form. However, this time you're going to place the check box on the Group Box control.

To place a control on a group box, you can use one of the following techniques:

- Add the control to the form, cut the control from the form, select the group box, and paste the control on the group box.
- Draw the control directly on the group box.
- Drop the control on the group box.

You're going to use the third method—dropping a new control directly on the group box. Follow these steps:

1. Click the group box to select it.
2. Click the CheckBox item in the toolbox and drag it to the group box.
3. Release the mouse when you are over the group box.

You should now have a check box on your group box like the one shown in Figure 7.13.

FIGURE 7.13

Container controls hold other controls.

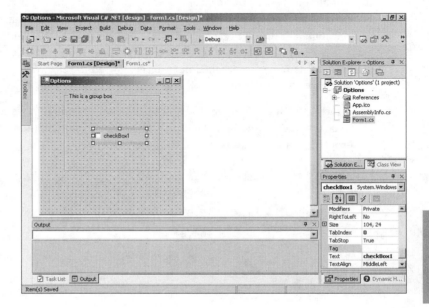

Move the check box around by clicking and dragging it. You'll notice that you can't move the check box outside the group box's boundaries. This is because the check box is a child of the group box, not of the form. Set the properties of the check box as follows:

Property	Value
Name	chkMyCheckBox
Location	16,24
Size	120,24
Text	This is a check box

When the user clicks the check box, it changes its visible state from checked to unchecked. To see this behavior, press F5 to run the project and click the check box a few times.

When you're done experimenting, stop the running project. To determine the state of the check box in code, use its Checked property. You can also set this property at design time using the Properties window.

Working with Radio Buttons

Check boxes are excellent controls for displaying true/false values. Check boxes work independently of one another, however. If you have five check boxes on a form, each of them could be checked or unchecked. Radio buttons, on the other hand, are mutually exclusive to the container on which they are placed. This means that only one radio button per container may be selected at a time. Selecting one radio button automatically deselects any other radio buttons on the same container. Radio buttons are used to offer a selection of items to a user when the user is allowed to select only one item. To better see how mutual exclusivity works, you're going to create a small group of radio buttons.

Click the RadioButton item in the toolbox to begin dragging, move the pointer over the group box, and then release the button to drop a new radio button on the group box. Set the properties of the radio button as follows:

Property	Value
Name	optOption1
Location	19,65
Size	104,24
Text	This is option 1

You're going to copy this radio button and paste a copy of the control on the group box. Begin by right-clicking the radio button and choosing Copy from its context menu. Next, click the group box to select it, right-click the group box, and choose Paste from its context menu to create a new radio button. Set the properties of the radio button as follows:

Property	Value
Name	optOption2
Checked	true
Location	19,96
Text	This is option 2

Now that you have your two radio buttons (see Figure 7.14), run the project by pressing F5.

FIGURE 7.14
Radio buttons restrict a user to selecting a single item.

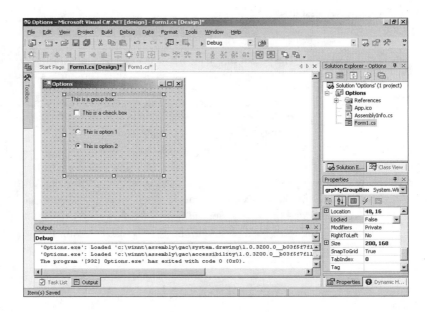

Click the first radio button to select it, and notice how the second radio button becomes deselected automatically (its Checked property is set to false). Two radio buttons are sufficient to demonstrate the mutual exclusivity, but be aware that you could add as many radio buttons to the group box as you care to and the behavior would be the same. The important thing to remember is that mutual exclusivity is shared only by radio buttons

7

placed on the same container. To create radio buttons that behave independently of one another, you would need to create a second set. You could easily create a new group box (or panel for that matter) and place the second set of radio buttons on the new container. The two sets of radio buttons would behave independently of one another, but mutual exclusivity would still exist among the buttons within each set.

Stop the running project and save your work.

Displaying a List with the List Box

The list box is used to present a list of items to a user. You can add items to and remove items from the list at any time with very little C# code. In addition, you can set up a list box so that a user can select only a single item or multiple items. When a list box contains more items than it can show because of the size of the control, scrollbars are automatically displayed.

> The cousin of the list box is the combo box, which looks like a text box with a down-arrow button at its right side. Clicking a combo box's button causes the control to display a drop-down list box. Working with the lists of a combo box is pretty much identical to working with a list box, so I'll discuss the details of list manipulation in this section. In the next section, I'll discuss features specific to the combo box.

Create a new project titled **Lists**. Change the name of the default form to **fclsLists** and set its Text property to **Lists Example**. Next, change the entry point Main() to reference fclsLists instead of Form1. Set the form's Size property to **300,320**. Add a new list box control to the form by double-clicking the ListBox item in the toolbox. Set the properties of the list box as follows:

Property	Value
Name	lstPinkFloydAlbums
Location	72,32
Size	160,121

Every item contained in a list box is a member of the list box's Items collection. Working with items, including adding and removing items, is performed using the Items collection. Most often, you'll manipulate the Items collection using code (which I'll show you a little bit later in this hour), but you can also work with the collection at design time using the Properties window.

Manipulating Items at Design Time

The Items collection is available as a property of the list box. Locate the Items property in the Properties window and click it to select it. The familiar button with three dots appears, indicating that you can do advanced things with this property. Click the button now to show the String Collection Editor. To add items to the collection, simply enter the items into the text box—one item to a line.

Enter the following items:

- Atom Heart Mother
- Saucer Full of Secrets
- Wish You Were Here
- Animals
- Echoes
- Piper at the Gates of Dawn

When you're finished, your screen should look like that shown in Figure 7.15. Click OK to commit your entries and close the window. Notice that the list box contains the items that you entered.

FIGURE 7.15

Use this dialog box to manipulate an Items collection at design time.

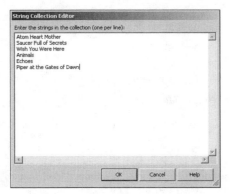

Manipulating Items at Runtime

In Hour 3, "Understanding Objects and Collections," you learned all about objects, properties, methods, and collections. All this knowledge comes into play when manipulating lists at runtime. The Items property of a list box (and a combo box) is an object property

7

that returns a collection (collections in many ways are like objects—they have properties and methods). To manipulate list items, you manipulate the Items collection.

> Whether you choose to set values at design time or runtime depends on the situation. For example, if you don't know the values at design time, you'll have to set them at runtime. I recommend that you set values at design-time whenever possible.

A list may contain duplicate values, as you'll see in this example. Because of this, C# needs another mechanism to treat each item in a list as a unique item. This is done by assigning each item in an Items collection a unique index. The first item in the list has an index of 0, the second an index of 1, and so on. The index is the ordinal position of an item relative to the first item in the Items collection, not the top item visible in the list.

Adding Items to a List

New items are added to the Items collection using the Add method of the collection. You're now going to create a button that adds an album to the list. Add a new button to the form and set its properties as follows:

Property	Value
Name	btnAddItem
Location	104,160
Size	96,23
Text	Add an Item

Double-click the button to access its Click event and add the following code:

```
lstPinkFloydAlbums.Items.Add("Dark Side of the Moon");
```

Notice that the Add method accepts a string argument—the text to add to the list.

> Unlike items added at design time, items added through code aren't preserved when the program is ended.

Press F5 to run the project now and click the button. When you do, the new album is added to the bottom of the list. Clicking the button a second time adds another item to the list with the same album name. The list box doesn't care whether the item already exists in the list; each call to the Add method of the Items collection adds a new item to the list. The Add method of the Items collection can be called as a function, in which case it returns the index (ordinal position of the newly added item in the underlying collection), as in the following:

```
int intIndex;
intIndex = lstPinkFloydAlbums.Items.Add("Dark Side of the Moon");
```

Stop the running project and save your work before continuing.

> To add an item to an Items collection at a specific location in the list, use the Insert method. The Insert method accepts an index in addition to text. For instance, to add an item at the top of the list, you could use a statement such as lstPinkFloydAlbums.Items.Insert(0,"Dark Side of the Moon");. Remember, the first item in the list has an index of 0.

Removing Items from a List

Removing an individual item from a list is as easy as adding an item and requires only a single method call: a call to the Remove method of the Items collection. The Remove method accepts a string, which is the text of the item to remove. You're now going to create a button that will remove an item from the list. Create a new button and set its properties as follows:

Property	Value
Name	btnRemoveItem
Location	104,192
Size	96,23
Text	Remove an Item

Double-click the new button to access its Click event and enter the following statement:

```
lstPinkFloydAlbums.Items.Remove("Dark Side of the Moon");
```

The Remove method tells C# to search the Items collection, starting at the first item (index = 0), and when an item is found that matches the specified text, to remove that item. As I stated earlier, you can have multiple items with the same text. The Remove method will remove only the first occurrence; after the text is found and removed, C#

7

stops looking. Press F5 to run the project now. Click the Add an Item button a few times to add Dark Side of the Moon to the list (see Figure 7.16). Next, click the Remove an Item button and notice how C# finds and removes one instance of the item.

FIGURE 7.16

The list box may contain duplicate entries, but each entry is a unique item in the Items collection.

 To remove an item at a specific index, use the RemoveAt method. For instance, to remove the first item in the list, you could use a statement such as `lstPinkFloydAlbums.Items.RemoveAt(0);`.

Stop the running project and save your work.

Clearing a List

To completely clear the contents of a list box, use the Clear method. You are now going to add a button to the form that will clear the list when clicked. Add a new button to the form now and set the button's properties as follows:

Property	Value
Name	btnClearList
Location	104,224
Size	96,23
Text	Clear List

Double-click the new button to access its Click event and enter the following statement:

```
lstPinkFloydAlbums.Items.Clear();
```

Press F5 to run the project, and then click the Clear List button. The Clear method doesn't care if an item was added at design time or runtime; Clear() always removes all items from the list. Stop the project and again save your work.

Remember, the Add, Insert, Remove, RemoveAt, and Clear methods are all methods of the Items collection, not of the list box itself. If you forget that these are members of the Items collection, you might get confused when you don't find them when you enter a period after typing a list box's name in code.

Retrieving Information About the Selected Item in a List

By default, a list box allows only a single item to be selected by the user at one time. Whether a list allows multiple selections is determined by the SelectionMode property of the list box. You will need to understand how to work with the selected item in a list box that allows only a single selection (list boxes that allow multiple selections are more complex and are beyond the scope of the book).

Two properties provide information about the selected item: SelectedItem and SelectedIndex. It's important to note that these are properties of the list box itself, not of the Items collection of a list box. The `SelectedItem` method returns the text of the currently selected item. If no item is selected, an empty string is returned. At times, it's desirable to know the index of the selected item. This is returned by the SelectedIndex property of the list box. As you know, the first item in a list has the index of 0. If no item is selected, SelectedIndex returns a –1, which is never a valid index for an item.

You're now going to add a button to the form that, when clicked, displays the selected item's text and index in the Output window. First, change the Height property of the form to 320 to accommodate one more button. As you build your interfaces, you'll often have to make small tweaks such as this because it's nearly impossible to anticipate everything ahead of time. Add a new button to the form and set its properties as follows:

Property	Value
Name	btnShowItem
Location	104,256
Size	96,23
Text	Show Selected

Double-click the new button to access its Click event and enter the following statements:

```
System.Diagnostics.Debug.WriteLine(lstPinkFloydAlbums.SelectedItem);
System.Diagnostics.Debug.WriteLine(lstPinkFloydAlbums.SelectedIndex);
```

7

System.Diagnostics.Debug.WriteLine sends text to the Output window. If you are planning to write several debug statements, it may be helpful to declare the System.Diagnostics namespace at the beginning of your class. This permits you to use the methods of the namespace without having to qualify the entire namespace. For example, after the namespace System.Diagnostics is declared in the class, you could use a statement like the following:

```
Debug.WriteLine(lstPinkFloydAlbums.SelectedItem);
```

Notice how you don't have to reference System.Diagnostics on this line; the compiler is able to determine this automatically.

To specify a namespace so that you can reference its objects without explicitly referencing the namespace, you add a using statement in the header of the class file (with the other using statements that C# automatically places in the header). For example, to reference the System.Diagnostics namespace, you could add a statement like this to the class's header:

```
using System.Diagnostics;
```

Again, after you've added the namespace with a using statement, you can reference the namespace's objects without explicitly referencing System.Diagnostics, as seen next:

```
Debug.WriteLine(lstPinkFloydAlbums.SelectedItem);
Debug.WriteLine(lstPinkFloydAlbums.SelectedIndex);
```

Press F5 to run the project and click the Show Selected button. Take a look at the Output window. You'll see a blank line (the empty string returned by SelectedItem) and a –1, returned by SelectedIndex denoting that no item is selected. Click an item in the list to select it, and then click Show Selected again. This time, you'll see the text of the selected item and its index in the Output window (see Figure 7.17).

FIGURE 7.17

The SelectedItem and SelectedIndex properties make it easy to determine which item is selected.

Stop the running project and save your work.

Sorting a List

List boxes and combo boxes have a `Sorted` property. By default, this property is set to false. Changing this property value to true causes C# to sort the contents of the list alphabetically. When the contents of a list are sorted, the index of each item in the Items collection is changed; therefore, you can't use an index value obtained prior to setting Sorted to true. Sorted is a property, not a member. You don't have to call Sorted to sort the contents of a list. Instead, as long as the Sorted property is set to true, C# enforces a sort order. This means that all items added using the Add method are automatically inserted into the proper location, in contrast to being inserted at the end of the list, which is the behavior of an unsorted list.

Creating Drop-Down Lists Using the Combo Box

List boxes are great, but they have two shortcomings. First, they take up quite a bit of space. Second, users can't enter their own values; they have to select from the items in the list. If you need to conserve space or if you want to allow a user to enter a value that may not exist in the list, use the Combo Box control.

Combo boxes have an Items collection that behaves exactly like that of the List Box control (refer to the previous section for information on manipulating lists). Here I will show you the basics of how a combo box works.

Add a new combo box to the form by double-clicking the ComboBox item in the toolbox. Set the combo box's properties as follows:

Property	Value
Name	cboColors
Location	72,8
Size	160,21
Text	(make blank)

The first thing you should note is that the combo box has a Text property, whereas the list box doesn't. This works the same as the Text property of a text box. When the user selects an item from the drop-down list, the value of the selected item is placed in the Text property of the text box. The default behavior of a combo box is to allow the user to enter any text in the text box portion of the control—even if the text doesn't exist in the list. Shortly, I'll show you how to change this behavior.

7

Select the Items property of the combo box in the Properties window and click the button that appears. Add the following items to the String Collection editor and click OK to commit your entries.

- Black
- Blue
- Gold
- Green
- Red
- Yellow

Press F5 to run the project. Click the arrow at the right side of the combo box and a drop-down list appears (see Figure 7.18).

FIGURE 7.18

Combo boxes conserve space.

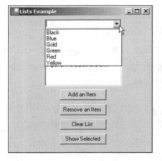

Next, try typing in the text **Magenta**. C# lets you do this. Indeed, you can type any text that you desire. Often, you'll want to restrict a user to entering only values that appear in the list. To do this, you change the DropDownStyle property of the combo box. Close the form to stop the running project and change the DropDownStyle property of the combo box to DropDownList. Press F5 to run the project again and try to type text into the combo box. You can't. However, if you enter a character that is the start of a list item, C# will select the closest matching entry.

As a matter of fact, clicking in the "text box" portion of the combo box opens the list the same as if you clicked the drop-down arrow. When set as a DropDownList, a combo box won't allow any text entry; therefore, the user is limited to selecting items from the list.

Stop the running project now and save your work. As you can see, the combo box and list box offer similar functionality. In fact, the coding of their lists is identical. However, each one of these controls serves a slightly different purpose. Which one is better? That depends entirely on the situation. As you use professional applications, pay attention to their interfaces; you'll start to get a feel for which control is appropriate in a given situation.

Summary

In this hour you learned how to present text to a user. You learned that the Label control is perfect for displaying static text (text the user can't enter) and that the text box is the control to use for displaying edited text. You can now create text boxes that contain many lines of text, and you know how to add scrollbars when the text is greater than what can be displayed in the control.

I don't think I've ever seen a form without at least one button on it. You've now learned how to add buttons to your forms and how to do some interesting things, such as adding a picture to a button. For the most part, working with buttons is a simple matter of adding one to a form, settings its Name and Text properties, and adding some code to its Click event—all of which you now know how to do.

Check boxes and option buttons are used to present true/false and mutually exclusive options, respectively. In this hour, you learned how to use each of these controls and how to use group boxes to logically group sets of related controls.

Last, you learned how to use list boxes and combo boxes to present lists of items to a user. You now know how to add items to a list at design time as well as runtime, and you know how to sort items. The List Box and Combo Box are powerful controls, and I encourage you to dig deeper into the functionality they possess.

Without controls, users would have nothing to interact with on your forms. In this hour, you learned how to use the standard controls to begin building functional interfaces. Keep in mind that I only scratched the surface of each of these controls and that most do far more than I've hinted at here. Mastering these controls will be easy for you, as you'll be using them a lot.

Q&A

Q. Can I place radio buttons directly on a form?

A. Yes. The form is a container, so all radio buttons placed on a form are mutually exclusive to one another. If you wanted to add a second set of mutually exclusive buttons, they'd have to be placed on a container control. In general, I think it's best to place radio buttons on a group box rather than on a form because the group box provides a border and a caption for the radio buttons and makes it much easier to move the set of radio buttons around when you're designing the form.

7

Q. I've seen what appears to be list boxes that have a check box next to each item in the list. Is this possible?

A. Yes. In C#, this is accomplished using an entirely different control: the checked list box.

Workshop

The Workshop is designed to help you anticipate possible questions, review what you've learned, and get you thinking about how to put your knowledge into practice. The answers to the quiz are in Appendix A, "Answers to Quizzes/Exercises."

Quiz

1. Which control would you use to display text that the user can't edit?
2. What common property is shared by the Label control and text box and whose value determines what the user sees in the control?
3. To change the Height of a text box, you must set what property?
4. What is the default event of a Button control?
5. A button whose Click event is triggered when the user presses Enter, regardless of the control that has the focus, is called an…?
6. Which control would you use to display a yes/no value to a user?
7. How would you create two distinct sets of mutually exclusive option buttons?
8. To manipulate items in a list, you use what collection?
9. What method adds an item to a list in a specific location?

Exercises

1. Create a form with a text box and a combo box. Add a button that, when clicked, adds the contents of the text box to the combo box.
2. Create a form with two list boxes. Add a number of items to one list box at design time using the Properties window. Create a button that, when clicked, removes the selected item in the first list and adds it to the second list.

Hour 8

Advanced Controls

The standard controls presented in the previous hour enable you to build many types of functional forms. However, to create truly robust and interactive applications, you've got to use the more advanced controls. As a Windows user, you've encountered many of these controls, such as the Tab control, which presents data on tabs, and the Tree View control, which displays hierarchical lists such as the one in Explorer. In this hour, you'll learn about these advanced controls and learn how to use them to make professional interfaces like those you're accustomed to seeing in commercial products.

The highlights of this hour include the following:

- Creating timers
- Creating tabbed dialog boxes
- Storing pictures in an Image List
- Building enhanced lists using the List View control
- Creating hierarchical lists with the Tree View control

In many of the examples in this hour, I show you how to add items to collections at design time. Keep in mind that almost everything you can do at design time can also be accomplished with C# code at runtime.

Creating Timers

One thing that all the controls you used in Hour 7, "Working with Traditional Controls," have in common is that the user can interact with them. However, not all controls have this capability—or restriction, depending on how you look at it. Some controls are designed for use only by the developer. One such control is the Open File Dialog control you used in your Picture Viewer application in Hour 1, "A C# Programming Tour." Another control that is invisible at runtime is the Timer control. The Timer control's sole purpose is to trigger an event at a specified interval of time.

Create a new Windows Application titled **Timer Example**. Change the name of the default form to **fclsTimerExample** and then set its Text property to **Timer Example**. Next, be sure to set the Main() entry point of the project to fclsTimerExample or the project won't run. Add a new Timer control to your form by double-clicking the Timer item in the toolbox. Because the Timer control is invisible at runtime, it's added to the gray area at the bottom of the screen rather than placed on the form (see Figure 8.1). Set the properties of the Timer control as follows:

Property	Value
Name	tmrClock
Enabled	True
Interval	1000

You probably noticed that there are very few properties for the Timer control, compared to the other controls with which you've worked. The key property of the Timer control is the Interval property. The Interval property determines how often the Timer control fires its Tick event. The Interval is specified in milliseconds, so a setting of 1,000 is equal to 1 second. The best way to understand how the timer works is to use it. Using the Timer and a Label control, you're now going to create a simple clock. The way the clock will work is that the timer will fire its Tick event once every second (because you'll set the Interval = 1000 milliseconds), and within the Tick event, the label's Text property will be updated with the current system time.

FIGURE 8.1

Invisible-at-runtime controls are shown at the bottom of the designer, not on the form.

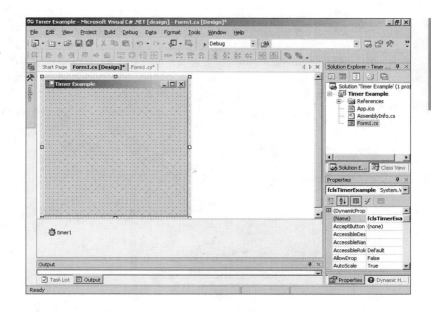

Add a new label to the form and set its properties as follows:

Property	Value
Name	lblClock
BorderStyle	FixedSingle
Location	96,120
Size	100,23
Text	*(make blank)*
TextAlign	MiddleCenter

Next, double-click the Timer control to access its Tick event. When a timer is first enabled, it starts counting, in milliseconds, from 0. When the amount of time specified in the Interval property passes, the Tick event fires and the timer starts counting from 0 again. This continues until the timer is disabled (that is, when its Enabled property is set to False). Because you've set the Enabled property of the timer to True at design time, it will start counting as soon as the form on which it is placed is loaded. Enter the following statement in the Tick event:

```
DateTime dtCurrentTime = DateTime.Now;
lblClock.Text = dtCurrentTime.ToLongTimeString();
```

The .NET Framework provides date/time functionality in the System namespace. The Now property of the DateTime class returns the current time. Using the ToLongTimeString method returns a string with a time format of hh:mm:ss. Using this class, property, and method, we set the Text property of the label to the current time of day, and it does this once a second. Press F5 to run the project now and you'll see the Label control acting as a clock, updating the time every second (see Figure 8.2).

FIGURE 8.2

Timers make it easy to execute at specified intervals.

Stop the running project now and save your work. Timers are powerful, but you must take care not to overuse them. For a timer to work, Windows must be aware of the timer and must constantly compare the current internal clock to the interval of the timer. It does all this so that it can notify the timer at the appropriate time to execute its Tick event. In other words, timers take system resources. This isn't a problem for an application that uses a few timers, but I wouldn't overload an application with a dozen timers unless I had no other choice.

Creating Tabbed Dialog Boxes

Windows 95 was the first version of Windows to introduce a tabbed interface. Since then, tabs have been unanimously adopted as a primary interface element. Tabs provide two primary benefits: the logical grouping of controls and the reduction of required screen space. Although tabs may look complicated, they are, in fact, extremely easy to build and use.

Create a new Windows Application named **Tabs Example**. Change the name of the default form to reference **fclsTabs** instead of Form1, set its Text property to **Tabs Example**, and modify the Main() entry point to fclsTabs. Next, add a new Tab control to your form by double-clicking the TabControl item in the toolbox. At first, the new control looks more like a panel than a set of tabs because it has no tabs. Set the Tab control's properties as follows:

8

Property	Value
Name	tabMyTabs
Location	8,16
Size	272,208

The tabs on a Tab control are part of the control's TabPages collection. Click the TabPages property of the Tab control in the Properties window and then click the small button that appears. C# then shows the TabPage Collection Editor. As you can see, your Tab control has no tabs. Click Add now to create a new tab (see Figure 8.3).

FIGURE 8.3

New Tab controls have no tabs; you must create them.

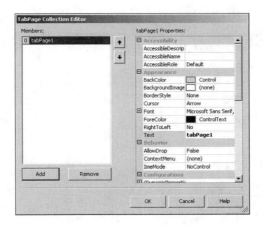

Each tab in the collection is called a page. C# names each new page with TabPageX, in which X is a unique number. It's usually not necessary to change the name of a page, but you can if you choose. Each page has a number of properties, but the property you'll be concerned with most is the Text property because the value in the Text property is the text the user will see on the tab. Change the Text property of your tab page to **Contacts**, and then click Add to create a second page. Change the Text property of the second page to **Appointments** and click OK to close the dialog box. Your Tab control now has two tabs (pages).

> A shortcut to adding or removing a tab is to use the shortcuts provided in the description pane at the bottom of the Properties window.

Each page on a Tab control acts as a container, much like the Panel and Group Box controls. This is why you can't drag the Tab control by clicking in the middle of it; to drag a container control, you have to click and drag the dotted border around the control. Add a text box to the first tab now by dragging the TextBox item from the toolbox and dropping in on the tab page. After it's on the page, drag it to approximately the center of the page. Next, click the Appointments tab, the same as if you were a user switching tabs. As you can see, the Appointments tab comes to the front, and the text box is no longer visible. C# has hidden the first page and shown you the second. Drag a check box from the toolbox and drop it on the tab page, and then click Contacts once more. Again, C# handles the details of showing and hiding the tab pages; you no longer see the check box, but you do see the text box (see Figure 8.4).

FIGURE 8.4

The Tab control makes it easy to create a tabbed interface.

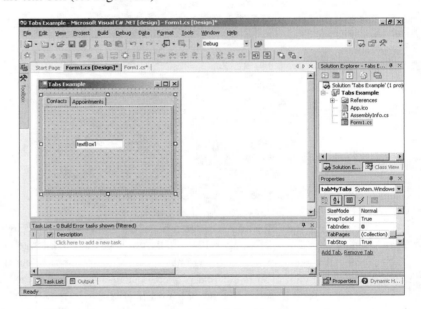

By understanding two simple programming elements, you'll be able to do 99% of what you need to with the Tab control. The first is that you will, at times, need to know which tab is selected. The SelectedIndex property of the control (not of the TabPages collection) sets and returns the index of the currently selected tab—0 for the first tab, 1 for the second, and so forth. The second thing you need to know is how to tell when the user switches tabs. The Tab control has a SelectedIndexChanged event, which fires whenever the selected tab is changed. In this event, you can check the value of SelectedIndex to determine the tab that has been selected. The only tricky part here is that each tab page has its own set of events, so to get to the events of the Tab control itself, you'll have to use the techniques discussed in Hour 4, "Understanding Events."

Storing Pictures in an Image List

Many of the controls I'll be discussing in this hour support the capability to attach pictures to different types of items. For instance, the Tree View control, which is used in Explorer for navigating folders, displays images next to each folder node. Not all these pictures are the same; the control uses specific pictures to denote information about each node. It would have been possible for Microsoft to make each control store its images internally, but that would be highly inefficient because it wouldn't allow controls to share the same pictures; you'd have to store the pictures in each control that needed them. Instead, Microsoft created a control dedicated to storing pictures and serving them to other controls: the Image List.

Create a new Windows Application named **Lists and Trees**. Change the name of the default form to **fclsListsAndTrees**, set its Text property to **Lists and Trees Example**, and set the entry point of the project to reference fclsListsAndTrees instead of Form1. Next, add a new Image List control by double-clicking the ImageList item in the toolbox. Like the timer, the Image List is an invisible-at-runtime control, so it appears below the form. Change the name of the Image List to **imgMyImages**.

The sole purpose of an Image List control is to store pictures and make them available to other controls. The pictures of an Image List are stored in the Images collection of the control. Click the Images property of the control in the Properties window and then click the small button that appears. C# then displays the Image Collection Editor, which is similar to other editors you've used in this hour. Click Add to display the Open dialog box and use this dialog box to locate and select a 16×16 pixel bitmap. If you don't have a 16×16 pixel bitmap, you can create one using Microsoft Paint, or you can download samples I've provided at `http://www.samspublishing.com/` `detail_sams.cfm?item=0672322870`. After you've added an image, click OK to close the Image Collection Editor.

Take a look at the ImageSize property of the Image control. It should read 16,16. If it doesn't, the bitmap you selected is not 16×16 pixels; this property sets itself to the dimensions of the first picture added to the Image List.

You can't always rely on the background where a picture will be displayed to be white—or any other color for that matter. Because of this, the Image List has a TransparentColor property. By default, this is set to Transparent, which essentially means that no color in the picture is transparent (if the pictures in the Image List are icons, rather than bitmaps, the transparent portion of the icons will remain transparent). If you designate a specific color for the TransparentColor property, when a picture is served from the Image List to another control, all occurrences of the specified color will appear transparent—the background will show through. This gives you the power to create pictures that can be served to controls without concern about the color on which the picture will appear.

That's all there is to adding images to an Image List. The power of the Image List resides in its capability to be linked to by other controls that can access the pictures it stores.

Building Enhanced Lists Using the List View

The List View control is like a list box on steroids—and then some. The List View can be used to create simple lists, multicolumn grids, and icon trays. The right pane in Explorer is a List View. (You may not know it, but you can change the appearance of the List View in Explorer by right-clicking it and using the View submenu of the context menu that appears.) The primary options you have available for changing the appearance of your List Views are Large Icons, Small Icons, List, and Details. These correspond exactly to the display options available for a List View by way of its View property. You're going to create a List View with a few items on it and experiment with the different views— including showing a picture for the items.

I can only scratch the surface of this great control here. After you've learned the basics in this hour, I highly recommend that you spend some time with the control, the help text, and whatever additional material you can find. I use the List View all the time; it's a very powerful tool to have in your arsenal because displaying lists is so common.

Add a List View to your form now by double-clicking the ListView item in the toolbox. Set the properties of the List View as follows:

Property	Value
Name	lvwMyListView
Location	8,8
Size	275,97
SmallImageList	imgMyImages
View	Details

As you can see, you can attach an Image List to a control via the Properties window (or with code). Not all controls support the Image List, but those that do make it as simple as setting a property to link to an Image List. The List View actually allows linking to two

Image Lists: one for large icons (32×32 pixels) and one for small images. In this example, you're going to use only small pictures. If you wanted to use the large format, you could hook up a second Image List containing larger images to the List View's LargeImageList control.

Creating Columns

When you changed the View property to Details, an empty header was placed at the top of the control. The contents of this header are determined by the columns defined in the Columns collection.

Select the Columns property on the Properties window and click the small button that appears. C# then displays the ColumnHeader Collection Editor window. Click Add to create a new header and change its Text to **Name** and its Width to **120**. Click Add once more to create a second column and change its Text to **State**. Click OK to save your column settings and close the window. Your list view should now have two named columns (see Figure 8.5).

FIGURE 8.5

List Views enable you to present multicolumn lists.

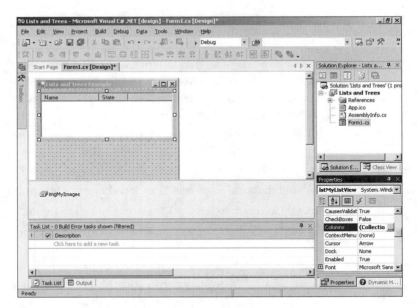

Adding List Items

You're now going to add two items to the list view.

1. Click the Items property in the Properties window and then click the small button that appears, which displays the ListViewItem Collection Editor dialog box.

2. Click Add to create a new item, and change the item's Text to **James Foxall**.

3. Next, open the drop-down list for the ImageIndex property. Notice how the list contains the picture in the linked Image List control (see Figure 8.6). Select the image.

FIGURE 8.6

Pictures from a linked Image List are readily available to the control.

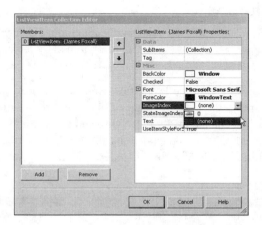

4. The Text property of an item determines the text displayed for the item in the List View. If the View property is set to Details and multiple columns have been defined, the value of the Text property appears in the first column. Subsequent column values are determined by the SubItems collection.

5. Click the SubItems property and then click the small button that appears, which displays the ListViewSubItem Collection Editor. The item that appears in the list refers to the text of the item itself, which you don't want to change.

6. Click Add to create a new sub item and change its text to **Nebraska**.

7. Click OK to return to the ListViewItem Collection Editor.

8. Click the Add button to create another item. This time, change the Text property to your name and use the techniques you just learned to add a sub item. For the Text property of the sub item, enter your state of residence.

9. When you're finished, click OK to close the ListViewItem Collection Editor. Your List View should now contain two list items (see Figure 8.7).

10. Next, experiment with the View property of the List View control to see how the various settings affect the appearance of the control. The Large Icons setting doesn't display an icon, because you didn't link an Image List control to the LargeImageList property of the List View.

FIGURE 8.7

List views offer much more functionality than a standard list box.

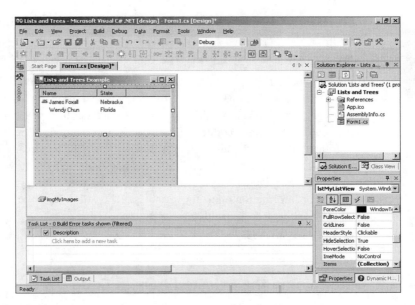

11. Press F5 to run the project and try selecting your name by clicking your state. You can't. The default behavior of the List View is only to consider the clicking of the first column as selecting an item.

12. Stop the project and change the FullRowSelect property to True; then run the project once more.

13. Click your state again, and this time your name becomes selected (actually, the entire row becomes selected). Personally, I prefer to set up all my List Views with FullRowSelect set to True, but this is just a personal preference. Stop the project now and save your work.

Manipulating a List View Using Code

You've just learned the basics of working with a List View control. Although you performed all the steps in Design view, you'll probably manipulate your list items using code because you won't necessarily know ahead of time what to display in the list, so I'll show you how.

Adding List Items Using Code

Adding an item using code is very simple—if the item you are adding is simple. To add an item to your list view, you use the Add method of the Items collection, like this:

```
lstMyListView.Items.Add("Mark Haro");
```

If the item is to have a picture, you can specify the index of the picture as a second parameter, like this:

```
lstMyListView.Items.Add("Luis Haro",0);
```

If the item has sub items, things get more complicated. The Add method allows you only to specify the text and image index. To access the additional properties of a list item, you need to get a reference to the item in code. Remember that new items have only one sub item; you have to create additional items. The Add method of the Items collection returns a reference to the newly added item. Knowing this, you can create a new variable to hold a reference to the item, create the item, and manipulate anything you choose to about the item using the variable (see Hour 12, "Using Constants, Data Types, Variables, and Arrays," for information on using variables). The following code creates a new item and appends a sub item to its SubItems collection:

```
ListViewItem objListItem;
objListItem = lstMyListView.Items.Add("Yvette Webster", 0);
objListItem.SubItems.Add("Tennessee");
```

Determining the Selected Item in Code

The List View control has a collection that contains a reference to each selected item in the control: the SelectedItems collection. If the MultiSelect property of the List View is set to True, as it is by default, the user can select multiple items by holding down the Ctrl or Shift keys when clicking items. This is why the List View supports a SelectedItems collection rather than a SelectedItem property. To gather information about a selected item, you refer to it by its index. For example, to print the text of the first selected item (or the only selected item if just one is selected), you could use code like this:

```
if (lstMyListView.SelectedItems.Count > 0)
System.Diagnostics.Debug.WriteLine(lstMyListView.SelectedItems[0].Text);
```

The reason you check the Count property of the SelectedItems collection is that if no items are selected, you would cause a runtime error by attempting to reference element 0 in the SelectedItems collection.

Removing List Items Using Code

To remove a list item, use the Remove method of the Items collection. The Remove Item method accepts and expects a reference to a list item. For instance, to remove the currently selected item, you could use a statement such as

```
lstMyListView.Items.Remove(lstMyListView.SelectedItems[0]);
```

or

```
lstMyListView.Items.RemoveAt(0);
```

Again, you'd want to make sure an item is actually selected before using this statement.

Removing All List Items

If you're filling a List View using code, you'll probably want to clear the contents of the List View first. That way, if the code to fill the List View is called a second time, you won't create duplicate entries. To clear the contents of a List View, use the Clear method of the Items collection, like this:

```
lstMyListView.Items.Clear();
```

The List View control is an amazingly versatile tool. As a matter of fact, I rarely use the standard list box now, preferring to use the List View because of its added functionality, such as displaying an image for an item. I've barely scratched the surface here, but you now know enough to begin using this awesome tool in your own development.

Creating Hierarchical Lists with the Tree View

The Tree View control is used to present hierarchical data. Perhaps the most commonly used Tree View control is found in Explorer, where you can use the Tree View to navigate the folders and drives on your computer. The Tree View is perfect for displaying hierarchical data, such as a departmental display of employees. In this section, I'll teach you the basics of the Tree View control so that you can use this great interface element in your applications.

The Tree View's items are contained in a Nodes collection. To add items to the tree, you append them to the Nodes collection. As you can probably see by now, after you understand the basics of objects and collections, you can apply that knowledge to almost everything in C#. For instance, the skills you learned in working with the Items collection of the List View control are similar to the skills needed for working with the Nodes collection of the Tree View control.

Add a Tree View control to your form now by double-clicking the TreeView item in the toolbox. Set the Tree View control's properties as follows:

Property	Value
Name	tvwLanguages
ImageList	imgMyImages
Location	8,128
Size	272,97

Adding Nodes to a Tree View

To add a node, call the Add method of the Nodes collection. Add a new button to your form and set its properties as follows:

Property	Value
Name	btnAddNode
Location	8,240
Size	75,23
Text	Add Node

Double-click the button to access its Click event and enter the following code:

```
tvwLanguages.Nodes.Add("Sam Chun");
tvwLanguages.Nodes.Add("C#");
```

Press F5 to run the project, and then click the button. Two nodes will appear in the tree, one for each Add method call (see Figure 8.8).

FIGURE 8.8

Nodes are the items that appear in a tree.

Notice how both nodes appear at the same level in the hierarchy; neither node is a parent or child of the other. If all your nodes are going to be at the same level in the hierarchy, you should consider using a List View instead, because what you're creating is simply a list.

Stop the project and return to the button's Click event. Any given node can be both a parent to other nodes and a child of a single node. For this to work, each node has its own Nodes collection. This can get confusing, but if you realize that children nodes belong to the parent node, it starts to make sense (but it still gets confusing in practice). You're now going to create a new button that adds the same two nodes as before but makes the second node a child of the first. Create a new button and set its properties as shown:

Property	Value
Name	btnCreateChild
Location	96,240
Size	80,23
Text	Create Child

Double-click the new button to access its Click event and add the following code:

```
TreeNode objNode;
objNode = tvwLanguages.Nodes.Add("Wendy Chun");
objNode.Nodes.Add("C#");
```

This code is similar to what you created in the List View example. The Add method of the Nodes collection returns a reference to the newly created node. Thus, this code creates a variable of type TreeNode (variables are discussed in detail in Hour 12), creates a new node whose reference is placed in the variable, and then adds a new node to the Nodes collection of the first node. To see the effect that this has, press F5 to run the project and click the new button. You'll see a single item in the list, with a plus sign to the left of it. This plus sign indicates that child nodes exist. Click the plus sign, and the node is expanded to show its children (see Figure 8.9).

FIGURE 8.9

You can create as deep a hierarchy as you need.

This example is a simple one—a single parent node having a single child node. However, the principles used here are the same as those used to build complex trees with dozens or hundreds of nodes.

Removing Nodes

Removing a node is simply a matter of calling the Remove method of the Nodes collection. The Remove method accepts and expects a valid node, so you must know which node to remove. Again, the Nodes collection works very much like the Items collection in the List View control, so the same ideas apply. For example, the currently selected node is returned in the SelectedNode property of the Tree View. So, to remove the currently selected node, you could use this statement:

```
tvwLanguages.Nodes.Remove(tvwLanguages.SelectedNode);
```

If this statement is called when no node is selected, an error would occur. In Hour 12, you'll learn all about data types and equalities, but here's a preview: If an object variable doesn't reference an object, it is equivalent to the C# keyword null. Knowing this, you could validate whether an item is selected with a little bit of logic, like this:

```
if (!(tvwLanguages.SelectedNode == null))
tvwLanguages.Nodes.Remove(tvwLanguages.SelectedNode);
```

 Removing a parent node causes all its children to be removed as well.

Clearing All Nodes

To clear all nodes in a Tree View, invoke the Clear method of the Nodes collection, like this:

```
tvwLanguages.Nodes.Clear();
```

As with the List View, I've only scratched the surface of the Tree View. Spend some time becoming familiar with the basics of the Tree View, as I've shown here, and then dig a bit deeper to discover the not-so-obvious power and flexibility of this control.

Summary

C# includes a number of controls that go beyond the standard functionality of the traditional controls discussed in Hour 7. In this hour, I discussed the most commonly used advanced controls. You learned how to use the Timer control to trigger events at predetermined intervals. You also learned how to use the tab to create the tabbed dialog boxes with which you're so familiar.

Also in this hour, you learned how to add pictures to an Image List so that other controls can use them. The Image List makes it easy to share pictures among many controls, making it a very useful tool. Finally, I taught you the basics of the List View and Tree View controls; two controls you can use to build high-end interfaces that present structured data. The more time you spend with all these controls, the better you will become at creating great interfaces.

Q&A

Q. What if I need a lot of timers, but I'm concerned about system resources?

A. When possible, use a single timer for multiple duties. This is extremely easy when two events occur at the same interval—why bother creating a second timer? When two events occur at different intervals, you can use some decision skills along with static variables (discussed in Hour 12) to share Timer events.

Q. What else can I do with an Image List?

A. You can assign a unique picture to a node in a Tree View when the node is selected. You can also display an image in the tab of a tab page in a Tab control. There are a lot of uses, and as you learn more about advanced controls, you'll see additional opportunities for using images from an Image List.

Workshop

The Workshop is designed to help you anticipate possible questions, review what you've learned, and get you thinking about how to put your knowledge into practice. The answers to the quiz are in Appendix A, "Answers to Quizzes/Exercises."

Quiz

1. What increment of time is applied to the `Interval` property of the Timer control?

2. What collection is used to add new tabs to a Tab control?

3. What property returns the index of the currently selected tab?

4. True or False: You should use different Image List controls for storing images of different sizes.

5. To see columns in a List View control, the View property must be set to what?

6. The additional columns of data that can be attached to an item in a list view are stored in what collection?

7. What property of what object would you use to determine how many items are in a List View?

8. Each item in a Tree View is called a what?

9. How do you make a node the child of another node?

Exercises

1. Add a second Image List to your project with the List View. Place an icon (32×32 pixels) in this Image List and link the Image List to the LargeImageList property of the List View control. Change the View to Large Icons. Does the icon appear next to a list item? If not, is there a property of an item you can set so that it does?

2. Create a new project and add a List View, a button, and a text box to the default form. When the button is clicked, create a new item in the List View using the text entered into the text box.

HOUR 9

Adding Menus and Toolbars to Forms

The use of a Graphical User Interface (GUI) for interacting with and navigating programs is one of the greatest features of Windows. In spite of this, a fair number of Windows users still rely primarily on the keyboard, preferring to use a mouse only when absolutely necessary. Data-entry people in particular never take their hands off the keyboard. Many software companies receive support calls from angry customers because a commonly used function is accessible only by using a mouse. Menus are the easiest way for a user who relies on the keyboard to navigate your program. Visual Studio and C# make it easier than ever to create menus for your applications. In this hour, you'll learn how to build, manipulate, and program menus on a form. In addition, I'll teach you how to use the Toolbar control to create attractive and functional toolbars. Finally, you'll learn how to "finish off" a form with a status bar.

The highlights of this hour include the following:

- Adding, moving, and deleting menu items
- Creating checked menu items
- Programming menus
- Implementing context menus
- Assigning shortcut keys
- Creating toolbar items
- Defining toggle buttons and separators
- Creating a status bar

Building Menus

When I said that C# makes building menus easier than ever, I wasn't kidding. Building menus is now an immediately gratifying process. I can't stress enough how important it is to have good menus, and now that it's so easy to do, there is no excuse for not putting menus in an application.

> When running an application for the first time, users often scan the menus before opening a manual. (Most users never open the manual!) When you provide comprehensive menus, you make your program easier to learn and use.

Adding Menu Items

Adding menus to a form is accomplished by way of a control: the Main Menu control. The Main Menu control is a bit odd in that it's the only control I know of that sits at the bottom of the form in the space reserved for controls without an interface (like a Timer control), yet actually has a visible interface on the form. Start by creating a new Windows Application project named **Menus and More**.

1. Change the name of the default form to **fclsMenusAndMore**, set its Text to **Menus and More**, and change the Main entry point of the project to reference **fclsMenusAndMore** instead of Form1.

2. Next, add a new Main Menu control to your form by double-clicking the MainMenu item in the toolbox. As you can see, the control is added to the pane at the bottom of the form designer. Take a look at the top of the form—you'll see the text Type Here (see Figure 9.1).

3. Click this text and type **&File**. As you begin typing, C# displays two new boxes that say Type Here (see Figure 9.2).

FIGURE 9.1

A menu has no items when first added to a form.

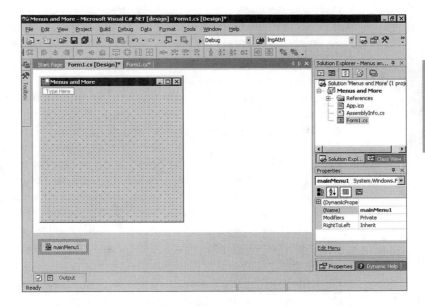

FIGURE 9.2

Creating a menu item automatically prepares the control for more items.

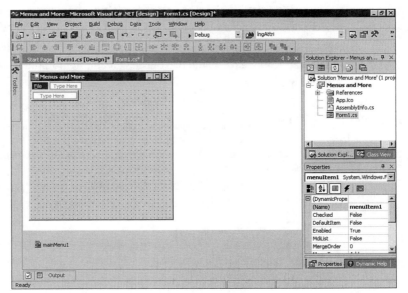

Notice the Properties window (if it's not visible, press F4 to show it). The text you just entered created a new menu item. Each menu item is an object; therefore, the item has properties. (You may have to press Tab to commit your entry and then click the text you typed once more to see its properties.)MenuItem1 isn't very descriptive, so change the name of the item to **mnuFileMenu**.

NEW TERM You may have been wondering why I had you enter the ampersand (&) in front of the word File. Take a look at your menu now, and you'll see that C# doesn't display the ampersand; instead, it displays the text with the F underlined, as in File. The ampersand, when used in the Text property of a menu item, tells C# to underline the character immediately following it. For top-level menu items, such as the File item you just created, this underlined character is known as an *accelerator key*. Pressing Alt+ an accelerator key opens the menu as if the user had clicked it. You should avoid assigning the same accelerator key to more than one top-level menu item on a given menu. When the menu item appears on a drop-down menu, in contrast to being a top-level item, the underlined character is called a *hotkey*. When a menu is visible (open), the user can press a hotkey to trigger the corresponding menu item the same as if it was clicked. Again, don't use the same hotkey for more than one item on the same menu.

4. Click the Type Here text that appears to the immediate right of the File item and enter the text **&Help**. C# gives you two more Type Here items, the same as when you entered the File item. Adding new menu items is a matter of clicking a Type Here box and entering the text for an item.

5. Press Tab to commit your entry and then click the text you typed once more to select it. Change the name of your new menu item in the Properties window to **mnuHelpMenu**.

 If you click a Type Here box below an existing menu item, you'll add a new item to the same menu as the item above the box. If you click the Type Here box to the right of a menu item, you'll create a submenu using the menu to the left of the box as the entry point for the submenu. As you've already seen, clicking the Type Here box along the top of the menu bar creates a top-level menu.

6. Click once more on the File item to display a Type Here box below the item. Click this box and enter the text **&Quit**.

7. Press Tab to commit your entry and then click the new item once more to select it. Change the name of the new item to **mnuQuit**. Now is a good time to save your work, so click Save All on the toolbar.

Moving and Deleting Menu Items

Deleting and moving menu items are even easier processes than adding new items. To delete a menu item, right-click it and choose Delete from the context menu that appears. To move an item, drag it from its current location and drop it in the location in which you want it placed.

Creating Checked Menu Items

A menu item that isn't used to open a submenu can display a check mark next to its text. Check marks are used to create menu items that have state—the item is either selected or it is not selected. You're now going to create a checked menu item. Click the Type Here box below the Quit menu item and enter **Ask before closing** and then change the name of this new item (remember to press Tab to commit your entry and then click the item again to select it) to **mnuAskBeforeClosing**. Next, change the Checked property of the new item to true. Notice that the menu item now has a check mark next to it (see Figure 9.3).

9

FIGURE 9.3

Menu items can be used to indicate state.

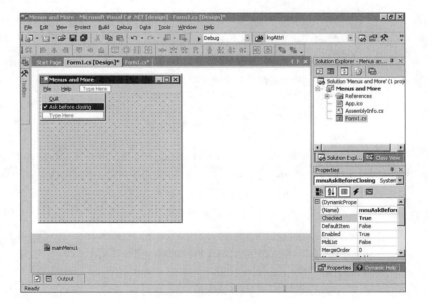

Press F5 to run the project. The menu will appear on your form, just as you designed it (see Figure 9.4). Click the File menu to open it and then click Quit; nothing happens. In the next section, I'll show you how to add code to menu items to make them actually do something. Stop the project before continuing.

FIGURE 9.4

What you see (at design time) is what you get (at runtime).

Programming Menus

As I've said before, every menu item is a unique object—this is why you were able to change the name for each item you created. Although individual menu items aren't controls, per se, adding code behind them is very similar to adding code behind a control. You're now going to add code to the Quit and Ask Before Closing menu items.

1. Click the File menu now to open it.

2. Double-click the Quit menu item. Just as when you double-click a control, C# displays the code editor with the default event for the menu item you've clicked. For menu items, this is the Click event.

3. Enter the following code:

```
this.Close();
```

As you know by now, this code closes the current form, which has the effect of stopping the project because this is the only form and it's designated as the Main entry point object.

4. Switch back to the form designer (click the Form1.cs [Design] tab).

You're now going to create the code for the Ask Before Closing button. This code will invert the Checked property of the menu item; if Checked = True, it will be set to false and vice versa.

1. Double-click the Ask Before Closing item to access its Click event and enter the following code:

```
mnuAskBeforeClosing.Checked = (!mnuAskBeforeClosing.Checked);
```

The logical negation operator (!) is used to perform a negation of a Boolean value. Don't worry, I discuss this in detail in Hour 13, "Performing Arithmetic, String Manipulation, and Date/Time Adjustments." For now, realize that if the current value of the Checked property is true, (!Checked) returns false. If Checked is currently false, (!Checked) returns true. Therefore, the checked value will toggle between true and false each time the menu item is clicked.

2. Press F5 to run the project. Open the File menu by pressing Alt+F (remember, the F is the accelerator key).

3. Next, click the Ask Before Closing button—it becomes unchecked. Click the menu item once more and it becomes checked again.

4. Click it a third time to remove the check mark, and then click Quit to close the form.

Did you notice that you weren't asked whether you really wanted to quit? This is because the quit code hasn't been written to consider the checked state of the Ask Before Closing button.

1. Return to the Click event of the Quit button and change its code to look like this:

```
if (mnuAskBeforeClosing.Checked)
{
    if (MessageBox.Show("Do you really wish to exit?","Quit
        Verification",MessageBoxButtons.YesNo) == DialogResult.No)
        return;
}
this.Close();
```

Now when the user selects the Quit button, C# considers the checked state of the Ask Before Closing menu item. If the item is checked, C# asks users whether they really want to exit. If a user chooses No, the procedure quits and the form doesn't unload. This code may be a bit foreign to you now, but you'll learn the ins and outs of making decisions (executing code based on conditions) and message boxes in later hours.

2. Press F5 to run the project. Open the File menu, click the Ask Before Closing item to select it, and then click Quit.

3. This time, C# asks you to confirm your intentions rather than immediately closing the form. Go ahead and close the form, and then click Save All on the toolbar to save your work.

When designing your menus, look at some of the many popular Windows applications available and consider the similarities and differences between their menus and yours. Although your application may be quite unique and therefore may have very different menus from other applications, similarities probably exist as well. When possible, make menu items in your application follow the same structure and design as similar items in the popular programs. This will shorten the learning curve of your application, reduce user frustration, and save you time.

9

Implementing Context Menus

Context menus are the pop-up menus that appear when you right-click an object on a form. Context menus get their name from the fact that they display context-sensitive choices—menu items that relate directly to the object that's right-clicked. Most C# controls have a default context menu, but you can assign custom context menus if you desire. Add a new text box to the form and set its properties as follows:

Property	Value
Name	txtMyTextbox
Location	96,122
Size	100,20
Text	(*make blank*)

Press F5 to run the project, and then right-click the text box to display its context menu (see Figure 9.5). This menu is the default context menu for the Text Box control; it is functional but limited. Stop the project now and return to Design view.

FIGURE 9.5

Most items have a default context menu.

Creating context menus is very much like creating regular menus. Context menus, however, are created using a different control: the Context Menu control.

1. Add a new context menu to the form by double-clicking the ContextMenu item in the toolbox. Like the Main_Menu control, the Context Menu control is placed in the pane below the form designer. When the control is selected, a Context Menu item appears at the top of the form.

2. Clicking the Context Menu box opens the context menu, which is empty by default. Click the Type Here box and enter the text **Clear text box** (see Figure 9.6). You've just created a context menu with a single menu item.

FIGURE 9.6

Context menus are edited much like regular menus.

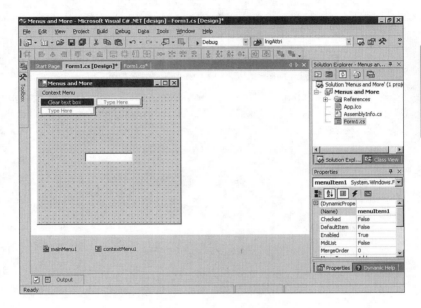

3. Change the name of the new menu item to **mnuClearTextbox**, and then double-click the item to access its Click event.

   Enter the following code:

   ```
   txtMyTextbox.Text = "";
   ```

4. Linking a control to a context menu is accomplished by setting a property. Display the form designer once more, and then click the Text Box control to select it and display its properties in the Properties window.

5. Change the ContextMenu property of the text box to **ContextMenu1**; the context menu is now linked to the text box. Press F5 to run the project.

6. Enter some text into the text box and then right-click the text box; your custom context menu appears in place of the default context menu.

7. Choose Clear Text Box from the context menu, and the contents of the text box will clear. Stop the project and save your work.

Assigning Shortcut Keys

If you've spent any time learning a Microsoft application, you've most likely learned some keyboard shortcuts. For instance, pressing Alt+P in any application that prints has the same effect as opening the File menu and choosing Print. You can add the same type of shortcuts to your menus by following these steps:

1. Click the Main Menu control at the bottom of the form designer, click File on its menu, and then click Quit to select the Quit menu item.

2. Next, click the Shortcut property in the Properties window and then click the down arrow that appears. This list contains all the shortcut keys that can be assigned to a menu item.

3. Locate and select CtrlQ (for Quit) in the list (see Figure 9.7).

FIGURE 9.7

A shortcut key is assigned using the shortcut property of a menu item.

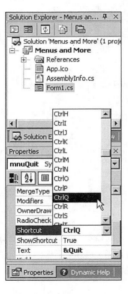

4. Press F5 to run the project once more. Next, press Ctrl+Q, and the application will behave just as though you opened the File menu and clicked the Quit item.

> Although it's not always possible, try to assign logical shortcut key combinations. The meaning of F6 is hardly intuitive, for example, but when assigning modifiers such as Ctrl with another character, you have some flexibility. For instance, the key combination of Ctrl+Q might be a more intuitive shortcut key for Quit than Ctrl+T.

Using the Toolbar Control

Generally speaking, when a program has a menu (as most programs should), it should also have a toolbar. Toolbars are one of the easiest ways for a user to access program functions. Unlike menu items, toolbar items are always visible and therefore are immediately available. In addition, toolbar items have ToolTips, which allow a user to discover a toolbar button's purpose simply by hovering the pointer over the button.

Toolbar items are really shortcuts for menu items; every item on a toolbar should have a corresponding menu item. Remember that some users prefer to use the keyboard, in which case they need to have keyboard access to functions via menus.

The actual items you place on a toolbar depend on the features supported by the application. However, the mechanics of creating toolbars and toolbar items is the same, regardless of the buttons you choose to use. Toolbars are created using the Toolbar control.

1. Add a new Toolbar control to your form now by double-clicking the ToolBar item in the toolbox. A new toolbar is then added to the top of your form (see Figure 9.8). Change the name of the toolbar to **tbrMainToolbar**.

FIGURE 9.8

New toolbars default to the top of the form and have no buttons.

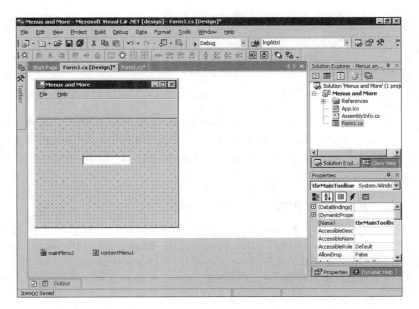

Every toolbar you've used displays pictures on buttons. The Toolbar control gets the pictures for its buttons from an Image List control.

2. Go ahead and add an Image List control to the form now and change its name to **imgMyPictures**.

3. Add a new 16×16 pixel bitmap to the Images collection of the Image List control (you can use a picture you created or use one from the samples I've made available on the Web site).

4. When you're finished adding the new button, close the Image Collection Editor and select the Toolbar control on the form.

5. Set the ImageList property of the toolbar to use the image list you've just created.

Adding Toolbar Buttons Using the Buttons Collection

Like many other controls you've already learned about, the Toolbar control supports a special collection: the Buttons collection. The Buttons collection contains the buttons that appear on the toolbar. Click the Buttons property in the Properties window and then click the small button that appears; the ToolBarButton Collection Editor displays. The list of button members is empty because new toolbars have no buttons. Click Add to create a new button, and set its properties as follows:

Property	Value
Name	tbbQuit
ImageIndex	0
Text	Quit
ToolTipText	Quit this application

Click OK to close the ToolBarButton Collection Editor. Your new button is now visible on the toolbar. As you can see, text appears below the picture in the button, but this is *not* how most toolbars appear. Not a problem—access the Buttons collection once more and clear the Text property of the button.

Programming Toolbars

Unlike menus, where each menu item receives its own Click event, the Toolbar control has one common Click event that fires when the user clicks any button on the toolbar. Double-click the Toolbar control on the form to access the toolbar's ButtonClick event (close the button editor first if it's open). Enter the following code:

```
if (e.Button == tbbQuit)
    this.Close();
```

In a nontrivial program, the ideal way to set this up would be to create a method that is called both by the Click event of the menu item and by clicking the equivalent toolbar button. This reduces duplication of code and eliminates bugs (the Quit button doesn't honor the Ask Before Closing option in this example, even though the menu item does).

9

The e object is discussed in detail in Hour 11, "Creating and Calling Methods." For now, realize that the Button property of the e object is an object property that holds a reference to the button that is clicked. This code uses an if statement to determine if the clicked button is the Quit button. If the Quit button was clicked, the form closes. When you have many buttons on a toolbar, a switch_statement is much more useful than an if statement, as you'll see in the next section. (Decision-making constructs such as if and switch statements are discussed in Hour 14, "Making Decisions in C# Code.")

Creating Toggle Buttons

The button that you've created for your toolbar is a standard push-style button. When the user clicks it with the mouse, the button will appear to be pressed while the user holds down the mouse button and will return to a normal state when the user releases the mouse button. Although this is the style you'll use for most of your toolbar buttons, the Toolbar control supports other styles as well. One such style is the toggle button. A toggle button, much like the check mark of a menu item, is used to denote state. When a toggle button is clicked, it appears in a pressed state and stays that way until clicked again, in which case it returns to its normal appearance. Microsoft Word has a number of such buttons. For instance, the paragraph alignment buttons are all toggle buttons—the button that corresponds to the current paragraph's alignment appears to be pressed.

Add a new button to your toolbar now and change its name to **tbbInvisible**. Change its Text property to Invisible and its Style to ToggleButton. Click OK to close the editor and the new button will appear on the toolbar. Take note that you didn't have to designate a picture for the toolbar item (but you usually should). Because you don't want the toolbar's height to be larger than necessary, change the TextAlign property of the Toolbar control to Right. Your toolbar should now look like the one in Figure 9.9.

Again, double-click the toolbar to access its ButtonClick event. Now that there are two buttons, the simple if statement is no longer suited to determining the button pushed. Change the code in your procedure to match the following:

```
switch (tbrMainToolbar.Buttons.IndexOf(e.Button))
{
    case 0:
```

```
            this.Close();
            break;
    case 1:
            txtMyTextbox.Visible = (!tbbInvisible.Pushed);
            break;
}
```

FIGURE 9.9

Toolbar items can display a picture, text, or a combination of both.

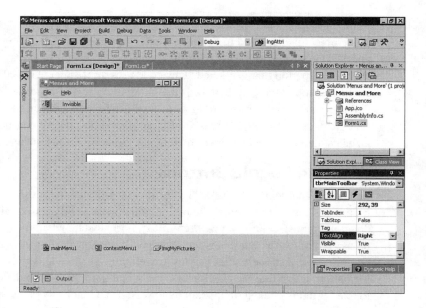

This code is a bit more complex than the previous code. The switch construct compares one value to many possible values, looking for a match. In this case, the IndexOf() method of the Buttons collection is used to determine the index of the clicked tool button (the first button is 0, the second is 1, and so forth). The index is then compared to values using the case statements, and when a match is found, the appropriate code executes. Again, don't worry too much about the details of the switch statement, because you'll learn everything you need to know about it in Hour 14, "Making Decisions in C# Code." The new statement that you're interested in at the moment is where the Visible property of the text box is set. Remember, the logical negation operator (!) negates a value. Therefore, this statement sets the Visible property of the text box to the negation of the pushed state of the tbbInvisible button. In other words, when the button is pushed, the text box is hidden, and when the button is not pushed, the text box is visible.

Press F5 to run the project now and notice that the text box is visible. Click the Invisible button on the toolbar and note that its appearance changes to a pushed state and the text box becomes hidden (see Figure 9.10). Click the button again to return the button's state to normal, and the text box reappears. When you're finished, stop the project and save your work.

FIGURE 9.10

Toggle-style buttons appear "pressed" when clicked.

9

Creating Separators

As you add more and more buttons to a toolbar, it becomes evident that you need a way to logically group buttons. Placing related buttons next to one another is a great start toward building a good toolbar. However, a toolbar may be a bit difficult to use even if its buttons are placed in a logical order, unless the buttons are separated into groups. Placing a space between sets of related buttons creates button groups. You're now going to add a separator space to your toolbar.

Add a new button to your toolbar using the Buttons collection in the Properties window. Change its name to **tbbSeparator1** and change its Style to Separator. When you change the Style property of the button to Separator, it disappears from the toolbar, or at least it seems to. When a button is designated as a separator, it's simply an empty placeholder used to create a space between two buttons. Because this separator is at the end row of buttons, you can't see it. Move it to the second position by selecting it in the ToolBarButton Collection Editor and clicking the up arrow that appears to the right of the Members list; this arrow and the one below it are used to move a button up or down in the list. Click OK to save your changes and your toolbar will now have a space between the two buttons (see Figure 9.11).

Press F5 to run the project once more and click the Invisible button; the text box no longer becomes hidden. This is a common problem when working with toolbars. Remember how the switch statement looks at the index of the clicked button? The index is the ordinal position of a button in the Buttons collection. When you changed the order of the buttons by moving the separator button up in the list, you changed the index of the separator button and the button it displaced—the tbbInvisible button. The tbbInvisible button now has an index of two (because it's the third button). Change the case statement in the ButtonClick event that compares the case to 1 so that it compares it to 2, and your code will work again. As you fine-tune your toolbars, you need to be conscious of any code that's been written to work with the indexes of buttons in the Buttons collection.

FIGURE 9.11

Separators are used to create spaces between groups of buttons.

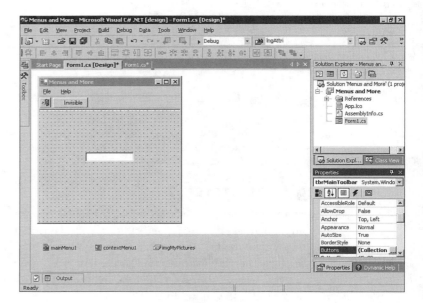

Creating Drop-Down Menus for Toolbar Buttons

You need to be familiar with one last type of toolbar button. Create a new button using the Buttons collection in the Properties window. Change the name of the new button to **tbbDropdown**, clear the Text property, and set the button's Style property to DropDownButton. Finally, set the DropDownMenu property to ContextMenu1 and click OK to commit your changes. Notice how the button has a drop-down arrow on it. Press F5 to run the project and click the drop-down arrow; the menu that you designated in the DropDownMenu property appears (see Figure 9.12). As you can see, the DropDownMenu property makes it easy to integrate drop-down menus with your toolbars.

FIGURE 9.12

Toolbar buttons can be used to display drop-down menus.

9

Creating a Status Bar

The last control I'm going to show you is the Status Bar control. The status bar isn't nearly as fancy, or even as useful, as other controls, such as the Toolbar or the Main Menu. It's also not that hard to work with. Nevertheless, a status bar adds value to an application in that it makes additional information available, and users have come to expect it. In its simplest form, a status bar displays a text caption and sizing grip—the three diagonal lines to the right of the control that the user can drag with the mouse to change the size of the form.

Add a new status bar to the form now by double-clicking the StatusBar item in the toolbox. Change the name of the status bar to **sbrMyStatusBar**. The Text property determines the text displayed in the left side of the status bar. Notice that the Text is set to the default name of the control. Change the Text property to **Menus and Toolbars Example** now, and notice how the text in the status bar changes (see Figure 9.13).

If a form's border is sizable, the user can click and drag the sizing grip at the right side of the status bar to change the size of the form. The status bar isn't smart enough to realize when a form's border can't be resized; you'll have to change the SizingGrip property of the status bar to false to hide the grip.

The default behavior of the status bar is quite simple, consisting of text and a sizing grip. However, you can create more complex status bars with this control. The Status Bar control contains a Panels collection. To see how a panel works, select the Panels property in the Properties window and click the small button that appears. On the StatusBarPanel Collection Editor, click Add to create a new panel. Set the Text of the panel to **Panel Text**, set the AutoSize property to Contents, and click OK to save your changes. Nothing looks different, right? This is because one last thing is required to display the status bar panels. Change the ShowPanels property of the status bar to true now, and the status bar will display its panel (see Figure 9.14). You can add multiple panels to a Status Bar control and even tailor the appearance of each panel by changing the border style or displaying an image from a linked Image List control. The status bar is such a simple control that you may overlook using it. However, I encourage you to use it when appropriate.

FIGURE 9.13

Status bars dress out a form.

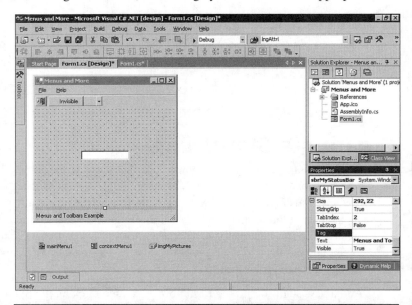

FIGURE 9.14

Status bars can display custom panels.

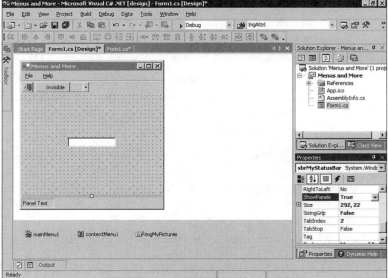

Summary

Menus, toolbars, and status bars add tremendous value to an application by greatly enhancing its usability. In this hour, you learned how to use the Main Menu control to build comprehensive menus for your applications. You learned how to add, move, and delete menu items and how to define accelerator and shortcut keys to facilitate better navigation via the keyboard. You also saw how toolbars provide shortcuts for accessing common menu items. You learned how to use the Toolbar control to create functional toolbars complete with bitmaps, drop-downs, and logical groupings. Finally, you discovered how to use the status bar to "dress out" the application. Implementing these items is an important part of the interface design process for an application, and you now have the skills necessary to start putting them into your own programs.

Q&A

Q. I have a number of forms with nearly identical menus. Do I really need to take the time to create menus for all these forms?

A. Not as much as you think. Create a Main Menu control that has the common items on it, and then copy and paste the control to other forms. You can then build on this menu structure, saving you a lot of time.

Q. I've seen applications that allow the end user to customize the menus and toolbars. Can I do that with the C# menus and toolbars?

A. No. To accomplish this behavior, you would have to purchase a third-party component.

Workshop

The Workshop is designed to help you anticipate possible questions, review what you've learned, and get you thinking about how to put your knowledge into practice. The answers to the quiz are in Appendix A, "Answers to Quizzes/Exercises."

Quiz

1. True or False: Form menu bars are created using the Context Menu control.
2. To create an accelerator or hotkey, preface the character with a(n):
3. If you've designed a menu using a Main Menu control, but that menu isn't visible on the form designer, how do you make it appear?
4. To place a check mark next to a menu item, you set what property of the item?
5. How do you add code to a menu item?

6. Toolbar items are part of what collection?

7. To create a separator on a toolbar, you create a new button and set what property?

8. True or False: Every button on a toolbar has its own Click event.

9. What must you do to have panels appear on a status bar?

Exercises

1. Modify the code you created for the toolbar that closes the form to take into consideration the checked status of the Ask Before Closing menu item.

2. Implement a toggle button that works just like the Ask Before Closing menu item.

HOUR 10

Drawing and Printing

C# provides an amazingly powerful array of drawing capabilities. However, this power comes at the price of a steep learning curve. Drawing isn't intuitive; you can't sit down for a few minutes with the online Help text and start drawing graphics. After you learn the basic principles involved, however, you'll find that drawing isn't that complicated. In this hour, you'll learn the basic skills for drawing shapes and text to a form or other graphical surface. You'll learn about pens, colors, and brushes. In addition, you'll learn how to persist graphics on a form—and even how to create bitmaps that exist solely in memory.

The highlights of this hour include the following:

- Understanding the Graphics object
- Working with pens
- Using system colors
- Working with rectangles
- Drawing shapes
- Drawing text
- Persisting graphics on a form

Understanding the Graphics Object

NEW TERM   The code within the Windows operating system that handles drawing *everything* to the screen, including text, lines, and shapes, is called the *Graphics Device Interface* (GDI). The GDI processes all drawing instructions from applications as well as from Windows itself and generates the proper output for the current display. Because the GDI generates what you see onscreen, it has the responsibility of dealing with the particular display driver installed on the computer and the settings of the driver, such as resolution and color depth. This means that applications don't have to worry about these details; you write code that tells the GDI what to output and the GDI does whatever is necessary to produce that output. This behavior is called *device independence* because applications can instruct the GDI to display text and graphics using code that is independent of the particular display device.

C# code communicates with the GDI primarily via a Graphics object. The basic process is the following:

- An object variable is created to hold a reference to a Graphics object.
- The object variable is set to a valid Graphics object (new or existing).
- To draw or print, you call methods of the Graphics object.

Creating a Graphics Object for a Form or Control

If you want to draw directly to a form or control, you can easily get a reference to the drawing surface by calling the CreateGraphics() method of the object in question. For example, to create a Graphics object that draws to a text box, you could use code such as:

```
System.Drawing.Graphics objGraphics;
objGraphics = this.textBox1.CreateGraphics();
```

When you call CreateGraphics(), you're setting the object variable to hold a reference to the Graphics object of the form or control's client area. The client area of a form is the gray area within the borders and title bar of the form. The client area of a control is usually the entire control. All drawing and printing done using the Graphics object is sent to the client area. In the code shown previously, the Graphics object references the client area of a text box, so all drawing methods called on the Graphics object would draw on the text box only.

When you draw directly to a form or control, the object in question doesn't persist what is drawn on it. If the form is obscured in any way, such as by a window covering it or by minimizing the form, the next time the form is painted, it won't contain anything that was drawn on it. Later in this hour, I'll teach you how to persist graphics on a form.

Creating a Graphics Object for a New Bitmap

You don't have to set a Graphics object to the client area of a form or control; you can also set a Graphics object to a bitmap that exists only in memory. For performance reasons, you might want to use a memory bitmap to store temporary images or to use as a place to build complex graphics before sending them to a visible element. To do this, you first have to create a new bitmap. To create a new bitmap, you declare a variable to hold a reference to the new bitmap, and then you create a new bitmap using the following syntax:

```
Bitmap variable = new Bitmap(width, height, pixelformat);
```

The *width* and *height* arguments are exactly what they appear to be: the width and height of the new bitmap. The *pixelformat* argument, however, is less intuitive. This argument determines the color depth of the bitmap and may also specify whether the bitmap has an alpha layer (used for transparent portions of bitmaps). Table 10.1 lists a few of the common values for PixelFormat (see C#'s online Help for the complete list of values and their meanings). Note that the *pixelformat* parameter is referenced as `System.Drawing.Imaging.PixelFormat.formatenumeration`.

TABLE 10.1 Common Values for PixelFormat

Value	Description
Format16bppGrayScale	The pixel format is 16 bits per pixel. The color information specifies 65,536 shades of gray.
Format16bppRgb555	The pixel format is 16 bits per pixel. The color information specifies 32,768 shades of color, of which 5 bits are red, 5 bits are green, and 5 bits are blue.
Format24bppRgb	The pixel format is 24 bits per pixel. The color information specifies 16,777,216 shades of color, of which 8 bits are red, 8 bits are green, and 8 bits are blue.

For example, to create a new bitmap that is 640 pixels wide by 480 pixels tall and has a pixel depth of 24 bits, you could use the following statement:

```
objMyBitMap =  new Bitmap(640, 480,
       System.Drawing.Imaging.PixelFormat.Format24bppRgb);
```

After the bitmap is created, you can create a Graphics object that references the bitmap using the FromImage() method, like this:

```
objGraphics = Graphics.FromImage(objMyBitMap);
```

Now, any drawing or printing done using objGraphics would be performed on the memory bitmap. For the user to see the bitmap, you'd have to send the bitmap to a form or control. You'll do this in the section "Persisting Graphics on a Form."

Disposing of an Object

When you're finished with a Graphics object, you should call its Dispose() method to ensure that all resources used by the Graphics object are freed. Simply letting an object variable go out of scope doesn't ensure that the resources used by the object are freed. Graphics objects can use considerable resources, so you should always call Dispose() when you're finished with any graphics object (including Pens and other types of objects).

C# also supports a way of automatically disposing object resources. This can be accomplished utilizing C#'s using statement. The using statement wraps a declared object or objects in a block and disposes of those objects after the block is done. As a result, after the code is executed in a block, the block is exited and the resources are disposed of on exit. Following is the syntax for the using statement and a small sample:

```
using (expression | type identifier = initializer)
{
    // Statements to execute
}

using (MyClass objClass = new MyClass())
{
    objClass.Method1();
    objClass.Method2();
}
```

One thing to keep in mind is that the using statement acts as a wrapper for an object within a specified block of code; therefore, it is only useful for declaring objects that are used and scoped within a method (scope is discussed in Hour 12, "Using Constants, Data Types, Variables, and Arrays").

Working with Pens

A *pen* is an object that defines line-drawing characteristics. Pens are used to define color, line width, and line style (solid, dashed, and so on), and pens are used with almost all the drawing methods you'll learn about in this hour.

C# supplies a number of predefined pens, and you can also create your own. To create your own pen, use the following syntax:

```
Pen variable = new Pen(color, width);
```

After a pen is created, you can set its properties to adjust its appearance. For example, all Pen objects have a DashStyle property that determines the appearance of lines drawn with the pen. Table 10.2 lists the possible values for DashStyle.

TABLE 10.2 Possible Values for DashStyle

Value	Description
Dash	Specifies a line consisting of dashes.
DashDot	Specifies a line consisting of a pattern of dashes and dots.
DashDotDot	Specifies a line consisting of alternating dashes and double dots.
Dot	Specifies a line consisting of dots.
Solid	Specifies a solid line.
Custom	Specifies a custom dash style. The Pen object contains properties that can be used to define the custom line.

The enumeration for DashStyle is part of the Drawing.Drawing2D object. Therefore, to create a new pen and use it to draw an ellipse, for example, you could use the following code:

```
Pen objMyPen = new Pen(System.Drawing.Color.DarkBlue, 3);
objMyPen.DashStyle = System.Drawing.Drawing2D.DashStyle.Dot;
```

C# includes many standard pens, which are available via the System.Drawing.Pens class, as in the following:

```
objPen = System.Drawing.Pens.DarkBlue;
```

When drawing using the techniques discussed shortly, you can use custom pens or system-defined pens—it's your choice.

Using System Colors

At some point, you may have changed your Windows theme, or perhaps you changed the image or color of your desktop. What you may not be aware of is that Windows enables you to customize the colors of almost all Windows interface elements. The colors that Windows allows you to change are called *system colors*. To change your system colors, right-click the desktop and choose Properties from the shortcut menu to display the Display Properties dialog box, and then click the Appearance tab (see Figure 10.1). To change the color for a specific item, you can select the item from the Item drop-down list, or you can click the element in the top half of the tab.

10

On Windows XP, you'll need to click Advanced on the Appearance tab to change your system colors.

FIGURE 10.1

The Display Properties dialog box lets you select the colors of most Windows interface elements.

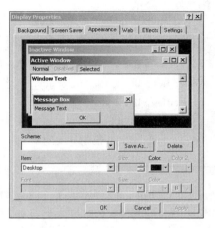

When you change a system color using the Display Properties dialog box, all loaded applications should change their appearance to match your selection. In addition, when you start any new applications, they should also match their appearance to your selection. If you had to write code to manage this behavior, you would have to write a *lot* of code, and you would be justified in avoiding the whole thing. However, making an application adjust its appearance to match the user's system color selections is actually quite trivial; therefore, there's no reason not to do it.

To designate that an interface color should stay in sync with a user's system colors, you assign a system color to a color property of the item in question (see Figure 10.2). Table 10.3 lists the system colors you can use. For example, if you wanted to ensure that the color of a button matches the user's corresponding system color, you would assign the system color named Control to the BackColor property of the Button control.

FIGURE 10.2

System colors are assigned using the System palette tab.

Fortunately, when you create new forms and when you add controls to forms, C# automatically assigns the proper system color to the appropriate properties. Another good thing is that when a user changes a system color using the Display Properties dialog box, C# automatically updates the appearance of objects that use system colors; you don't have to write a single line of code to do this.

Be aware that you aren't limited to assigning system colors to their logically associated properties. You can assign system colors to any color property you want, and you can also use system colors when drawing. This allows you, for example, to draw custom interface elements that match the user's system colors. Be aware, however, that if you do draw with system colors, C# won't update the colors automatically when the user changes system colors; you would have to redraw the elements with the new system color.

 Users don't just change their system colors for aesthetic purposes. I work with a programmer who is color blind. He's modified his system colors so that he can see things better on the screen. If you don't allow your applications to adjust to the color preferences of the user, you may make using your program unnecessarily difficult, or even impossible, for someone with color blindness.

10

TABLE 10.3   Properties of the SystemColors Class

Enumeration	Description
ActiveBorder	The color of the filled area of an active window border.
ActiveCaption	The color of the background of an active caption bar (title bar).
ActiveCaptionText	The color of the text of the active caption bar (title bar).
AppWorkspace	The color of the application workspace. The application workspace is the area in a multiple-document view that is not being occupied by child windows.
Control	The color of the background of push buttons and other 3D elements.
ControlDark	The color of shadows on a 3D element.
ControlDarkDark	The color of darkest shadows on a 3D element.
ControlLight	The color of highlights on a 3D element.
ControlLightLight	The color of lightest highlights on a 3D element.
ControlText	The color of the text on buttons and other 3D elements.
Desktop	The color of the Windows desktop.
GrayText	The color of the text on a user-interface element when it's unavailable.

TABLE 10.3 continued

Enumeration	Description
Highlight	The color of the background of highlighted text. This includes selected menu items as well as selected text.
HighlightText	The color of the foreground of highlighted text. This includes selected menu items as well as selected text.
HotTrack	The color used to represent hot tracking.
InactiveBorder	The color of an inactive window border.
InactiveCaption	The color of the background of an inactive caption bar.
InactiveCaptionText	The color of the text of an inactive caption bar.
Info	The color of the background of the ToolTip.
InfoText	The color of the text of the ToolTip.
Menu	The color of the menu background.
MenuText	The color of the menu text.
ScrollBar	The color of the scrollbar background.
Window	The color of the background in the client area of a window.
WindowFrame	The color of the frame around a window.
WindowText	The color of the text in the client area of a window.

Working with Rectangles

Before learning how to draw shapes, you need to understand the concept of a rectangle as it relates to C# programming. A rectangle isn't necessarily used to draw a rectangle (although it can be). Rather, a rectangle is a structure used to hold bounding coordinates used to draw a shape. Obviously, a square or rectangle can fit within a rectangle. However, so can circles and ellipses. Figure 10.3 illustrates how most shapes can be bound by a rectangle.

To draw most shapes, you must have a rectangle. The rectangle you pass to a drawing method is used as a bounding rectangle; the proper shape (circle, ellipse, and so on) is always drawn. Creating a rectangle is easy. First, you set the dimensions of a variable as Rectangle and then you set the X, Y, Width, and Height properties of the object variable. The X, Y value is the coordinate of the upper-left corner of the rectangle. For example, the following code creates a rectangle that has its upper-left corner at coordinate 0,0, has a width of 100, and a height of 50:

```
Rectangle rectBounding = new Rectangle();
rectBounding.X = 0;
rectBounding.Y = 0;
```

```
rectBounding.Width = 100;
rectBounding.Height = 50;
```

FIGURE 10.3

Rectangles are used to define the bounds of most shapes.

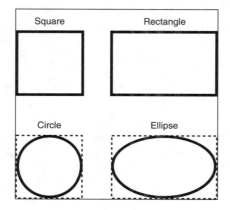

The Rectangle object enables you to send the X, Y, Height, and Width values as part of its initialize construct. Using this technique, you could create the same rectangle with only a single line of code:

```
Rectangle rectBounding = new Rectangle(0,0,100,50);
```

You can do a number of things with a rectangle after it's defined. Perhaps the most useful is the capability to enlarge or shrink the rectangle with a single statement. You enlarge or shrink a rectangle using the Inflate() method. The most common syntax of Inflate() is the following:

```
object.Inflate(changeinwidth, changeinheight);
```

When called this way, the rectangle width is enlarged (the left side of the rectangle remains in place) and the height is enlarged (the top of the rectangle stays in place). To leave the size of the height or width unchanged, pass 0 as the appropriate argument. To shrink a dimension, specify a negative number.

If you're going to do much with drawing, you'll use a lot of Rectangle objects, and I strongly suggest that you learn as much about them as you can.

Drawing Shapes

Now that you've learned about the Graphics object, pens, and rectangles, you'll probably find drawing shapes to be fairly simple. Shapes are drawn by calling methods of a

Graphics object. Most methods require a rectangle, which is used as the bounding rectangle for the shape, as well as a pen. In this section, I'll show you what you need to do to draw different shapes.

 I've chosen to discuss only the most commonly drawn shapes. The Graphics object contains many methods for drawing additional shapes.

Drawing Lines

Drawing lines is accomplished with the DrawLine() method of the Graphics object. DrawLine() is one of the few drawing methods that doesn't require a rectangle. The syntax for DrawLine() is

```
object.DrawLine(pen, x1, y1, x2, y2);
```

Object refers to a Graphics object and *pen* refers to a Pen object, both of which have already been discussed. X1, Y1 is the coordinate of the starting point of the line, whereas X2, Y2 is the coordinate of the ending point; C# draws a line between the two points, using the specified pen.

Drawing Rectangles

Drawing rectangles (and squares for that matter) is accomplished using the DrawRectangle() method of a Graphics object. As you might expect, DrawRectangle() accepts a pen and a rectangle. Following is the syntax for calling DrawRectangle() in this way:

```
object.DrawRectangle(pen, rectangle);
```

If you don't have a Rectangle object (and you don't want to create one), you can call DrawRectangle() using the following format:

```
object.DrawRectangle(pen, X, Y, width, height);
```

Drawing Circles and Ellipses

Drawing circles and ellipses is accomplished by calling the DrawEllipse() method. If you're familiar with geometry, you'll note that a circle is simply an ellipse that has the same height as it does width. This is why no specific method exists for drawing circles; DrawEllipse() works perfectly. Like the DrawRectangle() method, DrawEllipse() accepts a Pen and a Rectangle. The rectangle is used as a bounding rectangle—the width of the ellipse is the width of the rectangle, whereas the height of the ellipse is the height of the rectangle. DrawEllipse() has the following syntax:

```
object.DrawEllipse(pen, rectangle);
```

In the event that you don't have a Rectangle object defined (and again you don't want to create one), you can call DrawEllipse() with this syntax:

```
object.DrawEllipse(pen, X, Y, Width, Height);
```

Clearing a Drawing Surface

To clear the surface of a Graphics object, call the Clear() method, passing it the color to paint the surface, like this:

```
objGraphics.Clear(Drawing.SystemColors.Control);
```

Drawing Text

Printing text on a Graphics object is very similar to drawing a shape, and the method name even contains the word Draw, in contrast to Print. To draw text on a Graphics object, call the DrawString() method. The basic format for DrawString() looks like this:

```
object.DrawString(stringoftext, font, brush, topX, leftY);
```

A few of these items are probably new to you. The argument *stringoftext* is fairly self-explanatory; it's the string you want to draw on the Graphics object. The *topX* and *leftY* arguments represent the coordinate at which drawing will take place; they represent the upper-left corner of the string, as illustrated in Figure 10.4.

FIGURE 10.4
The coordinate specified in DrawString() represents the upper-left corner of the printed text.

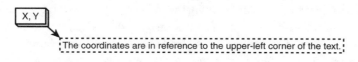

The arguments *brush* and *font* aren't so obvious. Both arguments accept objects. A brush is similar to a pen. However, whereas a pen describes the characteristics of a line, a brush describes the characteristics of a fill. For example, both pens and brushes have a color, but where pens have an attribute for defining a line style, such as dashed or solid, a brush has an attribute for a fill pattern, such as solid, hatched, weave, or trellis. When drawing text, a solid brush is usually sufficient. You can create brushes in much the same way as you create pens, or you can use one of the standard brushes available from the System.Drawing.Brushes class.

A Font object defines characteristics used to format text, including the character set (Times New Roman, Courier, for example), size (point size), and style (bold, italic, normal, underline, and so on). To create a new Font object, you could use code such as the following:

```
Font objFont;
objFont = new System.Drawing.Font("Arial", 30);
```

The text Arial in this code is the name of a font installed on my computer. In fact, Arial is one of the few fonts installed on all Windows computers. If you supply the name of a font that doesn't exist, C# will use a default font. The second parameter is the point size of the text. If you want to use a style other than normal, you can provide a style value as a third parameter, like this:

```
objFont = new System.Drawing.Font("Arial Black", 30,FontStyle.Bold);
```

or

```
objFont = new System.Drawing.Font("Arial Black", 30,FontStyle.Italic);
```

In addition to creating a Font object, you can also use the font of an existing object, such as a Form. For example, the following statement prints text to a Graphics object using the font of the current form:

```
objGraphics.DrawString("This is the text that prints!",
                       this.Font,System.Drawing.Brushes.Azure, 0, 0);
```

Persisting Graphics on a Form

You'll often use the techniques discussed in this hour to draw to a form. However, you may recall from earlier hours that when you draw to a form (actually, you draw to a Graphics object that references a form), the things that you draw aren't persisted; the next time the form paints itself, the drawn elements will disappear. For example, if the user minimizes the form or obscures the form with another window, the next time the form is painted, it will be missing any and all drawn elements that were obscured. You can use a couple of approaches to deal with this behavior:

- Place all code that draws to the form in the form's Paint event.
- Draw to a memory bitmap and copy the contents of the memory bitmap to the form in the form's Paint event.

If you're drawing only a few items, placing the drawing code in the Paint event might be a good approach. However, consider a situation in which you've got a lot of drawing code. Perhaps the graphics are drawn in response to user input, so you can't re-create them all at once. In these situations, the second approach is clearly better.

Build a Graphics Project Example

You're now going to build a project that uses the skills you've already learned to draw to a form. In this project, you'll use the technique of drawing to a memory bitmap to persist the graphics each time the form paints itself.

> The project you're about to build is perhaps the most difficult yet. I'll explain each step of the process of creating this project, but I won't spend any time explaining the objects and methods that I've already discussed.

To make things interesting, I've used random numbers to determine font size as well as the X, Y coordinate of the text you're going to draw to the form. The Random class and its Next() method will be used to generate pseudo-random numbers. To generate a random number within a specific range (such as a random number between 1 and 10), you use the following:

```
randomGenerator.Next(1,10);
```

I don't want you to dwell on the details of how the ranges of random numbers are created. However, at times, you may need to use a random number, so I thought I'd spice things up a bit and teach you something cool at the same time.

Start by creating a new Windows Application titled **Persisting Graphics**.

Change the name of the default form to **fclsMain**, set the form's Text property to **Persisting Graphics**, and change the entry point of the project to reference fclsMain instead of Form1. The interface of your form will consist of a text box and a button. When the user clicks the button, the contents of the text box will be drawn on the form in a random location and a random font size. Add a new text box to your form and set its properties as follows:

Property	Value
Name	txtInput
Location	56,184
Size	100,20
Text	(*make blank*)

10

Add a new button to the form and set its properties as follows:

Property	Value
Name	btnDrawText
Location	160,184
Text	Draw Text

Let the code fly!

As I mentioned earlier, all drawing is going to be performed using a memory bitmap, which will then be drawn on the form. You will reference this bitmap in multiple places, so you're going to make it a module-level variable by following these steps:

1. Double-click the Form to access its Load event.
2. Locate the statement public class fclsMain : System.Windows.Forms.Form and position your cursor immediately *after* the left bracket ({) on the next line.
3. Press Enter to create a new line.
4. Enter the following statement:

```
private System.Drawing.Bitmap m_objDrawingSurface;
```

For the bitmap variable to be used, it must reference a Bitmap object. A good place to initialize things is in the form's Load event, so put your cursor back in the Load event now and enter the following code:

```
// Create a drawing surface with the same dimensions as the client
// area of the form.
m_objDrawingSurface = new Bitmap(this.ClientRectangle.Width,
   this.ClientRectangle.Height,
System.Drawing.Imaging.PixelFormat.Format24bppRgb);
InitializeSurface();
```

Your procedure should now look like the one shown in Figure 10.5.

The first statement creates a new bitmap in memory. Because the contents of the bitmap are to be sent to the form, it makes sense to use the dimensions of the client area of the form as the size of the new bitmap—which is exactly what you've done. The final statement calls a procedure that you haven't yet created.

Position the cursor after the closing bracket (}) of the fclsMain_Load event and press Enter to create a new line. You're now going to write code to initialize the bitmap. The code will clear the bitmap to the system color named Control and then draw an ellipse that has the dimensions of the bitmap. (I've added comments to the code so that you can follow along with what's happening; all the concepts in this code have been discussed already.) Enter the following in its entirety:

```
private void InitializeSurface()
{
   Graphics objGraphics;
   Rectangle rectBounds;

   // Create a Graphics object that references the bitmap and clear it.
   objGraphics = Graphics.FromImage(m_objDrawingSurface);

   objGraphics.Clear(SystemColors.Control);

   //Create a rectangle the same size as the bitmap.
   rectBounds = new Rectangle(0, 0,
             m_objDrawingSurface.Width,m_objDrawingSurface.Height);
   //Reduce the rectangle slightly so the ellipse won't appear on the  border.
   rectBounds.Inflate(-1, -1);

   // Draw an ellipse that fills the form.
   objGraphics.DrawEllipse(Pens.Orange, rectBounds);

   // Free up resources.
   objGraphics.Dispose();
}
```

FIGURE 10.5

Make sure your code appears exactly as it does here.

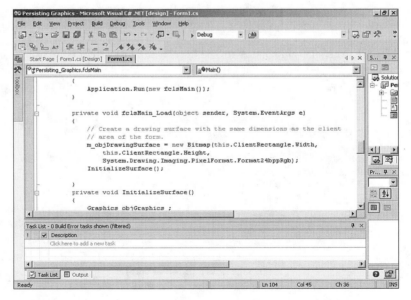

Your procedure should now look like the one shown in Figure 10.6.

If you run your project now, you'll find that nothing is drawn to the form. This is because the drawing is being done to a bitmap in memory, and you haven't yet added the code to copy the bitmap to the form. The place to do this is in the form's Paint event so

that the contents of the bitmap are sent to the form every time the form paints itself. This
ensures that the items you draw always appear on the form.

FIGURE 10.6

*Again, verify that
your code is entered
correctly.*

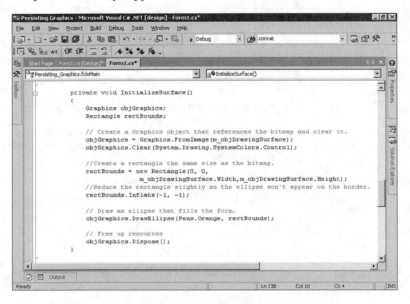

Create an event handler for the form's Paint event by first returning to the form designer and
selecting the form. Click the Event icon (the lightning bolt) in the Properties window and
then double-click Paint to create a Paint event. Add the following code to the Paint event:

```
Graphics objGraphics ;
//You can't modify e.Graphics directly.
objGraphics = e.Graphics;
// Draw the contents of the bitmap on the form.
objGraphics.DrawImage(m_objDrawingSurface, 0,0,
   m_objDrawingSurface.Width,
   m_objDrawingSurface.Height);
objGraphics.Dispose();
```

The previous code can be rewritten as follows when utilizing the using
statement mentioned earlier in this chapter; notice how the Dispose()
method is not required anymore.

```
using (Graphics objGraphics = e.Graphics)
{
objGraphics.DrawImage(m_objDrawingSurface,0,0,
m_objDrawingSurface.Width
m_objDrawingSurface.Height);
}
```

The e parameter of the Paint event has a property that references the Graphics object of the form. However, you can't modify the Graphics object using the e parameter (it's read-only), which is why you've created a new Graphics object to work with and then set the object to reference the form's Graphics object. The method DrawImage() draws the image in a bitmap to the surface of a Graphics object, so the last statement is simply sending the contents of the bitmap to the form.

If you run the project now, you'll find that the ellipse appears on the form. Furthermore, you can cover the form with another window or even minimize it, and the ellipse will always appear on the form when it's displayed again.

The last thing you're going to do is write code that draws the contents entered into the text box on the form. The text will be drawn with a random size and location. Return to the form designer and double-click the button to access its Click event. Add the following code:

```
Graphics objGraphics;
Font objFont;
int intFontSize, intTextX, intTextY;

Random randomGenerator = new Random();

// If no text has been entered, get out.
if (txtInput.Text == "") return;

// Create a graphics object using the memory bitmap.
objGraphics = Graphics.FromImage(m_objDrawingSurface);

// Create a random number for the font size. Keep it between 8 and 48.
intFontSize = randomGenerator.Next(8,48);
// Create a random number for the X coordinate of the text.
intTextX = randomGenerator.Next(0,this.ClientRectangle.Width);
// Create a random number for the Y coordinate of the text.
intTextY = randomGenerator.Next(0,this.ClientRectangle.Height);

// Create a new font object.
objFont = new System.Drawing.Font("Arial", intFontSize, FontStyle.Bold);
// Draw the user's text.
objGraphics.DrawString(txtInput.Text, objFont,
System.Drawing.Brushes.Red, intTextX, intTextY);
// Clean up.
objGraphics.Dispose();
// Force the form to paint itself. This triggers the Paint event.
this.Invalidate();
```

The comments I've included should make the code fairly self-explanatory. However, the last statement bears discussing. The Invalidate() method of a form invalidates the client rectangle. This operation tells Windows that the appearance of the form is no longer accurate and that the form needs to be repainted. This, in turn, triggers the Paint event of the form. Because the Paint event contains the code that copies the contents of the memory bitmap to the form, invalidating the form causes the text to appear. If you don't call Invalidate() here, the text won't appear on the form (but it is still drawn on the memory bitmap).

> If you draw elements that are based on the size of the form, you'll need to call Invalidate() in the Resize event of the form; resizing a form doesn't trigger the form's Paint event.

The last thing you need to do is make sure you free up the resources used by your module-level Graphics object. Using the Properties window, add an event handler for the Closed event of the form now and enter the following statement:

```
m_objDrawingSurface.Dispose();
```

Your project is now complete! Click Save All on the toolbar to save your work, and then press F5 to run the project. You'll notice immediately that the ellipse is drawn on the form. Type something into the text box and click the button. Click it again. Each time you click the button, the text is drawn on the form using the same brush, but with a different size and location (see Figure 10.7).

FIGURE 10.7

Text is drawn on a form, much like ordinary shapes.

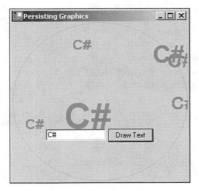

Summary

You won't need to add drawing capabilities to every project you create. However, when you need the capabilities, *you need the capabilities*. In this hour, you learned the basic skills for drawing to a graphics surface, which can be a form, control, memory bitmap, or one of many other types of surfaces. You learned that all drawing is done using a Graphics object, and you now know how to create a Graphics object for a form or control and even how to create a Graphics object for a bitmap that exists in memory.

Most drawing methods require a pen and a rectangle, and you can now create rectangles and pens using the techniques you learned in this hour. After learning pens and rectangles, you've found that the drawing methods themselves are pretty easy to use. Even drawing text is a pretty easy process when you've got a Graphics object to work with.

Persisting graphics on a form can be a bit complicated, and I suspect this will confuse a lot of new C# programmers who try to figure it out on their own. However, you've now built an example that persists graphics on a form, and you'll be able to leverage the techniques involved when you have to do this in your own projects.

I don't expect you to be able to sit down for an hour and create an Adobe Photoshop knock-off. However, you now have a solid foundation on which to build. If you're going to attempt a project that performs a lot of drawing, you'll want to dig deeper into the Graphics object.

10

Q&A

Q. What if I need to draw a lot of lines, one starting where another ends? Do I need to call DrawLine() for each line?

A. The Graphics object has a method called DrawLines(), which accepts a series of points. The method draws lines connecting the sequence of points.

Q. Is there a way to fill a shape?

A. The Graphics object includes methods that draw filled shapes, such as FillEllipse() and FillRectangle().

Workshop

The Workshop is designed to help you anticipate possible questions, review what you've learned, and get you thinking about how to put your knowledge into practice. The answers to the quiz are in Appendix A, "Answers to Quizzes/Exercises."

Quiz

1. What object is used to draw to a surface?

2. To set a Graphics object to draw to a form directly, you call what method of the form?

3. What object defines the characteristics of a line? A fill pattern?

4. How do you make a color property adjust with the user's Windows settings?

5. What object is used to define the bounds of a shape to be drawn?

6. What method do you call to draw an irregular ellipse? A circle?

7. What method do you call to print text on a Graphics surface?

8. To ensure that graphics persist on a form, the graphics must be drawn on the form in what event?

Exercises

1. Modify the example in this hour to use a font other than Arial. If you're not sure what fonts are installed on your computer, open the Start menu and choose Settings and then Control Panel. You'll have an option on the Control Panel for viewing your system fonts.

2. Create a project that draws an ellipse that fills the form, much like the one you created in this hour. However, draw the ellipse directly to the form in the Paint event. Make sure that the ellipse is redrawn when the form is sized. (Hint: Invalidate the form in the form's Resize event.)

PART III

Making Things Happen— Programming!

An attractive interface is useless if it doesn't *do* something. In this part, you'll get into the nuts and bolts of programming. You'll learn about the C# syntax and how to create reusable code. You'll learn how to make decisions in code and how to build loops. Some or all of these concepts may be new to you, and chances are you'll make mistakes and create bugs. Actually, all developers create bugs, regardless of their skill level. In this part, you'll learn how to use C#'s powerful debugging features to track down and correct problems in your code. Finally, you'll be exposed to object-oriented programming, and you'll learn some very useful techniques for optimizing the user experience in your application.

- Hour 11: Creating and Calling Methods
- Hour 12: Using Constants, Data Types, Variables, and Arrays
- Hour 13: Performing Arithmetic, String Manipulation, and Date/Time Adjustments
- Hour 14: Making Decisions in C# Code
- Hour 15: Looping for Efficiency
- Hour 16: Debugging Your Code
- Hour 17: Designing Objects Using Classes
- Hour 18: Interacting with Users

HOUR 11

Creating and Calling Methods

You've now spent about 11 hours building the basic skills necessary to navigate C# and to create an application interface. Creating a good interface is extremely important, but it's only one step toward creating a Windows program. After you've created the basic interface of an application, you need to enable the program to do something. The program may perform an action all on its own, or it may perform actions based on a user interacting with the interface—either way, to make your application perform tasks, you write C# code. In this hour, you'll learn how to create sets of code (called classes), and how to create and call isolated code routines (called methods).

The highlights of this hour include the following:

- Creating static class members
- Creating methods
- Calling methods
- Exiting methods

- Passing parameters
- Avoiding recursive methods
- Working with tasks

Creating Class Members

NEW TERM A *class* is a place to store the code you write. Before you can begin writing C# code, you must start with a class. As mentioned in previous hours, a class is used as a template to create an object (which may have properties and/or methods). Properties and methods of classes can be either instance members or static members. *Instance members* are associated with an instance of a class—an object created from a class using the keyword new. On the other hand, *static members* belong to the class as a whole, not to a specific instance of a class. You've already worked with one class using instance members to create a form (refer to Hour 5, "Building Forms—Part I, for more information).When you double-click an object on a form, you access events that reside in the form's class module.

Other languages, such as Visual Basic, differentiate between class methods and public methods that are globally available outside of a class. C# requires all methods to exist in the context of a class, but a globally available method can be achieved by defining static methods in your class. Static methods are always available regardless of whether an instance of the class exists. In fact, you can't access a static member through an instance of a class, and attempting to do so results in an exception (error).

Classes are used as templates for the instantiation of objects. I discuss the specifics of creating objects in Hour 17, "Designing Objects Using Classes." Most of the techniques discussed in this hour apply to class modules with instance members (methods that are part of an instantiated object), but I'm going to focus this discussion on static members because they are easier to use (you can create and use static methods without getting into the complications of creating objects).

Although you could place all your program's code into a single class module, it's best to create different modules to group different sets of code. In addition, it's best not to place code that isn't specifically related to a form within a form's class module; place such code in the logical class or in a specialized class module.

The current development trend centers on object-oriented programming, which revolves around class modules. I'll give you a primer on object-oriented programming in Hour 17, but this is a very advanced topic so I won't be covering it in detail. I highly recommend that you read a dedicated object-oriented book, such as *Sams Teach Yourself Object-Oriented Programming in 21 Days*, after you are comfortable with the material in this book.

One general rule for using static members is that you should create classes to group related sets of code. This isn't to say you should create dozens of classes. Rather, group related methods into a reasonably sized set of classes. For instance, you might want to create one class that contains all your printing routines and another that holds your data-access routines. In addition, I like to create a general-purpose class in which to place all the various routines that don't necessarily fit into a more specialized class.

Start C# now and create a new Windows Application project named **Static Methods**.

Change the name of the default form to **fclsExample**, set its Text property to **Method Example,** and set the Main() entry point of the project to reference **fclsExample** instead of Form1. Change the Size property of the form to **371, 300**. Next, add a new class to the project by choosing Add Class from the Project menu. C# then displays the Add New Item dialog box, as shown in Figure 11.1.

11

FIGURE 11.1

All new project items are added using this dialog box.

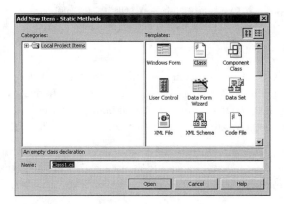

Note that this is the same dialog box used to add new forms. Change the name of the
class to **clsStaticExample.cs** and click Open. C# then creates the new class and positions
you in the code window—ready to enter code (see Figure 11.2).

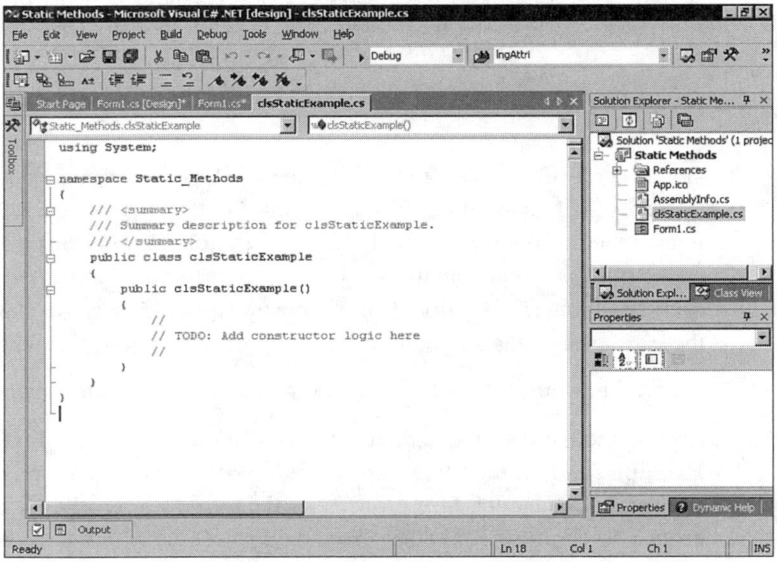

Figure **11.2**

Classes have no
graphical interface,
so you always work
with them in the code
editor.

Save your project now by clicking Save All on the toolbar.

Writing Methods

NEW TERM   After you've created the class(es) in which to store your code, you can begin
            writing methods. A *method* is a discrete set of code that can be executed.
Methods are much like events, but rather than being executed by a user interacting with a
form or control, methods are executed when called by a code statement.

The first thing to keep in mind is that every method should perform a specific function,
and it should do it very well. You should avoid creating methods that perform many
tasks. As an example of the use of methods, consider that you want to create a set of
code that, when called, draws an ellipse on a form. You also want a second method to
clear the form. If you placed both sets of code into the same method, the ellipse would
be drawn and then would immediately be erased. By placing each set of code in its own
method, you can draw the ellipse by calling one method and then erase it at any time by
calling the other method. By placing these routines in a class rather than attaching them
to a specific form, you also make the methods available to any form that may need them.

There are two types of methods in C#:

- Methods that return a value
- Methods that do not return a value (void)

There are many reasons to create a method that returns a value. For example, a method can return true or false, depending on whether it was successful in completing its task. You could also write a method that accepts certain parameters (data passed to the method, in contrast to data returned by the method) and returns a value based on those parameters. For example, you could write a method that lets you pass it a sentence, and in return it passes back the number of characters in the sentence. The possibilities are limited only by your imagination. Just keep in mind that a method doesn't have to return a value.

Declaring Methods That Don't Return Values

Because you've already created a class, you're ready to create methods (to create a method, you first declare it within a class).

Position the cursor to the right of the closed brace (}) that signifies the end of the public clsStaticExample block and press Enter to create a new line. Enter the following three statements:

```
public static void DrawEllipse(System.Windows.Forms.Form frm)
{
}
```

Next, position your cursor to the right of the open brace ({) and press Enter to create a new line between the two braces. This is where you'll place the code for the method.

The declaration of a method (the statement used to define a method) has a number of parts. The first word, public, is a keyword (a word with a special meaning in C#). The keyword public defines the scope of this method, designating that the method can be called from code contained in modules other than the one containing the defined method (scope is discussed in detail in the next hour). You can use the keyword private in place of public to restrict access of the method to code only in the module in which the method resides.

The word static is another C# keyword. As mentioned earlier, static members belong to a class as a whole, not to a specific instance of a class. This will allow the DrawEllipse() method to be accessed from other classes without having to instantiate an clsStaticExample object.

11

The word void is another C# keyword. The void keyword is used to declare a method that doesn't return a value. Later in this hour, you will learn how to create methods that do return values.

The third word, DrawEllipse, is the actual name of the method and can be any string of text you want it to be. Note, however, that you can't assign a name that is a keyword, nor can you use spaces within a name. In this example, the method is going to draw an ellipse on the form, so you used the name DrawEllipse. You should always give method names that reflect their purpose. You can have two methods with the same name only if they have different scope (discussed in the next hour).

> Some programmers prefer the readability of spaces in names, but in many instances, such as when naming a method, spaces can't be used. A common technique is to use an underscore (_) in place of a space, such as in Draw_Ellipse. This isn't a recommended practice, however.

New Term Immediately following the name of the method is a set of parentheses surrounding some text. Within these parentheses you can define *parameters*—data to be passed to the method by the calling program. In this example, you've created a parameter that accepts a reference to a form. The routine will draw an ellipse on whatever form is passed to the parameter.

> Parentheses must always be supplied, even when a procedure doesn't accept any parameters (in which case nothing is placed between the parentheses).

Add the following code to your DrawEllipse method:

```
System.Drawing.Graphics objGraphics;
System.Drawing.Rectangle recDrawRectangle;
recDrawRectangle = frm.DisplayRectangle;
recDrawRectangle.Inflate(-5, -5);
objGraphics = frm.CreateGraphics();
objGraphics.Clear(System.Drawing.SystemColors.Control);
objGraphics.DrawEllipse(System.Drawing.Pens.Blue, recDrawRectangle);
objGraphics.Dispose();
```

Much of this code is similar to a code example discussed in Hour 3, "Understanding Objects and Collections," so I'm not going to go over it in detail. Basically, this routine creates a rectangle with the same dimensions as the client rectangle of the supplied form. Then, the Inflate method is used to reduce the size of the rectangle by 5 pixels in each dimension. Finally, a graphics object is created and set to reference the client area of the supplied form, and a rectangle is drawn within the boundaries of the rectangle.

When you've finished entering your code, it should look like that in Figure 11.3.

FIGURE 11.3

All code for a method must reside between the open and close braces of the method.

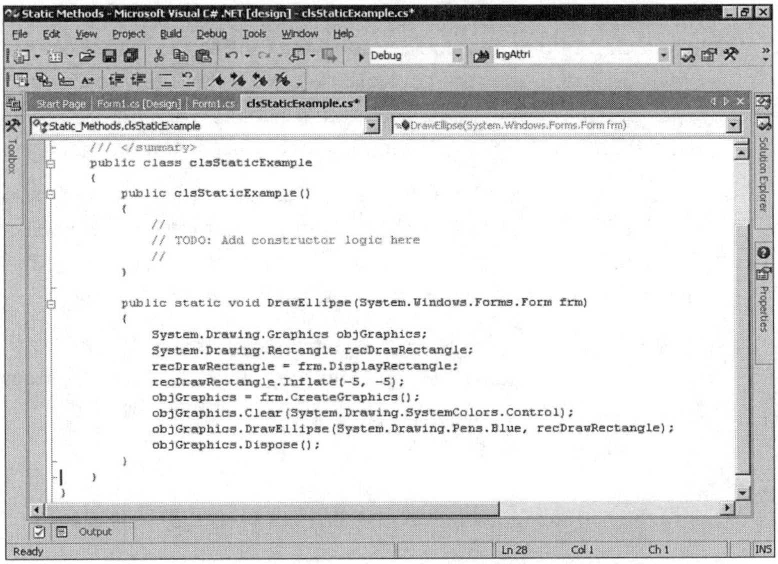

Now you're going to create a procedure that erases the ellipse from a form. Place the caret (cursor) at the end of the closing brace (}) for the DrawEllipse() method and press enter to create a new line. Enter the following three statements:

```
public static void ClearEllipse(System.Windows.Forms.Form frm)
{
}
```

Add the following line of code to the ClearEllipse() method on a new line between the opening and closing braces:

```
frm.Refresh();
```

This single line of code forces the designated form to refresh itself. Because the ellipse that was drawn by the first procedure isn't part of the form (it was simply drawn onto the form), the ellipse is cleared.

Declaring Methods That Return Values

NEW TERM   The two methods you've created so far don't return values. You're now going to declare a method that returns a value. Here's the general syntax for the method you will create:

```
[modifiers] datatype MethodName(parameters)
```

You'll notice one key difference between declaring a method that doesn't return a value and declaring one that does: you have to define the data type of the value returned. Previously, you used the keyword void to declare that no value was being returned. Data types are discussed in detail in the next hour, so it's not important that you fully understand them now. It is important, however, that you understand what is happening.

The data type entered before the method name denotes the type of data returned by the method. The method that you're about to enter returns a numeric value of type integer. If the method were to return a string of text, it would be declared as string. It is very important that you declare the proper data type for your functions.

Position the cursor to the right of the closing brace for the ClearEllipse() method, press Enter to create a new line, and enter the following three statements:

```
public static int ComputeLength(string strText)
{
}
```

Add the following code to a new line between the two braces:

```
return strText.Length;
```

When you create a method that returns a value, you use the C# keyword return to return whatever value you want the method to return. In this example, you're using the built-in Length() method of the string class to determine the number of characters within the string that's passed to the method. This value is returned as the value of the method. (You could, of course, avoid writing the function altogether and just use the String.Length() method in the calling code, but this makes a good example.) Your methods should now look like the one in Figure 11.4.

Creating the User Interface of Your Project

Now that you've written this example's procedures, you need to create the interface for the project. Click the Form1.cs [Design] tab in the IDE to display the form designer for the default form.

FIGURE 11.4

Classes often contain many methods.

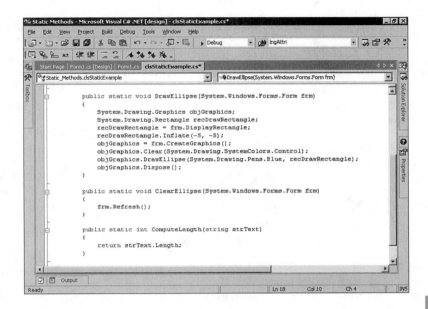

```
public static void DrawEllipse(System.Windows.Forms.Form frm)
{
    System.Drawing.Graphics objGraphics;
    System.Drawing.Rectangle recDrawRectangle;
    recDrawRectangle = frm.DisplayRectangle;
    recDrawRectangle.Inflate(-5, -5);
    objGraphics = frm.CreateGraphics();
    objGraphics.Clear(System.Drawing.SystemColors.Control);
    objGraphics.DrawEllipse(System.Drawing.Pens.Blue, recDrawRectangle);
    objGraphics.Dispose();
}

public static void ClearEllipse(System.Windows.Forms.Form frm)
{
    frm.Refresh();
}

public static int ComputeLength(string strText)
{
    return strText.Length;
}
```

You'll need three buttons on this form—one to call each of your methods. Add the first button to the form by double-clicking the Button icon in the toolbox and then set its properties as follows:

Property	Value
Name	btnDrawEllipse
Location	0,0
Size	80,23
Text	Draw Ellipse

Add a second button to the form and set its properties as follows:

Property	Value
Name	btnClearEllipse
Location	283,0
Size	80,23
Text	Clear Ellipse

11

Finally, add the third button to the form and set its properties as follows:

Property	Value
Name	btnComputeLength
Location	0,250
Size	100,23
Text	Compute Length

The last control you need to add to your form is a text box. When the user clicks the Compute Length button, the button's Click event will call the ComputeLength function, passing it the text entered into the text box. It will then display the length of the text in the Output window (this works only when running in the IDE, not when compiled as an application).

 The Output window is a Visual Studio design window to which you can print text. I use the Output window a lot in examples throughout the remaining hours. When you send text to the Output window, Visual Studio ensures that the Output window is visible. You can display it at any time while working in the IDE by choosing Other Windows from the View menu and then selecting Output. Be aware that the Output window is not available to a compiled component.

Add a text box to the form by double-clicking the Textbox icon in the toolbox. Set the new text box's properties as follows:

Property	Value
Name	txtInputForLength
Location	110,250
Text	(make blank)

Your form should now look like the one shown in Figure 11.5. You're now ready to write the C# code to call your methods.

FIGURE 11.5
*This form is not all
that attractive, but it's
functional enough for
our purposes.*

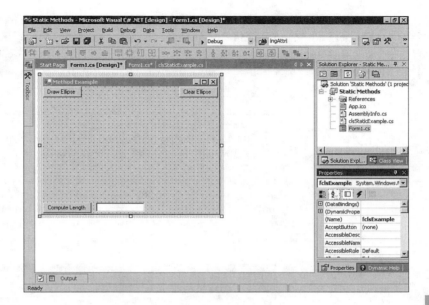

Calling Methods

Calling a method is fairly simple. However, just as methods that return values are declared differently from methods that do not, calling these two types of methods differs as well. You're first going to write code to call the two methods you declared as *void* (methods that don't return values). Double-click the Draw Ellipse button to access its Click event and take a look at the event declaration:

```
private void btnDrawEllipse_Click(object sender, System.EventArgs e)
{
}
```

As you can see, event handlers are methods. The only real difference is that event methods are called automatically in response to the user doing something, rather than being called by code you write. In this case, the btnDrawEllipse_Click() event is called when the user clicks the btnDrawEllipse button. This method is declared as private, so only methods within this module could call this method (yes, you can call event methods). Add the following statement to this Click event:

```
clsStaticExample.DrawEllipse(this);
```

To call the DrawEllipse method, you must precede it with the name of the class in which it is defined. The method name and parentheses always come next. If the method expects one or more parameters, place them within the parentheses. In this case, the DrawEllipse() procedure expects a reference to a form. By specifying the keyword this, you're passing a reference to the current form.

When you type in the class name clsStaticExample followed by a period, C# displays the methods defined for the clsStaticExample class. Also, notice that when you type in the left parenthesis for the DrawEllipse() method, C# displays a ToolTip showing the parameters expected by the method (see Figure 11.6). It can be difficult to remember the parameters expected by all methods (not to mention the proper order in which to pass them), so this little feature will save you a great deal of time and frustration.

FIGURE 11.6

C# displays the parameters expected of a method.

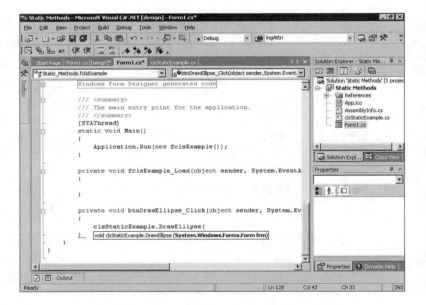

You're now going to place a call to the ClearEllipse() method in the Click event of the Clear Ellipse button. Display the form in Design view again and double-click the Clear Ellipse button to access its Click event. Add the following statement:

```
clsStaticExample.ClearEllipse(this);
```

All that's left to do is add code that computes the length of the string entered by the user. Again, display the form in Design view. Double-click the Compute Length button to access its Click event and enter the following statements (recall from Hour 7, "Working with Traditional Controls," that Debug.WriteLine() sends text to the Output window.):

```
int intLength;
intLength = clsStaticExample.ComputeLength(txtInputForLength.Text);
System.Diagnostics.Debug.WriteLine("length = " + intLength);
```

The first line creates a new variable to hold the return value of the ComputeLength() method (the next hour covers variables). The second statement calls the ComputeLength() method. When calling a method that returns a value, think of the method in terms of the value it returns. For example, when you set a form's Height property, you set it with code like this:

```
MyForm.Height = 200;
```

This statement sets a form's height to 200. Suppose you had a method that returned a value that you wanted to use to set the form's Height property. Thinking of the method in terms of the value it returns, you could replace the literal value with a method call, as in the following:

```
MyForm.Height = MyClass.MyMethod();
```

Try to look at the statement you just entered using this way of thinking. When you do, you see that the statement in this example really says, "Set the variable intLength equal to the value returned by the method ComputeLength()." If ComputeLength() returned the value 20, for example, the line of code would behave as though it were written like this:

```
intLength = 20;
```

When calling methods, you must treat the method call the same as you would treat the literal value returned by the method. This often means placing a method call on the right side of an equal sign.

The last line of code you entered outputs the result of the method call to the Output window in the IDE (refer to Hour 7). The text *"length ="* and the value of intLength are concatenated (joined together), to produce one string of text that gets displayed. You'll learn about concatenation in Hour 13, "Performing Arithmetic, String Manipulation, and Date/Time Adjustments." The project is now complete. Click Save All on the toolbar to save your work, and then press F5 to run the project. Click the Draw Ellipse button and an ellipse is drawn on the form (see Figure 11.7).

11

FIGURE 11.7

Clicking the button calls the method that draws the ellipse in the house that Jack built.

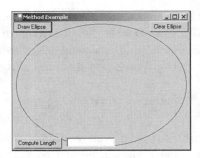

Here's what is happening when you click the Draw Ellipse button:

1. The Draw Ellipse button's Click event is triggered.
2. The method call statement within the Click event is executed.
3. Code execution jumps to the DrawEllipse() method.
4. All code within the DrawEllipse() method gets executed.
5. Execution returns to the Click event.

Click the Clear Ellipse button now to clear the form. When you click this button, the following occurs:

1. The Clear Ellipse button's Click event is triggered.
2. The method call statement within the Click event is executed.
3. Code execution jumps to the ClearEllipse() method.
4. All code within the ClearEllipse() method gets executed.
5. Execution returns to the Click event.

Finally, enter some text into the text box and click the Compute Length button. Here's what happens:

1. The Compute Length button's Click event is triggered.
2. The reference to the ComputeLength method causes code execution to jump to that method.
3. The ComputeLength() method determines the length of the string. This value is passed back as the result of the method.
4. Execution returns to the Click event.
5. The result of the method is placed in the variable intLength.
6. The rest of the code within the Click event executes. The final result is the length of the string, which is printed in the Output window (see Figure 11.8).

FIGURE 11.8

System.Diagnostics.D
ebug.WriteLine *sends*
text to the Output
window.

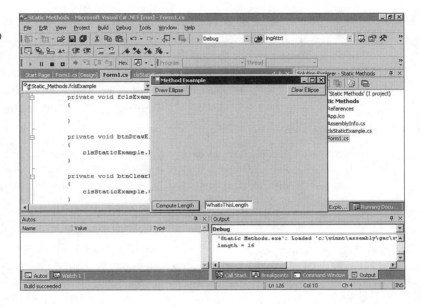

Passing Parameters

Parameters are used within a method to allow the calling code to pass data into the
method; methods help eliminate module and global variables. You've already seen how
parameters work—parameters are created within the parentheses of a method declaration.
A parameter definition consists of the data type and a name for the parameter, as shown
here:

```
public static void MyMethod(string strMyStringParameter)
```

> After you've read about variables in Hour 12, "Using Constants, Data Types,
> Variables, and Arrays," this structure will make a lot more sense. Here, I just
> want you to get the general idea of how to define and use parameters.

You can define multiple parameters for a method by separating them with a comma, like
this:

```
public static void MyMethod(string strMyStringParameter,
                            int intMyIntegerParameter)
```

NEW TERM   A calling method passes data to the parameters by way of arguments. This is
            mostly a semantic issue; when defined in the declaration of a method, the item is
called a *parameter*. When the item is part of the statement that calls the method, it's
called an *argument*. Arguments are passed within parentheses—the same as parameters
are defined. If a procedure has multiple arguments, you separate them with commas. For
example, you could pass values to the method just defined using a statement such as this:

```
MyClass.MyProcedure("This is a string", 11);
```

The parameter acts like an ordinary variable within the method. Hour 12 discusses variables in depth. For now, just realize that variables are storage entities whose values can
be changed. In the call statement shown previously, I sent literal values to the procedure.
I could have also sent the values of variables like this:

```
MyClass.MyProcedure(strAString, intAnInteger);
```

NEW TERM   An important thing to note about passing variables in C# is that parameters are
            passed *by value* rather than *by reference*. When passed by value, the method
receives a copy of the data; changes to the parameter don't affect the value of the original
variable. When passed by reference, the parameter is actually a pointer to the original
variable. Changes made to the parameter within the method propagate to the original
variable. To pass a parameter by reference, you preface the parameter definition with the
keyword ref as shown here:

```
public static void MyMethod(ref string strMyStringParameter,
                            int intMyIntegerParameter)
```

Parameters defined without ref are passed by value; this is the default behavior of parameters in C#. Therefore, in this declaration, the first parameter is passed by reference,
whereas the second parameter is passed by value.

Avoiding Recursive Methods

It's possible to call methods in such a way that a continuous loop occurs. Consider the
following procedures:

```
public static void DoSomething()
{
    DoSomethingElse();
}
public static void DoSomethingElse()
{
    DoSomething();
}
```

Calling either of these methods produces an infinite loop of methods calls and results in
the error shown in Figure 11.9.

FIGURE 11.9

Infinite recursion results in a Stack Overflow Exception (error).

NEW TERM This endless loop is known as a *recursive* loop. Without getting too technical, C# allocates some memory for each method call in an area known as the stack. Only a finite amount of space is on the stack, so infinite recursion eventually uses all the available stack space and an exception occurs. This is a serious error, and steps should be taken to avoid such recursion.

Legitimate uses exist for recursion, most notably in the use of algorithms such as those used in calculus. Deliberate recursion techniques don't create infinite recursion, however. There is always a point where the recursion stops (hopefully, before the stack is consumed). If you have an interest in such algorithms, you should consider reading a book dedicated to the subject.

Exiting Methods

Ordinarily, code within a method executes from beginning to end—literally. However, when a return statement is reached, execution immediately returns to the statement that made the method call; you can force execution to leave the method at any time by using a return statement. If C# encounters a return statement, the method terminates immediately, and code returns to the statement that called the method.

As you build your applications, you'll find that the number of methods and classes expands rather quickly. At times, you'll realize that a method isn't finished or that you had to use a "hack" (a less-desirable solution) to solve a problem. You'll need an easy way to keep these things straight so that you can revisit the code as needed. You'll learn a powerful way to do this in the next section.

Working with Tasks

One of the most exciting IDE enhancements from previous versions of Visual Studio, in my opinion, is the new Task List. Tasks are really all about managing code. If your Task List window isn't displayed, show it now by choosing Show Tasks from the View menu and then choosing All. Tasks are used to keep track of critical spots in code or things that need to be done. C# automatically creates some tasks for you, and you can create your own as needed.

11

One instance in which C# creates tasks is when your code has compile (build) errors. Because C# knows the exact error and the offending statement, it creates an appropriate task. Figure 11.10 shows the Task List containing a build error. Notice how the task's description tells you the exact problem. Double-clicking a system-generated task takes you directly to the related statement (double-clicking a task that you created has a different effect, as discussed shortly). If the task exists in a class that isn't loaded, C# loads the class and then takes you to the statement. This greatly simplifies the process of addressing compile errors in code; you can simply work through the list of tasks rather than compile, fix an error, try compiling again, fix the next error, and so on.

FIGURE 11.10

Tasks help you keep track of critical spots in code.

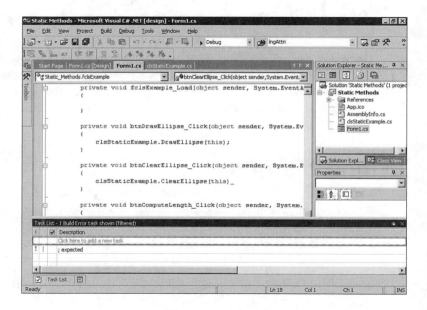

In addition to system-generated tasks, you can create your own tasks as often and wherever needed. In the past, it was common to place certain comments such as "TODO" in code where you needed to address something. These comments often were forgotten. When you wanted to address the issues, you had to perform a text search in your code. This was a highly inefficient process.

Now you can create a task wherever you need to. Creating a task is easy. Right-click the code statement to which you want to attach the task and choose Add Task List Shortcut from the context menu. C# creates a task shortcut at the statement (as indicated by a blue arrow in the left margin of the code window) and adds the task to the Task List window. The default description for the next task is the actual code statement you flagged (see Figure 11.11). To change this text, click the description in the Task List to put it in Edit mode and then change the text. To go directly to the statement to which a task is attached, double-click the shortcut arrow next to the task in the Task List (the arrow is the same one that appears in the left margin of the code window).

Another way to create a task is to insert a comment that literally starts with TODO:—Visual Studio .NET will then automatically create a task using the comment.

FIGURE 11.11

Tasks make it easy to track issues that need to be addressed.

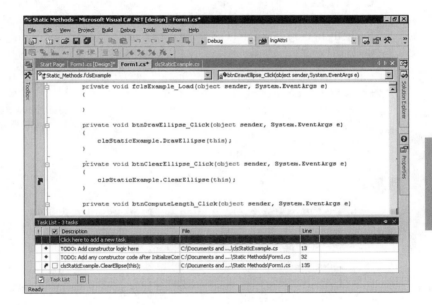

You don't have to attach a task to a code statement. To create a task that isn't attached to code, click the first row of the Task List. The default text Click here to add a new task goes away, and you're free to enter the description for your new task.

To delete a task you created, click once on the task in the Task List to select it, and then right-click the task and choose Delete from the context menu. You can't delete a task that was created by C# as a result of a build error—you must correct the error to make the task go away.

Tasks are an incredibly simple, yet useful, tool. I highly encourage you to use them in your development.

Summary

In this hour, you learned how a method is a discrete set of code designed to perform a task or related set of tasks. Methods are where you write C# code. Some methods may be as short as a single line of code, whereas others are pages in length. You learned how to define methods and how to call them. Creating and calling methods is critical to your success in programming with C#; be sure to avoid creating recursive methods! Because you use methods so often, they'll become second nature to you in no time.

Classes are used to group methods. In this hour, I focused on the class module (which is little more than a container for methods) and static methods. Remember to group related methods in the same class and to give each class a descriptive name. In Hour 17, you'll build on your experience with classes and methods and work with instance classes.

Finally, you learned about Visual Studio's new Task List feature. You now know that C# creates some tasks for you but that you are free to create tasks as you see fit. You learned how to easily jump to a statement that's related to a task and how to create tasks that aren't related to a specific code statement. The Task List is a powerful tool to have in your arsenal, and I encourage you to use it.

Q&A

Q. Do I need to pay much attention to scope when defining my methods?

A. It may be tempting to create all your methods as public static, but this is bad coding practice for a number of reasons. For one thing, you will find that in larger projects, you'll have methods with the same name that do slightly different things. Usually, these routines are relevant only within a small scope. If the method isn't needed at the public level, don't define it for public access.

Q. How many classes is a "reasonable" amount?

A. This is hard to say. There really is no right answer. Instead of worrying about an exact count, you should strive to make sure that your classes are logical and that they contain only appropriate methods and properties.

Workshop

The Workshop is designed to help you anticipate possible questions, review what you've learned, and get you thinking about how to put your knowledge into practice. The answers to the quiz are in Appendix A, "Answers to Quizzes/Exercises."

Quiz

1. What are the entities called that are used to house methods?

2. True or False: To access methods in a class module, you must first create an object.

3. Data that has been passed into a method by a calling statement is called a

4. To pass multiple arguments to a method, separate them with a

5. The situation in which a method or set of methods continue to call each other in a looping fashion is called

6. How do you attach a task to a code statement?

Exercises

1. Create a method as part of a form that accepts a string and outputs to the string. Add code to the TextChanged event of a text box to call the procedure, passing the contents of the text box as the argument.

2. Create a single method that calls itself. Call this method from the Click event of a button and observe the error that results.

11

Hour 12

Using Constants, Data Types, Variables, and Arrays

NEW TERM As you write your C# methods, you'll regularly need to store and retrieve various pieces of information. In fact, I can't think of a single application I've written that didn't need to store and retrieve data in code. For example, you might want to keep track of how many times a method has been called, or you may want to store a property value and use it at a later time. Such data can be stored as *constants*, *variables*, or *arrays*. Constants are named values that you define once at design time but that can be referenced as often as needed. Variables, on the other hand, are like storage bins; you can retrieve or replace the data in a variable as often as you need to. Arrays act like grouped variables, allowing you to store many values in a single array variable.

NEW TERM   Whenever you define one of these storage entities, you must decide the type of data it will contain. For example, is a new variable going to hold a string value (text) or perhaps a number? If it will hold a number, is the number a whole number, an integer, or something else entirely? After you determine the type of data to store, you must choose the level of visibility that the data has to other methods within the project (this visibility is known as *scope*). In this hour, you'll learn the ins and outs of C# new data types, how to create and use these "storage" mechanisms, and you'll learn how to minimize problems in your code by reducing scope.

The highlights of this hour include the following:

- Understanding data types
- Determining data type
- Converting data to different data types
- Defining and using constants
- Dimensioning and referencing variables
- Working with arrays
- Determining scope
- Using a naming convention

 I cover a lot of important material in this hour, but you'll notice a lack of hands-on examples. You're going to use variables throughout the rest of this book, and you've already used them in earlier hours. I've used the space in this hour to teach you the meat of the subject; you'll get experience with the material in other hours.

Understanding Data Types

In any programming language, it's critical that the compiler, the part of the Visual Studio framework that interprets the code you write into a language the computer can under-stand, fully understands the type of data you're manipulating in code. For example, if you asked the compiler to add the following values, it would get confused:

```
659 / "Dog"
```

NEW TERM   When the compiler gets confused, it either refuses to compile the code (which is the preferred situation because you can address the problem before your users run the application), or it will halt execution and display an exception (error) when it reaches the confusing line of code. (These two types of errors are discussed in detail in

Hour 16, "Debugging Your Code.") Obviously, you can't subtract 659 by the word "Dog"; these two values are different types of data. In C#, these two values are said to have two different *data types*. In C#, constants, variables, and arrays must always be defined to hold a specific type of information.

Determining Data Type

NEW TERM *Data typing*—the act of defining a constant, a variable, or an array's data type—can be confusing. To C#, a number is not a number. A number that contains a decimal value is different from a number that does not. C# can perform arithmetic on numbers of different data types, but you can't store data of one type in a variable with an incompatible type. Because of this limitation, you must give careful consideration to the type of data you plan to store in a constant, a variable, or an array at the time you define it. C# supports two categories of data types: value types and reference types. The main difference between these two types is how their values are stored in memory. As you continue to create more complex applications, this difference may have an impact on your programming. For this book, however, this distinction is minimal. Table 12.1 lists the C# data types and the range of values they can contain.

TABLE 12.1 The C# Data Types

Data Type—Value	Value Range
bool	true or false
byte	0 to 255
char	a single character
decimal	–79,228,162,514,264,337,593,543,950,335 to –7.9228162514264337593543950335. Use this data type for currency values
double	–1.79769313486232E308 to –4.94065645841247E-324 for negative values; 4.94065645841247E–324 to 1.79769313486232E308 for positive values
float	–3.402823E38 to –1.401298E–45 for negative values; 1.401298E–45 to 3.402823E38 for positive values
int	–2,147,483,648 to 2,147,483,647.
long	–9,223,372,036,854,775,808 to 9,223,372,036,854,775,807
sbyte	–128 to 127
short	–32,768 to 32,767
uint	Integers in the range from 0 to 4,294,967,295

12

TABLE 12.1   continued

Data Type—Value	Value Range
ulong	Integers in the range from 0 to 10^20
ushort	Integers in the range from 0 to 65,535

Data Type—Reference	Value Range
string	0 to approximately 2 billion characters
object	Any type can be stored in a variable type Object

C# supports unsigned data types for short, int, and long (the types prefaces with u, such as uint). Because negative numbers are excluded (there is no sign) this has the effect of doubling the positive values for a short, an int, or a long. Signed data types are preferable and should be used unless you have a very good reason for doing otherwise (such as declaring a variable that will never hold a negative value).

Tips for Determining Data Type

The list of data types may seem daunting at first, but you can follow some general guidelines for choosing among them. As you become more familiar with the different types, you'll be able to fine-tune your data type selection.

Following are some helpful guidelines for using data types:

- If you want to store text, use the string data type. The string data type can be used to store any valid keyboard character, including numbers and nonalphabetic characters.
- If you want to store only the values true or false, use the bool data type.
- If you want to store a number that contains no decimal places and is greater than −32,768 and smaller than 32,767, use the short data type.
- If you need to store numbers with no decimal places but with values larger or smaller than short allows, use the int or long data types.
- If you need to store numbers that contain decimal places, use the float data type. The float data type should work for almost all your values containing decimals, unless you're writing incredibly complex mathematical applications or need to store very large numbers; in that case, use a double.
- If you need to store currency amounts, use the decimal data type.
- If you need to store a single character, use the char data type.

Casting Data from One Data Type to Another

NEW TERM Under some circumstances, C# won't allow you to move data of one type into a variable of another type. The process of changing a value's data type is known as *casting*. C# supports two types of casting: implicit and explicit. *Implicit* conversions are done automatically by the compiler. These conversions guarantee that no data is lost in the conversion. For instance, you can set the value of a variable declared as double to the value of a variable declared as float without an explicit cast because there is no risk of losing data; (the double data type holds a higher value than does a float.

Explicit casting is required when a potential exists for data loss or when converting a larger data type into a smaller data type. If you tried to place a value in a variable when the value was higher than the variable's supported data type, some data would be lost. Therefore, C# requires that these types of conversions be explicitly written using the cast operator. For instance, you can set the value of a variable declared as short to the value of a variable declared as integer using the following syntax:

```
short MyShortInterger;
int MyInteger = 1000;
MyShortInterger = (short) MyInteger;
```

Notice here that 1000 would fit in a short, so data wouldn't actually be lost if no explicit cast were performed. However, C# doesn't care; it's the *potential* for data loss that causes C# to require explicit casts.

Table 12.2 lists some of the type conversions that can be done implicitly with no loss of information.

12

TABLE 12.2 Safe Conversions

Type	Can Be Safely Converted To
byte	char, short, int, long, float, double, decimal
short	int, long, float, double, decimal
int	long, float, double, decimal
long	float, double, decimal
float	double, decimal
double	decimal

Defining and Using Constants

When you hard-code numbers in your code (such as in intVotingAge = 19;), a myriad of things can go wrong. Hard-coded numbers are generally referred to as "magic numbers" because they're often shrouded in mystery; the meaning of such a number is obscure because the digits themselves give no indication as to what the number represents. Constants are used to eliminate the problems of magic numbers.

You define a constant as having a specific value at design time, and that value never changes throughout the life of your program. Constants offer the following benefits:

- Elimination or reduction of data entry problems   It is much easier, for example, to remember to use a constant named c_pi than it is to enter 3.14159265358979 everywhere that pi is needed. The compiler will catch misspelled or undeclared constants, but it doesn't care one bit what you enter as a literal value. (Incidentally, you can retrieve the value of pi using System.Math.PI, so you don't have to worry about creating your own constant!)

- Code is easier to update   If you hard-coded a mortgage interest rate at 6.785, and rates were changed to 7.00, you would have to change every occurrence of 6.785 in code. In addition to the possibility of data entry problems, you'd run the risk of changing a value of 6.785 that had nothing to do with the interest rate—perhaps a value that represented a savings bond yield. With a constant, you change the value once, and all code uses the new value.

- Code is easier to read   Magic numbers are often anything but intuitive. Well-named constants, on the other hand, add clarity to code. For example, which of the following statements makes the most sense?

```
decInterestAmount = ((decLoanAmount * 0.075) * 12);
```

or

```
decInterestAmount = ((decLoanAmount * c_fltInterestRate) * _
                      c_intMonthsInTerm);
```

Constant definitions have the following syntax:

```
const datatype name = value;
```

For example, to define a constant to hold the value of pi, you could use a statement such as this:

```
const float c_pi = 3.14159265358979;
```

Note how I prefix the constant name with c_. I do this so that it's easier to determine what's a variable and what's a constant when reading code. See the section on naming conventions later in this hour for more information.

After a constant is defined, you can use the constant's name anywhere in code in place of the constant's value. For example, to output the result of two times the value of pi, you could use a statement like this (the * character is used for multiplication and is covered in the next hour):

```
Debug.WriteLine(c_pi * 2);
```

Using the constant is much easier and less error prone than typing this:

```
Debug.WriteLine(3.14159265358979 * 2);
```

Constants can be referenced only in the scope in which they are defined. I discuss scope in the section "Determining Scope."

Declaring and Referencing Variables

Variables are similar to constants in that when you reference a variable's name in code, C# substitutes the variable's value in place of the variable name when the code executes. This doesn't happen at compile time, however. Instead, it happens at runtime—the moment the variable is referenced. This is because variables, unlike constants, may have their values changed at any time.

Declaring Variables

NEW TERM The act of defining a variable is called *declaring*. (Variables with scope other than local are dimensioned in a slightly different way, as discussed in the section on scope.) You've already defined variables in previous hours, so the statement should look familiar to you:

datatype *variablename* = *initialvalue*;

> It's possible to declare multiple variables of the same type on a single line. However, this is often considered bad form because it tends to make the code harder to read.

You don't have to specify an initial value for a variable, although being able to do so in the declaration statement is very cool and useful. For example, to create a new string variable and initialize it with a value, you could use two statements, such as the following:

```
string strName;
strName = "Chris Bermejo";
```

However, if you know the initial value of the variable at design time, you can include it on the declaration statement, like this:

```
string strName = "Chris Bermejo";
```

Note, however, that supplying an initial value doesn't make this a constant; it's still a variable, and the content of the variable can be changed at any time. This method of creating an initial value eliminates a code statement and makes the code a bit easier to read because you don't have to go looking to see where the variable is initialized.

It's important to note that C# is a strongly typed language; therefore, you must always declare the data type of a variable. In addition, C# requires that all variables be initialized before they're used.

 Visual Basic programmers should note that C# will not default numeric variables to 0 or strings to empty strings.

For example, the following statements would result in a compiler error in C#: Type or namespace "single" could not be found.

```
single sngMyValue;
Debug.WriteLine(sngMyValue + 2);
```

 You cannot use a reserved word to name a constant or a variable. For instance, you couldn't use public or private as variable names.

Passing Literal Values to a Variable

The syntax of passing a *literal* value (a hard-coded value such as 6 or "test") to a variable depends on the data type of the variable.

For strings, you must pass the value in quotes, like this:

```
strCollegeName = "Bellevue University";
```

There is one caveat when assigning literal values to strings: C# interprets slashes (\) as being a special type of escape sequence. If you pass a literal string containing one or more slashes to a variable, you'll get an error. What you have to do in such instances is preface the literal with the symbol @, like this:

```
strFilePath = @"c:\Temp";
```

When C# encounters the @ symbol, it knows not to treat slashes in the string as escape sequences.

To pass a literal value to a char variable, use single quotes instead of double quotes, like this:

```
chaMyCharacter = 'j';
```

For numeric values, you don't enclose the value in anything:

```
IntAnswerToEverything = 42;
```

Using Variables in Expressions

Variables can be used anywhere an expression is expected. The arithmetic functions, for example, operate on expressions. You could add two literal numbers and store the result in a variable like the following:

```
IntMyVariable = 2 + 5;
```

You could replace either or both literal numbers with numeric variables or constants, as shown next:

```
IntMyVariable = intFirstValue + 5;
IntMyVariable = 2 + intSecondValue;
IntMyVariable = intFirstValue + intSecondValue;
```

Variables are a fantastic way to store values during code execution, and you'll use variables all the time—from performing decisions and creating loops to using them only as a temporary place to stick a value. Remember to use a constant when you know the value at design time and the value won't change. When you don't know the value ahead of time or the value may change, use a variable with a data type appropriate to the function of the variable.

In C#, variables are created as objects. Feel free to create a variable and explore the members of the variable. You do this by entering the variable name and pressing a period (this will work only after you've entered the statement that defines the variable).

Working with Arrays

An array is a special type of variable—it's a variable with multiple dimensions. Think of an ordinary variable as a single mail slot. You can retrieve or change the contents of the mail slot by referencing the variable. An array is like having an entire row of mail slots (called elements). You can retrieve and set the contents of any of the individual mail slots at any time by referencing the single array variable. You do this by using an index that points to the appropriate slot.

Declaring Arrays

Before you can use an array, you must first declare it (the same as you have to declare variables). Consider the following statements:

```
string[] strMyArray;
strMyArray = new string[10];
```

The first statement declares strMyArray as an array, and the second statement defines the array as having 10 string elements.

The number in brackets specifies how many "mail slots" the array variable will contain, and it can be a literal value, a constant, or the value of another variable.

Referencing Array Variables

To place a value in an array index, you specify the index number when referencing the variable. Most computer operations consider 0 to be the first value in a series—not 1, as you might expect. This is how array indexing behaves. For example, for an array dimensioned with 10 elements, you would reference the elements sequentially using the indexes 0, 1, 2, 3, 4, 5, 6, 7, 8, and 9. Notice that the upper index is one fewer than the total elements because 0 is the first index, not 1. Therefore, to place a value in the first element of the array variable, you would use 0 as the index, like this:

```
strMyArray[0] = "This value goes in the first element";
```

The data type specified for the array variable is used for all the elements in the array. This is where the object data type can come in handy. For example, suppose you wanted to store the following pieces of information in an array: Name, City, State, Age, and DateOfBirth. As you can see, you need to store string values for Name, City, and State, but you need to store a number for Age. By dimensioning an array variable as data type object, you can store all these different types of data in the array; C# will determine the data type of each element as the data is placed into it. The following shows an example of a declaration of such an array:

```
object[] objPersonalInfo;
objPersonalInfo = new object[10];
```

Again, after it's defined, you can reference the array variable as you would an ordinary variable, with the exception that you must include an index. For example, you could populate the array using code like this:

```
objPersonalInfo[0] = "James Foxall";
objPersonalInfo[1] = "Papillion";
objPersonalInfo[2] = "Nebraska";
objPersonalInfo[3] = 32;
```

Creating Multidimensional Arrays

Array variables require only one declaration, yet they can store numerous pieces of data; this makes them perfect for storing sets of related information. The array example shown previously is a single-dimension array. Arrays can be much more complex than this example and can have multiple dimensions of data. For example, a single array variable could be defined to store the personal information shown previously for different people. Multidimensional arrays are declared with multiple parameters such as the following:

```
int[,] intMeasurements;
intMeasurements = new int[3,2];
```

These statements create a two-dimensional array. The first dimension (defined as having three elements) serves as an index to the second dimension (defined as having two elements). Suppose you wanted to store the height and weight of three people in this array. You reference the array as you would a single-dimension array, but you include the extra parameter index. The two indexes together specify an element, much like coordinates in Battleship relate to specific spots on the game board. Figure 12.1 illustrates how the elements are related.

Elements are grouped according to the first index specified; think of the first set of indexes as being a single-dimension array. For example, to store the height and weight of a person in the array's first dimension, you could use code such as the following:

```
intMeasurements[0,0] = FirstPersonsHeight;
intMeasurements[0,1] = FirstPersonsWeight;
```

I find it helpful to create constants for the array elements, which makes array references much easier to understand. Consider the following:

```
const int c_Height = 0;
const int c_Weight = 1;
intMeasurements[0,c_Height] = FirstPersonsHeight;
intMeasurements[0,c_Weight] = FirstPersonsWeight;
```

12

FIGURE 12.1

Two-dimensional arrays are like a wall of mail slots.

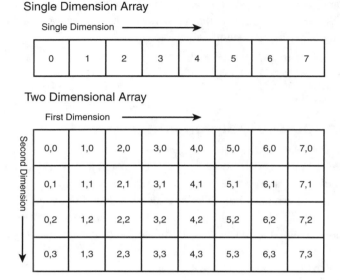

Single Dimension Array

Single Dimension ⟶

0	1	2	3	4	5	6	7

Two Dimensional Array

First Dimension ⟶

Second Dimension ⟶

0,0	1,0	2,0	3,0	4,0	5,0	6,0	7,0
0,1	1,1	2,1	3,1	4,1	5,1	6,1	7,1
0,2	1,2	2,2	3,2	4,2	5,2	6,2	7,2
0,3	1,3	2,3	3,3	4,3	5,3	6,3	7,3

You could then store the height and weight of the second and third person like this:

```
intMeasurements[1,c_Height] = SecondPersonsHeight;
intMeasurements[1,c_Weight] = SecondPersonsWeight;
intMeasurements[2,c_Height] = ThirdPersonsHeight;
intMeasurements[2,c_Width] = ThirdPersonsWeight;
```

In this array, I've used the first dimension to differentiate people. I've used the second dimension to store a height and weight for each element in the first dimension.

Because I've consistently stored heights in the first slot of the array's second dimension and weights in the second slot of the array's second dimension, it becomes easy to work with these pieces of data. For example, you can retrieve the height and weight of a single person as long as you know the first dimension index used to store the data. You could, for instance, print out the total weight of all three people using the following code:

```
Debug.WriteLine(intMeasurements[0,c_Weight] + intMeasurements[1,c_Weight] +
                intMeasurements[2,c_Weight]);
```

When working with arrays, keep the following points in mind:

- The first element in any dimension of an array has an index of 0.
- Dimension an array to hold only as much data as you intend to put into it.
- Dimension an array with a data type appropriate to the values to be placed in the array's elements.

Arrays are an extremely powerful and easy way to store and work with related sets of data in C# code. Arrays can make working with larger sets of data much simpler and more efficient than using other methods. To maximize your effectiveness with arrays, study the for loop discussed in Hour 15, "Looping for Efficiency." Using a for loop, you can quickly iterate through all the elements in an array.

This section discussed the rectangular type of a C# multidimensional array. C# also supports another type of multidimensional array called *jagged*. Jagged arrays are an array of one-dimensional arrays, each of which can be of different lengths. However, teaching jagged arrays is beyond the scope of this book.

Determining Scope

Constants, variables, and arrays are extremely useful ways to store and retrieve data in C# code. Hardly a program is written that doesn't use at least one of these elements. To properly use them, however, it's critical that you understand *scope*.

You had your first encounter with scope in Hour 11, "Creating and Calling Methods," with the keywords private and public. You learned that code is written in procedures and that procedures are stored in modules. Scope refers to the level that a constant, a variable, an array, or a procedure can be "seen" in code. For a constant or variable, scope can be one of the following:

- Block level
- Method level (local)
- Private level

12

Scope has the same effect on array variables as it does on ordinary variables. For the sake of clarity, I'll reference variables in this discussion on scope, but understand that what I discuss applies equally to arrays.

The different levels of scope are explained in the following sections.

Understanding Block Scope

 NEW TERM *Block scope*, also called structure scope, is when a variable is declared within a structure, and if so, it gives the variable block scope.

Structures are coding constructs that consist of two statements as opposed to one. For example, the standard do structure is used to create a loop; it looks like this:

> C# uses the word structure to mean a user-defined type. However, when talking about code, structure is also used to mean a block of code that has a beginning and an end. For the purpose of this discussion, it is this code block that I am referring to.

```
do
    <statements to execute in the loop
while(i <10)
```

Another example is the for loop, which looks like this:

```
for (int I = 1; i<10;i++)
{
    <statements to execute when expression is True>
}
```

If a variable is declared within a structure, the variable's scope is confined to the structure; the variable isn't created until the declaration statement occurs, and it's destroyed when the structure completes. If a variable is needed only within a structure, think about declaring it within the structure to give it block scope. Consider the following example:

```
if (blnCreateLoop)
{
    int intCounter ;

for (intCounter=1; intCounter<=100; intCounter++)
    // Do something
}
```

By placing the variable declaration statement within the if structure, you ensure that the variable is created only if it is needed. In fact, you can create a block simply by enclosing statements in opening and closing braces like this:

```
{
    int intMyVariable = 10;
    Console.WriteLine(intMyVariable);
}
```

The various structures, including looping and decision-making structures, are discussed in later hours.

Understanding Method-Level (Local) Scope

NEW TERM When you declare a constant or variable within a method, that constant or variable has *method-level,* or *local,* scope. Most of the variables you'll create will have method scope. In fact, all the variables you've created in previous hours have had method-level scope. You can reference a local constant or variable within the same method, but it isn't visible to other methods. If you try to reference a local constant or variable from a method other than the one in which it's defined, C# returns a compile error to the method making the reference (the variable or constant doesn't exist). It's generally considered the best practice to declare all your local variables at the top of a method, but C# doesn't care where you place declaration statements within a method. Note, however, that if you place a declaration statement within a structure, the corresponding variable will have block scope, not local scope.

Understanding Private-Level Scope

When a constant or variable has private-level scope, it can be viewed by all methods within the class containing the declaration. To methods in all other classes, however, the constant or variable doesn't exist. To create a constant or variable with private-level scope, you must place the declaration within a class but not within a method. Class member declarations are generally done at the beginning of the class (right after the opening brace of the class). Use private-level scope when many methods must share the same variable and when passing the value as a parameter is not a workable solution.

For all modules other than those used to generate forms, it's easy to add code to the declarations section; simply add the declaration statements just after the class declaration line and prior to any method definitions, as shown in Figure 12.2.

Classes used to generate forms have lots of system-generated code within them, so it might not be so obvious where to place private-level variables. C# inserts many private statements in classes used to build forms, so place your variable declarations after any and all form-type declaration statements in such classes (see Figure 12.3).

12

FIGURE 12.2

The declarations section exists above all declared methods.

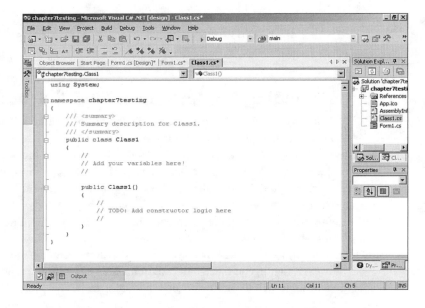

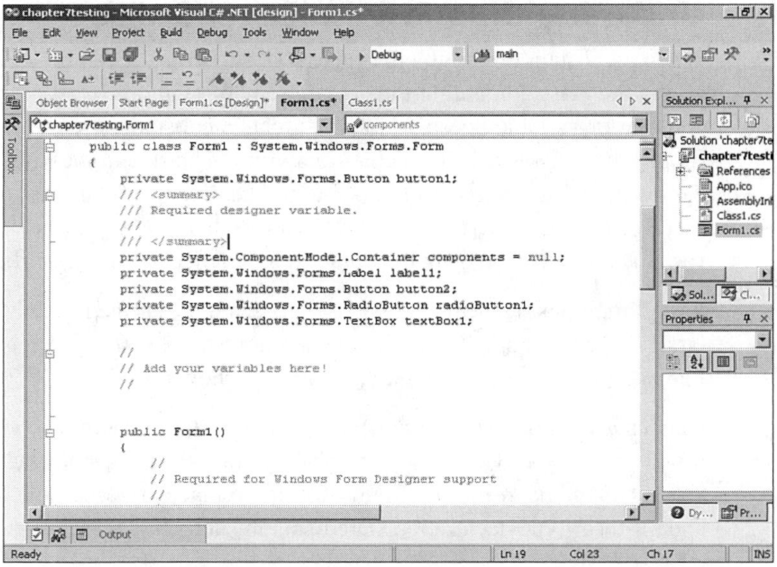

FIGURE 12.3

The declarations section includes the C# generated statements.

In general, the smaller the scope the better. When possible, give a variable block or local scope. If you have to increase scope, attempt to make the variable a private-level variable. You should use public variables only when absolutely necessary (and there are times when it is necessary to do so). The higher the scope, the more possibilities exist for problems and the more difficult it is to debug those problems.

Naming Conventions

To make code more self-documenting (always an important goal) and to reduce the chance of programming errors, you need an easy way to determine the exact data type of a variable or the exact type of a referenced control in C# code.

Variable naming conventions have long been a hot topic. With the release of .NET, Microsoft has officially recommended that you *not* use naming conventions (although it's hard to imagine why). As a professional developer, I find this idea counterproductive, and most other developers I have spoken with have no plans to abandon using naming conventions. Because I so firmly believe in them and because they aid the learning process, I have used them, and I teach them in this book. Please be aware that if you don't like naming conventions, you don't have to use them. However, I *strongly* recommend that you do use naming conventions; the benefits they provide are considerable.

12

Using Prefixes to Denote Data Type

Table 12.3 lists the prefixes of the common data types.

TABLE 12.3 Prefixes for Common Data Types

Data Type	Prefix	Value
Boolean	bln	blnLoggedIn
Byte	byt	bytAge
Char	chr	chrQuantity
Decimal	dec	decSalary
Double	dbl	dblCalculatedResult
Integer	int	intLoopCounter
Long	lng	lngCustomerID

TABLE 12.3   continued

Data Type	Prefix	Value
Object	obj	objWord
Short	sho	shoTotalParts
String	str	strFirstName

> The prefix of obj should be reserved for when a specific prefix isn't available. The most common use of this prefix is when referencing Automation libraries of COM applications. For instance, when automating Microsoft Word, you create an instance of Word's Application object. Because no prefix exists specifically for Word objects, obj works just fine (that is, `Word.Application objWord = new Word.Application);`.

Denoting Scope Using Variable Prefixes

Prefixes are useful not only to denote data types, they also can be used to denote scope (see Table 12.4). In particularly large applications, a scope designator is almost a necessity. Again, C# doesn't care whether you use prefixes, but consistently using prefixes benefits you as well as others who have to review your code.

TABLE 12.4   Prefixes for Variable Scope

Prefix	Description	Example
g	Global	g_strSavePath
m	Private to class	m_blnDataChanged
(no prefix)	Nonstatic variable, local to method	

Other Prefixes

Prefixes aren't just for variables. All standard objects (including forms and controls) can use a three-character prefix. There are simply too many controls and objects to list all the prefixes here, although you will find that I use control prefixes throughout this book.

Summary

In this hour, you learned how to eliminate magic numbers by creating constants. By using constants in place of literal values, you increase code readability, reduce the possibilities of coding errors, and make it much easier to change a value in the future.

In addition, you learned how to create variables for data elements in which the initial value isn't known at design time or for elements whose values will be changed at run-time. You learned how arrays add dimensions to variables and how to declare and reference them in your code.

C# enforces strict data typing, and in this hour you learned about the various data types and how they're used, as well as tips for choosing data types and functions for converting data from one type to another. Finally, you learned about scope—a very important programming concept—and how to manage scope within your projects.

Writing code that can be clearly understood even by those who didn't write it is a worthwhile goal. Naming prefixes goes a long way toward accomplishing this goal. In this hour you learned the naming prefixes for the common data types, and you learned to use prefixes to denote scope.

Q&A

Q. Are any performance tricks related to the many data types?

A. One trick when using whole numbers (values with no decimal places) is to use the data type that matches your processor. For instance, most current home and office computers have 32-bit processors. The C# integer data type is made up of 32 bits. Believe it or not, C# can process an integer variable faster than it can process a short variable, even though the short variable is smaller. This has to do with the architecture of the CPU, memory, and bus. The explanation is complicated, but the end result is that you should usually use integer rather than short, even when working with values that don't require the larger size of the integer.

Q. Are arrays limited to two dimensions?

A. Although I showed only two dimensions (that is, intMeasurements[3,1]), arrays can have many dimensions, such as intMeasurements[3,3,3,4]. The technical maximum is 60 dimensions, but you probably won't use more than three.

12

Workshop

The Workshop is designed to help you anticipate possible questions, review what you've learned, and get you thinking about how to put your knowledge into practice. The answers to the quiz are in Appendix A, "Answers to Quizzes/Exercises."

Quiz

1. What data type would you use to hold currency values?
2. Which data type can be used to hold any kind of data and essentially serves as a generic data type?
3. What values does C# support for type bool?
4. What can you create to eliminate magic numbers by defining a literal value in one place?
5. What type of data element can you create in code that can have its value changed as many times as necessary?
6. What are the first and last indexes of an array dimensioned using `string_strMyArray[5]`?
7. What word is given to describe the visibility of a constant or variable?
8. In general, is it best to limit the scope of a variable or to use the widest scope possible?

Exercises

1. Create a project with a text box, a button, and a label control. When the user clicks the button, move the contents of the text box to a variable, and then move the contents of the variable to the Text property of the label. (Hint: a string variable will do the trick.)
2. Rewrite the following code so that a single array variable is used rather than two standard variables. (Hint: Do not use a multidimensional array.)

```
string strFirstName;
string strLastName ;
strFirstName = "Allison";
strLastName = "Bermejo";
```

HOUR 13

Performing Arithmetic, String Manipulation, and Date/Time Adjustments

Just as arithmetic is a necessary part of everyday life, it's also vital to developing Windows programs. You probably won't write an application that doesn't add, subtract, multiply, or divide some numbers. In this hour, you'll learn how to perform arithmetic in code. You'll also learn about order of operator precedence, which determines how C# evaluates complicated expressions (or equations). After you understand operator precedence, you'll learn how to compare equalities—something you'll do all the time.

NEW TERM   *Boolean logic* is the logic C# itself uses to evaluate expressions in decision-making constructs. If you've never programmed before, Boolean logic may be a new concept to you. However, in this hour I explain what you need to know about Boolean logic to create efficient code that performs as expected. Finally, I show you how to manipulate strings and work with dates and times.

The highlights of this hour include the following:

- Performing arithmetic
- Understanding the order of operator precedence
- Comparing equalities
- Understanding Boolean logic
- Manipulating strings
- Working with dates and times

Performing Basic Arithmetic

To be a programmer, you have to have solid math skills; you'll be performing a lot of basic arithmetic when writing C# applications. To get the results you're looking for in any given calculation, you must

- Know the mathematical operator that performs the desired arithmetic function.
- Understand and correctly use order of precedence.

Using the correct mathematical operator is simple. Most are easy to commit to memory, and you can always look up the ones you're not quite sure of. I'm not going to go into great detail on any of the math functions (if you've made it this far, I'm sure you have a working grasp of math), but I will cover them all.

In Hour 7, "Working with Traditional Controls," I mentioned how the System.Diagnostics.Debug.WriteLine() method prints text to the Output window. I use this method in the examples throughout this hour. You will not be asked to create a project in this chapter, but you may want to try some of these examples in a test project. Because we are planning to use several debug statements, it will be helpful to declare the System.Diagnostics namespace in the header of your class. This permits you to use the methods of the namespace without having to qualify the entire namespace. The following is the line you need to add at the beginning of your class (put it with the other using statements created automatically by C#):

```
using System.Diagnostics;
```

For more specific information on the Debug object, refer to Hour 16, "Debugging Your Code."

Performing Addition

Simple addition is performed using the standard addition symbol, the **+** character. The following line prints the sum of 4, 5, and 6:

```
Debug.WriteLine(4 + 5 + 6);
```

You don't have to use a hard-coded value with arithmetic operators. You can use any of the arithmetic operators on numeric variables and constants. For example:

```
const int c_FirstValue = 4;
const int c_SecondValue = 5;
Debug.WriteLine(c_FirstValue + c_SecondValue);
```

This bit of code prints the sum of the constants c_FirstValue and c_SecondValue, which, in this case, is 9.

Performing Subtraction and Negation

Like the addition operator, you're most likely familiar with the subtraction operator because it's the same one you would use on a calculator or when writing an equation: the – character. The following line of code prints 2 (the total of 6–4):

```
Debug.WriteLine(6 - 4);
```

As with written math, the – character is also used to denote a negative number. For example, to print the value –6, you would use a statement such as the following:

```
Debug.WriteLine(-6);
```

Performing Multiplication

If you work with adding machines, you already know the multiplication operator. The multiplication character is the asterisk (*) character. You can enter this character using Shift+8 or by pressing the * key located in the upper row of the keypad section of the keyboard. Although you would ordinarily use an "×" when writing multiplication equations such as $6 = 3×2$ on paper, you'll receive an error if you try this in code; you have to use the * character. The following statement prints 20 (5 multiplied by 4):

```
Debug.WriteLine(5 * 4);
```

Performing Division

Division is accomplished using the slash (/) operator. This operator is easy to remember if you think of division as fractions. For example, one-eighth is written as 1/8, which literally means one divided by eight. The following statement prints 8 (32 divided by 4):

```
Debug.WriteLine(32 / 4);
```

13

C# overloads the division operator. This means that based on the input arguments, the results may vary. For example, C# division will return an integer when dividing integers, but it will return a fractional number if a float, a double, or a decimal data type is used. Hence, 32 / 5 will return 6, dropping the remainder (2, in this case). If you wanted to return the actual value of the operation 32 / 5, you would have to specify the numbers with decimal places (that is, 32.0 / 5.0).

> The modulus operator (%) can be used to find the remainder of an integer division.

Performing Modulus Arithmetic

NEW TERM | *Modulus arithmetic* is the process of performing division on two numbers but keeping only the remainder. Modulus arithmetic is performed using the % operand, in contrast to using a slash (/) operator symbol. The following are examples of modulus statements and the values they would print:

```
Debug.WriteLine(10 % 5);     // Prints 0

Debug.WriteLine(10 % 3);     // Prints 1

Debug.WriteLine(12 % 4.3);   // Prints 3.4

Debug.WriteLine(13.6 % 5);   // Prints 3.6
```

The first two statements are relatively easy to understand: 5 goes into 10 twice with no remainder and 3 goes into 10 three times with a remainder of 1. C# processes the third statement as 4.3 going into 12 three times with a remainder of 3.4. In the last statement, C# performs the modulus operation as 5 going into 13.6 twice with a remainder of 3.6.

Determining the Order of Operator Precedence

NEW TERM | When several arithmetic operations occur within a single equation (called an expression), C# must resolve the expression in pieces. The order in which these pieces are evaluated is known as *operator precedence*. To fully understand operator precedence, you have to brush up a bit on your algebra (most of the math you perform in code is algebraic).

Consider the following expression:

```
Debug.WriteLine(6 * 5 + 4);
```

Two arithmetic operations occur in this single expression. To evaluate the expression, C# must perform both operations: multiplication and addition. Which operation does C#

perform first? Does it matter? Absolutely. If C# performs the multiplication before the addition, you end up with the following:

Step 1: 6 * 5 = 30

Step 2: 30 + 4 = 34

The final result would be that of C# printing 34. Now look at the same equation with the addition performed prior to multiplication:

Step 1: 5 + 4 = 9

Step 2: 6 * 9 = 54

In this case, C# would print 54—a drastically different number from the one computed when the multiplication is performed first. To prevent these types of errors, C# consistently performs arithmetic operations in the same order—the order of operator precedence (in this case, multiplication and then addition). Table 13.1 lists the order of operator precedence for *arithmetic* and *Boolean operators*. (Boolean operators are discussed later in this hour.) If you're familiar with algebra, you'll note that the order of precedence used by C# is the same as that used in algebraic formulas.

TABLE 13.1   C#'s Order of Operator Precedence, Highest to Lowest

Category	Operators
Multiplicative	* / %
Additive	+ -
Equality	== (equal), != (not equal)
Logical AND	&
Logical XOR	^
Logical OR	|
Conditional AND	&&
Conditional OR	||
Conditional	?:

13

Notice that two equal signs are used to denote equality, not one as you might expect.

NEW TERM   All *comparison operators* (discussed in the next section) have an equal precedence. When operators have an equal precedence, C# evaluates them from left to right. Notice that the multiplication and division operators have an equal precedence, so in an expression that has both, the operators would be evaluated from left to right. The same holds true for addition and subtraction. When expressions contain operators from more than one category (arithmetic, comparison, or logical), arithmetic operators are evaluated first, comparison operators are evaluated next, and *logical operators* are evaluated last.

Just as when writing an equation on paper, you can use parentheses to override the order of operator precedence. Operations placed within parentheses are always evaluated first. Consider the previous example:

```
Debug.WriteLine(6 * 5 + 4);
```

Using the order of operator precedence, C# evaluates the equation like this:

```
Debug.WriteLine((6 * 5) + 4);
```

The multiplication is performed first, and then the addition. If you wanted the addition performed prior to the multiplication, you could write the statement like this:

```
Debug.WriteLine(6 * (5 + 4));
```

> When writing complex expressions, you absolutely must keep in mind the order of operator precedence and use parentheses to override the default operator precedence when necessary. Personally, I try to always use parentheses so that I'm sure of what is happening and my code is easier to read.

Comparing Equalities

Comparing values, particularly variables, is even more common than performing arithmetic (but you need to know how C# arithmetic works before you can understand the evaluation of equalities).

Comparison operators are most often used in decision-making structures, as explained in the next hour. Indeed, these operators are best understood using a simple if decision structure. In an if construct, C# considers the expression on the if statement, and if the expression equates to true, the code statement(s) are executed. For example, the following is an if operation (a silly one at that) expressed in English, not in C# code:

IF DOGS BARK, THEN SMILE.

If this were in C# code format, C# would evaluate the if condition, which in this case is *dogs bark*. If the condition is found to be true, the code following the expression is performed. Because dogs bark, you'd smile. Notice how these two things (dogs barking and you smiling) are relatively unrelated. This doesn't matter; the point is that if the condition evaluates to true, certain actions (statements) occur.

You'll often compare the value of one variable to that of another variable or to a specific value when making decisions. The following are some basic comparisons and how C# evaluates them:

```
Debug.WriteLine(6 > 3);        //  Evaluates to true

Debug.WriteLine(3 == 4);       //  Evaluates to false

Debug.WriteLine(3 >= 3);       //  Evaluates to true

Debug.WriteLine(5 <= 4);       //  Evaluates to false
```

Performing comparisons is pretty straightforward. If you get stuck writing a particular comparison, attempt to write it in English before creating it in code.

Understanding Boolean Logic

Boolean logic is a special type of arithmetic/comparison. Boolean logic is used to evaluate expressions down to either true or false. This may be a new concept to you, but don't worry; it's not difficult to understand. Boolean logic is performed using a logical operator. Consider the following sentence:

If black is a color and wood comes from trees then print "ice cream."

At first glance, it might seem that this is nonsensical. However, C# could make sense of this statement using Boolean logic. First, notice that three expressions are actually being evaluated within this single sentence. I've added parentheses in the following sentence to clarify two of the expressions. *If (black is a color) and (wood comes from trees) then print "ice cream."*

Boolean logic evaluates every expression to either true or false. Therefore, substituting true or false for each of these expressions yields the following:

if (true) And (true) then print "ice cream."

Now, for the sake of clarity, here is the same sentence with parentheses placed around the final expression to be evaluated:

If (True And True) then print "ice cream."

This is the point where the logical operators come into play. The And (**&&**) operator returns true if the expressions on each side of the And (**&&**) operator are true (see Table

13

13.2 for a complete list of logical operators). In the sentence we're considering, the expressions on both sides of the And (**&&**) operator are true, so the expression evaluates to true. Replacing the expression with true yields:

If True then print "ice cream."

This would result in the words "ice cream" being printed. If the expression had evaluated to false, nothing would be printed. As you'll see in the next hour, the decision constructs always fully evaluate their expressions to either true or false, and statements execute according to the results.

TABLE 13.2   Logical (Boolean) Operators

Operator	Description
And (&&)	Evaluates to true when the expressions on both sides are true.
Not (!)	Evaluates to true when its expression evaluates to false; otherwise, it returns false (the true/false value of the expression is negated, or reversed).
Or (‖)	Evaluates to true if an expression on either side evaluates to true.
Xor (^)	Evaluates to true if one, and only one, expression on either side evaluates to true.

Each of these is discussed in the following sections.

Using the And (&&) Operator

The And (&&) operator is used to perform a logical conjunction. If the expressions on both sides of the And (&&) operator evaluate to true, the And (&&) operation evaluates to true. If either expression is false, the And (&&) operation evaluates to false, as illustrated in the following examples:

```
Debug.WriteLine(true && true);          // Prints true

Debug.WriteLine(true && false);         // Prints false

Debug.WriteLine(false && true);         // Prints false

Debug.WriteLine(false && false);        // Prints false

Debug.WriteLine((32 > 4) && (6 == 6));  // Prints true
```

Using the Not(!) Operator

The Not(!) operator performs a logical negation. That is, it returns the opposite of the expression. Consider the following examples:

```
Debug.WriteLine(! (true));        // Prints false

Debug.WriteLine(! (false));       // Prints true

Debug.WriteLine(! (5 == 5));      // Prints false

Debug.WriteLine(!(4 < 2));        // Prints true
```

The first two statements are easy enough; the opposite of true is false and vice versa. For the third statement, remember that C#'s operator precedence dictates that arithmetic operators are evaluated first (even if no parentheses are used), so the first step of the evaluation would look like this:

```
Debug.WriteLine( ! (true));
```

The opposite of true is false, of course, so C# prints false.

The fourth statement would evaluate to:

```
Debug.WriteLine( !(false));
```

This happens because 4 is *not* less than 2, which is the expression C# evaluates first. Because the opposite of false is true, this statement would print true.

Using the Or (||) Operator

The Or(||) operator is used to perform a logical disjunction. If the expression to the left *or* right of the Or(||) operator evaluates to true, the Or(||) operation evaluates to true. The following are examples using Or(||) operations, and their results:

```
Debug.WriteLine(true || true);         // Prints true

Debug.WriteLine(true || false);        // Prints true

Debug.WriteLine(false || true);        // Prints true

Debug.WriteLine(false || false);       // Prints false

Debug.WriteLine((32 < 4) || (6 == 6)); // Prints true
```

Using the Xor (^) Operator

The Xor(^) operator performs a nifty little function. I personally haven't had to use it much, but it's great for those times when its functionality is required. If one—and only one—of the expressions on either side of the Xor(^) operator is true, the Xor(^) operation evaluates to true. Take a close look at the following statement examples to see how this works:

```
Debug.WriteLine(true ^ true);          // Prints false

Debug.WriteLine(true ^ false);         // Prints true
```

13

```
Debug.WriteLine(false ^ true);              // Prints true

Debug.WriteLine(false ^ false);             // Prints false

Debug.WriteLine((32 < 4) ^ (6 == 6));       // Prints true
```

Manipulating Strings

Recall from the previous hour that a string is text. Although string manipulation isn't technically arithmetic, the things that you do with strings are very similar to things you do with numbers, such as adding two strings together; string manipulation is much like creating equations. Chances are you'll be working with strings a lot in your applications. C# includes a number of methods that enable you to do things with strings, such as retrieve a portion of a string or find one string within another. In the following sections, you'll learn the basics of string manipulation.

Concatenating Strings of Text

NEW TERM C# makes it possible to "add" two strings of text together to form one string. Although purists will say it's not truly a form of arithmetic, it's very much like performing arithmetic on strings, so this hour was the logical place in which to present this material. The process of adding two strings together is called *concatenation*. Concatenation is very common. For example, you may want to concatenate variables with hard-coded strings to display meaningful messages to the user, such as Are you sure you wish to delete the user XXX?, where XXX is the contents of a variable.

To concatenate two strings, you use the + operator as shown in this line of code:

```
Debug.WriteLine("This is" + "a test.");
```

This statement would print:

```
This isa test.
```

Notice that there is no space between the words *is* and *a*. You could easily add a space by including one after the word *is* in the first string or before the *a* in the second string, or you could concatenate the space as a separate string, like this:

```
Debug.WriteLine("This is" + " " + "a test.");
```

NEW TERM Text placed directly within quotes is called a *literal*. Variables are concatenated in the same way as literals and can even be concatenated with literals. The following code creates two variables, sets the value of the first variable to "Allan," and sets the value of the second variable to the result of concatenating the variable with a space and the literal "Reed":

```
string strFullName;
string strFirstName = "Allan";

strFullName = strFirstName + " " + "Reed";
```

The final result is that the variable strFullName contains the string Allan Reed. Get comfortable concatenating strings of text—you'll do this often.

In C#, strings are *immutable*. What this means is that they never change. When you concatenate two strings together, neither is modified; instead a new string is created. Eventually, the garbage collector (discussed in Hour 24, "The 10,000-Foot View") will clean up the unused strings. However, if you're going to be concatenating a lot of strings, this could have an adverse effect on system resources (until the garbage collector springs into action). C# includes a highly efficient way to concatenate strings via System.Text. StringBuilder. Although I can't go into the details here, I highly encourage you to research this if you plan to concatenate a lot of strings at once.

Using the Basic String Methods and Properties

The .NET Framework includes a number of functions that make working with strings of text considerably easier than it might be otherwise. These functions let you easily retrieve a piece of text from a string, compute the number of characters in a string, and even determine whether one string contains another. The following sections summarize the basic string functions.

Determining the Number of Characters Using Length

The Length property of the string object returns the variable's length. The following statement prints 26, the total number of characters in the literal string "Pink Floyd reigns supreme." Remember, the quotes that surround the string tell C# that the text within them is a literal; they are not part of the string.

```
Debug.WriteLine(("Pink Floyd reigns supreme.").Length);      // Prints 26
```

Retrieving Text from a String Using the Substring() Method

The Substring() method retrieves a part of a string.

The Substring() method can be used with the following parameters:

```
public string Substring(startposition,numberofcharacters);
```

13

For example, the following statement prints Queen, the first five characters of the string.

```
Debug.WriteLine(("Queen to Queen's Level Three.").Substring(0,5));
```

The arguments used in this Substring example are 0 and 5. The 0 indicates starting at the 0 position of the string (beginning). The 5 indicates the specified length to return (characters to retrieve).

The Substring() method is commonly used with the IndexOf() method (discussed shortly) to retrieve the path portion of a variable containing a filename and path combination, such as c:\Myfile.txt. If you know where the \ character is, you can use Substring() to get the path.

> If the number of characters requested is greater than the number of characters in the string, an exception (error) occurs. If you're unsure about the number of characters in the string, use the Length property of the string to find out. (Exception handling is reviewed in Hour 16, "Debugging Your Code.")

Determining Whether One String Contains Another Using IndexOf() Method

At times you'll need to determine whether one string exists within another. For example, suppose you let users enter their full name into a text box, and that you want to separate the first and last names before saving them into individual fields in a database. The easiest way to do this is to look for the space in the string that separates the first name from the last. You could use a loop to examine each character in the string until you find the space, but C# includes a string method that does this for you, faster and easier than you could do it yourself: the IndexOf() method. The basic IndexOf() method has the following syntax:

```
MyString.IndexOf(searchstring);
```

The IndexOf() method of a string searches the string for the occurrence of a string passed as an argument. If the string is found, the location of character at the start of the string is returned. If the search string is not found within the other string, -1 is returned. The IndexOf() method can be used with the following arguments:

- `public int IndexOf(searchstring);`
- `public int IndexOf(searchstring, startinglocation);`
- `public int IndexOf(searchstring, startinglocation, numberofcharacterstosearch);`

The following code searches a variable containing the text "Jayson Goss", locates the space, and uses the Substring() method and Length property to place the first and last names in separate variables.

```
string strFullName = "Jayson Goss";
string strFirstName, strLastName;
int intLocation, intLength;

intLength = strFullName.Length;
intLocation = strFullName.IndexOf(" ");

strFirstName = strFullName.Substring(0,intLocation );
strLastName = strFullName.Substring(intLocation + 1);
```

> This code assumes that a space will be found and that it won't be the first or last character in the string. In your applications, your code may need to be more robust, including checking to ensure that IndexOf() returned a value other than -1, which would indicate that no space was found.

When this code runs, IndexOf() returns 6, the location in which the first space is found. Notice how I subtracted an additional character when using SubString() to initialize the strLastName variable; this was to take the space into account.

Trimming Beginning and Trailing Spaces from a String

As you work with strings, you'll often encounter situations in which spaces exist at the beginning or ending of strings. The .NET Framework includes the following four methods for automatically removing spaces from the beginning or end of a string:

Method	Description
String.Trim	Removes white spaces from the beginning and end of a string.
String.TrimEnd	Removes characters specified in an array of characters from the end of a string.
String.TrimStart	Removes characters specified in an array of characters from the beginning of a string.
String.Remove	Removes a specified number of characters from a specified index position in a string.

13

Working with Dates and Times

Dates are a unique beast. In some ways, they act like strings, in which you can concatenate and parse pieces. In other ways, dates seem more like numbers in that you can add to or subtract from them. Although you'll often perform math-type functions on dates (such as adding a number of days to a date or determining the number of months between two dates), you don't use the typical arithmetic operations. Instead, you use functions specifically designed for working with dates.

Understanding the DateTime Data Type

Working with dates is very common (suppose, for example, that you want your program to determine when a service contract expires). No matter the application, you'll probably need to create a variable to hold a date using the DateTime data type. You can get a date into a DateTime variable in several ways. Recall that when setting a string variable to a literal value, the literal is enclosed in quotes. When setting a numeric variable to a literal number, the number is not closed in quotes:

```
string strMyString = "This is a string literal" ;
int intMyInteger = 69 ;
```

The more common way to set a DateTime variable to a literal date is to instantiate the variable passing in the date, like this (year, month, day):

```
DateTime objMyBirthday = new DateTime(1969,7,22);
```

You cannot pass a string directly to a DateTime variable. For instance, if you let the user enter a date into a text box and you want to move the entry to a DateTime variable, you'll have to parse out the string to be able to adhere to one of the allowable DateTime constructors. The DateTime data type is one of the more complicated data types. This chapter will expose you to enough information to get started, but this is only the tip of the iceberg. I suggest reviewing the MSDN documentation of this curious data type for more information.

It's important to note that DateTime variables store a date and a time—always. For example, the following code:

```
DateTime objMyBirthday = new DateTime(1969,7,22);
Debug.WriteLine(objMyBirthday.ToString());
```

Produces this output:

```
7/22/1969 12:00:00 AM
```

Although a DateTime variable always holds a date and a time, on occasion, you'll only be concerned with either the date or the time. Notice that the previous example printed the time `12:00:00` AM, even though no time was specified for the variable. This is the default time placed in a DateTime variable when only a date is specified. Later, I'll show you how to use the GetDateTimeFormats() method to retrieve just a date or a time.

Adding to or Subtracting from a Date or Time

To add a specific amount of time (such as one day or three months) to a specific date or time, you use methods of the DateTime class (see Table 13.3). These methods do not change the value of the current DataTime variable; instead, they return a new DateTime instance whose value is the result of the operation.

TABLE 13.3   Available Data Adding Methods (Source MSDN)

Method	Description
Add	Adds the value of the specified TimeSpan instance to the value of this instance.
AddDays	Adds the specified number of days to the value of this instance.
AddHours	Adds the specified number of hours to the value of this instance.
AddMilliseconds	Adds the specified number of milliseconds to the value of this instance.
AddMinutes	Adds the specified number of minutes to the value of this instance.
AddMonths	Adds the specified number of months to the value of this instance.
AddSeconds	Adds the specified number of seconds to the value of this instance.
AddYears	Adds the specified number of years to the value of this instance.

For instance, to add six months to the date 7/22/69, you could use the following statements:

```
DateTime objMyBirthday = new DateTime(1969,7,22);
DateTime objNewDate = objMyBirthday.AddMonths(6);
```

After this second statement executes, `objNewDate` contains the date `1/22/1970` `12:00:00` AM.

The following code shows sample addition methods and the date they would return:

```
objNewDate = objMyBirthday.AddYears(2);      // Returns 7/22/1971   12:00:00 AM

objNewDate = objMyBirthday.AddMonths(5);     // Returns 12/22/1971   12:00:00 AM

objNewDate = objMyBirthday.AddMonths(-1);    // Returns 6/22/1971   12:00:00 AM

objNewDate = objMyBirthday.AddHours(7);      // Returns 7/22/1969   7:00:00 AM
```

13

Retrieving Parts of a Date

Sometimes, it can be extremely useful to know just a part of a date. For example, you may have let a user enter his or her birth date, and you want to perform an action based on the month in which they were born. To retrieve part of a date, the DateTime class exposes properties such as Month, Day, Year, Hour, Minute, Second, and so on.

The following should illustrate the retrieval of some properties of the DateTime class(the instance date is still 7/21/1969):

```
objMyBirthday.Month          // Returns 7

objMyBirthday.Day            // Returns 22

objMyBirthday.DayOfWeek      // Returns DayOfWeek.Monday
```

The Hour property will return the hour in military format. Also, note that DayOfWeek returns an enumerated value.

Formatting Dates and Times

As I stated earlier, at times you'll want to work with only the date or a time within a DateTime variable. In addition, you'll probably want to control the format in which a date or time is displayed. All this and more can be accomplished via the DateTime class by way of the following:

- Using the DateTime methods to retrieve formatted strings
- Using standard-format strings
- Using custom-format strings

I can't possibly show you everything regarding formatting a DateTime value here, but I do want to show you how to use formatting to output either the date portion or the time portion of a DateTime variable. (The DateTime class is comprehensive; you'll most likely want to investigate it more thoroughly as you continue in your programming efforts.)

The following illustrates some basic formatting methods available with the DateTime class. (Note that the instance date is still 7/22/1969 12:00:00 AM)

```
objMyBirthday.ToLongDateString();    // Returns Monday, July 21, 1969

objMyBirthday.ToShortDateString();   // Returns 7/21/1969

objMyBirthday.ToLongTimeString();    // Returns 12:00:00 AM

objMyBirthday.ToShortTimeString();   // Returns 12:00 AM
```

Retrieving the Current System Date and Time

C# gives you the capability to retrieve the current system date and time. Again, this is accomplished by way of the DateTime class. For example, the Today property returns the current system date. To place the current system date into a new DateTime variable, for example, you could use a statement such as this:

```
DateTime objToday =  DateTime.Today;
```

To retrieve the current system date *and* time, use the Now property of DateTime, like this:

```
DateTime objToday =  DateTime.Now;
```

Commit DateTime.Today and DateTime.Now to memory. You'll need to retrieve the system date and/or time in an application, and this is by far the easiest way to get that information.

Summary

Being able to work with all sorts of data is crucial to your success as a C# developer. Just as you need to understand basic math to function in society, you need to be able to perform basic math in code to write even the simplest of applications. Knowing the arithmetic operators and understanding the order of operator precedence will take you a long way in performing math using C# code.

Boolean logic is a special form of evaluation used by C# to evaluate simple and complex expressions alike down to a value of true or false. In the following hours, you'll learn how to create loops and how to perform decisions in code. What you learned here about Boolean logic is critical to your success with loops and decision structures; you'll use Boolean logic perhaps even more often than you'll perform arithmetic.

Manipulating strings and dates each takes special considerations. In this hour, you learned how to work with both types of data to extract portions of values and to add pieces of data together to form a new whole. String manipulation is pretty straightforward, and you'll get the hang of it soon enough as you start to use some of the string functions. Date manipulation, on the other hand, can be a bit tricky. Even experienced developers need to refer to the online help at times. You learned the basics in this hour, but don't be afraid to experiment on your own.

13

Q&A

Q. **Should I always specify parentheses to ensure that operators are evaluated as I expect them to be?**

A. C# never fails to evaluate expressions according to the order of operator precedence, so using parentheses isn't necessary when the order of precedence is correct for an expression. However, using parentheses assures you that the expression is being evaluated and may make the expression easier to read by other people. This really is your choice.

Q. **I would like to learn more about the properties and methods available in the DateTime structure; where can I find all the members listed?**

A. I would look at the DateTime members documentation found within the .NET Framework documentation. This is available on the MSDN and as an installable option when installing Visual Studio .NET.

Workshop

The Workshop is designed to help you anticipate possible questions, review what you've learned, and get you thinking about how to put your knowledge into practice. The answers to the quiz are in Appendix A, "Answers to Quizzes/Exercises."

Quiz

1. To get only the remainder of a division operation, you use which operator?
2. Which operation is performed first in the following expression—the addition or the multiplication?

   ```
   x = 6 + 5 * 4
   ```
3. Does this expression evaluate to true or to false?

   ```
   ((true || true) && false) == !true
   ```
4. Which Boolean operator performs a logical negation?
5. The process of appending one string to another is called?
6. What property can be used to return the month of a given date?

Exercises

1. Create a project that has a single text box on a form. Assume the user enters a first name, a middle initial, and a last name into the text box. Parse the contents into three variables—one for each part of the name.
2. Create a project that has a single text box on a form. Assume the user enters a valid birthday into the text box. Use the date functions as necessary to tell the user the number of the month in which they were born.

HOUR 14

Making Decisions in C# Code

In Hour 11, "Creating and Calling Methods," you learned how to separate code into multiple methods to be called in any order required. But if you had to separate each small code routine into its own method, your projects would quickly become unmanageable. Instead of creating numerous methods, you can use decision-making techniques to execute or omit specific lines of code within a single method. Decision-making constructs or coding structures allow you to execute (or omit) code based on the current situation, such as the value of a variable. C# includes two constructs that allow you to make any type of branching decision you can think of: if...else and switch.

In this hour, you'll learn how to use the decision constructs provided by C# to perform robust yet efficient decisions in C# code. In addition, you'll learn how to use the goto statement to redirect code. You'll probably create decision constructs in every application you build, so the quicker you master these skills, the easier it will be to create robust applications.

The highlights of this hour include the following:

- Making decisions using if statements
- Expanding the capability of if statements using else
- Evaluating an expression for multiple values using the switch statement
- Redirecting code flow using goto

Making Decisions Using if Statements

By far the most common decision-making construct used in programming is the if construct. A simple if construct looks like this:

```
if (expression)
    ... statement to execute when expression is true;
```

The if construct uses Boolean logic, as discussed in Hour 13, "Performing Arithmetic, String Manipulation, and Date/Time Adjustments," to evaluate an expression to either true or false. The expression may be simple (if (x == 6)) or complicated (if (x==6 && y>10)). If the expression evaluates to true, the statement or block of statements (if enclosed in braces) gets executed. If the expression evaluates to false, C# doesn't execute the statement or statement block for the if construct.

Remember that compound, also frequently called *block* statements, can be used anywhere a statement is expected. A compound statement consists of zero or more statements enclosed in braces ({}). Following is an example of the if construct using a block statement:

```
if (expression)
    {
    statement 1 to execute when expression is true;
    statement 2 to execute when expression is true;
    … statement n to execute when expression is true;
    }
```

You're going to create a simple if construct in a C# project. Create a new Windows Application named **Decisions**. Rename the default form to **fclsDecisions**, set the Text property of the form to **Decisions Example**, and update the entry point Main() to reference **fclsDecisions** instead of Form1.

Add a new text box to the form by double-clicking the Textbox icon in the toolbox. Set the properties of the text box as follows:

Property	Value
Name	txtInput
Location	44,44
Text	(make blank)

Next, add a new button to the form by double-clicking the Button icon in the toolbox. Set the button's properties as follows:

Property	Value
Name	btnIsLessThanHundred
Location	156,42
Size	100,23
Text	Is text < 100?

Your form should now look like the one in Figure 14.1.

FIGURE 14.1

You'll use the if state-ment to determine whether the value of the text entered into the text box is less than 100.

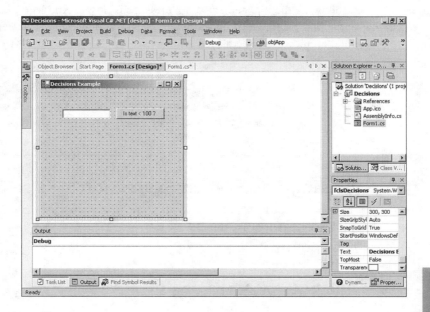

14

You're now going to add code to the button's Click event. This code will use a simple if construct and the int.Parse() method. The int.Parse() method is used to convert text into its numeric equivalent, and you'll use it to convert the text in txtInput into an integer. The if statement will then determine whether the number entered into the text box is less than 100. Double-click the button now to access its Click event, and enter the following code:

```
if (int.Parse(txtInput.Text)< 100 )
    MessageBox.Show("The text entered is less than 100.");
```

This code is simple when examined one statement at a time. Look closely at the first statement and recall that a simple if statement looks like this:

```
if (expression)
    statement;
```

In the code you entered, *expression* is

```
int.Parse(txtInput.Text)< 100
```

What you are doing is asking C# to evaluate whether the parsed integer is less than 100. If it is, the evaluation returns true. If the value is greater than or equal to 100, the expression returns false. If the evaluation returns true, execution proceeds with the line immediately following the if statement and a message is displayed. If the evaluation returns false, the line statement (or block of statements) following the if statement doesn't execute and no message is displayed.

If the user leaves the text box empty or enters a string, an exception will be thrown. Therefore, you'd normally implement exception handling around this type of code. You'll learn about exception handling in Hour 16, "Debugging Your Code."

Executing Code When *Expression* Is False

If you want to execute some code when *expression* evaluates to false, include the optional else keyword, like this:

```
if (expression)
    statement to execute when expression is true;
else
    statement to execute when expression is false;
```

> If you want to execute code only when *expression* equates to false, not
> when true, use the not-equal operator (!=) in the expression. Refer to Hour
> 13 for more information on Boolean logic.

By including an else clause, you can have one or more statements execute when *expression* is true and other statements execute when the *expression* is false. In the example you've built, if a user enters a number less than 100, the user will get a message. However, if the number is greater than or equal to 100, the user receives no feedback. Modify your code to look like the following, which ensures that the user always gets a message:

```
if (int.Parse(txtInput.Text)< 100 )
    MessageBox.Show("The text entered is less than 100.");
else
    MessageBox.Show("The text entered is greater than or equal to 100.");
```

Now, if the user enters a number less than 100, the message The text entered is less than 100 is displayed, but nothing more. When C# encounters the else statement, it ignores the statement(s) associated with the else statement. The statements for the else condition execute only when *expression* is false. Likewise, if the user enters text that is greater than or equal to 100, the message The text entered is greater than or equal to 100 is displayed, but nothing more; when *expression* evaluates to false, execution immediately jumps to the else statement.

Click Save All on the toolbar to save your work and then press F5 to run the project. Enter a number into the text box and click the button. A message box appears, telling you whether the number you entered is less than or greater than 100 (see Figure 14.2).

FIGURE 14.2
As implied with this message box, if gives you great flexibility in making decisions.

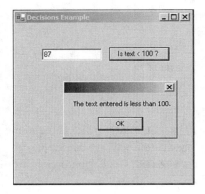

14

Feel free to enter other numbers and click the button as often as you like. When you're satisfied that the code is working, choose Stop Debugging from the Debug menu.

> Get comfortable with if; chances are you'll include at least one in every project you create.

Nesting if Constructs

As mentioned earlier, you can nest if statements to further refine your decision making. The format you use can be something like the following:

```
if ( expression1 )
    if ( expression2 )
    ...
    else
        ...
else
    ...
```

Evaluating an Expression for Multiple Values Using switch

At times, the if construct isn't capable of handling a decision situation without a lot of extra work. One such situation is when you need to perform different actions based on numerous possible values of an expression, not just true or false. For instance, suppose you wanted to perform actions based on a user's profession. The following shows what you might create using if:

```
if (strProfession =="programmer")
    ...
else if (strProfession =="teacher")
    ...
else if (strProfession =="accountant")
    ...
else
    ...
```

As you can see, this structure can be a bit hard to read. If the number of supported professions increases, this type of construction will get harder to read and debug. In addition, executing many if statements like this is rather inefficient from a processing standpoint.

The important thing to realize here is that each else...if is really evaluating the same expression (strProfession) but considering different values for the expression. C# includes a much better decision construct for evaluating a single expression for multiple possible values: switch.

A switch construct looks like the following:

```
switch (expression)
{
    case  value1:
            ...
        jump-statement

    default:
            ...
        jump-statement

}
```

> default is used to define code that executes only when *expression* doesn't evaluate to any of the values in the case statements. Use of default is optional.

Here's the Profession example shown previously, but this time switch is used:

```
switch (strProfession)
{
case "teacher" :
        MessageBox.Show("You educate our young");
        break;
    case "programmer":
        MessageBox.Show("You are most likely a geek");
        break;
    case "accountant":
        MessageBox.Show("You are a bean counter");
        break;
    default:
        MessageBox.Show("Profession currently not supported in switch
➥statement");
        break;
}
```

The flow of the switch statement is as follows: When the case expression is matched, the code statement or statements within the case are executed. This must be followed by a jump-statement, such as break, to transfer control out of the case body.

14

If you create a case construct but fail to put code statements or a jump-statement within the case, execution will fall through to the next case statement, even if the expression doesn't match.

The switch makes decisions much easier to follow. Again, the key with switch is that it's used to evaluate a single expression for more than one possible value.

Building a switch Example

You're now going to build a project that uses expression evaluation in a switch construct. This simple application will display a list of animals in a combo box to the user. When the user clicks a button, the application will display the number of legs of the animal in the list (if an animal is selected). Create a new Windows Application named **Switch Example**. Rename the default form to **flcsSwitchExample,** set the form's Text property to **Switch Example,** and update the entry point in procedure Main() to reference **flcsSwitchExample** instead of Form1.

Next, add a new combo box to the form by double-clicking the ComboBox item on the toolbox. Set the combo box's properties as follows:

Property	Value
Name	cboAnimals
Location	80,100
Text	(make blank)

Next, you'll add some items to the list. Click the Items property of the combo box, and then click the Build button that appears in the property to access the String Collection Editor for the combo box. Enter the text as shown in Figure 14.3; be sure to press Enter at the end of each list item to make the next item appear on its own line.

Next you'll add a Button control. When the button is clicked, a switch construct will be used to determine which animal the user has selected and to tell the user how many legs the selected animal has. Add a new button to the form by double-clicking the Button tool in the toolbox. Set the button's properties as follows:

Property	Value
Name	btnShowLegs
Location	102,140
Text	Show Legs

FIGURE 14.3

Each line you enter here becomes an item in the combo box at runtime.

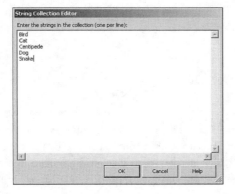

Your form should now look like the one in Figure 14.4. Click Save All on the toolbar to save your work before continuing.

FIGURE 14.4

This example uses only a combo box and a button control.

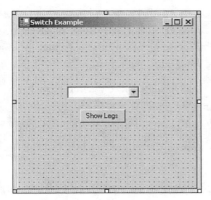

All that's left to do is add the code. Double-click the Button control to access its Click event, and then enter the following code:

```
switch (cboAnimals.Text)
{
   case "Bird":
     MessageBox.Show("The animal has 2 legs.");
     break;
   case "Dog":
     // Notice there is no code here to execute.
   case "Cat":
     MessageBox.Show("The animal has 4 legs.");
     break;
   case "Snake":
     MessageBox.Show("The animal has no legs.");
```

14

```
      break;
   case "Centipede":
      MessageBox.Show("The animal has 100 legs.");
      break;
   default:
      MessageBox.Show("You did not select from the list!");
      break;
}
```

NEW TERM Here's what's happening: The switch construct compares the content of the cboAnimals combo box to a set of predetermined values. Each case statement is evaluated in the order in which it appears in the list. Therefore, the expression is first compared to "Bird." If the content of the combo box is Bird, the MessageBox.Show() method immediately following the case statement is called, followed by the break statement, which transfers control outside of the switch construct. If the combo box doesn't contain Bird, C# looks to see if the content is "Dog," and so on. Notice that the Dog case contains no code, therefore the execution of the code in the following case (Cat) is executed if the text Dog was selected (this is known as *execution falling through*). In this situation, you end up with the correct output. However, what happens if you move the Snake case in front of Cat? You'd end up telling the user that the dog has no legs! When using this technique, you must be careful that all situations will produce desired behavior.

Each successive case statement is evaluated in the same way. If no matches are found for any of the case statements, the MessageBox.Show() method in the default statement is called. If there were no matches and no default statement, no code would execute.

As you can see, adding a new animal to the list can be as simple as adding a case statement.

Press F5 to run your project now and give it a try. Select an animal from the list and click the button. Try clearing the contents of the combo box and clicking the button. When you're finished, choose Stop Debugging from the Debug menu to stop the project and click Save All on the toolbar.

Branching Within Code Using goto

NEW TERM Decision structures are used to selectively execute code. When a decision statement is encountered, C# evaluates an expression and diverts code according to the result. You don't have to use a decision structure to divert code, however, because C# includes a statement that can be used to jump code execution to a predetermined location within the current procedure: the goto statement. Before I talk about how to use goto, I want to say that under most circumstances, it's considered bad coding practice to use a goto. Code that's heavily laden with gotos is difficult to read and debug because the execution path is so convoluted. Such code is often called *spaghetti code*, and should be avoided at all costs. I'd say that in 90% of the situations in which goto is used, a better approach to the problem exists, and I'll show an example of just such a case shortly. Nevertheless, goto, like all other statements, is a tool. Although it's not needed as often as some of the other C# statements are, it's still a useful tool to have at your disposal—when used judiciously.

NEW TERM   To jump to a specific location in code, you must first define the jump location using a *code label*. A code label is not the same as a Label control that you place on a form. You create a code label by positioning the cursor on a new line in a method, typing in a name for the label followed by a colon, and pressing Enter. Code labels can't contain spaces and they can't be a C# reserved word. For instance, you can't create a code label called try, because try is a reserved word in C#. However, you could create a label called TryThis, because TryThis isn't a reserved word. Code labels act as pointers that you can jump to using goto. The following shows an example using goto to jump code execution to a label.

```
private void btnGoto_Click(object sender, System.EventArgs e)
{
   long lngCounter = 0;

IncrementCounter:
   lngCounter++;
   if (lngCounter < 5000) goto IncrementCounter;
}
```

This code does the following:

- Dimensions a long variable called lngCounter.
- Sets the new variable to 0.
- Defines a code label titled IncrementCounter. One or more goto statements can be used to jump code execution to this label at any time.
- Increments lngCounter by 1.
- Uses an if statement to determine if lngCounter has exceeded 5000. If it hasn't, a goto statement forces code execution back to the IncrementCounter label, where lngCounter is incremented and tested again, creating a loop.

This code works, and you're welcome to try it. However, this is *terrible* code. Remember how I said that the use of a goto can often be replaced by a better coding approach? In this case, C# has specific looping constructs that you'll learn about in the next hour. These looping constructs are far superior to building your own loop under most conditions, so you should avoid building a loop using a goto statement. In fact, one of the

14

biggest misuses of goto is using it in place of one of C#'s internal looping constructs. In case you're interested, here's the loop that would replace the use of goto in this example:

```
for(long lngCounter = 0; lngCounter<=5000; lngCounter++)
    ...
```

This discussion may leave you wondering why you would ever use goto. One situation in which I commonly use goto statements is to create single exit points. As you know, you can force execution to leave a method at any time using return. Often, clean-up code is required before a method exits. In a long method, you may have many return statements. However, such a method can be a problem to debug because clean-up code may not be run under all circumstances. Because all methods have a single entry point, it makes sense to give them a single exit point. With a single exit point, you use a goto statement to go to the exit point, rather than use a return statement. The following procedure illustrates using goto to create a single exit point:

```
private void btnGoto_Click(object sender, System.EventArgs e)
{
    ...
    ...
    // If it is necessary to exit the code, perform a goto to
    // the PROC_EXIT label, rather than using an Exit statement.
PROC_EXIT:
    ...
    return;
}
```

Summary

In this hour you learned how to use C#'s decision constructs to make decisions in C# code. You learned how to use if statements to execute code when an expression evaluates to true and to use else to run code when the expression evaluates to false. For more complicated decisions, you learned how to use else...if to add further comparisons to the decision construct and nest if structures for more flexibility.

In addition to if, you learned how to use switch to create powerful decision constructs to evaluate a single expression for many possible values. You learned how you can check for multiple possible values using a fall through case statement. Finally, you learned how to use goto to jump to any predefined position in code.

Decision-making constructs are often the backbone of applications. Without the capability to run specific sets of code based on fluctuating situations, your code would be very linear and hence very limited. Get comfortable with the decision constructs and make a conscious effort to use the best construct for any given situation. The better you are at writing decision constructs, the faster you'll be able to product solid and understandable code.

Q&A

Q. What if I want to execute code only when an expression in an if statement is false, not true? Do I need to place the code in an else clause, and no code after the if?

A. This is where Boolean logic helps. What you need to do is make the expression evaluate to true for the code you want to run. This is accomplished using the not operator (!) in the expression, like this:

```
if (!expression)
. . .
```

Q. How important is the order in which case statements are created?

A. This all depends on the situation. In the example given in the text in which the selected animal was considered and the number of legs it has was displayed, the order of the Dog case was important. If all case statements contained code, the order has no effect.

Workshop

The Workshop is designed to help you anticipate possible questions, review what you've learned, and get you thinking about how to put your knowledge into practice. The answers to the quiz are in Appendix A, "Answers to Quizzes/Exercises."

Quiz

1. Which decision construct should you use to evaluate a single expression to either true or false?

2. Evaluating expressions to true or false for both types of decision constructs is accomplished using _____ logic.

3. If you want code to execute when the expression of an if statement evaluates to false, include an _____ clause.

4. Which decision construct should you use when evaluating the result of an expression that may equate to one of many possible values?

5. Is it possible that more than one case statement may have its code execute?

6. True or False: You can use goto to jump code execution to a different method.

14

7. To use goto to jump execution to a new location in code, what must you create as a pointer to jump to?

Exercises

1. Create a project that allows the user to enter text into a text box. Use an if construct to determine whether the text entered is Circle, Triangle, Square, or Pentagon, and display the number of sides the entered shape has. If the text doesn't match one of these shapes, let the users know that they must enter a shape.

2. Rewrite the following code using only an if structure; the new code should *not* contain a goto.

```
...
if (!blnAddToAge) goto SkipAddToAge;
lngAge++;
SkipAddToAge:
...
```

HOUR 15

Looping for Efficiency

NEW TERM As you develop your C# programs, you'll encounter situations in which you'll need to execute the same code statement or statements repeatedly. Often, you'll need to execute these statements a specific number of times, but you may need to execute them as long as a certain condition persists (an expression is true) or until a condition occurs (an expression becomes true). C# includes constructs that enable you to easily define and execute these repetitive code routines: *loops*. This hour shows you how to use the two major looping constructs to make your code smaller, faster, and more efficient.

The highlights of this hour include the following:

- Looping a specific number of times using for statements
- Looping an indeterminate number of times using do...while and while statements

Looping a Specific Number of Times Using for Statements

The simplest type of loop to create is the for loop, which has been around since the earliest forms of the BASIC language. With a for loop, you instruct C# to begin a loop by starting a counter at a specific value. C# then executes the code within the loop, increments the counter by a defined incremental value, and repeats the loop until the counter reaches an upper limit you've set. The following is the syntax for the basic for loop:

```
for ([initializers]; [expression]; [iterators]) statement
```

Initiating the Loop Using For

The for statement both sets up and starts the loop. The for statement has the components shown in Table 15.1.

TABLE 15.1 Components of the for Statement

Part	Description
initializers	A comma-separated list of expressions or assignment statements to initialize the loop counters.
expression	An expression that can be implicitly converted to boolean. The expression is used to test the loop-termination criteria.
iterators	Expression statement(s) to increment or decrement the loop counters.
statement	The embedded statement(s) to execute.

The following is a simple example of a for loop, followed by an explanation of what it's doing:

```
for (int intCounter = 1; intCounter <= 100; intCounter++)
    Debug.WriteLine(intCounter);
```

This for statement initializes an Integer named intCounter at 1; the condition intCounter <= 100 is tested and returns true; therefore, the statement debug.WriteLine(lngCounter) is executed. After the statement(s) are executed, the variable intCounter is incremented (intCounter++). This loop would execute 100 times, printing the numbers 1 through 100 to the Output debug window.

To use the Debug object, you need to use the System.Diagnostics namespace.

To execute multiple statements within a for loop, braces { } are used; a single line for statements does not require braces. Here is the previous for loop written to execute multiple statements:

```
for (int intCounter = 1; intCounter <= 100; intCounter++)
{
   Debug.WriteLine(intCounter);
   Debug.WriteLine(intCounter-1);
}
```

Exiting a for Loop Early

There may be times when you'll want to terminate a for loop before the expression evaluates to true. To exit a for loop at any time, use the break statement.

Building a for Loop Example

You're now going to create a method containing two for loops—one nested within the other. The first loop is going to count from 1 to 100 and set the Width property of a Label control to the current counter value; this will emulate a Windows progress meter. The second loop will be used to slow the execution of the first loop—an old programmer's trick using a for loop.

Create a new Windows Application named **ForExample**. Set the form's Text to **For Statement Example**. Add a Label control to the form by double-clicking the Label tool in the toolbox. Set the label's properties as follows:

Property	Value
Name	lblMeter
BackColor	*(Set to a light blue or any color you like.)*
Location	100,100
Text	*(make blank)*
Size	100,17

15

Next, add a button to the form by double-clicking the Button item in the toolbox. Set the button's properties as follows:

Property	Value
Name	btnForLoop
Location	88,125
Size	125,23
Text	Run a For Loop

Your form should look like the one shown in Figure 15.1.

FIGURE 15.1

This simple project will emulate a progress meter.

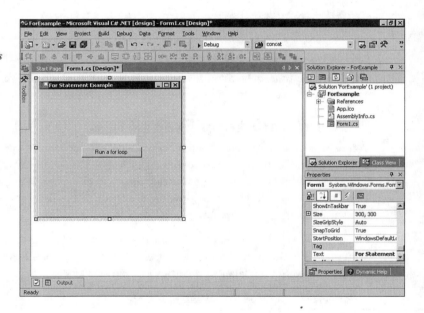

All that's left to do is to write the code. Double-click the button to access its Click event and enter the following:

```
for (int intLabelWidth=1; intLabelWidth<=100; intLabelWidth++)
{
   lblMeter.Width = intLabelWidth;
   lblMeter.Refresh();
   for (int intPauseCounter=1; intPauseCounter<=600000; intPauseCounter++);
}
```

Using a loop to create a delay is actually a very poor and outdated coding technique. Other options can be used for creating a delay, such as calling System.Threading.Thread.Sleep(). This example is designed to illustrate nested loops—which it does, not to show the best way to create a delay.

Remember that C# is case sensitive. (Hint: for, int, and long are all lowercase).

The first line starts the first for loop. It starts by creating and initializing the variable intLabelWidth; next comes an expression used to evaluate the variable, and the third part is the iterator, which increments intLabelWidth by one each time the loop completes.

The first statement within this for loop sets the width of the Label control to the value of intLabelWidth. The next statement calls the Refresh method of the Label control to ensure that it paints itself. Often, painting catches up when the CPU has idle time. Because you want the transition from a small label to a large one to be smooth, you need to make sure the label paints itself after each update to its Width property. After all the statements within the braces execute, intLabelWidth is incremented by one (intLabelWidth++) and the expression is evaluated once more. This means that the code within the loop will execute 100 times.

The next statement starts a second for loop using the intPauseCounter variable, creating and initializing intPauseCounter to 1 and setting the upper limit of the loop to 600,000. Following this for statement is a semicolon(;) with no statement before it. This creates an empty statement. Why is there no code for this for statement of the lngPauseCounter loop? This loop is used simply to create a delay within the processor. Most computers are so fast that if you didn't add a delay here, the first for loop would update the label's width from 1 to 100 so fast that you might not even see it update!

I wrote this code on a 1.33GHz (1,333MHz) machine; you may have to alter this value if your processor speed is much different. If you have a slower CPU, reduce this value. If you have a much faster processor, increase this value. Wait until you test this code before making changes to the upper limit, however. Again, using another method, such as calling System.Threading.Thread.Sleep(), would allow precise control over the delay, regardless of the speed of the machine.

Click Save All on the toolbar and press F5 to run the project. The label starts with a width of 100. Click the button, and you'll see the label's width change to 1 and then increment to 100. If the speed is too slow or too fast, stop the project and adjust the upper limit of the inner for loop.

If you were to forgo a loop and write each and every line of code necessary to draw the label with a width from 1 to 100, it would take 100 lines of code. Using a simple for loop, you performed the same task in just a few lines. In addition, a for loop allowed you to create a pause during the update.

A for loop is best when you know the number of times you want the loop to execute. This doesn't mean that you have to actually know the number of times you want the loop to execute at design time; it simply means that you must know the number of times you want the loop to execute when you first start the loop. You can use a variable to define any of the arguments of the for loop, as illustrated in the following code:

```
int intUpperLimit=100;
for (int intCounter=1; intCounter<=intUpperLimit;intCounter++)
    Debug.WriteLine(intCounter);
```

One of the keys to writing efficient code is to eliminate redundancy. If you find yourself typing the same (or a similar) line of code repeatedly in the same procedure, chances are it's a good candidate for a loop (and you may even want to place the duplicate code in its own method).

Using do...while to Loop an Indeterminate Number of Times

In some situations, you won't know the exact number of times a loop needs to be performed—not even when the loop begins. When you need to create such a loop, using the do...while loop is the best solution.

The do...while comes in a number of flavors. Its most basic form has the following syntax:

do statement **while** (expression);

The following is used to execute multiple statements:

```
do
{
    [Statements]
} while (expression);
```

Ending a do...while

A do...while without some sort of exit mechanism or defined condition is an endless loop. In its most basic form, nothing is present to tell the loop when to stop looping. At times you may need an endless loop (game programming is an example), but more often, you'll need to exit the loop when a certain condition is met. Like the for loop, you can use the break statement to exit a do...while loop at any time. For example, you could expand the do...while we're discussing to include a break statement like the following:

```
do
{
   [Statements]
   if (expression)
      break;
} while (x==x);
```

In this code, the loop would execute until *expression* evaluates to true. Generally, the expression is based on a variable that's modified somewhere within the loop. Obviously, if the expression never changes, the loop never ends.

The second flavor of the while loop is the while...do loop. The following is a simple while...do loop:

```
while (expression) statement
```

As long as *expression* evaluates to true, the loop continues to occur. If *expression* evaluates to false when the loop first starts, the code between the statement(s) doesn't execute—not even once.

The difference between the do...while and the while...do loops is that the code statements within the do...while loop *always* execute at least once; *expression* isn't evaluated until the loop has completed its first cycle. Therefore, such a loop executes at least once, regardless of the value of expression. The while loop evaluates the expression first; therefore, the statements associated with it may not execute at all.

Creating a do...while Example

You're now going to create an example using a do...while loop that updates a label to once again simulate a progress meter. This loop performs the same purpose as the for loop you created in the previous example, but its structure is quite different.

If your for example is currently running, choose Stop Debugging from the Debug menu. Add another button to the formand set the new button's properties as follows:

Property	Value
Name	btnDoLoop
Location	88,160
Size	125,23
Text	Run a Do Loop

Your form should now look like the one shown in Figure 15.2.

FIGURE 15.2

You'll use the same form for both loop examples.

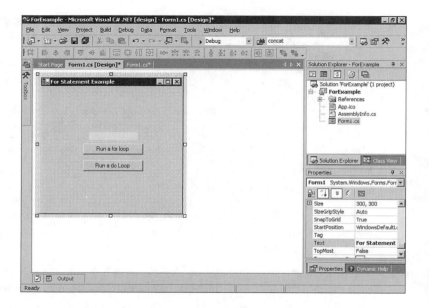

Double-click the new button to access its Click event and then enter the following code:

```
int intLabelWidth=1;

while (intLabelWidth != 100)
{
   lblMeter.Width = intLabelWidth;
   lblMeter.Refresh();
   intLabelWidth++;   // Increment by one.
   for (int intPauseCounter=1; intPauseCounter<=600000; intPauseCounter++);
}
```

15

Again, this code is more easily understood when broken down, as shown in the following list:

- The first line creates the intLabelWidth variables and sets it to 1.

- A while statement is used to start a loop. This loop will execute until intLabelWidth has the value 100. It can also be read as "the statements will execute while intLabelWidth does not equal 100."

- The Label's Width property is set to the value of intLabelWidth.

- The Label is forced to refresh its appearance.

- The intLabelWidth variable is incremented by 1.

- A for loop is used to slow down the procedure, just as it was in the previous example. Again, this is just to illustrate nested loops. Calling System.Threading.Thread.Sleep() would be a better way to create a delay.

- Click Save All on the toolbar to save the project, and then press F5 to run it. Click the Run a Do Loop button to see the progress meter set itself to 1 pixel and then update itself by 1 until it reaches 100 pixels.

> I wanted to show you how both types of loops could be used to accomplish the same task. In this example, however, the for loop is clearly the best approach because you know the starting values and the number of times to loop when the loop starts.

You've now seen how to perform the same function with two entirely different coding techniques. This is fairly common when creating programs; usually, multiple ways exist to approach a solution to a given problem. Simply being aware of your options makes writing code that much easier. When you hear of people optimizing their code, they're usually looking for a different, faster approach to a problem they've already solved.

Summary

Looping is a powerful technique that allows you to write tighter code. Tighter code is code consisting of fewer lines, is more efficient, and is usually—but not always—more readable. In this hour, you learned to write for loops for situations in which you know the precise number of times you want a loop executed. Remember, it's not necessary to know the number of iterations at design time, but you must know the number at runtime to use a for loop. You learned how to use iterators to increment the counter of a for loop, and even how to exit a loop prematurely using break.

In this hour, you also learned how to use the very powerful do...while loop. The do...while loop enables you to create very flexible loops that can handle almost any looping scenario. You learned how evaluating *expression* in a do...while loop makes the loop behave differently than when evaluating the expression in a while...do loop. If a for loop can't do the job, some form of the do...while or while...do loop will.

In addition to learning the specifics about loops, you've seen firsthand how multiple solutions to a problem can exist. Often, one approach is clearly superior to all other approaches, although you may not always find it. Other times, one approach may be only marginally superior, or multiple approaches may all be equally applicable. Expert programmers are able to consistently find the best approaches to any given problem. With time, you'll be able to do the same.

Q&A

Q. Are there any specific cases in which one loop is appropriate over another?

A. Usually, when you have to walk an index or sequential set of elements (such as referencing all elements in an array), the for loop is the best choice.

Q. Should I be concerned about the performance differences between the two types of loops?

A. With today's fast processors, chances are good that the performance difference between the two loop types in any given situation will be overshadowed by the readability and functionality of the best choice of loop. If you have a situation in which performance is critical, write the loop using all the ways you can think of, benchmark the results, and choose the fastest loop.

Workshop

The Workshop is designed to help you anticipate possible questions, review what you've learned, and get you thinking about how to put your knowledge into practice. The answers to the quiz are in Appendix A, "Answers to Quizzes/Exercises."

Quiz

1. True or False: You have to know the start and end values of a for loop at design time to use this type of loop.

2. Is it possible to nest loops?

3. What type of loop would you most likely need to create if you didn't have any idea how many times the loop would need to occur?

4. If you evaluate the expression in a do...while on the while statement, is it possible that the code within the loop may never execute?

5. What statement do you use to terminate a do...while without evaluating the expression on the do or while statements?

Exercises

1. The status meter example using do...while has a deliberate "bug." The meter will display only to 99 (the label's width will adjust only to 99 pixels, not 100). The problem has to do with how the expression is evaluated. Find and correct this problem.

2. Use two for loops nested within each other to size a label in two dimensions. Have the outer loop change the Width of the label from 1 to 100 and have the inner loop change the Height from 1 to 100. Don't be surprised by the result—the end result is rather odd.

15

HOUR **16**

Debugging Your Code

No one writes perfect code. You're most certainly familiar with those problems that prevent code from executing properly—they're called bugs. Being new to C#, your code will probably contain a fair number of bugs. As you gain proficiency, the number of bugs in your code will decrease, but they will never disappear entirely. Debugging is a skill and an art. This book can't teach you how to debug every possible build or runtime error you may encounter; however, in this hour you will learn the basic skills necessary to trace and correct most bugs in your code.

The highlights of this hour include the following:

- Adding comments to your code
- Identifying the two basic types of errors
- Working with break points
- Using the Command window
- Using the Output window
- Creating a structured error handler

The Task List window is useful for addressing build errors in code. However, because its use goes beyond this simple debugging application, I discuss the Task List in Hour 11, "Creating and Calling Methods."

Before proceeding, create a new Windows Application project named **Debugging Example**. Change the name of the default form to **fclsDebuggingExample**, set its Text property to **Debugging Example**, and change the Main() entry point of the project to reference fclsDebuggingExample instead of Form1.

Add a new text box to the form by double-clicking the TextBox item in the toolbox. Set the text box's properties as follows:

Property	Value
Name	txtInput
Location	88,112
Size	120,20
Text	(make blank)

Next, add a new button to the form by double-clicking the Button item in the toolbox, and then set its properties as follows:

Property	Value
Name	btnPerformDivision
Location	96,144
Size	104,23
Text	Perform Division

Your form should now look like the one shown in Figure 16.1.

All this little project will do is divide 100 by whatever is entered into the text box. As you write the code to accomplish this, various bugs will be introduced (on purpose), and you'll learn to correct them. Save your project now by clicking the Save All button on the toolbar.

FIGURE 16.1

This simple interface will help teach you debugging techniques.

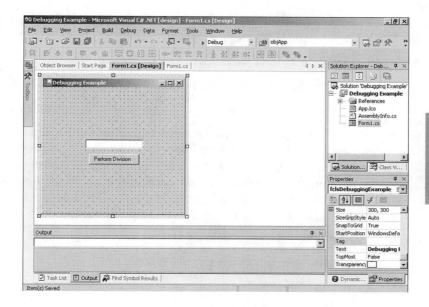

Adding Comments to Your Code

One of the simplest things you can do to reduce bugs from the start—and make tracking down existing bugs easier—is to add comments to your code. A code comment is simply a line of text that C# knows isn't actual code. Comment lines are stripped from the code when the project is compiled to create a distributable component, so comments don't affect performance. C#'s code window shows comments as green text. This makes it easier to read and understand procedures. You should consider adding comments to the top of each procedure stating the purpose of the procedure. In addition, you should add liberal comments throughout all procedures, detailing what's occurring in the code.

Comments are meant to be read by humans, not by computers. Strive to make your comments intelligible. Keep in mind that a comment that is hard to understand is not much better than no comment at all. Also, remember that comments serve as a form of documentation. Just as documentation for an application must be clearly written, code comments should also follow good writing principles.

To create a comment, precede the comment text with two forward slash marks (//). For example, a simple comment might look like this:

```
// This is a comment because it is preceded with double forward slashes.
```

Comments can also be placed at the end of a line of code, like this:

```
int intAge;        // Used to store the user's age in years.
```

Everything to the right of and including the double forward slashes in this statement is a comment. C# also supports a second type of comment. This allows for comments to span multiple lines without forcing the developer to add // characters to each line. The comment begins with an open comment mark of a forward slash, followed by an asterisk (/*), and the comment closes with a close mark of an asterisk followed by a forward slash (*/). For example, a comment can look like this:

```
/*      Chapter 16 in Sams TY C#
focuses on debugging code, a topic
every developer spends a lot of time on.   */
```

By adding comments to your code, you don't have to rely on memory to decipher the code's purpose or mechanics. If you've ever had to go back and work with code you haven't looked at in a while, or had to work with someone else's code, you probably already have a great appreciation for comments.

Double-click the button now to access its Click event and add the following two lines of code (comments, actually):

```
// This procedure divides 100 by the value entered in
// the text box txtInput.
```

Notice that after you enter the second forward slash, both slashes turn green. Comments, whether single line (//) or multiline (/* comments */), will be displayed in a green font in Visual Studio.

When creating code comments, strive to do the following:

- Document the purpose of the code (the *why*, not the *how*).
- Clearly indicate the thinking and logic behind the code.
- Call attention to important turning points in code.
- Reduce the need for readers to run a simulation of code execution in their heads.

C# also supports an additional type of comment denoted with three slashes (///). When the C# compiler encounters these comments, it processes them into an XML file. These types of comments are often used to create documentation for code. Creating XML files from comments is beyond the scope of this book, but if these features intrigue you, I highly recommend that you look into it.

16

Identifying the Two Basic Types of Errors

NEW TERM Essentially, two types of errors can occur in code: *compile errors* and *runtime errors*. A compile error (commonly called a *build* error) is an error in code that prevents C#'s compiler from being able to process the code. C# won't compile a project that has a build error in it. A method call with incorrect parameters, for example, will generate a build error. Runtime errors are errors that don't occur at compile time but are encountered when the project is being run. Runtime errors are usually a result of trying to perform an invalid operation on a variable.

For example, the following code won't generate a compile error:

```
intResult = 10 / intSomeOtherVariable;
```

Under most circumstances, this code won't even generate a runtime error. However, what happens if the value of intSomeOtherVariable is 0? Ten divided by zero is infinity, which won't fit into intResult (intResult is an Integer variable). Attempting to run the code with the variable having a value of 0 causes C# to return a runtime error. Runtime errors are called *exceptions*, and when an exception is created, it is said to be *thrown* (that is, C# throws an exception when a runtime error occurs). When an exception is thrown, code execution stops at the offending statement and C# displays an error message. You can prevent C# from stopping execution when an exception is thrown by writing special code to handle the exception (writing error handlers is discussed later in this hour).

Add the following statements to the Click event, right below the two comment lines:

```
long lngAnswer;

lngAnswer = 100 / long.Parse(txtInput.Text);
MessageBox.Show("100/" + txtInput.Text + " is " + lngAnswer)
```

The missing semicolon in the MessageBox.Show line is intentional; type in the preceding line of code exactly as it appears. Although you've missed the ending semicolon, C#

doesn't return an immediate error. However, notice how C# displays a wavy red line at the end of the statement. Notice the Description in the Task List following an exclamation point and a red, wavy line; C# displays a tip explaining the nature of the error (see Figure 16.2).

FIGURE 16.2

Using wavy under-lines, C# highlights build errors in the code window.

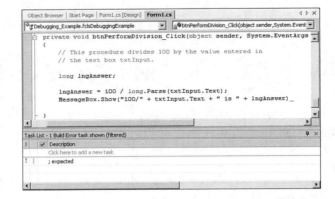

Press F5 to run the project. When you do, C# displays a message that a build error was found and asks you whether you want to continue. Because the code won't run, there's no point in continuing, so click No to return to the code editor. Take a look at the Task List (if it's not displayed, use the View menu to show it). All build errors in the current project appear in the Task List (see Figure 16.2). To view a particular offending line of code, double-click an item in the Task List.

Build errors are very serious errors in that they prevent code from being compiled; therefore, they completely prevent execution. Build errors must be corrected before you can run the project. Double-click the build error in the Task List to go directly to the error.

Correct the problem by adding a semicolon to the end of the line. After you've made this change, press F5 to run the project. C# no longer returns a build error; you've just successfully debugged a problem! Click the Perform Division button now, and you'll receive another error (see Figure 16.3).

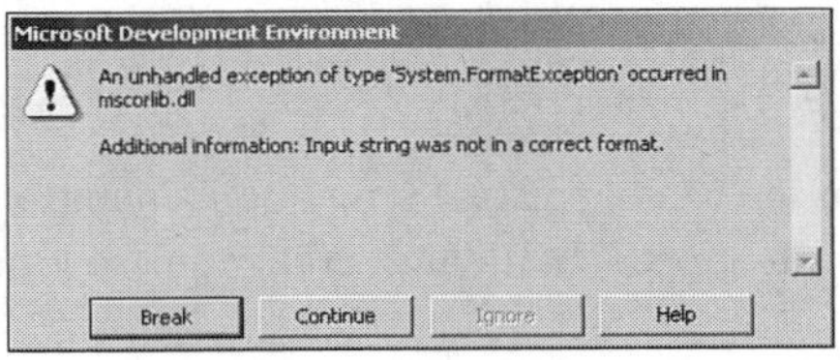

FIGURE 16.3

A runtime exception halts code execution at the offending line.

This time, the error is a runtime error, or exception. If an exception occurs, you know that the code compiled without a problem because build errors prevent code from compiling and executing. This particular exception is a Format exception. Format exceptions generally occur when you attempt to perform a method using a variable, and the variable is of an incompatible data type for the specified operation. Click Break to view the offending line of code. C# denotes the offending statement with a green arrow (the arrow indicates the current statement). At this point, you know that the statement has a "bug," and you know it is related to data typing. Choose Stop Debugging from the Debug menu now to stop the running project and return to the code editor.

Using C#'s Debugging Tools

C# includes a number of debugging tools to help you track down and eliminate bugs. In this section, you'll learn how to use break points, the Command window, and the Output window—three tools that form the foundation of any debugging arsenal.

Working with Break Points

NEW TERM The same way an exception halts the execution of a method, you can deliberately stop execution at any statement of code by creating a *break point*. When C# encounters a break point while executing code, execution is halted at the break statement, prior to it being executed. Break points enable you to query or change the value of variables at a specific instance in time, and they let you step through code execution one line at a time.

You're going to create a break point to help troubleshoot the exception in your MessageBox.Show() statement.

Adding a break point is simple. Just click in the gray area to the left of the statement at which you want to break code execution. When you do so, C# displays a red circle, denoting a break point at that statement (see Figure 16.4). To clear a break point, click the red circle.

Break points are saved with the project. This makes it much easier to suspend a debugging session; you don't have to reset all your break points each time you open the project.

FIGURE **16.4**

*Break points give you
control over code
execution.*

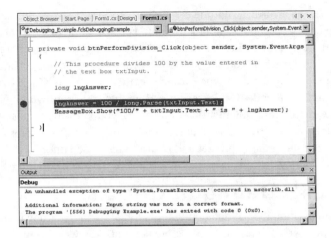

Set a new break point on the statement shown in Figure 16.4 (the statement where
lngAnswer is set). Do this by clicking in the gray area to the left of the statement. After
you've set the break point, press F5 to run the program. Again, click the button. When
C# encounters the break point, code execution is halted and the procedure with the break
point is shown. In addition, the cursor is conveniently placed at the statement with the
current break point. Notice the yellow arrow overlaying the red circle of the break point
(see Figure 16.5). This yellow arrow marks the next statement to be executed. It just so
happens that the statement has a break point, so the yellow arrow appears over the red
circle (the yellow arrow won't always be over a red circle, but it will always appear in
the gray area aligned with the next statement to execute).

FIGURE **16.5**

*A yellow arrow
denotes the next state-
ment to be executed.*

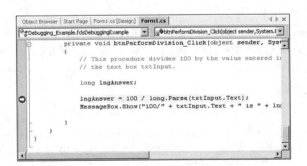

When code execution is halted at a break point, you can do a number of things. See
Table 16.1 for a list of the most common actions. For now, press F5 to continue program
execution. Again, you get the Format exception. Click Break to access the code procedure with the error.

TABLE 16.1   Actions That Can Be Taken at a Break Point

Action	Keystroke	Description
Continue Code Execution	F5	Continues execution at the current break statement.
Step Into	F11	Executes the statement at the break point and then stops at the next statement. If the current statement is a function call, F11 enters the function and stops at the first statement in the function.
Step Over	F10	Executes the statement at the break point and then stops at the next statement. If the current statement is a function call, the function is run in its entirety; then execution stops at the statement following the function call.
Step Out	Shift+F11	Runs all the statements in the current procedure and halts execution at the statement following the one that called the current procedure.

Using the Command Window

Break points themselves aren't usually sufficient to debug a procedure. In addition to break points, you'll often use the Command window to debug code. The Command window is a Visual Studio IDE window that generally appears only when your project is in Run mode. If the Command window isn't displayed, press Ctrl+Alt+A to display it now (or use the Other Views submenu of the View menu). Using the Command window, you can type in code statements that C# executes immediately. You'll use the Command window now to debug our problem statement example.

Type the following statement into the Command window and press Enter:

```
? txtInput.Text
```

Although not intuitive, the ? character has been used in programming for many years as a shortcut for the word "print." The statement that you entered simply prints the contents of the Text property of the text box.

Notice how the command window displays " " on the line below the statement you entered. This indicates that the text box contains an empty string (also called a *zero-length string*). The statement throwing the exception is attempting to use the `long.Parse()` method to convert the contents of the text box to a Long. The `long.Parse()` method expects data to be passed to it, yet the text box has no data (the Text property is empty). Consequently, a Format exception occurs.

Generally, when you receive a Format exception, you should look at any variables or properties being referenced to ensure that the data they contain is appropriate data for the statement. Often, you'll find that the code is trying to perform an operation that is inappropriate for the data being supplied.

You can do a number of things to prevent this error. The most obvious is to ensure that the text box contains a value before attempting to use the `long.Parse()` method. You'll do this now. C# doesn't allow you to modify code when in break mode, so choose Stop Debugging from the Debug menu before continuing.

Add the following statement to your method, right above the statement that throws the exception (the one with the break point):

```
if (txtInput.Text == "") return;
```

Press F5 to run the project once more, and then click the button. This time, C# won't throw an exception, and it won't halt execution at your break point; the test you just created causes code execution to leave the procedure before the statement with the break point is reached.

Type your name into the text box and click the button again. Now that the text box is no longer empty, execution passes the statement with the exit test and stops at the break point. Press F5 to continue executing the code, and again you'll receive an exception. Click Break to enter Break mode, and type the following into the Command window (be sure to press Enter when done):

```
? txtInput.Text
```

The Command window prints your name.

Well, you eliminated the problem of not supplying any data to the `long.Parse()` method, but something else is wrong. Press F5 to continue executing the code and take a closer look at the exception text. The last statement in the text says Input string was not in a correct format. It apparently still doesn't like what's being passed to the `long.Parse()` method. By now, it may have occurred to you that no logical way exists to convert alphanumeric text to a number; `long.Parse()` needs a number to work with. You can easily test this by entering a number into the text box. Do this now by clicking Break, choosing Stop Debugging from the Debug menu, and pressing F5 to run the project. Enter a number into the text box and click the button. Code execution again stops at the break point. Press F11 to execute the statement. No errors this time! Press F5 to continue execution and C# will display the message box (finally). Click OK to dismiss the message box and then close the form to stop the project.

> You can use the Command window to change the value of a variable in addition to printing the value.

16

Because the `long.Parse()` method expects a number, yet the text box contains no intrinsic way to force numeric input, you have to accommodate this situation in your code. You will learn how to deal with exceptions later on in this chapter using a catch statement.

Using the Output Window

The Output window (see Figure 16.6) is used by C# to display various status messages and build errors. The most useful feature of the Output window, for general use, is the capability to send data to it from a running application. This is especially handy when debugging applications.

FIGURE 16.6

The Output window displays a lot of useful information—if you know what you're looking for.

You've already used the Output window in previous hours, but you might not have seriously considered its application as related to debugging. As you can see from Figure 16.6, some data sent to the Output window by C# isn't that intuitive—in fact, you can ignore much of what is automatically sent to the Output window. What you'll want to use the Output window for is printing data for debugging (as you have done and will do throughout this book). Therefore, it's no coincidence that printing to the Output window is accomplished via the Debug object.

To print data to the Output window, use the WriteLine() method of the Debug object, like this:

```
Debug.WriteLine("Results = " + lngResults);
```

The Debug object is a member of the `System.Diagnostics` namespace. Therefore, to define the scope for `Debug.WriteLine` statements, you will need to add **using System.Diagnostics** to the header section of your class (along with the other using statements C# creates automatically.

If you do not add **using System.Diagnostics** to the top of your code file, you can still access Debug.WriteLine() by writing out the full expression: **System.Diagnostics.Debug.WriteLine()**.

Whatever you place within the parentheses of the WriteLine() method is what is printed to the Output window. Note that you can print literal text and numbers, variables, or expressions. WriteLine() is most useful in cases where you want to know the value of a variable, but you don't want to halt code execution using a break point. For instance, suppose you have a number of statements that manipulate a variable. You can sprinkle WriteLine() statements into the code to print the variable's contents at strategic points. When you do this, you'll want to print some text along with the variable's value so that the output makes sense to you. For example:

```
Debug.WriteLine("Results of area calculation = " + sngArea);
```

You can also use WriteLine() to create checkpoints in your code, like this:

```
Debug.WriteLine("Passed Checkpoint 1");
// Execute statement here
Debug.WriteLine("Passed Checkpoint 4");
// Execute another statement here
Debug.WriteLine("Passed Checkpoint 3");
```

Many creative uses exist for the Output window. Just remember that the Output window isn't available to a compiled component; calls to the Debug object are ignored by the compiler when creating distributable components.

Writing an Error Handler Using `try...catch...finally`

It's very useful to have C# halt execution when an exception occurs. When the code is halted while running with the IDE, you receive an error message and you're shown the offending line of code. However, when your project is run as a compiled program, unhandled exceptions will cause the program to terminate (crash to the desktop). This is one of the most undesirable things an application can do. Fortunately, you can prevent exceptions from stopping code execution (and terminating compiled programs) by writing code specifically designed to deal with exceptions. Exception-handling code is used to instruct C# on how to deal with an exception, rather than relying on C#'s default behavior.

NEW TERM C# supports *structured error handling* (a formal way of dealing with errors) in the form of a try block and/or catch block(s) and/or a finally block. Creating structured error-handling code can be a bit confusing at first, and like most coding principles, it is best understood by doing it.

Create a new Windows Application called **Structured Error Handling**. Change the name of the default form to **flcsErrorHandlingExample**, set its Text property to **Try...Catch...Finally**, and change the Main() entry point of the project to reference fclsErrorHandlingExample instead of Form1. Next, add a new button to the form and set its properties as follows:

Property	Value
Name	btnCatchException
Location	104,128
Size	96,23
Text	Catch Exception

Double-click the button and add the following code.

```
try
{
    Debug.WriteLine("Try");
}
catch
{
    Debug.WriteLine("Catch");
}
finally
{
    Debug.WriteLine("Finally");
}
Debug.WriteLine("Done Trying");
```

Remember to add **using System.Diagnostics** to the top of your class so that you can use the Debug.WriteLine() statement.

As you can see, the try, catch, and finally statements use the braces ({ }) to enclose statements. The try, catch, and finally structure is used to wrap code that may cause an exception; it provides the means of dealing with thrown exceptions. Table 16.2 explains the sections of this structure.

TABLE 16.2   *try, catch, and finally* Structure

Part	Description
try	The try section is where you place code that may cause an exception. You may place all of a procedure's code within the try section, or just a few lines.
catch	Code within a general catch clause executes only when an exception occurs; it's the code you write to catch any exception. There may be multiple catch clauses to handle specific exceptions.
finally	Code within the finally section occurs when the code within the try and/or code within the catch sections completes. This section is where you place your "clean up" code—code that you want always executed regardless of whether an exception occurs.

Three possible forms of try statements are the following:
- A try block followed by one or more catch blocks.
- A try block followed by a finally block.
- A try block followed by one or more catch blocks, followed by a finally block.

This example is using a try block followed by a catch block, followed by a finally block.

Press F5 to run the project and then click the button. Next, take a look at the contents of the Output window. The Output window should contain the following lines of text:

```
Try
Finally
Done Trying
```

Here's what happened:

1. The try block begins, and code within the try section executes.

2. No exception occurs, so code within the catch section doesn't execute.

3. When all statements within the try section finish executing, the code within the finally section executes.

4. When all statements within the finally section finish executing, execution jumps to the statement immediately following the try, catch, and finally statements.

Stop the project now by choosing Stop Debugging from the Debug menu. Now that you understand the basic mechanics of the try, catch, and finally structure, you're going to add statements within the structure so that an exception occurs and gets handled.

Change the contents of the code to match this code:

```
long lngNumerator = 10;
long lngDenominator = 0;
long lngResult;

try
{
    Debug.WriteLine("Try");
    lngResult = lngNumerator / lngDenominator;
}
catch
{
    Debug.WriteLine("Catch");
}
finally
{
    Debug.WriteLine("Finally");
}

Debug.WriteLine("Done Trying");
```

Again, press F5 to run the project; then click the button and take a look at the Output window. This time, the text in the Output window should read

```
Try
Catch
Finally
Done Trying
```

Notice that this time the code within the catch section is executed. This is because the statement that sets lngResult causes a DivideByZero exception. Had this statement not been placed within a catch block, C# would have raised the exception and an error dialog box would have appeared. However, because the statement is placed within the try block, the exception is "caught." This means that when the exception occurred, C# directed execution to the catch section (you do not have to use a catch section, in which case caught exceptions are simply ignored). Notice also how the code within the finally section executed after the code within the catch section. Remember, code within the finally section always executes, regardless of whether an exception occurs.

Dealing with an Exception

Catching exceptions so that they don't crash your application is a noble thing to do, but it's only part of the error-handling process. Usually, you'll want to tell the user (in a friendly way) that an exception has occurred. You'll probably also want to tell the user what type of exception occurred. To do this, you have to have a way of knowing what

16

exception was thrown. This is also important if you intend to write code to deal with specific exceptions. The catch statement enables you to specify a variable to hold a reference to an Exception object. Using this Exception object, you can get information about the exception. The following is the syntax used to place the exception in an Exception object:

```
catch ( Exception variablename)
```

Modify your catch section to match the following:

```
catch (Exception objException)
{
    Debug.WriteLine("Catch");
    MessageBox.Show("An error has occurred: " + objException.Message);
}
```

The Message property of the Exception object contains the text that describes the specific exception that occurs. Run the project, click the Catch Exception button, and C# displays your custom error message (see Figure 16.7).

FIGURE 16.7
Structured exception handling lets you decide what to do when an exception occurs.

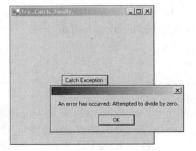

Handling an Anticipated Exception

At times, you'll anticipate a specific exception being thrown. For example, you may write code that attempts to open a file when the file does not exist. In such an instance, you'll probably want the program to perform certain actions when this exception is thrown. When you anticipate a specific exception, you can create a catch section designed specifically to deal with that one exception.

Recall from the previous section that you can retrieve information about the current exception using a catch statement such as catch (Exception). By creating a generic Exception variable, this catch statement will catch any and all exceptions thrown by statements within the try section. To catch a specific exception, change the data type of the exception variable to a specific exception type. Remember the code you wrote earlier that caused a Format exception when an attempt was made to pass an empty string to the long.Parse() method? You could have used a try structure to deal with the exception, using code such as this:

```
long lngAnswer;

try
{
    lngAnswer = 100 / long.Parse(txtInput.Text);
    MessageBox.Show("100/" + txtInput.Text + " is " + lngAnswer);
}
catch (System.FormatException)
{
MessageBox.Show("You must enter a number in the text box.");
}
catch
{
    MessageBox.Show("Caught an exception that wasn't a format exception.");
}
```

16

Notice that two catch statements are in this structure. The first catch statement is designed to catch only a Format exception; it won't catch exceptions of any other type. The second catch statement doesn't care what type of exception is thrown; it catches all of them. This second catch statement acts as a "catch all" for any exceptions that aren't Format exceptions, because catch sections are evaluated from top to bottom, much like case statements in the switch structure. You could add more catch sections to catch other specific exceptions if the situation calls for it.

Summary

In this hour, you learned the basics for debugging applications. You learned how adding useful and plentiful comments to your procedures makes debugging easier. However, no matter how good your comments are, you'll still have bugs.

You learned about the two basic types of errors: build errors and runtime errors (exceptions). Build errors are easier to troubleshoot because the compiler tells you exactly what line contains a build error and generally provides useful information about the error. Exceptions, on the other hand, can crash your application if not handled properly. You learned how to track down exceptions using break points, the Command window, and the Output window. Finally, you learned to how to make your applications more robust by creating structured error handlers using the try structure.

No book can teach you everything you need to know to write bug-free code. However, this hour taught you the basic skills to track down and eliminate many types of errors in your programs. As your skills as a programmer improve, so will your debugging abilities.

Q&A

Q. **Should I alert the user that an exception has occurred to just let the code keep running?**

A. If you've written code to handle the specific exception, then there's probably no need to tell the user about it. However, if an exception occurs that the code doesn't know how to address, you should provide the user with the exception information so that he or she can report the problem and you can fix it.

Q. **Should I comment every statement in my application?**

A. Probably not. However, you should consider commenting every decision-making and looping construct in your program. Usually, these sections of code are pivotal to the success of the procedure, and it's not always obvious what they do.

Q. **I'm tired of writing out the full qualifier System.Diagnostics.Debug.WriteLine(). Is there anyway to shorten this?**

A. Yes, by adding a using directive for the System.Diagnostics namespace, you will be able to access its members without having to specify the namespace. This will shorten all your System.Diagnostics.Debug.WriteLine() statements to Debug. WriteLine().

Workshop

The Workshop is designed to help you anticipate possible questions, review what you've learned, and get you thinking about how to put your knowledge into practice. The answers to the quiz are in Appendix A, "Answers to Quizzes/Exercises."

Quiz

1. What type of error prevents C# from compiling and running code?
2. What is the name of a runtime error: an error that usually occurs as a result of attempting to process inappropriate data?
3. What character is used to denote a single line comment?
4. To halt execution at a specific statement in code, you set a what?
5. Explain the yellow arrow and red circles that can appear in the gray area in the code editor.
6. What IDE window would you use to poll the contents of a variable in Break mode?
7. True or False: You must always specify a catch section in a try structure.

Exercises

1. In the code example that sets lngAnswer to the result of a division expression, change lngAnswer from a long to a single (call it sngAnswer). Next, remove the if statement that tests the contents of the text box *before* performing the division. Do you get the same exceptions that you did when the variable was a long? Why or why not?

2. Rewrite the code that sets lngAnswer to the result of a division expression so that the code is wrapped in a try structure. Remove the if statements that perform data validation, and create two catch sections—one for each of the possible exceptions that may be thrown.

16

HOUR 17

Designing Objects Using Classes

You learned about what makes an object an object in Hour 3, "Understanding Objects and Collections." Since that hour, you've learned how to manipulate objects such as forms and controls. The real power of leveraging objects comes from being able to design and implement custom objects of your own design. In this hour, you'll learn how to create your own objects by using classes (in contrast to using static methods). You'll learn how to define the template for an object and how to create your own custom properties and methods.

The highlights of this hour include the following:

- Encapsulating data and code using classes
- Comparing instance member classes with static member classes
- Constructors and destructors
- Creating an object interface

- Exposing object attributes as properties
- Exposing methods
- Instantiating objects from classes
- Binding an object reference to a variable
- Understanding object lifetime
- Releasing object references

> There is simply no way to become an expert on programming classes in a single hour. However, when you've finished with this hour, you'll have a working knowledge of creating classes and deriving custom objects from those classes; consider this hour a primer on object-oriented programming. I strongly encourage you to seek other texts that focus on object-oriented programming after you feel comfortable with the material presented throughout this book.

Understanding Classes

Classes enable you to develop applications using object-oriented programming (OOP) techniques (recall that I discussed OOP briefly in Hour 3). Classes are templates that define objects. Although you may not have known it, you have been programming with classes throughout this book. When you create a new form in a C# project, you are actually creating a class that defines a form; forms instantiated at runtime are derived from the class. Using objects derived from predefined classes, such as a C# Form class, is just the start of enjoying the benefits of object-oriented programming—to truly realize the benefits of OOP, you must create your own classes.

The philosophy of programming with classes is considerably different from that of "traditional" programming. Proper class-programming techniques can make your programs better, both in structure and in reliability. Class programming forces you to consider the logistics of your code and data more thoroughly, causing you to create more reusable and extensible object-based code.

Encapsulating Data and Code Using Classes

An object derived from a class is an encapsulation of data and code; that is, the object comprises its code *and* all the data it uses. For example, suppose that you need to keep track of employees in an organization and that you need to store many of pieces of information for each employee, such as Name, Date Hired, and Title. In addition, suppose you need methods for adding and removing employees, and you want all this information and functionality available to many functions within your application. You could use static methods to manipulate the data. However, this would most likely require many variable arrays, as well as code to manage the arrays.

NEW TERM A better approach is to *encapsulate* all the employee data and functionality (adding and deleting routines and so forth) into a single, reusable object. Encapsulation is the process of integrating data and code into one entity—an object. Your application, as well as external applications, could then work with the employee data through a consistent interface—the Employee object's interface (An *interface* is a set of exposed functionality—essentially, code routines.)

 Creating objects for use outside of your application is beyond the scope of this book. The techniques you'll learn in this hour, however, are directly applicable to creating externally creatable objects.

The encapsulation of data and code is the key detail of classes. By encapsulating the data and the routines to manipulate the data into a single object by way of a class, you free application code that needs to manipulate the data from the intricacies of data mainte-nance. For example, suppose company policy has changed so that when a new employee is added to the system, a special tax record needs to be generated and a form needs to be printed. If the data and code routines weren't encapsulated in a common object but were written in various places throughout your code, you would need to modify each and every module that contained code to create a new employee record. By using a class to create an object, you need to change only the code in one location: within the object. As long as you don't modify the interface of the object (discussed shortly), all the routines that use the object to create a new employee will instantly have the policy change in effect.

Comparing Instance Members with Static Members

You learned in Hour 11, "Creating and Calling Methods," that C# does not support global methods, but supports only class methods. By creating static methods, you create methods that can be accessed from anywhere in the project through the class.

Instance methods are similar to static methods in how they appear in the C# design envi-ronment and in the way in which you write code within them. However, the behavior of classes at runtime differs greatly from that of static members. With static members, all static data is shared by all members of the class. In addition, there are never multiple instances of the static class data. With instance member classes, objects are instantiated from a class and each object receives its own set of data. Static methods are accessed through the class, whereas nonstatic methods (also called instance methods) are accessed through instances of the class.

NEW TERM Instance methods differ from static methods in more ways than just in how their data behaves. When you define a static method, it is instantly available to other classes within your application. However, instant member classes aren't immediately available in code. Classes are templates for objects. At runtime, your code doesn't interact with the code in the class per se, but it instantiates objects derived from the class. Each object acts as its own class "module" and thus it has its own set of data. When classes are exposed externally to other applications, the application containing the class's code is called the *server*. Applications that create and use instances of objects are called *clients*. When you use instances of classes in the application that contains those classes, the application itself acts as both a client and a server. In this hour, I'll refer to the code instantiating an object derived from a class as *client code*.

Begin by creating a new Windows Application titled **Class Programming Example**. Change the name of the default form to **fclsClassExample** and set its Text property to **Class Example**. Next, change the entry point of the project in the method Main() to reference **fclsClassExample** instead of Form1. Add a new class to the project by choosing Add Class from the Project menu. Save the class with the name **clsMyClass.cs** (see Figure 17.1).

FIGURE 17.1

Classes are added to a project the same as other object files are added.

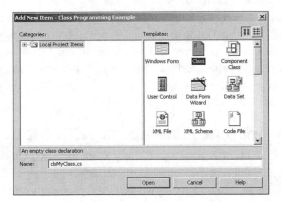

Constructors and Destructors

NEW TERM As you open your new class file, you'll notice that C# added the public class declaration and a method called clsMyClass(). This is known as the *class* *constructor*. A constructor has the same name as the class, includes no return type, and has no return value. A class constructor is called whenever a class object is instantiated. Therefore, it's normally used for initialization if some code needs to be executed automatically when a class is instantiated. If a constructor isn't specified in your class definition, the Common Language Runtime (CLR) will provide a default constructor.

> Objects consume system resources. The .NET Framework (discussed in Hour 24, "The 10,000-Foot View") has a built-in mechanism to free resources used by objects. This mechanism is called the *Garbage Collector* (and it is discussed in Hour 24 as well). Essentially, the garbage collector determines when an object is no longer being used and then destroys the object. When the garbage collector destroys an object, it calls the object's destructor method. If you aren't careful about how to implement a destructor method, you can cause problems. I recommend that you seek a book dedicated to object-oriented programming to learn more about constructors and destructors.

Creating an Object Interface

For an object to be created from a class, the class must expose an interface. As I mentioned earlier, an interface is a set of exposed functionality (essentially, code routines/methods). Interfaces are the means by which client code communicates with the object derived from the class. Some classes expose a limited interface, whereas some expose complex interfaces. The content and quantity of your class's interface is entirely up to you.

The interface of a class consists of one or more of the following members:

- Properties
- Methods
- Events

For example, assume that you are creating an Employee object (that is, a class used to derive employee objects). You must first decide how you want client code to interact with your object. You'll want to consider both the data contained within the object and the functions the object can perform. You might want client code to be able to retrieve the name of an employee and other information such as sex, age, and the date of hire. For client code to get these values from the object, the object must expose an interface member for each of the items. Recall from Hour 3 that values exposed by an object are called properties. Therefore, each piece of data discussed here would have to be exposed as a property of the Employee object.

In addition to properties, you can expose functions—such as a Delete or AddNew function. These functions may be simple in nature or very complex. The Delete function of the Employee object, for example, might be quite complex. It would need to perform all the actions necessary to delete an employee, including such things as removing the employee from an assigned department, notifying accounting to remove the employee from the payroll, notifying security to revoke the employee's security access, and so on. Publicly exposed functions of an object, as you should remember from Hour 3, are called methods.

Properties and methods are the most commonly used interface members. Although designing properties and methods may be new to you, by now using them isn't; you've been using properties and methods in almost every hour so far. Here, you're going to learn the techniques for creating properties and methods for your own objects.

For even more interaction between the client and the object, you can expose custom events. Custom object events are similar to the events of a form or a text box. However, with custom events you have complete control over the following:

- The name of the event
- The parameters passed to the event
- When the event occurs

Events in C# are based on delegates. Creating custom events is complicated, and I'll be covering only custom properties and methods in this hour.

Properties, methods, and events together make up an object's interface. This interface acts as a contract between the client application and the object. Any and all communication between the client and the object must transpire through this interface (see Figure 17.2).

FIGURE 17.2

Clients interact with an object via the object's interface.

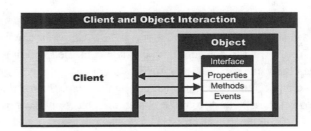

The technical details of the interaction between the client and the object by way of the interface are, mercifully, handled by C#. Your responsibility is to define the properties, methods, and events of an object so that its interface is logical, consistent, and exposes all the functionality a client needs to use the object.

Exposing Object Attributes as Properties

Properties are the attributes of objects. Properties can be read-only, or they can allow both reading and writing of their values. For example, you may want to let a client retrieve the value of a property containing the path of the component, but not let the client change it because you can't change the path of a running component.

You can add properties to a class in two ways. The first is to declare public variables. Any variable declared as public instantly becomes a property of the class (technically, it's referred to as a *field*). For example, suppose you have the following statement in the Declarations section of a class:

```
public long Quantity;
```

Clients could read from and write to the property using code such as the following:

```
objMyObject.Quantity = 139;
```

This works, but significant limitations exist that make this approach less than desirable:

- You can't execute code when a property value changes. For example, what if you wanted to write the quantity change to a database? Because the client application can access the variable directly, you have no way of knowing when the value of the variable changes.

- You can't prevent client code from changing a property, because the client code accesses the variable directly.

- Perhaps the biggest problem is this: How do you control data validation? For instance, how could you ensure that Quantity was never set to a negative value?

You simply can't work around these issues using a public variable. Instead of exposing public variables, you should create class properties using property procedures.

Property procedures enable you to execute code when a property is changed, to validate property values, and to dictate whether a property is read-only, write-only, or both readable and writable. Declaring a property procedure is similar to declaring a method, but with some important differences. The basic structure of a property looks like this:

```
Private int privatevalue;

public int  propertyname
{
```

17

```
      get
      {
        return privatevalue;    // Code to return the property's value .
      }
      set
      {
        privatevalue = value;   // Code that accepts a new value.
      }
}
```

The first word in the property declaration simply designates the scope of the property (public or private). Properties declared with public are available to code outside of the class (they can be accessed by client code). Properties declared as private are available only to code within the class. Immediately following public or private are the data type and property name.

Place your cursor after the left bracket following the statement `public class clsMyclass` and press Enter to create a new line. Type the following statements into your class:

```
private int m_intHeight;

public int Height
{
    get
    {
    }
    set
    {
    }
}
```

You might be wondering why you just created a module-level variable of the same name as your property procedure (with a naming prefix, of course). After all, I just finished preaching about the problems of using a module-level variable as a property. A property has to get its value from somewhere, and a module-level variable is usually the best place to store it. The property procedure will act as a wrapper for this variable. Notice here that the variable is private rather than public. This means that no code outside of the class can view or modify the contents of this variable; as far as client code is concerned, this variable doesn't exist.

Between the property declaration statement and its closing brace are two constructs: the get construct and a set construct. Each of these constructs is discussed in its own section.

Creating Readable Properties Using the get Accessor

The get accessor is used to place code that returns a value for the property when read by the client. If you remove the get accessor and its corresponding brackets, clients won't be able to read the value of the property. It's rare that you'll want to create such a property, but you can.

Think of the get accessor as a method; whatever you return as the result of the method becomes the property value. Add the following statement between the get brackets:

```
return m_intHeight;
```

You return the value of the property by using the return keyword followed by the value.

Creating Writable Properties Using the set Accessor

The set accessor is where you place code that accepts a new property value from client code. If you remove the set accessor (and its corresponding brackets), clients won't be able to change the value of the property. Leaving the get accessor and removing the set accessor creates a read-only property; clients can retrieve the value of the property but they cannot change it.

Add the following statement between the set brackets:

```
m_intHeight = value;
```

The set clause uses a special variable called value, which is provided automatically by C# and always contains the value being passed to the property by the client code. The statement you just entered assigns the new value to the module-level variable.

As you can see, the property method is a wrapper around the module-level variable. When the client code sets the property, the set accessor stores the new value in the variable. When the client retrieves the value of the property, the get accessor returns the value in the module-level variable.

So far, the property code, with its get and set accessor, doesn't do anything different from what it would do if you were to simply declare a public variable (only the property procedure requires much more code). However, look at this variation of the same set accessor:

```
set
{
if (value >=10)
   m_intHeight = value;
}
```

This set accessor restricts the client to setting the Height property to a value greater than 10. If a value less than 10 is passed to the property, the property procedure is exited without setting m_intHeight. You're not limited to performing only data validation; you can pretty much add whatever code you desire and even call other methods. Go ahead and add the verification statement to your code so that the set accessor looks like this one. Your code should now look like the procedure shown in Figure 17.3.

17

Figure 17.3

This is a property procedure, complete with data validation.

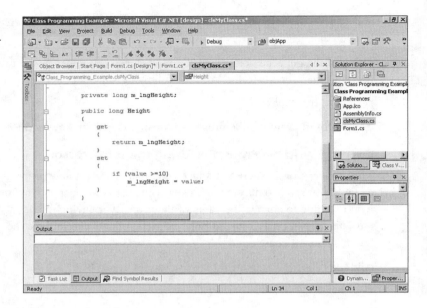

Exposing Functions as Methods

Unlike a property that acts as an object attribute, methods are functions exposed by an object. A method can return a value, but it doesn't have to. Create the following method in your class now. Enter this code on the line following the closing bracket for the declared public int Height property:

```
public long AddTwoNumbers(int intNumber1, int intNumber2)
{
    return intNumber1 + intNumber2;
}
```

Recall that methods defined with a data-type return values, whereas methods defined with void don't. To make a method private to the class and therefore invisible to client code, declare the method as private rather than public.

Instantiating Objects from Classes

After you obtain a reference to an object and assign it to a variable, you can manipulate the object using an object variable. You're going to do this now.

Click the Form1.cs Design tab to view the form designer and add a button to the form by double-clicking the Button item in the toolbox. Set the button's properties as follows:

Property	Value
Name	btnCreateObject
Location	104,120
Size	88,23
Text	Create Object

Next, double-click the button to access its Click event and enter the following code:

```
clsMyClass objMyObject = new clsMyClass();
MessageBox.Show(objMyObject.AddTwoNumbers(1,2).ToString());
```

The first statement creates a variable of type clsMyClass. (Declaring variables was discussed in Hour 12, "Using Constants, Data Types, Variables, and Arrays.") The new keyword tells C# to create a new object, and the text following new is the name of the class to use to derive the object (remember, classes are object templates). The last statement calls the AddTwoNumbers method of your class and displays the result in a message box after converting the return value to a string.

Notice that C# displayed an IntelliSense drop-down list with all the members of the class (see Figure 17.4).

FIGURE 17.4
*C# displays
IntelliSense drop-down
lists for members of
early-bound objects.*

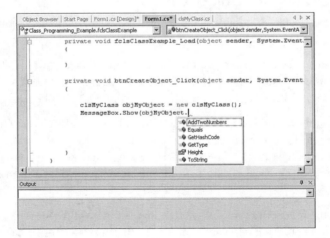

Go ahead and run the project by pressing F5, and then click the button to make sure everything is working correctly. When finished, stop the project and save your work.

Binding an Object Reference to a Variable

NEW TERM An object can contain any number of properties, methods, and events; every object is different. When you write code to manipulate an object, C# has to understand the interface of the object or your code won't work. Resolving the interface members (the properties, methods, and events of the object) occurs when an object variable is bound to an object. The two forms of binding are *early binding* and *late binding*. In addition, binding can occur at runtime or at compile time. It is important that you have at least a working understanding of binding if you are to create code based on classes. Although I can't explain the intricacies and technical details of early binding versus late binding in this hour, I will teach you what you need to know to perform each type of binding.

 Benefits exist to both types of binding, but early binding is generally superior to late binding because code that uses late-bound objects requires more work (time and resources) by C# than code that uses early-bound objects.

Late Binding an Object Variable

When you declare a variable using the generic data type Object, you are late binding to the object.

Unfortunately, C# requires you to handle additional details when late binding to an object (unlike Visual Basic, which handles the details for you). Late binding is beyond the scope of this book, so I'll be focusing on early binding in this hour.

Late binding requires a great deal of overhead, and it adversely affects the performance of an application. Therefore, late binding isn't the preferred method of binding. Late binding does have some attractive uses; however, most of these are related to using objects outside your application, not for using objects derived from classes within the project.

One of the main drawbacks of late binding is the inability for the compiler to check the syntax of the code manipulating an object. Because C# doesn't know anything about the members of a late-bound object, the compiler has no way of knowing whether you're using a member correctly—or even if the member you're referencing exists. This can result in a runtime exception or some other unexpected behavior.

As explained in the previous hour, runtime exceptions are more problematic than build errors because they're usually encountered by end users and under varying circumstances. When you late bind objects, it's easy to introduce these types of problems;

therefore, a real risk exists of throwing exceptions with late binding. As you'll see in the next section, early binding reduces a lot of these risks.

Early Binding an Object Variable

For a member of an object to be referenced, C# must determine and use the internal ID of the specified member. You don't have to know this ID yourself; just be aware that C# needs to know the ID of a member to use it. When an object is early bound (declared as a specific type of object), C# is able to gather the necessary ID information at compile time. This results in considerably faster calls to object members at runtime. In addition, C# can validate a member call at compile time, reducing the chance of errors in your code.

Early binding occurs when you declare a variable as a specific type of object, rather than just as object.

The following are important reasons to use early binding:

- Speed.
- More speed.
- Objects, their properties, and their methods appear in IntelliSense drop-down lists.
- The compiler can check for syntax and reference errors in your code so that many problems are found at compile time, rather than at runtime.

For early binding to take place, an object variable must be declared as a specific object type.

Releasing Object References

When an object is no longer needed, it should be destroyed so that all the resources used by the object can be reclaimed. Objects are destroyed automatically when the last reference to the object is released. Be aware, however, that objects aren't necessarily destroyed immediately when they are no longer referenced and that you don't have control over when they are destroyed. In Hour 24, you'll learn how the garbage collector cleans up unused objects. In this hour, I'm going to focus on what you should do with an object when you're finished with it.

One way to release a reference to an object is simply to let the object variable holding the reference go out of scope, letting the garbage collection of .NET regain the memory space.

To explicitly release an object, set the object variable equal to null, like this:

```
objMyObject = null;
```

17

When you set an object variable equal to null, you're assured that the object reference is fully released. However, just because the reference is released does not mean the object is destroyed! The garbage collector will periodically check for unused objects and reclaim the resources they consume, but this may occur a considerable length of time after the object is no longer used. Therefore, you should add a Dispose() method to all your classes. You should place clean-up code within your Dispose() method and always call Dispose() when you are finished with an object. One thing to keep in mind is that it is technically possible to have more than one variable referencing an object. When this occurs, calling Dispose() may cause clean-up code to execute and therefore cause problems for the code using the second object variable. As you can see, you need to consider many things when programming objects.

> If you don't correctly release resources used by your objects, your application may experience resource leaks, may become sluggish, and might consume more resources than it should. If your object uses resources (such as memory or hardware resources), you should implement a Dispose() method. In addition, you should always call the Dispose() method of an object you are finished with if the object has implemented a Dispose() method.

Understanding the Lifetime of an Object

An object created from a class exists until the garbage collector (see Hour 24) determines it is no longer used and then destroys the object. Fortunately, C# (or more specifically, the .NET Framework) handles the details of keeping track of the references to a given object; you don't have to worry about this when creating or using objects. When all the references to an object are released, C# destroys the object. Your primary responsibility for destroying objects is to call Dispose() on any objects that you are finished with and to create a Dispose() method for your own classes that use resources. Beyond that, the garbage collector handles the details of destroying the objects.

- An object is created (and hence referenced) when an object variable is declared using the keyword new (for example, `clsMyClass objMyObject = new clsMyClass();`).

- An object is referenced when an object variable is assigned an existing object (for example, `objThisObject = objThatObject;`).

- An object reference is released when an object variable is set to null (see the section "Releasing Object References") or goes out of scope.

- When the last reference to an object is released, the object becomes eligible for garbage collection. Many factors, including available system resources, determine when the garbage collector executes next and destroys unused objects.

Summary

Object-oriented programming is an advanced methodology that enables you to create more robust applications; programming classes is the foundation of OOP. In this hour, you learned how to create classes, which are the templates used to instantiate objects. You learned how to create a custom interface consisting of properties and methods and how to use the classes you've defined to instantiate and manipulate objects by way of object variables. You've also learned how you should implement a Dispose() method for classes that consume resources and how it is important to call Dispose() on objects that implement it to ensure that the object frees up its resources as soon as possible. Finally, you learned how objects aren't destroyed as soon as they are no longer needed; rather, they become eligible for garbage collection and are destroyed when the garbage collector next cleans up.

In this hour, you learned the basic mechanics of programming objects with classes. Object-oriented programming takes considerable skill, and you'll need to master the concepts in this book before you can really begin to take advantage of what OOP has to offer. Nevertheless, what you learned in this hour will take you further than you might think. Using an OOP methodology is as much a way of thinking as it is a way of programming; consider how things in your projects might work as objects, and before you know it, you'll be creating robust classes.

17

Q&A

Q. Should I always try to place code into instance classes rather than static classes?

A. Not necessarily. As with most things, there are no hard and fast rules. Correctly programming instance classes takes some skill and experience, and programming static is easier for the beginner. If you want to experiment with instance classes, I encourage you to do so. However, don't feel as though you have to place everything into instantiated classes.

Q. I want to create a general class with a lot of miscellaneous methods—sort of a "catchall" class. What is the best way to do this?

A. If you want to create some sort of utility class, I recommend calling the class something like clsUtility. Then you can use this class throughout your application to access the utility functions.

Workshop

The Workshop is designed to help you anticipate possible questions, review what you've learned, and get you thinking about how to put your knowledge into practice. The answers to the quiz are in Appendix A, "Answers to Quizzes/Exercises."

Quiz

1. To create objects, you must first create a template. This template is called a:

2. One of the primary benefits of object-oriented programming is that objects contain both their data and their code. This is called:

3. With static classes, public variables and routines are always available to code via the static class in other modules. Is this true with public variables and routines in classes?

4. True or False: Each object derived from a class has its own set of class-level data.

5. What must you do to create a property that can be read but not changed by client code?

6. What is the best way to store the internal value of a property within a class?

7. Which is generally superior, early binding or late binding?

8. What is the best way to release an object you no longer need?

Exercises

1. Add a new property to your class called DropsInABucket. Make this property a Long, and set it up so that client code can read the property value but not set it. Finally, add a button to the form that, when clicked, prints the value of the property to the Output window. When this is working, modify the code so that the property always returns 1,000,000.

2. Add a button to your form that creates two object variables of type clsMyClass(). Use the new keyword to instantiate a new instance of the class in one of the variables. Then set the second variable to reference the same object and print the contents of the Height property to the Output window.

HOUR 18

Interacting with Users

Forms and controls are the primary means by which users interact with an application, and vice versa. However, program interaction can and often does go deeper than that. For example, a program can display customized messages to a user, and it can be finely tuned to deal with certain keystrokes or mouse clicks. In this hour, you'll learn how to create functional and cohesive interaction between your application and the user. In addition, you'll learn how to program the keyboard and the mouse so that you can expand the interactiveness of your program beyond what is natively supported by a form and its controls.

The highlights of this hour include the following:

- Displaying messages using the MessageBox.Show() method
- Creating custom dialog boxes
- Interacting with the keyboard
- Using the common mouse events

Displaying Messages Using the MessageBox.Show() Method

A message box is a small dialog box that displays a message to the user. Message boxes are often used to tell the user the result of some action, such as `The file has been copied.` or `The file could not be found.` A message box is dismissed when the user clicks one of the message box's available buttons. Most applications have many message boxes, yet developers often don't display messages correctly. It's important to remember that when you display a message to a user, you're communicating with the user. In this section, I want to teach you not only how to use the MessageBox.Show() method to display messages, but how to use the statement effectively.

The MessageBox.Show() method can be used to tell a user something or ask the user a question. In addition to text, which is its primary function, you can also use this function to display an icon or display one or more buttons that the user can click. Although you are free to display whatever text you want, you must choose from a predefined list of icons and buttons.

A MessageBox.Show() method is an overloaded method. This means that the method was written with numerous constructs supporting various options. While coding in Visual Studio .NET, IntelliSense displays a drop-down scrolling list displaying any of the twelve overloaded MessageBox.Show method calls to aid in coding. Following are a few ways to call MessageBox.Show():

To display a message box with specified text, a caption in the title bar, and an OK button, use this syntax:

```
MessageBox.Show(MessageText, Caption);
```

To display a message box with specified text, caption, and one or more specific buttons, use this syntax:

```
MessageBox.Show(MessageText, Caption, Buttons);
```

To display a message box with specified text, caption, buttons, and icon, use this syntax:

```
MessageBox.Show(MessageText, Caption, Buttons, Icon);
```

In all these statements, *MessageText* is the text to display in the message box, *Caption* determines what appears in the title bar, *Buttons* determines which buttons the user sees, and *Icon* determines what icon (if any) appears in the message box. Consider the following statement, which produces the message box shown in Figure 18.1.

```
MessageBox.Show("This is a message.");
```

FIGURE 18.1

A message box in its simplest form.

As you can see, if you omit *Buttons*, C# displays only an OK button. You should always ensure that the buttons displayed are appropriate for the message.

The Visual Basic MsgBox() function defaults the caption for the message box to the name of the project. There is no default in C#.

Specifying Buttons and an Icon

The *Buttons* parameter contains the "meat" of the message box statement. Using the *Buttons* parameter, you can display a button (or buttons) in the message box. The *Buttons* parameter type is *MessageBoxButtons*, and the allowable values are shown in Table 18.1.

TABLE 18.1 Allowable Enumerators for MessageBoxButtons

Members	Description
AbortRetryIgnore	Displays Abort, Retry, and Ignore buttons.
OK	Displays OK button only.
OKCancel	Displays OK and Cancel buttons.
YesNoCancel	Displays Yes, No, and Cancel buttons.
YesNo	Displays Yes and No buttons.
RetryCancel	Displays Retry and Cancel buttons.

Because the *Buttons* parameter is an enumerated type, C# gives you an IntelliSense dropdown list when specifying a value for this parameter. Therefore, committing these values to memory isn't all that important; you'll fairly quickly commit the ones you use most often to memory.

The *Icon* parameter determines the symbol displayed in the message box. The Icon parameter is an enumeration from the MessageBoxIcon type. The MessageBoxIcon has the values shown in Table 18.2.

TABLE 18.2   Enumerators for MessageBoxIcon

Members	Description
Asterisk	Displays a symbol consisting of a lowercase letter i in a circle.
Error	Displays a symbol consisting of a white X in a circle with a red background.
Exclamation	Displays a symbol consisting of an exclamation point in a triangle with a yellow background.
Hand	Displays a symbol consisting of a white X in a circle with a red background.
Information	Displays a symbol consisting of a lowercase letter i in a circle.
None	Displays no symbol.
Question	Displays a symbol consisting of a question mark in a circle.
Stop	Displays a symbol consisting of a white X in a circle with a red background.
Warning	Displays a symbol consisting of an exclamation point in a triangle with a yellow background.

The *Icon* parameter is also an enumerated type; therefore, C# gives you an IntelliSense drop-down list when specifying a value for this parameter.

The message box in Figure 18.2 was created with the following statement:

```
MessageBox.Show("I'm about to do something...","MessageBox sample",
   MessageBoxButtons.OKCancel,MessageBoxIcon.Information);
```

FIGURE 18.2

Assign the Information icon to general messages.

The message box in Figure 18.3 was created with a statement almost identical to the previous one, except that the second button is designated the default button. If a user presses the Enter key with a message box displayed, the message box acts as though the user clicked the default button. You'll want to give careful consideration to the default button in each message box. For example, if the application is about to do something that the user probably doesn't want to do, it's best to make the Cancel button the default button—in case the user is a bit quick when pressing the Enter key. Following is the statement used to generate the message box in Figure 18.3.

```
MessageBox.Show("I'm about to do something...","MessageBox sample",
    MessageBoxButtons.OKCancel,MessageBoxIcon.Information,
    MessageBoxDefaultButton.Button2);
```

FIGURE 18.3

The default button has a dark border.

In Figure 18.4, the Error icon is shown. The Error icon is best used in rare circumstances, such as when an exception has occurred. Overusing the Error icon is like crying wolf—when a real problem emerges, the user might not take notice. Notice here how I've displayed only the OK button. If something has already happened and there's nothing the user can do about it, don't bother giving the user a Cancel button. The following statement generated the message box shown in Figure 18.4.

```
MessageBox.Show("Something bad has happened!","MessageBox sample",
    MessageBoxButtons.OK,MessageBoxIcon.Error);
```

In Figure 18.5, a question has been posed to the user, so I chose to display the Question icon. Also note how I assumed that the user would probably choose No, so I made the second button the default. In the next section, you'll learn how to determine which button the user clicks. Here's the statement used to generate the message box shown in Figure 18.5:

```
MessageBox.Show("Would you like to format your hard drive now?",
    "MessageBox sample",MessageBoxButtons.YesNo,MessageBoxIcon.Question,
    MessageBoxDefaultButton.Button2);
```

18

FIGURE 18.4

If users have no control over what has occurred, don't give them a Cancel button.

FIGURE 18.5

Message boxes can be used to ask a question.

As you can see, designating buttons and icons is not all that difficult. The real thought comes in determining which buttons and icons are appropriate for a given situation.

Determining Which Button Is Clicked

You'll probably find that many of your message boxes are simple, containing only an OK button. For other message boxes, however, you'll need to determine which button a user clicks. Why give the user a choice if you're not going to act on that choice? The MessageBox.Show() method returns the button clicked as a DialogResult enumeration. The DialogResult has the following values, as shown in Table 18.3.

TABLE 18.3 Enumerators for DialogResult

Members	Description
Abort	Return value Abort, usually sent from a button labeled Abort.
Cancel	Return value Cancel, usually sent from a button labeled Cancel.
Ignore	Return value Ignore, usually sent from a button labeled Ignore.

TABLE 18.3 continued

Members	Description
No	Return value No, usually sent from a button labeled No.
None	Nothing is returned from the dialog box. The model dialog will continue running.
OK	Return value OK, usually sent from a button labeled OK.
Retry	Return value Retry, usually sent from a button labeled Retry.
Yes	Return value Yes, usually sent from a button labeled Yes.

Performing actions based on the button clicked is a matter of using one of the decision constructs. For example:

```
if (MessageBox.Show("Would you like to do X?","MessageBox sample",
    MessageBoxButtons.YesNo,MessageBoxIcon.Question) == DialogResult.Yes)
    // Code to do X would go here.
```

As you can see, MessageBox.Show() is a method that gives you a lot of "bang for your buck"; it offers considerable flexibility.

Crafting Good Messages

The MessageBox.Show() method is surprisingly simple to use, considering all the different forms of messages it enables you to create. The real trick is in providing appropriate messages to users and appropriate times. In addition to considering the icon and buttons to display in a message, you should follow these guidelines for crafting message text.

- Use a formal tone. Don't use large words, and avoid using contractions. Strive to make the text immediately understandable and not overly fancy; a message box is not a place to show off your literary skills.

- Limit messages to two or three lines. Lengthy messages are not only harder for users to read, but they can also be intimidating. When a message box is used to ask a question, make the question as simple as possible.

- Never make users feel as though they've done something wrong. Users will, and do, make mistakes, but you should craft messages that take the sting out of the situation.

- Spell check all message text. Visual Studio's code editor doesn't spell check for you, so you should type your messages into a program such as Word and spell check the text before pasting it into your code. Spelling errors have an adverse effect on a user's perception of a program.

- Avoid technical jargon. Just because someone uses software doesn't mean that he or she is a technical person; explain things in plain English.

18

Creating Custom Dialog Boxes

Most of the time, the MessageBox.Show() method should be a sufficient means to display messages to a user. At times, however, the MessageBox.Show() method is too limited for a given purpose. For example, suppose you wanted to display a lot of text and therefore wanted a message box that was sizable by the user.

Custom dialog boxes are nothing more than standard modal forms with one notable exception: one or more buttons are designated to return a dialog result, the same as the buttons on a message box shown with the MessageBox.Show() method.

You're now going to create a custom dialog box. Create a new Windows Application titled **Custom Dialog Example**. Change the name of the default form to **fclsMain**, set its Text property to **Custom Dialog Box Example**, and set the Main() entry point of the project to reference **fclsMain** rather than Form1. Add a new button to the form and set its properties as follows:

Property	Value
Name	btnShowCustomDialogBox
Location	72,180
Size	152,23
Text	Show Custom Dialog Box

Next, you're going to create the custom dialog box. Add a new form to the project by choosing Add Windows Form from the Project menu. Save the new form with the name **fclsCustomDialogBox.cs**. Change the Text property of the new form to **This is a custom dialog box**. Add a new text box to the form and set its properties as follows:

Property	Value
Name	txtCustomMessage
Location	8,8
Locked	true
Multiline	true
Size	276,224
Text	Custom message goes here

For a custom dialog box to return a result like a standard message box does, it must have buttons that are designated to return a dialog result. This is accomplished by setting the DialogResult property of a button (see Figure 18.6).

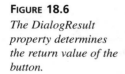

FIGURE **18.6**

The DialogResult property determines the return value of the button.

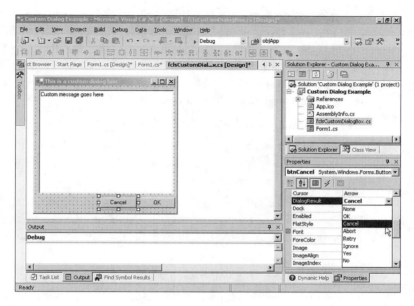

Add a new button to the form and set its properties as shown in the following table. This button will act as the custom dialog box's Cancel button.

Property	Value
Name	btnCancel
DialogResult	Cancel
Location	128,240
Size	75,23
Text	Cancel

Last, you need to create an OK button for the custom dialog box. Create another button and set its properties as shown in the following table:

Property	Value
Name	btnOK
DialogResult	OK
Location	208,240
Size	75,23
Text	OK

18

Specifying a dialog result for one or more buttons is the first step in making a form a custom dialog box. The second part of the process is in how the form is shown. As you learned in Hour 5, "Building Forms—Part I," forms are displayed by calling the Show method of the form or setting its visible property to true. However, to show a form as a custom dialog box, you call the ShowDialog method instead. When a form is displayed using ShowDialog, the following occurs:

- The form is shown modally.
- If the user clicks a button that has its DialogResult property set to return a value, the form is immediately closed and that value is returned as the result of the ShowDialog method call.

Notice how you don't have to write code to close the form; clicking a button with a dialog result closes the form automatically. This simplifies the process of creating custom dialog boxes. Return to the first form in the form designer by clicking the Form1.cs [Design] tab.

Double-click the button you created and add the following code:

```
fclsCustomDialogBox  objCustomDialogBox = new fclsCustomDialogBox();

if (objCustomDialogBox.ShowDialog() == DialogResult.OK)
    MessageBox.Show("You clicked OK.");
else
    MessageBox.Show("You clicked Cancel.");

objCustomDialogBox = null;
```

Press F5 to run the project, click the button to display your custom dialog box (see Figure 18.7), and then click one of the available dialog box buttons. When you're satisfied the project is working correctly, stop the project and save your work.

 If you click the Close (X) button in the upper-right corner of the form, the form is closed and the code behaves as if you've clicked Cancel; the else code occurs.

The capability to create custom dialog boxes is a powerful feature. Usually, a call to MessageBox.Show() will suffice, but when you need more control over the appearance and contents of a message box, creating a custom dialog box is the way to go.

FIGURE 18.7

The ShowDialog method enables you to create custom message boxes.

Interacting with the Keyboard

Most every control handles its own keyboard input; however, on occasion, you'll want to handle keyboard input directly. For example, you might want to perform an action when the user presses a specific button or releases a specific button. Most controls support three events that you can use to work directly with keyboard input. These are listed in Table 18.4.

TABLE 18.4 Events That Handle Keyboard Input

Event Name	Description
KeyDown	Occurs when a key is pressed down while the control has the focus.
KeyPress	Occurs when a key is pressed (the key has been pushed down and then released) while the control has the focus.
KeyUp	Occurs when a key is released while the control has the focus.

These events fire in the same order in which they appear in Table 18.4. Suppose, for example, that the user presses a key while a text box has the focus. The following list shows how the events would fire for the text box:

1. When the user presses a key, the KeyDown event fires.

2. When the user releases a key, the KeyPress event fires.

3. After the KeyPress event fires, the KeyUp event fires, completing the cycle of keystroke events.

You're now going to create a project that illustrates handling keystrokes. This project has a text box that will refuse to display the letter "k." Start by creating a new Windows

Application titled **Keyboard Example**. Change the name of the default form to **fclsKeyboardExample**, set its Text property to **Keyboard Example**, and set the Main() entry point of the project to reference **fclsKeyboardExample** instead of Form1. Add a new text box to the form and set its properties as shown in the following table:

Property	Value
Name	txtInput
Location	24,80
Multiline	true
Size	240,120
Text	*(make blank)*

You're going to add code to the KeyPress event of the text box to "eat" keystrokes made with the letter "k." Select the text box on the form and open the events list in the Properties window (Remember, this is the lightning bolt icon). Scroll through the list and locate the KeyPress event. Next, double-click the KeyPress event to access it in code. Your code editor should look now look like Figure 18.8.

FIGURE 18.8

The KeyPress event is a good place to handle keyboard entry.

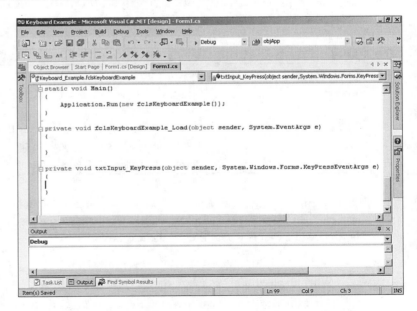

As you learned in Hour 4, "Understanding Events," the e parameter contains information about the occurrence of this event. In the keyboard events, the e parameter contains information about the key being pressed; therefore, it's what you'll be using to work with the keystroke made by the user.

The key being pressed is available as the KeyChar property of the e parameter. You are going to write code that handles the keystroke when the key being pressed is "k." Add the following code to the KeyPress event:

```
if (e.KeyChar == 'k')
        e.Handled = true;
```

Be sure to surround the k with single quotes, not double-quotes, because you're dealing with a character (char), not a string.

I would imagine that you're curious about the Handled property of the e object. When you set this property to true, you are telling C# that you handled the keystroke, and C# should ignore it. To see the effect this has, press F5 to run the project and enter the following into the text box:

Heard any good jokes lately?

What you'll end up with is the text shown in Figure 18.9.

FIGURE 18.9

Notice how the letter k was "eaten" by your code.

Go ahead, try to enter another "k"—you can't. Next, try to enter an uppercase "K"; C# allows you to do this because uppercase and lowercase characters are considered different characters. Want to catch all "Ks," regardless of case? You could do so by adding the OR (| |) operand to your decision construct, like this:

```
if (e.KeyChar == 'k'|| e.KeyChar == 'K')
    e.Handled = true;
```

It's not often that I need to catch a keypress, but every now and then I do. The three keystroke events have always made it easy to do what I need to do, but if there's any caveat I've discovered, it's that you need to give careful consideration to which event you choose (such as KeyPress or KeyUp, for example). Different events work best in different situations, and the best thing to do is to start with what seems like the most logical event, test the code, and change the event if necessary.

Using the Common Mouse Events

As with keyboard input, most controls support mouse input natively; you don't have to write code to deal with mouse input. However, at times you need more control than that offered by the native functionality of a control. C# supports six events that enable you to deal with mouse input directly. These events are listed in Table 18.5, in the order in which they occur.

TABLE 18.5   Events Used to Handle Mouse Input

Event Name	Description
MouseEnter	Occurs when the pointer enters a control.
MouseMove	Occurs when the pointer moves over a control.
MouseHover	Occurs when the pointer hovers over a control.
MouseDown	Occurs when the pointer is over a control and a button is pressed.
MouseUp	Occurs when the pointer is over a control and a button is released.
MouseLeave	Occurs when the pointer leaves a control.

You're now going to build a project that illustrates interacting with the mouse, using the MouseMove event. This project will allow a user to draw on a form, much like you can draw in a paint program. Begin by creating a new Windows Application titled **Mouse Paint**. Change the name of the default form to **fclsMousePaint**, set its Text property to **Paint with the Mouse**, and set the Main() entry point of the project to reference **fclsMousePaint** instead of Form1.

Next, double-click the form to access its default event, the Load event. Enter the following statement into the load event:

```
m_objGraphics = this.CreateGraphics();
```

You've already used a graphics object a few times. What you're doing here is setting a graphics object to the client area of the form; any drawing performed on the object will appear on the form. Because you're going to draw to this graphics object each time the mouse moves over the form, there's no point in creating a new graphics object each time you need to draw to it. Therefore, you're going to make m_objGraphics a module-level variable, which will be instantiated only once—in the Load event of the form. Enter this statement below the opening curly-brace after the *public class fclsMousePaint* class declaration:

```
private Graphics m_objGraphics;
```

As I've said previously, you should always destroy objects when you're done with them. In this case, you want the object to remain in existence for the life of the form. Therefore, you'll destroy it in the Closed event of the form, which occurs when the form is unloaded. Return to the Form1.cs[Design] tab, open the events list in the Property window and double-click the Closed event to create and open the code window to the Closed event. Enter the following statement in the Closed event:

```
m_objGraphics.Dispose();
```

Your form should now look like the one shown in Figure 18.10.

FIGURE 18.10

Code in many places often works together to achieve one goal.

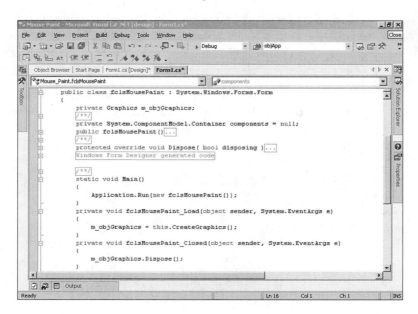

The last bit of code you need to add is the code that will draw on the form. You're going to place code in the MouseMove event of the form to do this. First, the code will make sure the left mouse button is held down. If it's not, no drawing will take place; the user must hold down the mouse button to draw. Next, a rectangle will be created. The coordinates of the mouse pointer will be used to create a very small rectangle that will be passed to the DrawEllipse method of the graphics object. This has the effect of drawing a tiny circle right where the mouse pointer is positioned. Again, Return to the Form1.cs[Design] tab, open the events list in the Property window, and double-click the MouseMove event to create and open the code window to the MouseMove event. Add the following code to this event:

```
Rectangle rectEllipse = new Rectangle() ;

if (e.Button != MouseButtons.Left) return;

rectEllipse.X = e.X - 1;
rectEllipse.Y = e.Y - 1;
rectEllipse.Width = 2;
rectEllipse.Height = 2;

m_objGraphics.DrawEllipse(System.Drawing.Pens.Blue, rectEllipse);
```

Like all events, the e object contains information related to the event. In this example, you are using the X and Y properties of the e object, which is the coordinate of the pointer when the event fires. In addition, you're checking the Button property of the object to make sure the user is pressing the left button.

Your project is now complete! Save your work by clicking Save All on the toolbar, and then press F5 to run the project. Move your mouse over the form—nothing happens. Now, hold down the left mouse button and move the mouse. This time, you'll be drawing on the form (see Figure 18.11).

FIGURE 18.11

Capturing mouse events opens many exciting possibilities.

Notice that the faster you move the mouse, the more space appears between circles. This shows you that the user is able to move the mouse faster than the MouseMove event can fire, so you can't get every single movement of the mouse. This is important to remember.

Summary

Forms and controls allow for a lot of flexibility in the way a user interacts with an application. However, solid interactivity goes beyond what is placed on a form. In this hour, you learned how to use the MessageBox.Show() method to create informational dialog boxes. You learned how to specify an icon, buttons, and even how to designate a specific button as the default button. You also learned some valuable tips to help you create the best messages possible. You'll create message boxes frequently, so mastering this skill is important.

Finally, you learned how to interact with the keyboard and the mouse directly, through numerous events. Sometimes, the mouse or keyboard capabilities of a control fall short of what you want to accomplish. By understanding the concepts presented in this hour, you can go beyond the native capabilities of controls to create a rich, interactive experience for your users.

18

Q&A

Q. Is it possible to capture keystrokes at the form level, rather than capturing them in control events?

A. Yes. For the form's keyboard-related events to fire when a control has the focus, however, you must set the form's KeyPreview property to true. The control's keyboard events will still fire, unless you set KeyAscii = 0 in the form's KeyPress event and KeyCode = 0 in the form's KeyDown event.

Q. You don't seem to always specify a button in your MessageBox.Show() statements throughout this book. Why?

A. If you don't explicitly designate a button or buttons, C# displays the OK button. Therefore, if all you want is an OK button, you do not need to pass a value to the *buttons* argument.

Workshop

The Workshop is designed to help you anticipate possible questions, review what you've learned, and get you thinking about how to put your knowledge into practice. The answers to the quiz are in Appendix A, "Answers to Quizzes/Exercises."

Quiz

1. What minimal argument should you supply when calling MessageBox.Show()?

2. If you don't supply a value for the *title* parameter of MessageBox.Show(), what gets displayed in the title bar of the message?

3. What type of data is always returned by the MessageBox.Show() method?

4. Which event fires first, the KeyUp or KeyPress event?

5. How do you determine which button is being pressed in a mouse-related event?

Exercises

1. Modify your custom dialog box project so that the OK button is the Accept button of the form. That way, the user has only to press Enter to dismiss the dialog box. Next, make the Cancel button the Cancel button of the form so that the user can press the Esc key to dismiss the form as well.

2. Modify your mouse paint project so that the form clears each time the user starts drawing. Hint: Clear the graphics object in the MouseDown event.

PART IV
Working with Data

Most applications written these days are data-centric. In this part, you'll learn
basic file operations, such as creating and deleting files and folders. You'll
also learn basic database skills, such as navigating and working with sets of
records. Last, you'll learn how to use Automation to control the behavior of
other applications such as Microsoft Word.

- Hour 19: Performing File Operations
- Hour 20: Controlling Other Applications Using Automation
- Hour 21: Working with a Database

HOUR 19

Performing File Operations

It's very difficult to imagine any application other than a tiny utility program that doesn't make use of the file system. In this hour, you'll learn how to use the controls to make it easy for a user to browse and select files. In addition, you'll learn how to use the System.IO.File and System.IO.Directory objects to manipulate the file system. Using these objects, you can delete files and directories, move them, rename them, and more. These objects are powerful, but please remember: play nice!

The highlights of this hour include the following:

- Using the Open File Dialog and Save File Dialog controls
- Manipulating files with System.IO.File
- Manipulating directories with System.IO.Directory

Using the Open File Dialog and Save File Dialog Controls

In Hour 1, "A C# Programming Tour," you used the Open File Dialog control to enable a user to browse for pictures to display in your Picture Viewer program. In this section, you'll move beyond those basics to learn important details about working with the Open File Dialog control, as well as its sister control, the Save File Dialog.

You're going to build a project to illustrate most of the file-manipulation concepts discussed in this hour. Before continuing, create a new Windows Application titled **Manipulating Files**. Change the name of the default form to **fclsManipulatingFiles**, set its Text to **Manipulating Files**, and then set the entry point of the project to fclsManipulatingFiles. Add a new text box to the form and set its properties as shown in the following table:

Property	Value
Name	txtSource
Location	95,8
Size	184,20
Text	*(make blank)*

Using the Open File Dialog Control

The Open File Dialog control is used to display a dialog box that enables the user to browse and select a file (see Figure 19.1). It's important to note that usually the Open File Dialog doesn't actually open a file, but it allows a user to select a file that is then opened by code within the application.

Add a new Open File Dialog to your project now by double-clicking the OpenFileDialog item in the toolbox. The Open File Dialog doesn't have an interface per se, so it appears in the area below the form rather than on it. For the user to browse for files, you have to manipulate the Open File Dialog using its properties and methods.

You're going to add a button to the form that, when clicked, allows a user to locate and select a file. If a user selects a file, the filename will be placed in the text box you've created. Go ahead and add a button to the form now, and set its properties as follows:

Property	Value
Name	btnOpenFile
Location	8,8
Size	80,23
Text	Source

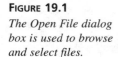

FIGURE 19.1

The Open File dialog box is used to browse and select files.

Next, double-click the button and add the following code to its Click event:

```
openFileDialog1.InitialDirectory = @"C:\";
openFileDialog1.Title = "Select a File";
```

The first statement specifies the directory to display when the dialog box is first shown. If you don't specify a directory for the InitialDirectory property, the active system directory is used (for example, the last directory browsed to with a different Open File dialog box).

The Title property of the Open File Dialog determines the text displayed in the title bar of the Open File dialog box. If you don't specify text for the Title property, C# displays the word Open in the title bar.

Different types of files have different extensions. The Filter property determines what types of files appear in the Open File dialog box (refer to Figure 19.1). A filter is specified in the following format:

```
Description|*.extension
```

The text that appears before the pipe symbol (|) is the descriptive text of the file type to filter on, whereas the text after the pipe symbol is the pattern used to filter files. For example, to display only Windows bitmap files, you could use a filter such as the following:

```
control.Filter = "Windows Bitmaps|*.bmp";
```

You can specify more than one filter type. To do this, add a pipe symbol (|) between the filters, like this:

```
control.Filter = "Windows Bitmaps|*.bmp|JPEG Files|*.jpg";
```

You're going to restrict your Open File dialog box to show only text files, so enter the following statement in your btnOpenFile_Click code:

```
openFileDialog1.Filter = "Text Files|*.txt";
```

19

When you have more than one filter, you can specify which filter appears selected by default using the FilterIndex property. Although you've specified only one filter type in this example, it's still a good idea to designate the default filter, so add this statement to your code:

```
openFileDialog1.FilterIndex = 1;
```

Finally, you need to show the Open File dialog box and take action based on whether the user selects a file. The ShowDialog() method of the Open File Dialog control acts much like the method of forms by the same name, returning a result that indicates the user's selection on the dialog box. Enter the following statements into your procedure:

```
if (openFileDialog1.ShowDialog() != DialogResult.Cancel)
    txtSource.Text = openFileDialog1.FileName;
else
    txtSource.Text = "";
```

This code just places the selected filename into the text box txtSource. If the user clicks Cancel, the contents of the text box are cleared.

Press F5 to run the project and click the button. You'll get the same dialog box shown in Figure 19.1 (with different files and directories, of course). Select a text file, click Open, and C# places the name of the file into the text box.

By default, the Open File Dialog won't allow the user to enter a filename that doesn't exist. You can override this behavior by setting the CheckFileExists property of the Open File Dialog to false.

The Open File Dialog control has the capability to allow the user to select multiple files. It's rare that you need to do this (I don't recall ever needing this capability in one of my projects), so I won't go into the details here. If you're interested, take a look at the Multiselect property of the Open File Dialog in the Help text.

The Open File Dialog control makes allowing a user to browse and select a file almost trivial. Without this code, you would have to write an amazing amount of very difficult code and would still probably not come up with all the functionality supported by this control.

Using the Save File Dialog Control

The Save File Dialog control is very similar to the Open File Dialog control, but it is used to allow a user to browse directories and specify a file to save, rather than open. Again, it's important to note that the Save File Dialog doesn't actually save a file, it is used to enable a user to specify a file to save; you'll have to write code to do something with the filename returned by the control.

You're going to use the Save File Dialog to let the user specify a filename. This filename will be the target of various file operations you'll learn about later in this hour. Create a new text box on your form and set its properties as follows:

Property	Value
Name	txtDestination
Location	95,40
Size	184,20
Text	*(make blank)*

You're now going to create a button that, when clicked, enables the user to specify a filename to save a file. Add a new button to the form and set its properties as shown in the following table:

Property	Value
Name	btnSaveFile
Location	8,40
Size	80,23
Text	Destination

Of course, none of this will work without adding a Save File dialog box. Double-click the SaveFileDialog item in the toolbox to add a new control to the project.

Next, double-click the new button (btnSaveFile) and add the following code to its Click event:

```
saveFileDialog1.Title = "Specify Destination Filename";
saveFileDialog1.Filter = "Text Files|*.txt";
saveFileDialog1.FilterIndex = 1;
saveFileDialog1.OverwritePrompt = true;
```

The first three statements set properties that are identical to those of the Open File Dialog. The OverwritePrompt property, however, is unique to the Save File Dialog. When this property is set to true, C# asks users to confirm their selections when they

19

choose a file that already exists, as shown in Figure 19.2. I highly recommend that you prompt the user about replacing files by ensuring the OverwritePrompt property is set to true.

FIGURE 19.2

It's a good idea to get confirmation before replacing an existing file.

If you want the Save File dialog box to prompt users when the file they specify *doesn't* exist, set the CreatePrompt property of the Save File Dialog control to true.

The last bit of code you need to add places the selected filename in the txtDestination text box. Enter the code as shown here:

```
if (saveFileDialog1.ShowDialog() != DialogResult.Cancel)
   txtDestination.Text = saveFileDialog1.FileName;
```

Press F5 to run the project. Then click each of the buttons and select a file. When you're satisfied that your selections are being sent to the appropriate text box, stop the project and save your work. If your selected filenames aren't being sent to the proper text box, verify that your code is correct.

The Open File Dialog and Save File Dialog controls are very similar in their design and appearance, but each serves a specific purpose. Throughout the rest of this hour, you'll be using the interface you've just created.

Manipulating Files with the File Object

.NET includes a powerful object called System.IO (technically, System and IO are Namespaces, but they behave like objects). Using various properties, methods, and object properties of System.IO, you can do just about anything you can imagine with the file system. In particular, the System.IO.File and System.IO.Directory objects provide you with extensive file and directory (folder) manipulation.

In the following sections, you'll continue to expand the project that you created earlier in this hour. You'll be writing code that manipulates the filenames selected using the Open File Dialog and Save File Dialog controls.

> The code you'll write in the following sections is "the real thing." For instance, the code for deleting a file really deletes a file. Don't forget this as you test your project; the files selected as the source and as the destination will be affected by your actions. I provide the cannon; it's up to you not to shoot yourself in the foot.

Determining Whether a File Exists

Before attempting any operation on a file, such as copying or deleting it, it's a good idea to make certain the file exists. For example, if the user doesn't click the Source button to select a file but types the name and path of a file into the text box instead, the user could type an incorrect filename. Attempting to manipulate a nonexistent file could result in an exception, which you don't want to happen. Because you're going to work with the source file selected by the user in many routines, you're going to write a central function that can be called to determine whether the source file exists. The function uses the Exists() method of the System.IO.File object to determine whether the file exists.

Add the following method to your Form class:

```
bool SourceFileExists()
{
if (!System.IO.File.Exists(txtSource.Text))
    {
        MessageBox.Show("The source file does not exist!");
        return false;
    }
    else
        return true;
}
```

The Exists() method accepts a string containing the filename (with path) of the file to verify. If the file exists, Exists() returns true; otherwise, it returns false.

Copying a File

Copying files is a common task. For instance, you may want to create an application that backs up important data files by copying them to another location. For the most part, copying is pretty safe—as long as you specify a destination filename that doesn't already exist. Copying files is accomplished using the Copy() method of the System.IO.File object.

You're now going to add a button to your form. When the user clicks this button, the file specified in the source text box will be copied to a new file with the name given in the

19

destination text box. Add a button to your form now and set its properties as shown in the following table:

Property	Value
Name	btnCopyFile
Location	96,80
Size	75,23
Text	Copy

Double-click the Copy button and add the following code:

```
if (!SourceFileExists()) return;
System.IO.File.Copy(txtSource.Text, txtDestination.Text);
MessageBox.Show("The file has been successfully copied.");
```

The Copy() method has two arguments. The first is the file that you want to copy, and the second is the name and path of the new copy of the file. In this example, you're using the filenames in the two text boxes.

Press F5 to run the project and test your copy code now by following these steps:

1. Click the Source button and select a text file.
2. Click the Destination button to display the Save File dialog box. Don't select an existing file. Instead, type a new filename into the File Name text box and click Save. If you are asked whether you want to replace a file, click No and change your filename; don't use the name of an existing file.
3. Click Copy to copy the file.

After you get the message box telling you the file was copied, you can use Explorer to locate the new file and open it. Stop the project and save your work before continuing.

Moving a File

When you move a file, the file is taken out of its current directory and placed into a new one. You can specify a new name for the file or use the original name. Moving a file is accomplished with the Move() method of the System.IO.File object. You're now going to create a button on your form that will move the file selected as the source to the path and the filename selected as the destination.

> I recommend that you use Notepad to create a text file and then use this temporary text file when testing this code and the rest of the examples that permanently alter or destroy a file.

Add a new button to the form and set its properties as follows:

Property	Value
Name	btnMove
Location	96,112
Size	75,23
Text	Move

Double-click the Move button and add the following code to its Click event:

```
if (!SourceFileExists()) return;
System.IO.File.Move(txtSource.Text, txtDestination.Text);
MessageBox.Show("The file has been successfully moved.");
```

Remember, if you specify a name for the destination that isn't the same as that of the source, the file will be given the new name when it's copied.

Deleting a File

Deleting a file can be a risky proposition. The Delete() method of System.IO.File deletes a file permanently—it doesn't send the file to the Recycle Bin. For this reason, you should take great care when deleting files. First and foremost, this means testing your code. When you write a routine to delete a file, be sure to test it under various conditions. For example, if you mistakenly referenced the destination text box instead of the source text box in this project, you could inadvertently delete the wrong file! Users aren't forgiving of such mistakes.

You're now going to add a button to your project that deletes the source file when clicked. Remember, be careful when testing this code. Add a button to the form now and set its properties as follows:

Property	Value
Name	btnDelete
Location	96,144
Size	75,23
Text	Delete

Next, double-click the button and add the following code to its Click event:

```
if (!SourceFileExists()) return;

if (MessageBox.Show("Are you sure you want to delete the source file?", "Delete
Verification",MessageBoxButtons.YesNo,MessageBoxIcon.Question) ==
➥DialogResult.Yes)
{
```

19

```
System.IO.File.Delete(txtSource.Text);
MessageBox.Show("The file has been successfully deleted.");
}
```

Notice that you've included a message box to confirm the user's intentions. It's a good idea to do this whenever you are about to perform a serious action that can't be undone. In fact, the more information you can give, the better. For example, I would suggest that if this were production code (code meant for end users) that you include the name of the file in the message box, so the user knows without a doubt what the program intends to do.

Renaming a File

When you rename a file, it remains in the same directory and nothing materially happens to the contents of the file—the name is changed to something else. Because the original file isn't altered, renaming a file isn't as risky as performing an action such as deleting the file. Nevertheless, it is frustrating trying to determine what happened to a file when it was mistakenly renamed. To rename a file, use the Move() method of System.IO.File, specifying a new filename but keeping the same path.

Retrieving a File's Properties

Although many don't realize it, files have a number of properties, such as the date the file was last modified. The easiest way to see these properties is to use Explorer. View the attributes of a file now by starting Explorer, right-clicking any file displayed in Explorer, and choosing Properties. Explorer then shows the File Properties window with information about the file (see Figure 19.3).

FIGURE 19.3

C# provides a means to easily obtain most file properties.

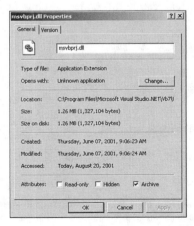

The System.IO.File object provides ways to get at most of the data displayed on the General tab of the File Properties dialog box shown in Figure 19.3. Some of this data is available directly from the File object, whereas others are accessed using a FileAttributes object.

Getting Date and Time Information About a File

Getting the last created, last accessed, and last modified dates of a file is easy; the System.IO.File object supports a method for each of these dates. Table 19.1 lists the applicable methods and what they return.

TABLE 19.1 File Object Methods to Retrieve Data Information

Property	Description
GetCreationTime	Returns the date and time the file was created.
GetLastAccessTime	Returns the date and time the file was last accessed.
GetLastWriteTime	Returns the date and time the file was last modified.

Getting the Attributes of a File

The attributes of a file (refer to the bottom of the dialog box shown in Figure 19.3) aren't available as properties or methods of the System.IO.File object. Just how you determine an attribute's value is a bit complicated. The GetAttributes() method of System.IO.File returns a FileAttributes enumeration. This, in turn, acts as a set of flags for the various attributes. The method used to store these values is called *bit packing*. Bit packing is pretty complicated and has to do with the binary method in which values are stored in memory and on disk. Teaching bit packing is beyond the scope of this book—what I want to show you is how to determine if a certain flag is set in a value that is bit packed.

The first step to determining the attributes is to get the file attributes. To do this, create a FileAttributes variable and call GetAttributes(), like this:

```
System.IO.FileAttributes  objfileAttributes ;
lngAttributes = System.IO.File.GetAttributes(txtSource.Text);
```

After you have the flags in the variable, by &ing the variable with one of the flags shown in Table 19.2 and then testing whether the result equals the flag, you can determine whether a particular attribute is set. For example, to determine whether a file's ReadOnly flag is set, you could use a statement like the following:

```
(objfileAttributes &
    System.IO.FileAttributes.ReadOnly == System.IO.FileAttributes.ReadOnly)
```

When you & a flag value with a variable, you'll get the flag value back if the variable contains the flag; otherwise, you'll get a zero back.

19

TABLE 19.2   File Attribute Flags

Attribute	Meaning
Archive	The file's archive status. Applications use this attribute to mark files for backup and removal.
Directory	The file is a directory.
Hidden	The file is hidden and therefore not included in an ordinary directory listing.
Normal	The file is normal and has no other attributes set.
ReadOnly	The file is a read-only file.
System	The file is part of the operating system or is used exclusively by the operating system.
Temporary	The file is a temporary file.

Writing Code to Retrieve a File's Properties

Now that you know how to retrieve the properties of an object, you're going to use this knowledge to display the properties of the file specified in the source text box on your form. Begin by adding a new button to your form and setting its properties as shown in the following table:

Property	Value
Name	btnGetFileProperties
Location	8,176
Size	80,56
Text	Get Properties of Source File

Next, add a text box to the form and set its properties as follows:

Property	Value
Name	txtProperties
Location	96,176
Multiline	True
ScrollBars	Vertical
Size	184,88
Text	(make blank)

The code you enter into the Click event of the button will be a bit longer than most of the code you've entered so far. Therefore, I'll show the code in its entirety, and then I'll explain what the code does. Double-click the button and add the following code to the button's Click event:

```
System.Text.StringBuilder stbProperties = new System.Text.StringBuilder("");
System.IO.FileAttributes  fileAttributes ;

if (!SourceFileExists()) return;
// Get the dates.
stbProperties.Append("Created: ");
stbProperties.Append(System.IO.File.GetCreationTime(txtSource.Text));

stbProperties.Append("\r\n");

stbProperties.Append("Accessed: ");
stbProperties.Append(System.IO.File.GetLastAccessTime(txtSource.Text));

stbProperties.Append("\r\n");

stbProperties.Append("Modified: ");
stbProperties.Append(System.IO.File.GetLastWriteTime(txtSource.Text));

// Get File Attributes
fileAttributes = System.IO.File.GetAttributes(txtSource.Text);

stbProperties.Append("\r\n");

stbProperties.Append("Normal: ");
stbProperties.Append(
    Convert.ToBoolean((fileAttributes & System.IO.FileAttributes.Normal)
                      ==System.IO.FileAttributes.Normal));

stbProperties.Append("\r\n");

stbProperties.Append("Hidden: ");
stbProperties.Append(
    Convert.ToBoolean((fileAttributes & System.IO.FileAttributes.Hidden)
                      ==System.IO.FileAttributes.Hidden));

stbProperties.Append("\r\n");

stbProperties.Append("ReadOnly: ");
stbProperties.Append(
    Convert.ToBoolean((fileAttributes & System.IO.FileAttributes.ReadOnly)
                      ==System.IO.FileAttributes.ReadOnly));

stbProperties.Append("\r\n");

stbProperties.Append("System: ");
stbProperties.Append(
    Convert.ToBoolean((fileAttributes & System.IO.FileAttributes.System)
                      ==System.IO.FileAttributes.System));
```

19

```
stbProperties.Append("\r\n");

stbProperties.Append("Temporary File: ");
stbProperties.Append(
        Convert.ToBoolean((fileAttributes & System.IO.FileAttributes.Temporary)
                            ==System.IO.FileAttributes.Temporary));

stbProperties.Append("\r\n");

stbProperties.Append("Archive: ");
stbProperties.Append(
        Convert.ToBoolean((fileAttributes & System.IO.FileAttributes.Archive)
                            ==System.IO.FileAttributes.Archive));

txtProperties.Text = stbProperties.ToString();
```

All the various properties of the file are appended to the StringBuilder variable stbProperties. The "\r\n" denotes a carriage return and a linefeed, and appending this into the string ensures that each property appears on its own line.

The first statement declares an empty StringBuilder variable called stbProperties. The StringBuilder object was designed for optimizing string concatenation. You'll be using the append method of the StringBuilder class to create the file properties text. The second set of statements simply call the GetCreateTime(), GetLastAccessTime(), and GetLastWriteTime() methods to get the values of the date-related properties. Next, the attributes are placed in a variable by way of the GetAttributes() method, and the state of each attribute is determined. The Convert.ToBoolean() method is used so that the words True and False appear. Lastly, you assign the txtProperties.Text value to the created StringBuilder string.

> You've previously used the + to concatenate strings, and this will also work. But, when concatenating a large number of strings, you should use the StringBuilder object. The reason for this is that strings are immutable in .NET—they can never be changed. So every concatenation operation creates an entirely new string object, discarding both of the other strings. This can have a negative affect on performance.

Press F5 to run the project, click Source to select a file, and then click the button to get and display the attributes. If you entered the code exactly as shown, the attributes of the file should appear in the text box as they do in Figure 19.4.

FIGURE 19.4
The System.IO.File object enables you to look at the properties of a file.

Manipulating Directories with the Directory Object

Manipulating directories (folders) is very similar to manipulating files. However, rather than using System.IO.File, you use System.IO.Directory. Notice that when you specify a directory path, double slashes are used instead of just one. If any of these method calls confuse you, see the previous section on System.IO.File for more detailed information. Following are the method calls:

- To create a directory, call the CreateDirectory() method of System.IO.Directory, passing the name of the new folder, like this: (Note: As discussed in Hour 12, you must preference literal strings containing slashes with the @ character.)

  ```
  System.IO.Directory.CreateDirectory(@"c:\my new directory");
  ```

- To determine whether a directory exists, call the Exists() method of System.IO.Directory, passing it the directory name in question, like this:

  ```
  MessageBox.Show(Convert.ToString(System.IO.Directory.Exists(@"c:\temp")));
  ```

- To move a directory, call the Move() method of System.IO.Directory. The Move() method takes two arguments. The first is the current name of the directory, and the second is the new name and path of the directory. When you move a directory, the contents of it are moved as well. The following illustrates a call to Move().

  ```
  System.IO.Directory.Move(@"c:\current directory name",
                           @"d:\new directory name");
  ```

- Deleting directories is even more perilous than deleting files; when you delete a directory, you also delete all files and subdirectories within the directory. To delete a directory, call the Delete() method of System.IO.Directory, passing it to the

19

directory to delete. I can't tell you often enough that you have to be careful when calling this method; it can you get you into a lot of trouble. The following statement illustrates deleting a directory:

```
System.IO.Directory.Delete(@"c:\temp");
```

Summary

The Open File Dialog and Save File Dialog controls coupled with System.IO enable you to do many powerful things with a user's file system. In this hour, you learned how to let a user browse and select a file for opening, and how to let a user browse and select a file for saving. Determining a user's file selection is only the first part of the process, however. You also learned how to manipulate files and directories, including renaming, moving, and deleting, by using System.IO. Finally, you learned how to retrieve the properties and attributes of a file.

With the techniques shown in this hour, you should be able to do most of what you'll need to do with files and directories. None of this material is very difficult, but don't be fooled by the simplicity; use care whenever manipulating a user's file system.

Q&A

Q. What if I want to perform an operation on a file, but something is preventing the operation, such as the file may be open or I don't have rights to the file?

A. All the method calls have one or more exceptions that can be thrown in the event that the method fails. These method calls are listed in the online Help. You can use the techniques discussed in Hour 16, "Debugging Your Code," to trap the exceptions.

Q. What if a user types a filename into one of the file dialog boxes, but the user doesn't include the extension?

A. By default, both file dialog controls have their AddExtension properties set to true. When this property is set to true, C# automatically appends the extension of the currently selected filter.

Workshop

The Workshop is designed to help you anticipate possible questions, review what you've learned, and get you thinking about how to put your knowledge into practice. The answers to the quiz are in Appendix A, "Answers to Quizzes/Exercises."

Quiz

1. True or False: The Open File dialog box automatically opens a file.
2. What symbol is used to separate a filter description from its extension?
3. What objects are used to manipulate files?
4. What arguments are required by System.IO.File.Copy()?
5. How would you rename a file?
6. True or False: Files deleted with System.IO.File.Delete() are sent to the Recycle Bin.
7. What objects are used to manipulate folders?

Exercises

1. Create a project that enables a user to select a file with the Open Dialog control. Store the filename in a text box. Provide another button that, when clicked, creates a backup of the file by making a copy of it with the extension .bak.
2. Create a project with a text box on it in which the user can type in a three-character file extension. Include a button that, when clicked, shows an Open File dialog box with the filter set to the extension entered by the user.

19

HOUR **20**

Controlling Other Applications Using Automation

NEW TERM In Hour 17, "Designing Objects Using Classes," you learned how to use classes to create objects. In that hour, I mentioned that objects could be exposed to outside applications—Excel, for example, exposes most of its functionality as a set of objects. The process of using objects from another application is called *Automation*. The externally accessible objects of an application compose its *object model*. Using Automation to manipulate a program's object model enables you to reuse components. For instance, you can use Automation with Excel to perform complex mathematical functions using the code that's been written and tested within Excel, rather than having to write and debug the complex code yourself.

Programs that expose objects are called *servers*, and the programs that consume those objects are called *clients*. Creating automation servers requires advanced skills, including a very thorough understanding of programming classes. Creating clients to use objects from other applications, on the other hand, is relatively simple. In this hour, you'll learn how to create a client application that uses objects of an external server application.

The highlights of this hour include the following:

- Creating a reference to an automation library
- Creating an instance of an automation server
- Manipulating the objects of an automation server

To understand Automation, you're going to build a Microsoft Excel client—a program that automates Excel via Excel's object model.

> This exercise is designed to work with Excel 2000 or Excel XP. If you don't have Excel installed on your computer, you won't be able to complete the exercise.

Create a new Windows Application named **Automate Excel**. Change the name of the default form to **fclsMain,** set its Text property to **Automate Excel,** and then set the entry point in Main() to reference **fclsMain** instead of Form1. Next, add a button to the form by double-clicking the Button item in the toolbox and set the button's properties as follows:

Property	Value
Name	btnAutomateExcel
Location	96,128
Size	104,23
Text	Automate Excel

Creating a Reference to an Automation Library

NEW TERM To use the objects of a program that supports Automation (a server), you have to reference the program's type library. A program's *type library* (also called object library) is a file that contains a description of the program's object model. After you've referenced the type library of an automation server (also called a component), you can access the objects of the server as though they were internal C# objects.

NEW TERM   To create a reference to a type library, first display the Add Reference dialog box by choosing Add Reference from the Project menu (do this now). A number of types of components support automation. Of course, .NET is the latest technology, but in the case of Excel, we're interested in the *COM* components. COM stands for Component Object Model, and it's been *the* technology for working with objects within windows for many years. Microsoft's .NET platform is designed to replace COM. This isn't going to happen overnight, however; literally thousands of objects are built on COM technology. In fact, all the Microsoft Office products up to and including Office XP are based on COM.

Click the COM tab now to display the available COM components (programs that have a type library) on your computer. Scroll the list and locate the Microsoft Excel *X* Object Library (where X is the version of Excel installed on your computer). Double-click the Excel item to add it to the list of selected components at the bottom of the Add Reference dialog box (see Figure 20.1).

FIGURE 20.1

To use an object library, you need to reference it first.

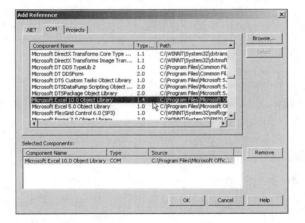

If you don't see an entry for Microsoft Excel, you probably don't have Excel installed on your computer; therefore, this code won't work.

NEW TERM   Click OK now to add the reference to your project. C# doesn't work directly with COM components. Instead, it interacts through a *wrapper*, a set of code and objects that works as an intermediary between C# and a COM component. Chances are

that your machine doesn't have an existing wrapper for Excel; if this is the case, C#
automatically creates the wrapper and references the component.

Creating an Instance of an Automation Server

Referencing a type library allows C# to integrate the available objects of the type library
with its own internal objects. After this is done, you can create object variables based on
object types found in the type library. Excel has an object called Application, which acts
as the primary object in the Excel object model. In fact, most Office programs have an
Application object. How do you know what objects an automation server supports? The
only sure way is to consult the documentation of the program in question or use the
Object Browser discussed in Hour 3, "Understanding Objects and Collections."

> In this example, you'll be using about a half-dozen members of an Excel
> object. This doesn't even begin to scratch the surface of Excel's object
> model, and it isn't intended to. What you should learn from this example is
> the mechanics of working with an automation server. If you choose to auto-
> mate a program in your own projects, you'll want to consult the program's
> developer documentation to learn about its object model; you're sure to be
> surprised at the functionality available to you.

Double-click the button to access its Click event, and then enter the following code,
which creates a new Excel Application:

```
Excel.Application objExcel = new Excel.Application();
```

Notice that C# included Excel in its IntelliSense drop-down list of available objects. It
was able to do this because you referenced Excel's type library. Excel is the reference to
the server and Application is an object supported by the server. This statement creates a
new Application object based on the Excel object model.

Manipulating the Server

After you have an instance of an object from an automation server, manipulating the
server (creating objects, setting properties, calling methods, and so forth) is accomplished by manipulating the object.

Forcing Excel to Show Itself

When Excel is started using Automation, it's loaded but not shown. By remaining hidden, it allows the developer to use its functionality and then close Excel without the user ever knowing what happened. For instance, you could create an instance of an Excel object, perform a complicated formula to obtain a result, close Excel, and return the result to the user—all without the user ever seeing Excel. In this example, you want to see Excel so that you can see what your code is doing. Fortunately, showing Excel couldn't be easier. Add the following statement to make Excel visible:

```
objExcel.Visible = true;
```

Creating an Excel Workbook and Worksheet

In Excel, a Workbook is the file in which you work and store your data; you can't manipulate data without a Workbook. When you first start Excel from the Start menu, an empty Workbook is created for you. However, when you start Excel via Automation, Excel doesn't create a Workbook; you have to do it yourself. To create a new Workbook, you use the Add method of the Workbooks collection. After the Workbook has been created, you need to set up a worksheet. Enter the following statements:

```
//start a new workbook and a worksheet.
Excel.Workbook objBook =
                objExcel.Workbooks.Add(System.Reflection.Missing.Value);
Excel.Worksheet objSheet = (Excel.Worksheet)objBook.Worksheets.get_Item(1);
```

> Notice how System.Reflection.Missing.Value is being passed into the Add() method. This is because the Add() method supports a default parameter and C# does not support default parameters. Using the System.Reflection.Missing.Value as the parameter in the Add() method enables the COM's late-binding service to use the default value for the indicated parameter value.

20

Working with Data in an Excel Workbook

In this section, you're going to manipulate data in the worksheet. The following describes what you'll do:

1. Add data to four cells in the worksheet.
2. Select the four cells.
3. Total the selected cells and place the sum into a fifth cell.
4. Bold all five cells.

To manipulate cells in the worksheet, you manipulate the Range object, which is an object property of the Worksheet object. Entering data into a cell involves first selecting a cell and then passing data to it. Selecting a cell is accomplished by setting a range object by calling the get_Range ()_method of the Worksheet object; the get_Range () method is used to select one or more cells. The get_Range () method accepts a starting column and row and an ending column and row. If you want to select only a single cell, as we do here, you can substitute the ending column and row with System.Reflection.Missing.Value parameter. After a range is set, you pass data to the selected range by using the set_Value() method on the Range object. Sound confusing? Well, it is to some extent. Programs that support Automation are often vast and complex, and programming them is usually far from intuitive.

range.set_Value(Missing.Value,"75") is used for Excel 10 (Excel XP). Use range.Value = "75" for Excel 9 (Excel 2000).

If the program you want to automate has a macro builder (as most Microsoft products do), you can save yourself a lot of time and headache by creating macros of the tasks you want to automate. The "macros" are actually code, and in the case of Microsoft products, they're VBA code.

The following section of code uses the techniques just described to add data to four cells. Enter this code into your procedure:

```
Excel.Range objRange;

objRange = objSheet.get_Range("A1", System.Reflection.Missing.Value);

// For EXCEL9 Use objRange.Value method in place of all of the
// objRange.set_Value() statements used in this example. i.e.
// objRange.Value = "75";

objRange.set_Value(System.Reflection.Missing.Value, 75 );

objRange = objSheet.get_Range("B1", System.Reflection.Missing.Value);
objRange.set_Value(System.Reflection.Missing.Value, 125 );

objRange = objSheet.get_Range("C1", System.Reflection.Missing.Value);
objRange.set_Value(System.Reflection.Missing.Value, 255 );

objRange = objSheet.get_Range("D1", System.Reflection.Missing.Value);
objRange.set_Value(System.Reflection.Missing.Value, 295 );
```

The next step is to have Excel total the four cells. You'll do this by using the get_Range() method to select the cell in which to place the total, and then use set_Value() method again to create the total by passing it a formula, rather than a literal value. Enter the following code into your procedure:

```
objRange = objSheet.get_Range("E1", System.Reflection.Missing.Value);
objRange.set_Value(System.Reflection.Missing.Value, "=SUM(RC[-4]:RC[-1])" );
```

Next, you'll select all five cells and bold them. Enter the following statements to accomplish this:

```
objRange = objSheet.get_Range("A1", "E1");
objRange.Font.Bold=true;
```

The last thing you need to do is destroy the object reference by setting the object variable to null. Excel will remain open even though you've destroyed the Automation instance (not all servers will do this). Add this last statement to your procedure:

```
objExcel=null;
```

To help you ensure that everything is entered correctly, Listing 20.1 shows the procedure in its entirety.

LISTING 20.1   Code to Automate Excel

```
private void btnAutomateExcel_Click(object sender, System.EventArgs e)
{
    Excel.Application objExcel = new Excel.Application();
    objExcel.Visible = true;

    //start a new workbook and a worksheet.
    Excel.Workbook objBook =
        objExcel.Workbooks.Add(System.Reflection.Missing.Value);

    Excel.Worksheet objSheet =
                Excel.Worksheet)objBook.Worksheets.get_Item(1);

    Excel.Range objRange;

    objRange = objSheet.get_Range("A1", System.Reflection.Missing.Value);

    // For EXCEL9 Use objRange.Value method in place of all of the
    // objRange.set_Value() statements used in this example. i.e.
    // objRange.Value = "75";

    objRange.set_Value(System.Reflection.Missing.Value, 75 );
```

20

LISTING 20.1   continued

```
        objRange = objSheet.get_Range("B1", System.Reflection.Missing.Value);
        objRange.set_Value(System.Reflection.Missing.Value, 125 );

        objRange = objSheet.get_Range("C1", System.Reflection.Missing.Value);
        objRange.set_Value(System.Reflection.Missing.Value, 255 );

        objRange = objSheet.get_Range("D1", System.Reflection.Missing.Value);
        objRange.set_Value(System.Reflection.Missing.Value, 295 );

        objRange = objSheet.get_Range("E1", System.Reflection.Missing.Value);
        objRange.set_Value(System.Reflection.Missing.Value,
                "=SUM(RC[-4]:RC[-1])" );

    objRange = objSheet.get_Range("A1", "E1");
    objRange.Font.Bold=true;

    objExcel=null;
}
```

Testing Your Client Application

Now that your project is complete, press F5 to run it and then click the button to automate Excel. If you entered the code correctly, Excel will start, data will be placed into
four cells, the total of the four cells will be placed into a fifth cell, and all cells will be
made bold (see Figure 20.2).

FIGURE 20.2

*You can control almost
every aspect of Excel
using its object model.*

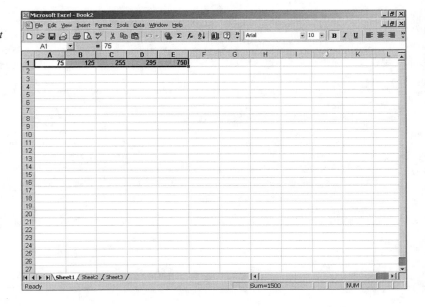

Automating applications, particularly Office products such as Excel and Word, requires a lot of system resources. If you intend to perform a lot of automation, you should use the fastest machine with the most RAM that you can afford.

Summary

In this hour, you learned how a program can make available an object model that client applications can use to manipulate the program. You learned that the first step in automating a program (server) is to reference the type library of the server. After the type library is referenced, the objects of the server are available as though they're internal C# objects. As you have seen, the mechanics of automating a program aren't that difficult—they build on the object-programming skills you've already learned in this book. The real challenge comes in learning the object model of a given server and in making the most productive use of the objects available.

Q&A

Q What are some applications that support Automation?

A All the Microsoft Office products, as well as Microsoft Visio, support Automation. You can create a useful application by building a client that makes use of multiple automation servers. For instance, you could calculate data in Excel and then format and print the data in Word.

Q Can you automate a component without creating a reference to a type library?

A Yes, but this gets considerably more complicated than when using a type library. First, you can't early bind to objects, because C# knows nothing about the objects. This means you have no IntelliSense drop-down list to help you navigate the object model; the chances for bugs in this situation are almost unbearably large. To use late binding in Visual C#, use the System.Type.InvokeMember method.

Workshop

The Workshop is designed to help you anticipate possible questions, review what you've learned, and get you thinking about how to put your knowledge into practice. The answers to the quiz are in Appendix A, "Answers to Quizzes/Exercises."

20

Quiz

1. Before you can early bind objects in an automation server, you must do what?
2. What is the most likely cause of not seeing a type library listed in the Add References dialog box?
3. For C# to use a COM library, it must create a:
4. To manipulate a server via automation, you manipulate:
5. To learn about the object library of a component, you should:

Exercises

1. Modify the Excel example to save the Workbook. Hint: Consider the SaveAs() method of the Workbooks collection.
2. If you have Word installed, add the Word type library to a new project, create an object variable that holds a reference to Word's Application object, create a new document, and send some text to the document.

HOUR **21**

Working with a Database

You've heard it so many times that it's almost a cliché: This is the information age. Information is data, and managing information means working with databases. Database design is a skill unto itself, and entire books are devoted to database design and management. In this hour, you'll learn the basics of working with a database using ADO.NET, Microsoft's newest database technology. Although high-end solutions are built around advanced database technologies such as Microsoft's SQL Server, the Microsoft Jet database (used by Microsoft Access) is more readily available and easier to learn, so you'll build working examples that use a Jet database.

The highlights of this hour include the following:

- Introduction to ADO.NET
- Connecting to a database
- Understanding DataTables
- Creating a DataAdapter

- Referencing fields in a DataRow
- Navigating records
- Adding, editing, and deleting records
- Building an ADO.NET example

 You'll learn a lot in this hour, but realize that this material is really the tip of the iceberg. Database programming can be, and often is, very complex. This hour is intended to get you writing database code as quickly as possible, but if you plan on doing a lot of database programming, you'll want to consult a dedicated book (or two) on the subject.

Start by creating a new Windows Application named **Database Example**. Change the name of the default form to **fclsMain** and set its Text property to **Database Example**. Next, click the View Code button on the Solution Explorer window to access the form's code, scroll down and locate the procedure Main(), and change the reference of Form1 to **fclsMain**. Finally, click the Form1.cs tab to return to the form designer.

Introduction to ADO.NET

ADO.NET is the .NET platform's new database technology, and it builds on ADO (Active Data Objects). ADO.NET defines DataSet and DataTable objects that are optimized for moving disconnected sets of data across intranets and Internets, including through firewalls. At the same time, ADO.NET includes the traditional Connection and Command objects, as well as an object called a DataReader that resembles a forward-only, read-only ADO recordset. Together these objects provide the very best performance and throughput for retrieving data from a database.

Connecting to a Database

To access data in a database, you must first establish a connection using an ADO.NET connection object. Two connection objects are included in the .NET Framework: the OleDbConnection object, for working with the same OLE DB data providers you would access through traditional ADO, and the SqlConnection object, for optimized access to Microsoft SQL Server. Because these examples connect to the Microsoft Jet Database, you'll be using the OleDbConnection object. To create an object variable of type OleDbConnection and initialize the variable to a new connection, you could use a statement such as the following:

```
OleDbConnection cnADONetConnection = new OleDbConnection();
```

To use ADO.NET, the first step that you need to take is to add the proper Namespace to your project. Double-click the form now to access its events. Scroll to the top of the class and add the following using statement on the line below the other using statements:

```
using System.Data.OleDb;
```

You're going to create a module-level variable to hold the connection, so place the cursor below the left bracket ({) that follows the statement public class fclsMain : System.Windows.Forms.Form and press Enter to create a new line. Enter the following statement:

```
OleDbConnection m_cnADONetConnection = new OleDbConnection();
```

Before using this connection, you must specify the data source to which you want to connect. This is done through the ConnectionString property of the ADO.NET connection object. The ConnectionString contains connection information such as the name of the provider, username, and password. The ConnectionString might contain many connection parameters; the set of parameters available varies depending on the source of data that you are connecting to. Some of the parameters used in the OLE DB ConnectionString are listed in Table 21.1. If you specify multiple parameters, separate them with a semicolon.

TABLE 21.1   Possible Parameters for ConnectionString

Parameter	Description
Provider=	The name of the data provider (Jet, SQL, and so on) to use.
Data Source=	The name of the data source (database) to connect to.
UID=	A valid username to use when connecting to the data source.
PWD=	A password to use when connecting to the data source.
DRIVER=	The name of the database driver to use. This isn't required if a DSN is specified.
SERVER=	The network name of the data source server.

The Provider= parameter is one of the most important at this point and is governed by the type of database you're accessing. For example, when accessing a SQL database, you specify the provider information for SQL; when accessing a Jet database, you specify the provider for Jet. In this example, you'll be accessing a Jet (Microsoft Access) database, so you'll use the provider information for Jet.

21

In addition to specifying the provider, you're also going to specify the database. I've provided a sample database at the Web site for this book. This code assumes that you've placed the database in a folder called C:\Temp. If you are using a different folder, you'll need to change the code accordingly.

To specify the ConnectionString property of your ADO.NET connection, place the following statement in the Load event of your form:

```
m_cnADONetConnection.ConnectionString =
@"Provider=Microsoft.Jet.OLEDB.4.0;Data Source=C:\temp\contacts.mdb";
```

After the connection string is defined, a connection to a data source is established by using the Open() method of the connection object. The Open() method has the following syntax:

```
objectvariable.Open();
```

Refer to the online documentation for information on the connection strings for providers other than Jet.

When you attach to an unsecured Jet database, it's not necessary to provide a username and password. When attaching to a secured Jet database, however, you'll have to provide a username and a password. This is done by passing the username and password as parameters in the ConnectionString property. The sample database I've provided isn't secured, so it's not necessary to provide a username and password.

Closing a Connection to a Data Source

You should always explicitly close a connection to a data source. This means that you should not rely on a variable going out of scope to close a connection, but you should force an explicit disconnect via code. This is accomplished by calling the Close() method of the connection object.

You're now going to write code to explicitly close the connection when the form is closed. Start by clicking the Form1.cs tab to return to the form designer. Next, click the Events button on the Properties window (the lightening bolt) to access the list of events for the form. Double-click the Closed event to create a new event handler. Enter the following statement in the Closed event:

```
m_cnADONetConnection.Close();
```

Manipulating Data

The easiest way to manipulate data using ADO.NET is to create a DataTable object containing the resultset of a table, query, or stored procedure. Using a DataTable, you can add, edit, delete, find, and navigate records. The following sections explain how to use DataTables.

Understanding DataTables

NEW TERM   *DataTables* contain a snapshot of the data in the data source. You generally start by filling a DataTable, and then you manipulate the results of the DataTable before finally sending the changes back to the data source. The DataTable is populated using the Fill() method of a DataAdapter object, and changes are sent back to the database using the Update() method of a DataAdapter. Any changes made to the DataTable appear only in the local copy of the data until you call the Update() method. Having a local copy of the data reduces contention by preventing users from blocking others from reading the data while it is being viewed. This is similar to the Optimistic Batch Client Cursor in ADO.

Creating a DataAdapter

NEW TERM   To populate a DataTable, you need to create a *DataAdapter*, an object that provides a set of properties and methods to retrieve and save data between a DataSet and its source data. The DataAdapter you're going to create will use the connection you've already defined to connect to the data source and will then execute a query you'll provide. The results of that query will be pushed into a DataTable.

Just as two ADO.NET connection objects are in the .NET Framework, there are two ADO.NET DataAdapter Objects as well: the OleDbDataAdapter and the SqlDataAdapter. Again, you'll be using the OleDbDataAdapter because you aren't connecting to Microsoft SQL Server.

The constructor for the DataAdapter optionally takes the command to execute when filling a DataTable or DataSet, as well as a connection specifying the data source. (You could have multiple connections open in a single project.) This constructor has the following syntax:

```
OleDbDataAdapter cnADONetAdapter = new
    OleDbDataAdapter([CommandText],[Connection]);
```

To add the DataAdapter to your project, first add the following statement immediately below the statement you entered to declare the m_cnADONewConnection object.

```
OleDbDataAdapter m_daDataAdapter = new OleDbDataAdapter();
```

21

Next, add the following statement to the Load event of the form, immediately following the statement that creates the connection:

```
_daDataAdapter =
new OleDbDataAdapter("Select * From Contacts",m_cnADONetConnection);
```

Because you're going to use the DataAdapter to update the original data source, you need to specify the insert, update, and delete statements to use to submit changes from the DataTable to the data source. ADO.NET lets you customize how updates are submitted by allowing you to manually specify these statements as database commands or stored procedures. In this case, you're going to have ADO.NET automatically generate these statements for you by creating a CommandBuilder object. Enter the following statement to create the CommandBuilder.

```
OleDbCommandBuilder m_cbCommandBuilder =
        new OleDbCommandBuilder(m_daDataAdapter);
```

When you create the CommandBuilder, you pass into the constructor the DataAdapter that you want the CommandBuilder to work with. The CommandBuilder then registers for update events on the DataAdapter and provides the insert, update, and delete commands as needed. You don't need to do anything further with the CommandBuilder.

> When using a Jet database, the CommandBuilder object can create the dynamic SQL code only if the table in question has a primary key defined.

Creating and Populating DataTables

You're going to create a module-level DataTable in your project. First, create the DataTable variable by adding the following statement on the line below the statement you entered previously to declare a new module-level m_daDataAdapter object:

```
DataTable m_dtContacts = new DataTable();
```

You are going to use an integer variable to keep track of the user's current position within the DataTable. To do this, add the following statement immediately below the statement you just entered to declare the new DataTable object:

```
int m_rowPosition = 0;
```

Next, add the following statement to the Load event of the form, immediately following the statement that creates the CommandBuilder:

```
m_daDataAdapter.Fill(m_dtContacts);
```

Because the DataTable doesn't hold a connection to the data source, it's not necessary to close it when you're finished.

Your class should now look like the one in Figure 21.1.

FIGURE 21.1

This code accesses a database and creates a DataTable that can be used anywhere in the class.

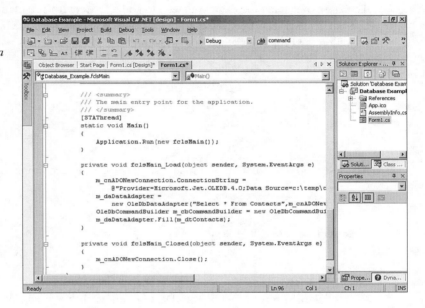

Referencing Columns in a DataRow

DataTables contain a collection of DataRows. To access a row within the DataTable, you specify the ordinal of that DataRow. For example, you could access the first row of your DataTable like this:

```
DataRow m_rwContact = m_dtContacts.Rows[0];
```

Data elements in a DataRow are called *columns*. For example, two columns, ContactName and State, are in the Contacts table I've created. To reference the value of a column, you can pass the column name to the DataRow like this:

```
m_rwContact["ContactName"] = "Bob Brown";
```

or

```
Debug.WriteLine(m_rwContact["ContactName"]);
```

21

> If you spell a column name incorrectly, an exception occurs when the statement executes at runtime.

You're now going to create a procedure that is used to display the current record in the database. To display the data, you need to add a few controls to the form. Create a new text box and set its properties as follows (you'll probably need to click the Properties button on the Properties window to view the text box's properties rather than its events):

Property	Value
Name	txtContactName
Location	48,112
Size	112,20
Text	(*make blank*)

Add a second text box to the form and set its properties according to the following table:

Property	Value
Name	txtState
Location	168,112
Size	80,20
Text	(*make blank*)

Next, click the Form1.cs tab in the IDE to return to the code window. Position the cursor after the right bracket that ends the fclsMain_Closed() event and press Enter a few times to create some blank lines. Next, enter the following procedure in its entirety:

```
private void ShowCurrentRecord()
{
   if (m_dtContacts.Rows.Count==0)
   {
      txtContactName.Text = "";
      txtState.Text = "";
      return;
   }
   txtContactName.Text =
      m_dtContacts.Rows[m_rowPosition]["ContactName"].ToString();
   txtState.Text = m_dtContacts.Rows[m_rowPosition]["State"].ToString();
}
```

Ensure that the first record is shown when the form loads by adding the following statement to the Load event, after the statement that fills the DataTable:

```
this.ShowCurrentRecord();
```

You've now ensured that the first record in the DataTable is shown when the form first loads. Next, you'll learn how to navigate and modify records in a DataTable.

Navigating and Modifying Records

The ADO.NET DataTable object supports a number of methods that can be used to access its DataRows. The simplest of these is the ordinal accessor that you used in your ShowCurrentRecord() method. Because the DataTable has no dependency on the source of the data, this same functionality is available regardless of where the data came from.

You're now going to create buttons that the user can click to navigate the DataTable.

The first button is used to move to the first record in the DataTable. Add a new button to the form and set its properties as follows:

Property	Value
Name	btnMoveFirst
Location	16,152
Size	32,23
Text	<<

Double-click the button and add the following code to its Click event:

```
m_rowPosition = 0;
this.ShowCurrentRecord();
```

A second button is used to move to the previous record in the DataTable. Add another button to the form and set its properties as shown in the following table:

Property	Value
Name	btnMovePrevious
Location	56,152
Size	32,23
Text	<

Double-click the button and add the following code to its Click event:

```
if  (m_rowPosition > 0)
{
   m_rowPosition = m_rowPosition-1;
   this.ShowCurrentRecord();
}
```

21

A third button is used to move to the next record in the DataTable. Add a third button to the form and set its properties as shown in the following table:

Property	Value
Name	btnMoveNext
Location	96,152
Size	32,23
Text	>

Double-click the button and add the following code to its Click event:

```
if  (m_rowPosition < m_dtContacts.Rows.Count-1)
{
   m_rowPosition = m_rowPosition + 1;
   this.ShowCurrentRecord();
}
```

A fourth button is used to move to the last record in the DataTable. Add yet another button to the form and set its properties as shown in the following table:

Property	Value
Name	btnMoveLast
Location	136,152
Size	32,23
Text	>>

Double-click the button and add the following code to its Click event:

```
If (m_dtContacts.Rows.Count !=0)
{
    m_rowPosition = m_dtContacts.Rows.Count-1;
    this.ShowCurrentRecord();
}
```

Editing Records

To edit records in a DataTable, simply change the value of a particular column in the desired DataRow. Remember, however, that changes are not made to the original data source until you call Update() on the DataAdapter, passing in the DataTable containing the changes.

You're now going to add a button that the user can click to update the current record. Add a new button to the form now and set its properties as follows:

Property	Value
Name	btnSave
Location	176,152
Size	40,23
Text	Save

Double-click the Save button and add the following code to its Click event:

```
if  (m_dtContacts.Rows.Count !=0)
{
    m_dtContacts.Rows[m_rowPosition]["ContactName"]= txtContactName.Text;
    m_dtContacts.Rows[m_rowPosition]["State"] = txtState.Text;
    m_daDataAdapter.Update(m_dtContacts);
}
```

Creating New Records

Adding records to a DataTable is performed very much like editing records. However, to create a new row in the DataTable, you must first call the NewRow() method. After creating the new row, you can set its column values. The row isn't actually added to the DataTable, however, until you call the Add() method on the DataTable's RowCollection.

You're now going to modify your interface so that the user can add new records. You'll use one text box for the contact name and a second text box for the state. When the user clicks a button you'll provide, the values in these text boxes will be written to the Contacts table as a new record.

Start by adding a group box to the form and set its properties as shown in the following table:

Property	Value
Name	grpNewRecord
Location	16,192
Size	264,64
Text	New Contact

Next, add a new text box to the group box and set its properties as follows:

Property	Value
Name	txtNewContactName
Location	8,24
Size	112,20
Text	(make blank)

21

Add a second text box to the group box and set its properties as shown:

Property	Value
Name	txtNewState
Location	126,24
Size	80,20
Text	*(make blank)*

Finally, add a button to the group box and set its properties as follows:

Property	Value
Name	btnAddNew
Location	214,24
Size	40,23
Text	Add

Double-click the Add button and add the following code to its Click event:

```
DataRow drNewRow = m_dtContacts.NewRow();
drNewRow["ContactName"] = txtNewContactName.Text;
drNewRow["State"] = txtNewState.Text;
m_dtContacts.Rows.Add(drNewRow);
m_daDataAdapter.Update(m_dtContacts);
m_rowPosition = m_dtContacts.Rows.Count-1;
this.ShowCurrentRecord();
```

Notice that after the new record is added, the position is set to the last row and the ShowCurrentRecord() procedure is called. This causes the new record to appear in the text boxes you created earlier.

Deleting Records

To delete a record from a DataTable, you call the Delete() method on the DataRow to be deleted. Add a new button to your form (not to the group box) and set its properties as shown in the following table.

Property	Value
Name	btnDelete
Location	224,152
Size	56,23
Text	Delete

Double-click the Delete button and add the following code to its Click event:

```
if  (m_dtContacts.Rows.Count !=0)
{
   m_dtContacts.Rows[m_rowPosition].Delete();
   m_daDataAdapter.Update(m_dtContacts);
   m_rowPosition=0;
   this.ShowCurrentRecord();
}
```

Your form should now look like that in Figure 21.2.

FIGURE 21.2

A basic data-entry form.

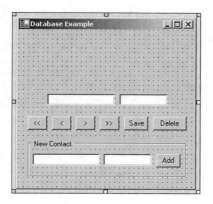

Running the Database Example

Press F5 to run the project. If you entered all the code correctly, and you placed the Contacts database into the C:\Temp folder (or modified the path used in code), the form should display without errors, and the first record in the database will appear. Click the navigation buttons to move forward and backward. Feel free to change the information of a contact, click the Save button, and your changes will be made to the underlying database. Next, enter your name and state into the New Contact section of the form and click Add. Your name will be added to the database and displayed in the appropriate text boxes.

Using the Data Form Wizard

Visual Basic .NET includes a tool to help introduce you to ADO.NET—the Data Form Wizard. In this section, you're going to use the Data Form Wizard to create a form that is bound to the same database you used in the previous example.

Start by creating a new Windows Application titled **Data Form Example**. The Data Form Wizard is run by adding it to your project as a form template. Choose Add

21

Windows Form from the Project menu to display the Add New Item dialog box, click the
Data Form Wizard icon, change the name to **fclsDataForm.cs** (see Figure 21.3), and
click Open to start the wizard.

FIGURE 21.3
*The Data Form Wizard
as a form template.*

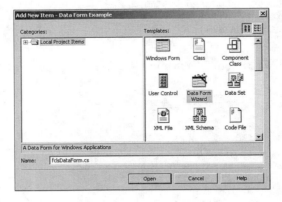

The first page of the wizard is simply an introduction. Click Next to get to the first "real"
page. This next page is used to choose the dataset you want to bind to the form.
ADO.NET datasets hold a collection of DataTables. Enter **AllContacts** into the text box
(see Figure 21.4) and click Next to continue.

FIGURE 21.4
*A DataTable is similar
to an ADO recordset.*

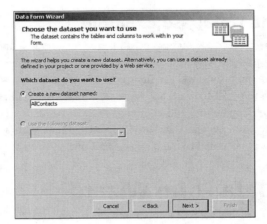

The next page of the wizard is used to specify a connection to a data source (see Figure
21.5). Note: Because you haven't previously defined a connection to the Contacts database, your drop-down list will be empty. Click the New Connection button to display the
Data Link Properties dialog box. Notice that this dialog box opens with the Connection

page visible. Click the Provider tab to see the list of installed providers on your computer (see Figure 21.6), choose Microsoft Jet 4.0 OLE DB Provider to select it, and then click the Connection tab once more.

FIGURE 21.5

Use this page to specify a data source.

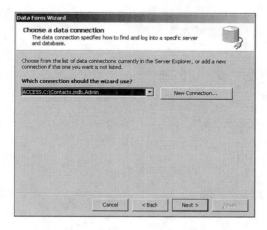

FIGURE 21.6

You must specify the appropriate provider for the type of data source to which you are connecting.

Now that you've selected the provider, you need to locate and select the data source (your Jet database). Click the build button next to the database name text box, and then locate and select the contacts.mdb database. Next, click Test Connection to make sure the information you have supplied creates a valid connection to the database. If the test succeeded, click OK to close the Data Link Properties dialog box. The database should now appear in the Connection drop-down list. Click Next to continue.

21

The next step in completing the wizard is to choose the table or tables you want to use (see Figure 21.7). The tables you choose here will be used to supply the data that is bound to your form. Double-click the Contacts table to add it to the Selected Items list and click Next to continue.

FIGURE 21.7

Use this page to choose the data to bind to the form.

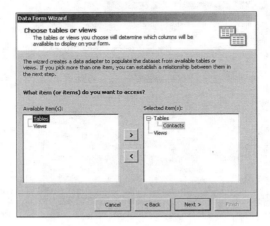

This page shown in Figure 21.8 is used to specify the columns that you want bound on the form. The two columns in your Contacts table are already selected by default, so click Next to continue.

FIGURE 21.8

You don't have to select all the fields in a table.

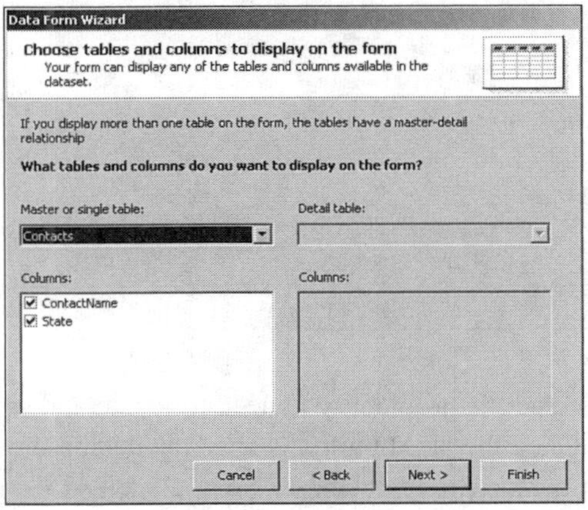

The last step of the wizard is specifying the style in which you want the data to appear (see Figure 21.9). Because the previous example had you add individual controls for each column, leave the All Records in a Grid radio button, selected (this will create a data grid). Click Finish to create your new data form, which will appear in the form designer (see Figure 21.10).

FIGURE 21.9

The Data Form Wizard gives you a number of choices for displaying your data.

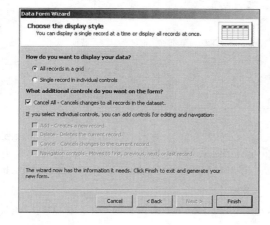

FIGURE 21.10

This bound grid was created by the Data Form Wizard.

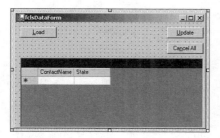

To test your form, you'll have to display it. Click Form1.cs to display the designer for the default form in your project and add a new button to the form. Set the button's properties as follows:

Property	Value
Name	btnShowDataForm
Location	96,120
Size	104,23
Text	Show Data Form

Next, double-click the button to access its Click event and add the following code:

```
fclsDataForm objDataForm = new fclsDataForm ();
objDataForm.Show();
```

21

Press F5 to run the project, and then click the button and your bound form will appear. To load the grid with records, click the Load button (see Figure 21.11).

FIGURE 21.11

This grid is bound to the record source.

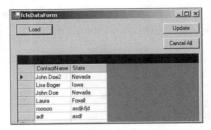

Stop the running project, click fclsDataForm.cs in the Solution Explorer, and then click the View Code button on the Solution Explorer to view the class. Notice that the Data Form Wizard created all the ADO.NET code for you, and even included rudimentary error handling.

The Data Form Wizard is a great way to get started with ADO.NET, but it will take you only so far. To create robust ADO.NET applications, you will need to find one or more dedicated resources that focus on the intricacies of ADO.NET.

Summary

Most commercial applications use some sort of database. Becoming a good *database* programmer requires extending your skills beyond being just a good programmer. There is so much to know about optimizing database and database code, creating usable database interfaces, creating a database scheme—the list goes on. However, writing any database application begins with the basic skills you learned in this hour. You learned how to connect to a database, create and populate a DataTable, and navigate the records in the DataTable. In addition, you learned how to edit records and how to add and delete records. Finally, you learned how to use the Data Form Wizard to create a basic ADO.NET bound form. You are now prepared to write simple, yet functional, database applications.

Q&A

Q. If I want to connect to a data source other than Jet, how do I know what connect string to use?

A. Not only is different connection information available for different types of data sources, but also for different versions of different data sources. The best way of determining the connection string is to consult the documentation for the data source to which you want to attach.

Q. What if I don't know where the database will be at runtime?

A. For file-based data sources such as Jet, you can add an Open File dialog control to the form and let the user browse and select the database. Then, concatenate the file with the rest of the connection information (such as the provider string).

Workshop

The Workshop is designed to help you anticipate possible questions, review what you've learned, and get you thinking about how to put your knowledge into practice. The answers to the quiz are in Appendix A, "Answers to Quizzes/Exercises."

Quiz

1. What is the name of the data access components used in the .NET Framework?

2. What is the name given to a collection of DataRows?

3. How do I get data into and out of a DataTable?

4. What object is used to connect to a data source?

5. What argument of a connection string contains information about the type of data being connected to?

6. The functionality of a DataTable (read-only, updateable, and so forth) is determined by what?

7. What are the two .NET data providers supplied as part of the .NET Framework?

8. What method of a DataTable object do you call to create a new row?

Exercises

1. Create a new project that connects to the same database used in this example. Rather than displaying a single record in two text boxes, put a list box on the form and fill the list box with the names of the people in the database.

2. Further extend the project you built in exercise 1 by adding a Name text box below the list. When the user clicks a name in the list, show the name in the text box. If the user clicks another name, update the database with any changes made in the text box to the previously selected name.

21

PART V

Deploying Solutions and Beyond

In this part, you'll learn how to take a completed project and distribute it to users. Taking advantage of C#'s Web development tools requires that you have a solid understanding of the material presented in this book. In Hour 23, I give you an overview of Web development using C#. In the last hour, you'll learn about the .NET platform at a higher level, such as how all the framework components fit together.

Hour 22

Deploying a Solution

Now you've learned how to create a C# application, and you're just itching to create some project and send it to the world. Fortunately, Visual Studio includes the tools you need to create a setup program for an application. In this hour, you'll learn how to use these tools to create a setup program that a user can run to install an application you've developed. In fact, you'll be creating a setup program for the Picture Viewer application you created in Hour 1, "A C# Programming Tour."

The highlights of this hour include the following:

- Creating a custom setup program
- Installing the output of a project
- Changing the installation location of a file
- Specifying build options
- Adding files to an installation
- Creating a custom folder on installation
- Creating a shortcut on the Start menu

Creating a Custom Setup Program

A custom setup program (the program the user runs to install a program) is the result of building a special type of project in C#. Throughout most of this book, you've created projects of the type Windows Application. To create a custom setup program, you start with a different type of project. Start Visual Studio and choose to create a new project now. On the New Project dialog box, click the Setup and Deployment Projects item to display its contents, and then click Setup Project (see Figure 22.1). This is the project type to use when you distribute Windows Applications; use the Web Setup Project item when distributing Web projects. Enter the name **TYCSharp Picture Viewer** and click OK to create the project.

FIGURE 22.1

Create a Setup Project to distribute Windows Applications.

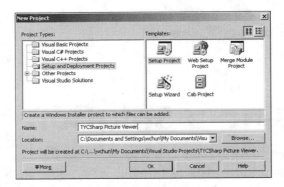

The name you give your Setup Project is the name that will appear in the setup wizard when the user installs your program. Unfortunately, the name you use for this project can't be the same as the one you used for the project whose output you are distributing (for reasons you'll learn shortly). This is why I had you put **TYCSharp** (for Teach Yourself C#) in the project name.

The interface for a Setup Project consists primarily of two panes. The pane on the left side represents the file system of the target machine (the computer on which the software is being installed).

The pane on the right shows the contents of the selected item in the left pane (see Figure 22.2). You really can do a lot when creating custom setup programs, but as you'll see, accessing the features to modify your setup program isn't all that intuitive.

FIGURE 22.2

The interface for creating a setup program isn't intuitive.

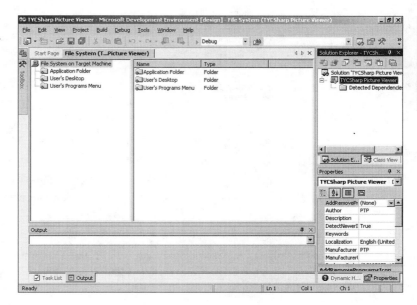

Adding the Output of a Project

At this point, the setup program doesn't install anything; you need to add the output of another project. For the purposes of creating a setup program, the final file (EXE, DLL, and so on) produced in building a C# project is called the *output* of the project. The setup program is used to install the output of a project on the user's computer. The first step to including a project's output is to add the project to the setup program project. Because you're creating a setup program for the Picture Viewer you created in Hour 1, you need to add the Picture Viewer project to the current solution.

Add the project to the solution now by right-clicking the solution name in the Solution Explorer window and then choosing Existing Project from the Add menu. Use the Add Existing Project dialog box to locate your Picture Viewer project and add it to the current solution. The Picture Viewer project should now appear in the Solution Explorer (see Figure 22.3).

Now that the Picture Viewer project is part of the solution, you have to tell the setup program to install the output of the Picture Viewer project. This is where things get a bit odd because the Project menu changes according to what project you have selected in the Project Explorer. What you're going to do next is have the Setup Project install the final executable of your Picture Viewer project.

FIGURE 22.3

To distribute the output of a project, the project must be part of the solution.

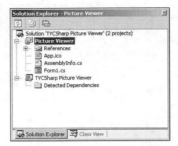

1. Click the TYCSharp Picture Viewer project in the Solution Explorer before continuing. If you don't do this, you won't find the appropriate menu items when you open the Project menu.

2. Open the Project menu and then open the Add submenu.

3. Choose Project Output to display the Add Project Output Group dialog box that appears in Figure 22.4. Make sure that the project selected is Picture Viewer and that Primary Output is selected as well.

FIGURE 22.4

Choosing Primary Output ensures that the distributable file of the project is installed on the user's machine.

4. Click OK to commit your selections.

5. Next, click the Application Folder in the left pane to view its contents. Notice that it now contains the primary output from the Picture Viewer project. This means that the EXE built by the Picture Viewer project will be installed in whatever folder the user designates as the application folder.

Changing the Installation Location of a File

You have complete control over where on the user's computer a file is installed. Most program files (such as the output of the Picture Viewer project) are installed in an application folder. The Application Folder has the following path by default:

22

```
[ProgramFilesFolder][\Manufacturer][\ProductName]
```

Users can change this when they run your setup program. However, you might want to change the default folder as well, which is what you'll do next.

Right-click the Application Folder in the left pane and choose Properties Window from its Context menu. In the Properties Window, notice that the DefaultLocation property contains the information that defines the default installation location. The items in brackets are tokens that get replaced when the user is running the setup program. The Manufacturer token pulls its value from the company name you entered when you installed C#. Go ahead and change the DefaultLocation property to the following:

```
[ProgramFilesFolder]\[ProductName]
```

This new property value eliminates one folder in the final path.

Specifying the Build Options of a Project's Output

At this point, the setup program installs the final output of the Picture Viewer program, which is an EXE. However, you have more control over the output of a project than just the file type. For example, you can specify the icon assigned to the EXE file. Right-click the Picture Viewer project in the Solution Explorer and choose Properties from its context menu to display the Picture Viewer Property Pages dialog box. Next, click General in the list on the left to display the General options for the project (see Figure 22.5).

FIGURE 22.5

Use this dialog box to tailor the output of a project.

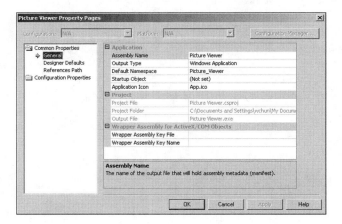

The icon specified appears wherever a shortcut is created for your program. The default icon assigned to executables isn't all that attractive (and even less meaningful), so I recommend that you assign a custom icon. Go ahead and click the Application Icon item to select it, and then click the Build button (. . .) that appears to the right of the Application Icon. Select the same icon that you used for the Picture Viewer's form.

Adding a File to the Install

You aren't limited to installing the output of a project; you can install any file that you choose. For example, you might want to include sample data or support files with your program. You're now going to install a bitmap with your application so that the user has something to view. Again, select the TYCSharp Picture Viewer project in the Solution Explorer or you won't have the appropriate items on the Project menu. Next, add a file by opening the Project menu and then choosing File from the submenu. Locate a BMP or JPG on your system, click it to select it, and then click Open to add the file to the install project.

Adding a Custom Folder to the Install

The pane on the left lists folders that correspond to folders on the user's computer. You can add other folders to this list. These folders may already exist on the user's computer (such as the user's Favorites folder) or may be a brand-new folder that your install creates. Add a new folder to the install now by right-clicking the File System on Target Machine item in the left pane (the first item) and choosing Add Special Folder from its context menu. As you can see, you can select from a number of folders that already exist on the user's computer. Now, however, you're going to create a custom folder:

1. Choose Custom Folder (see Figure 22.6). The new folder is added to the left pane.

2. Change the name of the new folder to Pictures.

FIGURE 22.6
It's easy to select existing folders or create new ones.

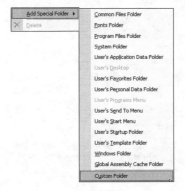

3. Click Application Folder again. Notice that the BMP file you selected for installation appears in the Application Folder.

4. Drag the bitmap to the Pictures folder you just created. Now, when the picture is installed, it will be installed in the Pictures folder.

Creating a Shortcut on the Start Menu

The Setup Project doesn't automatically create shortcuts for your application—you have to create these yourself. Most applications create a shortcut in the Programs folder on the Start menu (or in a subfolder of the Project folder). You're going to create a shortcut for the Picture Viewer program. This shortcut will be placed in the Programs folder on the Start menu.

Click the Application Folder to view its contents. Right-click the Primary Output from Picture Viewer item and choose Create Shortcut to Primary Output from Picture Viewer. C# creates the shortcut item and places it in the Application Folder. Drag the shortcut to the User's Programs Menu item in the left pane. Now, when the user installs your program, a shortcut will be placed in the Programs folder on the user's Start menu.

> Apparently, an issue with .NET prohibits the user from moving the shortcuts for .NET applications after they're installed. Hopefully, Microsoft will eventually correct this. As it stands, however, if the user moves the shortcuts, Windows will move them back. For this reason alone, you should pick a good name for your folder.

Defining the Build Configuration for the Setup Program

When you create a setup program, you can choose to include debug information. This information allows you to perform advanced debugging using techniques beyond the scope of this book. When distributing to other machines, you may want to leave out this debugging information and instead create a Release build. Release builds are smaller and faster than Debug builds. Change your installation to a Release build by choosing Configuration Manager from the Build menu and selecting Release from the drop-down list (see Figure 22.7). Click Close to save your changes.

FIGURE 22.7

Release builds are smaller and faster than Debug builds.

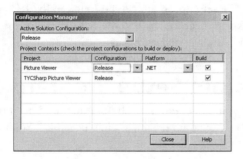

Installing the Common Language Runtime (CLR)

The Common Language Runtime (discussed in detail in Hour 24, "The 10,000-Foot View") allows any Visual Studio .NET language (C#, Visual Basic .NET, and so on) to run on a computer. For a user to run your C# application, the Common Language Runtime (CLR) must exist on the user's computer. By default, your new setup program contains the CLR; therefore, the CLR will be installed when your application is installed (if the current version of the CLR isn't already installed on the user's computer). If you know for a fact that your end user already has the CLR installed (such as when distributing an update to your application), you can omit the CLR from your installation—creating a much smaller installation file (14MB smaller in my tests). The CLR is listed in your Solution Explorer as `dotnetfxredist_x86_enu.msm` (see Figure 22.8). To remove the CLR from your installation, right-click the item and choose Exclude from its context menu.

FIGURE 22.8

The CLR looks like this in the Solution Explorer.

Building the Setup Program

That's it, you're done! All you have left is to actually build the program. Choose Build Solution from the Build menu to create the distributable file. As Visual Studio is building the file, a small animation appears in the status bar. This is because it can take some time to build a file, especially for large solutions compiling on slower machines with minimum RAM. When Visual Studio is done building the setup program, the status bar will read Build Succeeded. The setup program can be found in the Release subfolder of the TYCSharp Picture Viewer project folder. The file has the extension of MSI, which indicates that the file is a Windows Installer Package.

Running a Custom Setup Program

You should always test your setup programs before distribution. (I recommend that you test your setup wizard on a separate machine when possible.) You're now going to run the custom setup program that you've built, but you'll just do it on your current machine. Shut down C# now, saving your work if prompted. Double-click the installation program in the Release folder to start your custom setup program. The setup program is a wizard (see Figure 22.9), so installation for an end user is pretty simple. Click Next to pass the Welcome page.

FIGURE 22.9

Your final setup program is in the form of a wizard.

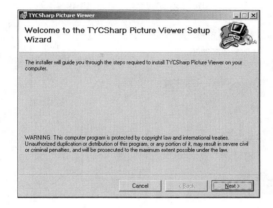

The second page in your setup program is where the user can specify the installation folder. Notice that the default path is what you specified when you created the setup program (see Figure 22.10). The wizard even allows the user to install the application for shared use; you don't have to worry about the details. Clicking Disk Cost shows all installed drives, their disk space, and the disk space required by the setup program. Click Next to accept the default path and continue.

FIGURE 22.10

The user can change your default installation path.

The last page of your setup wizard is used to ask for confirmation before installing the files (see Figure 22.11). You can add a lot more functionality to your setup program, and doing so might create additional pages in the final setup wizard. However, this example is pretty straightforward, so there's not much to the wizard. Click Next to install the Picture Viewer program. After the program is installed, users will get one last wizard page telling them the installation is complete (see Figure 22.12).

FIGURE 22.11

Clicking Next from here causes your program to be installed.

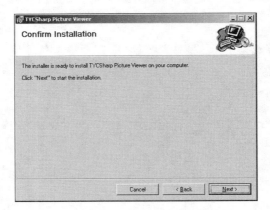

FIGURE 22.12

A successful installation!

Open up the Start menu and look at the contents of your Programs folder; you should see the shortcut to your Picture Viewer program. Click the shortcut to start your program. That's it! You've just created an installation program that installs the Picture Viewer program, and you can now distribute your program to other computers—even if they don't have C# installed.

Uninstalling an Application You've Distributed

All Windows applications should provide a facility for easily being removed from the user's computer. Most applications provide this functionality in the Add/Remove Programs dialog box, and yours is no exception. Open the Start menu, choose Settings, and then click Control Panel. Locate the Add/Remove Programs icon and double-click it. Scroll down in your Add/Remove programs dialog box until you find the Picture Viewer program (see Figure 22.13). To uninstall the program, click it to select it and then click Remove.

FIGURE 22.13

Your program can be uninstalled using the Add/Remove Programs dialog box.

Summary

In this hour, you learned how to create a custom setup program to distribute an application you've built using C#. You learned how to work with folders on the user's computer, how to create shortcuts, how to install files, and how to install the output of a C# project. Custom setup programs can get quite complex, but even the most advanced ones build on the foundation of skills you learned in this hour. Creating a useful program is a very rewarding experience. Nevertheless, your level of satisfaction will increase dramatically the first time you have a user running your creation on the user's own computer.

Q&A

Q. Should I always include the Common Language Runtime (CLR) in my setup programs?

A. That depends. If you're planning on distributing to a lot of users, it's probably best to include the CLR. If you're just distributing to a few users and you're sure they have the CLR, it may not be so important.

Q. Can I install multiple applications in a single setup program?

A. Yes. Just add each project as you did the Picture Viewer project, and be sure to include the output of each project.

Workshop

The Workshop is designed to help you anticipate possible questions, review what you've learned, and get you thinking about how to put your knowledge into practice. The answers to the quiz are in Appendix A, "Answers to Quizzes/Exercises."

Quiz

1. To create a custom setup program, you start by creating what type of Visual Studio project?

2. The final build file of a project (EXE, DLL, and so on) is referred to as the what?

3. True or False: To include the output of a project, the project must be added to the solution containing the setup program.

4. Which build option creates smaller and faster builds?

5. How do you add a file to an installation?

6. If the Project menu doesn't have the menu options for creating a setup program, what might be wrong?

7. How do you add folders to the custom setup program?

8. How do you create a shortcut for a file in a setup program?

Exercises

1. Modify the setup program you created in this hour so that the shortcut created appears on the Start menu with the name Picture Viewer. Also, give the shortcut the same icon you assigned to the Picture Viewer program.

2. Modify the setup program that you created in this hour so that it creates a custom folder within the Programs folder on the Start menu. Install the shortcut to this folder.

HOUR 23

Introduction to Web Development

Visual Studio .NET, more than any previous Microsoft technology, offers incredible Web development tools and functionality. In fact, .NET is very much about programming for the Web. Creating Web applications requires a thorough understanding of all the skills you've acquired in this book—and more. In addition to the complexities of programming that you've dealt with, such as creating forms, writing code, and so on, additional concerns exist, such as Web protocols, firewalls, Web servers, and scalability. Teaching you how to create Web applications is beyond the scope of this book. However, it's important that you're at least a little familiar with the concepts and technologies involved with Microsoft's .NET Internet programming strategy. This hour gives you an overview of the .NET Web programming technologies.

The highlights of this hour include the following:

- XML
- SOAP (Simple Object Access Protocol)

- ASP.NET
- Web Forms
- XML Web services

XML

XML (eXtensible Markup Language) is a universal format for transferring data across the Internet. On the surface, XML files are simply text files. However, this is oversimplifying things. The beauty in XML is that XML files themselves contain not only data, but self-describing information (metadata) about the data. The fact that XML files are text files makes it relatively easy to move them across boundaries (such as firewalls) and platforms.

NEW TERM Semantic tags are used to describe data in an XML file, and a starting and ending tag are used to define an *element*. The data between a starting and ending tag is the value of the element. Tags are similar to HTML tags and have the following format:

```
<tagname>data</tagname>
```

For example, you could store a color in an element titled BackColor, like this:

```
<BackColor>Blue</BackColor>
```

It's important to note that XML tags are case sensitive; therefore, BackColor is not the same as backcolor, and both elements could exist in the same XML file.

Elements can be nested as long as the starting and ending tags of elements don't overlap. For example, two customers could be stored in an XML file like this:

```
<Customer>
   <Name>John Smith</Name>
   <OrderItemID>Elder Scrolls: Morrowind</OrderItemID>
   <Price>$20.00</Price>
</Customer>
<Customer>
   <Name>Jane Aroogala</Name>
   <OrderItemID>Ultima VII: The Black Gate</OrderItemID>
   <Price>$62.00</Price>
</Customer>
```

XML files can be much more complex, but this simple example should suffice to show you that XML documents are text documents that can store just about any type of data you can think of. In fact, Microsoft is using XML in just about everything, from ADO.NET to XML Web services.

SOAP

To pass structured data across the Web (such as passing objects or calling methods on objects), the sender and receiver must agree on how the data will be transmitted. SOAP (Simple Object Access Protocol) is Microsoft's new protocol used to exchange structured data over the Web using an XML format. SOAP is lightweight (doesn't consume a lot of resources or bandwidth) and makes use of the widely accepted HTTP protocol. SOAP is fundamental to Microsoft's .NET strategy because it allows different applications on multiple platforms to share structured data and interoperate across the Web.

ASP.NET

23

ASP.NET is the next evolution of ASP (Active Server Pages). ASP.NET is a framework for creating applications that reside on a Web server and that are run from within a client browser. ASP.NET enables you to program Web-based client-server applications using tools and methodologies much like those used to create traditional applications.

ASP.NET solutions execute on a Web server running Microsoft Internet Information Server (IIS). Therefore, to create ASP.NET solutions, you'll need to have some knowledge of IIS.

In a nutshell, ASP.NET is used to dynamically generate Web pages by serving up Web Forms (discussed shortly). For example, you may create an e-commerce site where a user may choose to view all products by category. Using ASP.NET, you could dynamically build and display a Web page containing the appropriate list of products. The server would execute the code to build the new Web page and then send the page to the user's browser as an HTML document.

Web Forms

Web Forms are similar to Windows Forms applications (which you've been creating and programming throughout this book). However, Web Forms are designed specifically to run in a browser over the Web. Although Web Forms are designed to run within *any* browser by default, you can target deployment to a specific browser to take advantage of a particular browser's features.

To create a Web Forms application, you choose ASP.NET Web Application on the New Project dialog box (see Figure 23.1). Be aware that to create and test a Web Forms application, you will have to have a Web server installed. If you don't have a Web server installed and configured, you'll receive a message similar to that shown in Figure 23.2, and you'll be prevented from creating the project.

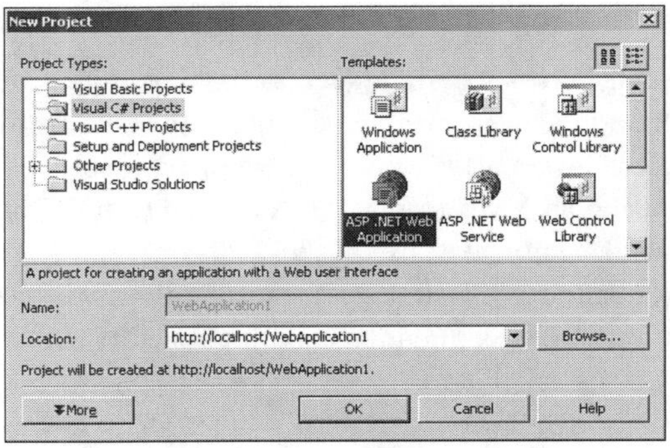

FIGURE 23.1

A Web Forms project is different from a Windows Forms project.

FIGURE 23.2

To create a Web Forms application, you will need to install and configure a Web server.

Comparing Windows Forms to Web Forms

Creating a Web Form application may offer many advantages. For example, to deploy a Web Form application, you have to deploy only to a Web server (not to all client machines). After it is set up on the server, users can run the program simply by pointing their browsers to the proper URL. Contrast this with the need to deploy a Windows Application to hundreds or thousands of users' computers. Another benefit of Web Forms is that applications are essentially platform independent because the code runs on the server and the browser is the only thing running on the client side. When deciding whether to make an application Windows-Forms based or Web-Forms based, consider the following.

Deployment

As mentioned previously, Windows applications built on Windows Forms are installed and executed on the user's machine. Web Forms, however, run within a browser and therefore do not require deployment to a client machine. Rather than having to install updates on every client as you do with a Windows Forms application, with a Web Forms application you need to update only the server (which must be running the .NET Framework).

Graphics

Windows Forms include the capability to interact with the Windows graphics device interface (refer to Hour 10, "Drawing and Printing," for information on the GDI) to create intricate graphics with excellent performance. Web Forms can access the GDI on a Web server. However, round-trips are required for screen updates, which can negatively affect the performance of drawing graphics.

Responsiveness

When an application requires a high degree of interactivity with the user (such as screen updates, lots of event code, and data validation), Windows Forms provide the best performance because they run on the client machine. Most interactive processes with Web Forms require round-trips to the server, which again can negatively affect the responsiveness of an application.

Text Formatting and Control Positioning

Windows Forms provide exceptional capability of placing controls (for example, Windows Forms support snapping to grids). Displaying text on a Windows Form, however, requires using controls such as a label or a text box. Making text flow on a Windows Form (such as flowing around other controls when adjusting to the sizing of a form) can be very difficult to accomplish. In addition, formatting text can be problematic because most controls support only one font at a time.

Web Forms, on the other hand, are served to clients as HTTP Web pages, which excel at formatting and flowing text. Web Forms aren't as precise as Windows Forms when it comes to placing controls, however.

.NET Platform Installation

To run a Windows Forms application, users must have the .NET Framework installed on their computer. Web Forms, however, are installed on the server; therefore, the .NET Framework must be installed on the server but isn't needed on the client. The client needs only a Web browser. It is important to note that future service packs of Windows will likely include the latest .NET Framework—but don't depend on this.

Security and System Resources

Windows Forms applications can have complete control over system resources such as the Registry and also may be restricted using the operating system's security features. Web Forms are restricted by the user's browser security settings and thus have very limited access to system resources.

23

XML Web Services

Perhaps the technology that Microsoft is most excited about in .NET is XML Web services. Microsoft describes an XML Web service as "a unit of application logic providing data and services to other applications." It's easiest to think of XML Web services as applications that reside on a server without a user interface, providing objects to clients. The following are a few practical examples of what can be done with XML Web services:

- A company could create stock quote XML Web services that clients could use to get real-time stock quotes.
- A doctor's office could expose scheduling functions so that clients could use their mobile devices to schedule appointments.
- A government office could expose tax-related objects, which businesses could use to get accurate tax rates.
- A company could expose data that is paid for by subscription. When clients access the data via the Web service's objects, a billing system could track the number of accesses.
- An auction company such as eBay could expose its bidding system as authenticated XML Web services, and third-party vendors could create their own front ends to placing bids on the auction site.

Obviously, this list just scratches the surface. Microsoft ambitiously envisions everyone exposing application logic as XML Web services. Although this may not become a reality in the near future (indeed, XML Web services may never take off like Microsoft hopes), many companies are generating a lot of excitement about this technology.

As a programmer, a lot of the details of XML Web services are handled for you by .NET. For example, SOAP and XML are used to marshal objects and method calls across the Web so that you don't have to worry about the details of the plumbing. Because a standard protocol is used to marshal this information, you don't have to worry about the language or the platform used to implement the XML Web services—almost any type of client can consume XML Web services (C#, Visual Basic, Java, and so on). Clients don't even have to be Windows based or even be PCs; Web-enabled phones and other wireless devices can consume XML Web services.

Writing code to consume XML Web services is actually similar to writing code to access an Automation server. First, you create a Web reference, which is much like creating a reference to an Automation library such as Excel or ADO. After you've got a reference to the XML Web services, the objects become available in code, and you can browse them as you would "traditional" objects.

To create XML Web services, you have to have a sound understanding of creating objects by programming classes, and you have to learn ASP.NET—the underlying technology of XML Web services. The .NET Framework handles the details of using SOAP to allow clients to interact with your XML Web services, so you focus most of your attention on creating useful objects rather than on details of the underlying plumbing.

Summary

Programming for the Web is an exciting proposition, and one that can't be entered into lightly. To create robust Web applications requires an understanding of a lot of technologies, including Web servers, protocols, firewalls, security, object-oriented programming concepts, and much more. By completing this book, you're gaining a solid understanding of application development with C#, and you're building a set of skills that you can use to move into Web programming. If you're interested in Web development, you should consider purchasing a book dedicated to the subject, such as *Sams Teach Yourself C# Web Programming in 21 Days*.

Q&A

Q. Can I use XML files within my applications?

A. Yes, you can design your own XML files and use them any way you see fit. For example, you could save a configuration file in an XML file with a scheme you've designed. For more information, look at the documentation on `System.Xml` in the online Help.

Workshop

The Workshop is designed to help you anticipate possible questions, review what you've learned, and get you thinking about how to put your knowledge into practice. The answers to the quiz are in Appendix A, "Answers to Quizzes/Exercises."

Quiz

1. What does XML stand for?
2. An element is designated in an XML document using the what?
3. True or False: XML tag names are case sensitive.
4. What is the name of the protocol used by .NET to marshal object requests across the Web?

5. What forms engine is used to create forms that run over the Internet?

6. Which forms engine provides for faster response to user interaction?

7. Where is the .NET Framework installed for Windows Forms applications? Web Forms applications?

8. What is the name of the ASP.NET technology used to expose application logic as objects over the Web?

Hour **24**

The 10,000-Foot View

You know a lot about C# by now. You can create projects, use forms and controls to build an interface, and you know how to add menus and toolbars to a form. You've also learned how to create modules and procedures and how to write code to make things happen. You can use variables, make decisions, perform looping, and even debug your code. The question you may be thinking now is, "Where to next?"

Throughout this book, I've focused my discussions on C#. When it comes to Microsoft's .NET platform, however, C# is just part of the picture. In this hour, I provide an overview of Microsoft's .NET platform so that you can see how C# relates to .NET as a whole. By the time you finish this hour, you'll understand the various pieces of .NET and how they are interrelated. Hopefully, you'll be able to combine this information with your current personal and professional needs to determine the facets of .NET that you want to explore in more detail.

The highlights of this hour include the following:

- Introduction to the .NET Framework
- Appreciating the Common Language Runtime (CLR)

- Understanding Microsoft Intermediate Language (IL)
- Working with namespaces
- The Common Type System
- Garbage collection

The .NET Framework

The components and technology that make up Microsoft .NET are collectively called the .NET Framework. The framework comprises numerous classes and includes components such as the Common Language Runtime, Microsoft Intermediate Language, and ADO.NET. In the following sections, I'll explain the various pieces that make up the .NET Framework.

Common Language Runtime (CLR)

A language runtime is what allows an application to run on a target computer; it consists of code that is shared among all applications developed using a supported language. A runtime contains the "guts" of language code, such as code that draws forms to the screen, handles user input, and manages data. The runtime of .NET is called the Common Language Runtime (CLR).

Unlike runtimes for other languages, the CLR is designed as a multilanguage runtime. For example, C# and Visual Basic both use the CLR. In fact, currently more than 15 language compilers are being developed to use the CLR.

Because all .NET languages share the CLR, they share the same IDE, the same forms engine, the same exception-handling mechanism, the same garbage collector (discussed shortly), and much more. One benefit of the multilanguage capability of the CLR is that programmers can leverage their knowledge of a given .NET language. For example, some developers on a team may be comfortable with C#, whereas others are more comfortable with Visual Basic. Because both languages share the same runtime, both can be integrated to deliver a solution. In addition, a common exception-handling mechanism is built into the CLR so that exceptions can be thrown from code written in one language and caught in code written in another .NET language.

NEW TERM Code that runs within the CLR is called *managed code* because the code and resources used by the code (variables, objects, and so on) are fully managed by the CLR. C# is restricted to working only in managed code, but some languages (such as C++) are capable of dropping to unmanaged code—code that isn't managed by the CLR. One big advantage with working in managed code is that the CLR provides garbage collection—the automatic freeing up of unused resources. You'll learn a bit more about garbage collection later in this hour.

Another advantage of the CLR is that all .NET tools share the same debugging and code-profiling tools. In the past, languages such as Visual Basic were limited to their own debugging tools, whereas languages such as C++ had many third-party debugging tools available. Now, all languages share the same tools. This means that as advancements are made to the debugging tools of one product, they're made to tools of all products because the tools are shared. This aspect goes beyond debugging tools. For example, add-ins to the IDE (such as code managers) are just as readily available to C# as they are to Visual Basic—or any other .NET language, for that matter.

Although Microsoft hasn't announced any official plans to do so, it's possible that Microsoft could produce a version of the CLR that runs on other operating systems, such as Macintosh or Linux. If this occurs, the applications that you've written for Windows should run on a newly supported operating system with little or no modification.

24

Microsoft Intermediate Language

As you can see in Figure 24.1, all .NET code, regardless of the language syntax used, compiles to Intermediate Language (IL) code. IL code is the only code the CLR under-stands; it doesn't understand C#, Visual Basic, or any other developer syntax. It's IL that gives .NET its multilanguage capabilities; as long as an original source language can be compiled to IL, it can become a .NET language. For example, people are developing a .NET compiler for COBOL—a mainframe language with a long history. This compiler will take existing COBOL code and compile it to IL so that it will run within the .NET Framework using the CLR. COBOL itself isn't a Windows language and doesn't support many of the features found in a true Windows language (such as a Windows Forms engine), so you can imagine the excitement of COBOL programmers at the prospect of being able to leverage their existing code and programming skills to create powerful Windows applications.

One of the potential drawbacks of IL is that it may be susceptible to reverse compilation. This has many people questioning the security of .NET code and the security of the .NET Framework, in general. If code security is a serious concern for you, I encourage you to research this matter on your own.

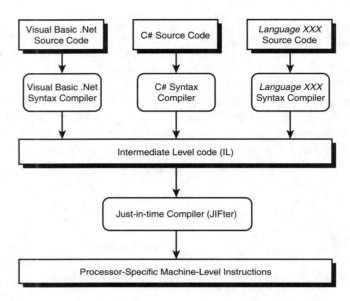

FIGURE 24.1

These are the steps taken to turn developer code into a running component.

NEW TERM IL code isn't the final step in the process of compiling and running an application. For a processor (CPU) to execute programmed instructions, those instructions must be in *machine-language* format. When you run a .NET application, a just-in-time compiler (called a *JITter*) compiles the IL to machine-language instructions that the processor can understand. IL code is *processor independent*, which again brings up the possibility that JITters could be built to create machine code for computers that are using something other than Intel-compatible processors. If Microsoft were to offer a CLR for operating systems other than Windows, much of the differences would lie in the way IL would be compiled by the JITter.

As .NET evolves, changes made to the CLR will benefit all .NET applications. For example, if Microsoft finds a way to further increase the speed at which forms are drawn to the screen by making improvements to the CLR, all .NET applications will immediately benefit from the improvement. Optimizations made to a specific syntax compiler, such as the one that compiles C# code to IL, are language specific, however. This means that even though all .NET languages compile to IL code and use the CLR, it's possible for one language to have small advantages over another because of the way in which the language's code is compiled to IL.

Namespaces

NEW TERM As I mentioned earlier, the .NET Framework is composed of classes—many classes. Namespaces are the method used to create a hierarchical structure of all these classes and they help prevent naming collisions. A *naming collision* occurs when two classes have the same name. Because namespaces provide a hierarchy, it's possible to have two classes with the same name, as long as they exist in different namespaces. Namespaces, in effect, create a scope for classes.

The base namespace in the .NET Framework is the System namespace. The System namespace contains classes for garbage collection (discussed shortly), exception handling, data typing, and so much more. The System namespace is just the tip of the iceberg. There are literally dozens of namespaces. Table 24.1 lists some of the more common namespaces, many of which you've used in this book. All the controls that you've placed on forms and even the forms themselves, for example, belong to the System.Windows.Forms namespace. Use Table 24.1 as a guide; if a certain namespace interests you, I suggest that you research it further in the Visual Studio .NET online help.

24

TABLE 24.1 Commonly Used Namespaces

Namespace	Description
Microsoft.CSharp	Contains classes that support compilation and code generation using the C# language.
Microsoft.VisualBasic	Contains classes that support compilation and code generation using the Visual Basic language.
System	Contains fundamental classes and base classes that define commonly used value and reference data types, event handlers, interfaces, attributes, and exceptions. This is the base namespace of .NET.
System.Data	Contains classes that constitute the ADO.NET architecture.
System.Diagnostics	Contains classes that enable you to debug your application and to trace the execution of your code.
System.Drawing	Contains classes that provide access to the Graphical Device Interface (GDI) basic graphics functionality.
System.IO	Contains classes that allow reading from and writing to data streams and files.
System.Net	Contains classes that provide a simple programming interface to many of the protocols found on the network.
System.Security	Contains classes that provide the underlying structure of the CLR security system.

TABLE 24.1 continued

Namespace	Description
System.Web	Contains classes that provide interfaces that enable browser/server communication.
System.Windows.Forms	Contains classes for creating Windows-based applications that take advantage of the rich user-interface features available in the Microsoft Windows operating system.
System.Xml	Contains classes that provide standards-based support for processing XML.

 All Microsoft-provided namespaces begin with either System or Microsoft. Other vendors can provide their own namespaces, and it's possible for you to create your own custom namespaces as well, but that's beyond the scope of this book.

Common Type System

The Common Type System in the CLR is the component that defines how data types are declared and used. The fact that the CLR can support cross-language integration to the level it does is largely because of the Common Type System. In the past, each language used its own data types and managed data in its own way. This made it very difficult for applications developed in different languages to communicate, because no standard way existed in which to pass data between them.

The Common Type System ensures that all .NET applications use the same data types, provides for self-describing type information (called metadata), and controls all the data manipulation mechanisms so that data is handled (stored and processed) in the same way among all .NET applications. This allows data (including objects) to be treated the same way in all .NET languages.

Garbage Collection

Although I've talked a lot about objects (you can't talk about anything .NET related without talking about objects), I've avoided discussing the underlying technical details of how .NET creates, manages, and destroys objects. Although you don't need to know the complex minutiae of how .NET works with objects, you do need to understand a few details of how objects are destroyed.

NEW TERM As I discussed in previous hours, setting an object variable to `null` or letting it go out of scope destroys the object. However, as I mentioned in Hour 17, "Designing Objects Using Classes," this isn't the whole story. The .NET platform uses a *garbage collector* for destroying objects. The specific type of garbage collection implemented by .NET is called *reference-tracing garbage collection*. Essentially, the garbage collector monitors the resources used by a program, and when resources reach a defined threshold, the garbage collector proceeds to look for unused objects. When the garbage collector finds an unused object, it destroys it, freeing all the memory and resources the object was using.

An important thing to remember about garbage collection is that releasing an object by setting it to null or letting an object variable go out of scope doesn't mean the object will be destroyed immediately. The object won't be destroyed until the garbage collector is triggered to go looking for unused objects.

Summary

Now that you've completed this book, you should have a solid working understanding of developing applications with C#. Nevertheless, you've just embarked on your journey. One of the things I love about developing applications is that there is always something more to learn, and there's always a better approach to a development problem. In this hour, I acquainted you with the "bigger picture" of Microsoft's .NET platform by exposing you to the .NET Framework and its various components. Consider the information you learned in this hour a primer; what you do with this information and where you go from here is entirely up to you.

I wish you the best of luck on your programming endeavors!

Q&A

Q. The .NET Framework seems incredibly complex and daunting. How should I go about learning it?

A. I wouldn't recommend that you attempt to learn the entire framework; I have no plans to do so, either. Instead, focus on areas of interest or research facets of the framework as the need arises. For instance, if security is very important to you, learn about System.Security. Attempting to learn everything you can about the framework may not be as productive as spending your time mastering user-interface design and general programming skills.

Q. Does an end user have to have the Common Language Runtime on his or her computer to run my .NET application?

A. Yes. In Hour 22, "Deploying a Solution," I discussed how to deploy a solution, as well as how to include the Common Language Runtime. If you know for a fact that your end user has the runtime, you can remove it from your setup, vastly reducing the size of your setup program.

Workshop

The Workshop is designed to help you anticipate possible questions, review what you've learned, and get you thinking about how to put your knowledge into practice. The answers to the quiz are in Appendix A, "Answers to Quizzes/Exercises."

Quiz

1. The classes and technology that make up .NET's underlying infrastructure are called what?

2. What is the name of the shared .NET runtime?

3. True or False: Each .NET language uses its own code editor and debugging tools.

4. True or False: Code that runs within the Common Language Runtime is called unmanaged code.

5. Code written in a .NET language such as C# is compiled to what?

6. What are namespaces?

7. One of the things that gives .NET its multilanguage capabilities is that all data is declared and managed in the same way across all languages. This is handled by .NET's what?

8. What destroys objects, freeing all the resources that they consume?

APPENDIX A

Answers to Hour 1

1. What type of Visual C# project creates a standard Windows program?

   Windows Application project

2. What window is used to change the attributes (location, size, and so on) of a form or control?

   Properties window

3. How do you access the default event (code) of a control?

   Double-click the control

4. What property of a PictureBox do you set to display an image?

   The Image property

5. What is the default event for a Button control?

   Click event

Answers to Hour 2

1. How can you make the Visual Studio Start Page appear at startup if this feature has been disabled?

   Change the At Startup property of the project.

2. Unless instructed otherwise, you are to create what type of project when building examples in this book?

Windows Application project

3. To make a docked design window appear when you hover over its tab and disappear when you move the mouse away from it, you change what setting of the window?

Auto Hide

4. How do you access the Toolbars menu?

Choose Toolbars from the View menu or right-click any toolbar.

5. What design window do you use to add controls to a form?

The toolbox

6. What design window is used to change the attributes of an object?

The Properties window

7. To modify the properties of a project, you must select the project in what design window?

Solution Explorer

8. Which Help feature adjusts the links it displays to match what it is you are doing?

Dynamic Help

Answers to Hour 3

1. True or False: C# is a true object-oriented language.

True.

2. An attribute that defines the state of an object is called a

Property

3. To change the value of a property, the property must be referenced on which side of an equal sign?

The left side

4. What is the term for when a new object is created from a template?

Instantiation

5. An external function of an object (one that is available to code using an object) is called a

Method

6. True or False: A property of an object can be another object.

   True. Such properties are called object properties.

7. A group of like objects is called a

   Collection

8. What tool is used to explore the members of an object?

   Object Browser

Answers to Hour 4

1. Name three things that can cause events to occur.

   The operating system, a user, objects

2. True or False: All objects support the same set of events.

   False. Each object supports a set of events specific to itself, or no events at all.

3. What is the default event type for a button?

   Click

4. The act of an event calling itself in a loop is called:

   Recursion

5. What is the easiest way to access a control's default event handler?

   Double-click the control in the form designer.

6. All control events pass a reference to the control causing the event. What is the name of the parameter that holds this reference?

   sender

Answers to Hour 5

1. True or False: The text displayed in the form's title bar is determined by the value in the TitleBarText property.

   False. The title bar text is determined by the Text property.

2. The named color Control is what kind of color?

   A system color. System colors are determined at runtime by the user's Windows settings.

3. In what three places are a form's icon displayed?

   In the form's title bar, in the taskbar when the form is minimized, and in the task list when the user presses Alt+Tab.

A

4. A window with a smaller than normal title bar is called:

A tool window

5. For a Minimize or Maximize button to be visible on a form, what other element must be visible?

The ControlBox must be visible.

6. What, in general, is the best value to use for the StartPosition property of a form?

CenterParent

7. To maximize, minimize, or restore a form in code, you set what property?

The WindowState property

8. True or False: To display a form, you must create a variable in code.

True

9. What property do you set to make a hidden form appear?

The form's Visible property.

Answers to Hour 6

1. True or False: The first control selected in a series is always made the active control.

False

2. How many methods are there to add a control to a form from the toolbox?

Three: double-click, drag and drop, select and draw

3. If you double-click a tool in the toolbox, where on the form is it placed?

Upper-left corner

4. Which property fixes an edge of a control to an edge of a form?

Anchor

5. Which property do you change to hide the grid on a form?

DrawGrid

6. Which menu contains the functions for spacing and aligning controls?

The Format menu

7. Which property do you set to make a form a MDI parent?

IsMdiContainer

Answers to Hour 7

1. Which control would you use to display text that the user can't edit?

   A Label control

2. What common property is shared by the Label control and text box and whose value determines what the user sees in the control?

   Text

3. To change the Height of a text box, you must set what property?

   You must set the MultiLine property to true.

4. What is the default event of a Button control?

   The Click event.

5. A button whose Click event is triggered when the user presses Enter, regardless of the control that has the focus, is called an...?

   Accept button.

6. Which control would you use to display a yes/no value to a user?

   A check box.

7. How would you create two distinct sets of mutually exclusive option buttons?

   Place each set of option buttons on a different container control, such as a group box.

8. To manipulate items in a list, you use what collection?

   The Items collection of the control.

9. What method adds an item to a list in a specific location?

   The Insert method of the Items collection.

Answers to Hour 8

1. What increment of time is applied to the Interval property of the Timer control?

   Milliseconds

2. What collection is used to add new tabs to a Tab control?

   The TabPages collection

3. What property returns the index of the currently selected tab?

   The SelectedIndex property of the control

4. True or False: You should use different Image List controls for storing images of different sizes.

   True

5. To see columns in a List View control, the View property must be set to:

Details

6. The additional columns of data that can be attached to an item in a list view are stored in what collection?

The SubItems collection

7. What property of what object would you use to determine how many items are in a List View?

The Count property of the Items collection

8. Each item in a Tree View is called a:

Node

9. How do you make a node the child of another node?

Add it to the Nodes collection of the first node.

Answers for Hour 9

1. True or False: Form menu bars are created using the Context Menu control.

False. They are created using the Main Menu control.

2. To create an accelerator or hotkey, preface the character with a(n):

Ampersand (&)

3. If you've designed a menu using a Main Menu control, but that menu isn't visible on the form designer, how do you make it appear?

Click the Main Menu control at the bottom of the form designer.

4. To place a check mark next to a menu item, you set what property of the item?

The Checked property.

5. How do you add code to a menu item?

Double-click the item while in Edit mode.

6. Toolbar items are part of what collection?

The Buttons collection

7. To create a separator on a toolbar, you create a new button and set what property?

The Style property to Separator.

8. True or False: Every button on a toolbar has its own Click event.

False. All buttons share a ButtonClick event.

9. What must you do to have panels appear on a status bar?

Set the ShowPanels property to true.

Answers to Hour 10

1. What object is used to draw to a surface?

Graphics

2. To set a Graphics object to draw to a form directly, you call what method of the form?

CreateGraphics()

3. What object defines the characteristics of a line? A fill pattern?

Pens define lines, brushes define fill patterns.

4. How do you make a color property adjust with the user's Windows settings?

Assign a system color to the property

5. What object is used to define the bounds of a shape to be drawn?

Rectangle

6. What method do you call to draw an irregular ellipse? A circle?

Ellipses and circles are both drawn using the DrawEllipse() method.

7. What method do you call to print text on a Graphics surface?

DrawString()

8. To ensure that graphics persist on a form, the graphics must be drawn on the form in what event?

The form's Paint event

Answers to Hour 11

1. What are the entities called that are used to house methods?

Classes

2. True or False: To access methods in a class module, you must first create an object.

False. Static methods do not require that an object be instantiated for the static methods to be called.

3. Data that has been passed into a method by a calling statement is called a

Parameter

4. To pass multiple arguments to a method, separate them with a

   Comma

5. The situation in which a method or set of methods continue to call each other in a looping fashion is called

   Recursion

6. How do you attach a task to a code statement?

   Right-click the statement and choose Add Task List Shortcut from the context menu.

Answers to Hour 12

1. What data type would you use to hold currency values?

   decimal

2. Which data type can be used to hold any kind of data and essentially serves as a generic data type?

   object

3. What values does C# support for type bool?

   true or false

4. What can you create to eliminate magic numbers by defining a literal value in one place?

   Constant

5. What type of data element can you create in code that can have its value changed as many times as necessary?

   Variable

6. What are the first and last indexes of an array dimensioned using `string_strMyArray[5]`?

   First index = 0, last index = 4

7. What word is given to describe the visibility of a constant or variable?

   Scope

8. In general, is it best to limit the scope of a variable or to use the widest scope possible?

   It is usually best to limit scope.

Answers to Hour 13

1. To get only the remainder of a division operation, you use which operator?

   %

2. Which operation is performed first in the following expression—the addition or the multiplication?

   x = 6 + 5 * 4

   Multiplication

3. Does this expression evaluate to true or to false?

   ((true || true) && false) == !true

   true

4. Which Boolean operator performs a logical negation?

   !

5. The process of appending one string to another is called?

   Concatenation

6. What property can be used to return the month of a given date?

   Month

Answers to Hour 14

1. Which decision construct should you use to evaluate a single expression to either true or false?

   if

2. Evaluating expressions to true or false for both types of decision constructs is accomplished using _____ logic.

   Boolean

3. If you want code to execute when the expression of an if statement evaluates to false, include an _____ clause.

   else

4. Which decision construct should you use when evaluating the result of an expression that may equate to one of many possible values?

   switch

A

5. Is it possible that more than one case statement may have its code execute?

   Yes, the case statement requires a jump-statement. A valid jump-statement is `goto case expression`, which transfers control to a specific switch-case label or the default label.

6. True or False: You can use goto to jump code execution to a different method.

   False. goto can be used only to divert code in the method in which the goto exists.

7. To use goto to jump execution to a new location in code, what must you create as a pointer to jump to?

   A code label

Answers to Hour 15

1. True or False: You have to know the start and end values of a for loop at design time to use this type of loop.

   False. You must know these values at runtime, but it isn't necessary to know them at design time.

2. Is it possible to nest loops?

   Yes, and this is a common thing to do.

3. What type of loop would you most likely need to create if you didn't have any idea how many times the loop would need to occur?

   do...while

4. If you evaluate the expression in a do...while on the while statement, is it possible that the code within the loop may never execute?

   No. When you evaluate the expression on the while statement, the code within the loop is guaranteed to execute at least once.

5. What statement do you use to terminate a do...while without evaluating the expression on the do or while statements?

   break

Answers to Hour 16

1. What type of error prevents C# from compiling and running code?

   A build error

2. What is the name of a runtime error: an error that usually occurs as a result of attempting to process inappropriate data?

   An exception

3. What character is used to denote a single line comment?

The double slashes character (//)

4. To halt execution at a specific statement in code, you set a

Break point

5. Explain the yellow arrow and red circles that can appear in the gray area in the code editor.

The yellow arrow denotes the next statement to be processed. Red circles are used to mark break points.

6. What IDE window would you use to poll the contents of a variable in Break mode?

The Command window

7. True or False: You must always specify a catch section in a try structure.

False

Answers to Hour 17

1. To create objects, you must first create a template. This template is called a what?

Class

2. One of the primary benefits of object-oriented programming is that objects contain both their data and their code. This is called a what?

Encapsulation

3. With static classes, public variables and routines are always available to code via the static class in other modules. Is this true with public variables and routines in classes?

No. To access the public variables and routines, an object must be instantiated from the class.

4. True or False: Each object derived from a class has its own set of class-level data.

True

5. What must you do to create a property that can be read but not changed by client code?

Create a property procedure that includes the get accessor, but not the set accessor.

6. What is the best way to store the internal value of a property within a class?

As a private class-level variable

7. Which is generally superior, early binding or late binding?

Early binding

A

8. What is the best way to release an object you no longer need?

Call the object's Dispose() method if it has one, and then set the object variable to null.

Answers to Hour 18

1. What minimal argument should you supply when calling MessageBox.Show()?

The *prompt* argument, the string for the message.

2. If you don't supply a value for the *title* parameter of MessageBox.Show(), what gets displayed in the title bar of the message?

Nothing

3. What type of data is always returned by the MessageBox.Show() method?

A DialogResult

4. Which event fires first, the KeyUp or KeyPress event?

KeyPress

5. How do you determine which button is being pressed in a mouse-related event?

Use the Buttons property of the e object in the event handler.

Answers for Hour 19

1. True or False: The Open File dialog box automatically opens a file.

False. The control returns the name of the file the user wants to open, but it doesn't open the file.

2. What symbol is used to separate a filter description from its extension?

The pipe (|) symbol

3. What objects are used to manipulate files?

System.IO.File and System.IO.FileInfo

4. What arguments are required by System.IO.File.Copy()?

Two arguments are required. The first is the name of the current file; the second is the name of the file to create as a result of the copy.

5. How would you rename a file?

Use System.IO.File.Move(), using the same path but a different filename.

6. True or False: Files deleted with System.IO.File.Delete() are sent to the Recycle Bin.

False

7. What objects are used to manipulate folders?

System.IO.Directory and System.IO.DirectoryInfo. Sometimes Microsoft calls them folders, sometimes directories. In .NET, however, it's usually directory.

Answers to Hour 20

1. Before you can early bind objects in an automation server, you must do what?

Create a reference to a type library.

2. What is the most likely cause of not seeing a type library listed in the Add References dialog box?

You don't have the component installed on your computer.

3. For C# to use a COM library, it must create a:

Wrapper

4. To manipulate a server via automation, you manipulate:

An object variable referencing an object in the server's object model

5. To learn about the object library of a component, you should:

Read the documentation or use the Object Browser.

Answers to Hour 21

1. What is the name of the data access components used in the .NET Framework?

ADO.NET

2. What is the name given to a collection of DataRows?

DataTable

3. How do I get data into and out of a DataTable?

Use the Fill() and Update() methods of the ADO.NET DataAdapter.

4. What object is used to connect to a data source?

The connection object appropriate to the data source (`SqlConnection` or `OleDbConnection`)

5. What argument of the OleDB connection string contains information about the type of data being connected to?

The Provider= argument

A

6. The functionality of a DataTable (read-only, updateable, and so forth) is determined by what?

    The DataTable always has the same functionality, regardless of the source of the data.

7. What are the two .NET data providers supplied as part of the .NET Framework?

    The OleDb .NET Data Provider and the SqlClient .NET Data Provider

8. What method of a DataTable object do you call to create a new row?

    NewRow()

Answers to Hour 22

1. To create a custom setup program, you start by creating what type of Visual Studio project?

    The project type is Setup Project, which can be found in the Setup and Deployment Projects folder.

2. The final build file of a project (EXE, DLL, and so on) is referred to as the:

    Output of the project

3. True or False: To include the output of a project, the project must be added to the solution containing the setup program.

    True

4. Which build option creates smaller and faster builds?

    Release builds are smaller and faster than Debug builds.

5. How do you add a file to an installation?

    Open the Project menu, open the Add submenu, and choose File.

6. If the Project menu doesn't have the menu options for creating a setup program, what might be wrong?

    You probably have a project other than the Setup Project selected in the Solution Explorer.

7. How do you add folders to the custom setup program?

    Right-click the File System on the Target Machine item in the left pane of the Setup Project.

8. How do you create a shortcut for a file in a setup program?

    Right-click the file and choose the appropriate menu item.

Answers for Hour 23

1. What does XML stand for?

   eXtensible Markup Language

2. An element is designated in an XML document using:

   Starting and ending tags

3. True or False: XML tag names are case sensitive.

   True

4. What is the name of the protocol used by .NET to marshal object requests across the Web?

   SOAP (Simple Object Access Protocol)

5. What forms engine is used to create forms that run over the Internet?

   Web Forms

6. Which forms engine provides for faster response to user interaction?

   Windows Forms

7. Where is the .NET Framework installed for Windows Forms applications? Web Forms applications?

   The .NET Framework is installed on the user's computer for Windows applications and on the Web server for Web Forms applications.

8. What is the name of the ASP.NET technology used to expose application logic as objects over the Web?

   XML Web services

Answers for Hour 24

1. The classes and technology that make up .NET's underlying infrastructure are called:

   The .NET Framework

2. What is the name of the shared .NET runtime?

   The Common Language Runtime (CLR)

3. True or False: Each .NET language uses its own code editor and debugging tools.

   False. All .NET languages share the same IDE and the same debugging tools. These are just a few of the benefits of the Common Language Runtime.

A

4. True or False: Code that runs within the Common Language Runtime is called unmanaged code.

   False. It is called managed code because it is managed by the runtime.

5. Code written in a .NET language such as C# is compiled to:

   Intermediate Language code (IL)

6. What are namespaces?

   Namespaces are the "nodes" in the hierarchical structure of classes in the .NET environment.

7. One of the things that gives .NET its multilanguage capabilities is that all data is declared and managed in the same way across all languages. This is handled by .NET's:

   Common Type System

8. What destroys objects, freeing all the resources that they consume?

   .NET's garbage collector

INDEX

M